German U-Boat Losses D

German U-Boat Losses During World War II

Details of Destruction

AXEL NIESTLÉ

FRONTLINE BOOKS, LONDON

German U-Boat Losses During World War II: Details of Destruction
This edition published in 2014 and reprinted in 2022 by Frontline Books,
an imprint of Pen & Sword Books Ltd,
47 Church Street, Barnsley, S. Yorkshire, S70 2AS
www.frontline-books.com

Copyright © Axel Niestlé, 2014, 2022

The right of Axel Niestlé to be identified as the author of this work has been asserted by him in
accordance with the Copyright, Designs and Patents Act 1988.

ISBN: 9 781 39908 283 9

CIP data records for this title are available from the British Library

For more information on our books, please visit
www.frontline-books.com, email info@frontline-books.com
or write to us at the above address.

Printed and bound by CPI Group (UK) Ltd, Croydon, CR0 4YY [TBC]

Typeset in 8.5/10.2 point Times New Roman by JCS Publishing Services Ltd

CONTENTS

LIST OF ILLUSTRATIONS

PREFACE

Why do we need another book on the whereabouts of the German U-boat fleet during World War II? As early as 1946, the basic data had been presented to the public in the official loss lists of the British Admiralty and the Office of the U.S. chief of naval operations, Navy Department. During the following five decades, several authors have also published in varying detail on this particular subject in the history of naval warfare.

The idea for it originated when I became aware that many of the wartime or postwar assessments on the loss of German U-boats were sometimes startlingly wrong. Wondering if other printed and published information was incorrect, I started a systematic check of all U-boat losses by using the existing German and Allied wartime records. This effort was greatly supported by the Naval Historical Branch of the British Ministry of Defence. In the end, the joint effort resulted in the reassessment of almost one-fifth of all front-line U-boat losses during the war with several others still under consideration.

With respect to the total number of U-boats, the tabular presentation of the data in abbreviated form offers the only way to limit the overall size of a book on the subject. My previous experience from having worked through the great amount of literature focusing on German U-boat operations and losses during World War II greatly helped to define the standard for its content and outline. The addition of background information on the individual U-boat provides a more complete set of facts on its last patrol and final fate. Extensive indexes were prepared to allow cross referencing and a quick search for specific data.

It is my hope that this volume will provide a handy compilation of updated information on the particulars of destruction of the German U-boats for future researchers and naval enthusiasts. It is certain that despite all my efforts to find the truth, there will remain a number of mistakes in the book for which the editors and the publisher cannot be blamed. I would appreciate any necessary corrections and additions to update the present information.

The completion of the book in its present form would not have been possible without the help of others. First of all, I would like to thank Robert M. Coppock of the Foreign Documents Section of the Naval Historical Branch of the British Ministry of Defence for exchanging the results of his work with me and for his willingness to discuss various cases. Credit belongs to the NHB and Coppock's work for a large number of reassessments of operational losses. I am greatly indebted to them for allowing this information to be included here.

Next I wish to thank Walter Cloots, Herentals, Belgium, for his lasting support. Without his relentless search for hitherto unnoticed records in various archives and institutions in Europe, the book would have been lacking much important information.

Flight Lieutenant (Ret.) Edmund "Eddie" Cheek, DSO, Barnstaple, Great Britain, generously provided his research on the achievements of the RAF Coastal Command during the war. I am also thankful to him for providing detailed insights into the Coastal Command procedure of anti-U-boat operations.

Herbert Ritschel, a long-time fellow in the research of the German U-boat operations, helped with important background data necessary for my research on individual U-boat losses.

Eberhard Rößler, author of many publications on the history of German U-boat design and construction, helped to define the general standard for my own research during our numerous discussions. His kind offer to allow me free access to his materials during the last decade is reflected here in many details on individual losses.

Among those persons and institutions who also provided necessary information on various aspects of the subject of U-boat losses, I am grateful to (alphabetically) David J. Lees, Romfield, Great Britain; Lennart Lindberg, Stockholm, Sweden; Lt. Comdr. Doug MacLean (RCN), Ontario, Canada; Dr. Sönke Neitzel, Mainz, Germany; Dr. Jürgen Rohwer, Weinheim, Germany; Dr. Roger Sarty, Directorate of History and Heritage, National Defence Headquarters, Ottawa, Canada; K. Kapt. (Ing) a.D. Klaus Schäle, Kiel, Germany; Stiftung Traditionsarchiv Unterseeboote e.V., Cuxhaven, Germany and Peter J. White, Maidenhead, Great Britain.

Special thanks go to the Public Record Office, London; the National Archives, Washington D.C.; the former Militärarchiv of the German Democratic Republic, Potsdam; the Bundesarchiv/Militärarchiv, Freiburg, Germany and the Air Photo Library at the University of Keele, Great Britain, for providing many of the official records and materials used in the research.

I also would like to thank all former servicemen of the U-boat arm of the German Kriegsmarine who shared with me their memories on the fate of many U-boats scuttled or destroyed in the final days of the war along the coasts of the North Sea and the Baltic.

Most important, I wish to thank my wife Katrin and my children for their patience and understanding during the long periods of my absence from our family life while I was working on the book. Without their support and encouragement the completion of this work would have been impossible.

PREFACE TO THE SECOND EDITION

Research into the final fate of German U-boats operating on all seven oceans during World War II seems to be a never-ending story. It is now a well-established fact that many of the immediate postwar assessments by the British Admiralty and its US counterpart were outright wrong. The work to correct previous mistakes has been carried on since the publication of the first edition of this book in 1998. The sheer number of changed U-boat fates and the fact that the first edition had been sold out for a long time, warrants a second edition of this work sixteen years later. Hence, I was very thankful for the offer from the publisher to prepare this updated and corrected edition of my work.

Much to my disappointment, the number of German U-boats still recorded as missing at this time could not be reduced significantly, despite all efforts to uncover their final fates. Although a number of long-standing mystery losses were finally solved, other wartime assessments had to be revised without finding out the real reasons for the relevant losses. Thus, there are still sixty-three boats at present which are recorded as missing or whose final fate has not been fully ascertained. It seems more than likely that a fair number of them were lost to human or material failure in the absence of enemy forces, while others may have succumbed to attacks without providing visual evidence of their destruction. The answer in all this cases is still hidden in the sometimes confusing wartime actions or the darkness of the oceans. However, from the new assessments it has been established that Allied sea mines were far more effective U-boat killers during the final inshore campaign around the British Isles in 1944/45 than previously known. In combination with many other reassessments within this period of the U-boat campaign, previous accounts on the operational history of the last phase of the German U-boat war must be rewritten in many cases.

Researching unsolved U-boat losses has much in common with a detective's work. Similar to the fact that one can see only what you know, historical researchers can only find out if they understand the underlying principles governing the historical action. Almost seventy years after the end of the catastrophic World War II, the majority of the wartime records are now freely available to the public, often on the Internet. It is therefore hoped that future research will help to unearth the truth about the final resting places of the missing German U-boat crews. The author always took great pride in the fact that his and others work helped to preserve the memory of so many young men who paid the utmost price in those dark days of war.

The work often would not have been possible without the valuable support from the ever-growing community of scuba divers, which helped to find and explore numerous U-boat wreck sites along the coasts of Britain and elsewhere. These fearless women and men have contributed much to correct former mistakes in the field of U-boat loss assessment. Likewise I am greatly indebted to many fellow researchers who shared their information and results with me. Particular thanks goes to Innes McCartney, Penzance, Great Britain, Eric Zimmermann, Calgary, Canada, Derek Waller, Arundel, Great Britain, and Jerry Mason, Victoria, Canada. Last but not least, I like to thank my wife Katrin, who, together with the rest of my family, continue to support and endure my obsession in U-boat history. Without their love my life would be meaningless.

INTRODUCTION

The U-boat campaign lay at the heart of the Allied strategy in World War II. Although victory over the U-boat alone would not guarantee overall success, defeat would have grave consequences. The imminent danger of the German U-boat campaign led to an ever-growing Allied interest in all aspects of the building and location of these German vessels. Soon after the beginning of the war, the British Admiralty set up the Antisubmarine Assessment Committee to centralize the evaluation and assessment of the large number of anti-U-boat attacks reported by British and other Allied ships and aircraft. After the U.S. entry into the war, a similar committee was formed at the Office of the Commander in Chief U.S. Fleet (Cominch). Thereafter, the British committee took responsibility for all attacks carried out by British ships and aircraft and those of other Allies operating under British command. Results were frequently discussed and exchanged between the two committees.

Apart from the safe and timely arrival of shipping, the destruction of U-boats was the prime interest of the Allies in the Atlantic campaign. From 1942 onward, the results of the efficient Allied system of air reconnaissance over the important U-boat building centers and the steady flow of "Ultra"-intelligence derived from the deciphered German wireless traffic were extensively used in the assessment and attribution of success to individual operations and attacks against German U-boats. Until the end of the war, these sources of intelligence also provided excellent help to Allied military commands in the course of strategic or operational decisions.

With the cessation of hostilities, the Allies were eager to make sure that no U-boat had escaped their attention in order to avoid any risk from possible hard-liners among German U-boat commanders and to prohibit the escape of top-ranking Nazi leaders to a safe haven by using a U-boat.

In a first step, the Allies ordered the staff of the Operational Division of the German U-boat Command to produce a list of all German U-boat losses at sea during front-line service. Although known to be incomplete due to lack of communication, the list comprised a total of 635 U-boats. Handed over to the British Admiralty in June 1945, it stated details on the U-boat number, the name of the commanding officer, the date of loss as assumed by the U-boat Command and the general area of its loss. At the same time, Allied naval inspection troops searched all occupied German ports and anchoring roads for the wrecks of U-boats sunk prior to the surrender or scuttled at the end of the war during the scuttling operation "Regenbogen."

The main sources of information on the whereabouts of all German front-line U-boats were the operational records of the German Kriegsmarine, which were captured by the Allies at the Tambach Castle Archive in late April 1945. The U-boat Command war diary was quickly translated in order to make its content available for further evaluation and the assessment of U-boat losses. Together with the Allied operational records and intelligence files on the individual U-boats prepared during the war, a broad base was available for a detailed assessment of the U-boat losses inflicted on the German Kriegsmarine.

The main obstacle in the process of assessing the reasons for the loss of more than six hundred U-boats was, however, the rapid disbanding of existing Allied commands and establishments after the victory in Europe. This included the British and the American assessment committees whose members were transferred to other commands or returned to private life. Once the war against the U-boat menace had been won, the prime interest was directed toward victory against Japan and the evaluation of operations in order to define future tactics. At the top command level, the assessment of U-boat losses was now probably considered of mere academic and historical importance. In the summer of 1945, the credits for the sinking of all those U-boats not rated as "known sunk" were attributed somewhat indiscriminately to those attacks considered as successful or promising during the war. Obviously, there had been often not enough time and/or personnel to verify the decisions by information from the available German records. Finally, in 1946 the British Admiralty and the office of the U.S. chief of naval operations reported their joint official results on the assessment of German U-boat losses to their governments and the public. According to these reports, a total of 781 German U-boats had been sunk or destroyed by Allied actions or other incidents during the war. Both reports differed only in the amount of detail given on the individual actions.

Soon after the war, steps were taken by all nations involved in the naval campaign against the Axis Powers to write the official views on the history of the war at sea during the Second World War. In 1947, the first volume on the Atlantic campaign appeared with Samuel E. Morison's *History of the United States Naval Operations in World War II*, followed by a second volume in 1956. The Canadian perspective on the anti-U-boat campaign was presented in 1950 by Joseph Schull in his book *Far Distant Ships.* In 1961, Captain Stephen Roskill finally completed the last volume of the official British history, *The War at Sea.*

In addition to these volumes, several important and often more detailed official monographs and works have been written on the German U-boat war and Allied anti-U-boat operations. Among these were the two volumes of *The Defeat of the Enemy Attack on Shipping* by Commander Freddy Barley and Lt. Commander David Waters, the eight-volume narrative *The RAF in the Maritime War* by Captain D. V. Peyton-Ward, and the three volumes of *The U-boat War in the Atlantic* by Fregattenkapitän a.D. Günter Hessler. The latter is probably still the best account on the German perspective of the U-boat campaign, although the influence of the Allied cryptographic success on the operation was not known to the author at the time of its writing. Unfortunately, all these works held what was considered to be classified information and access to them was limited to certain privileged persons.

All the listed works made extensive use of official postwar reports on the particulars of destruction of the German U-boats. Surprisingly, in only a few cases were the immediate postwar assessments on the loss of German U-boats ever questioned or altered. This is partly due to the fact that the number of available multilingual historians and researchers at this time was rather limited, which resulted in most of the works being entirely based on the records of only one side of the action.

The 1950s also saw the beginning of the large number of generally secondary, sometimes tertiary works on the wide-ranging subject of U-boat warfare history. Among these were several books or publications containing lists and compilations on the loss of individual U-boats. Though these works greatly varied in content, their authors usually assumed the information in the official loss list or the official histories was accurate. This practice consolidated previous mistakes by reiterating them despite sometimes wide discrepancies between the accepted official version and the actual facts reported in the war records.

Naturally, the works of German authors on the subject of U-boat losses dominated in the past. First came Erich Gröner's *Die Schiffe der deutschen Kriegsmarine und Luftwaffe 1939–1945 und ihr Verbleib* in 1953. A revised edition was published in 1972. Detailed data on U-boat losses were also included in Gröner's standard reference book on German naval ships *Die deutschen Kriegsschiffe 1815-1945*, first published in 1966. An expanded and revised edition of it appeared in 1985, now published by Dieter Jung and others. In 1960, Lohmann and Hildebrand included data on the loss of individual U-boats in their multiple-volume standard reference book *Die deutsche Kriegsmarine 1939-1945* on the organization and staff composition of the German Kriegsmarine. Other major compilations were published by Herbert Zeissler in 1956, Otto Mielke in 1959, and Bodo Herzog in 1968.

The number of non-German authors on the subject is even more limited. In 1965, Henry T. Lenton published his two-volume compilation *German Submarines*, which gave some details on the loss of German U-boats. Similar but less-detailed information is included in J. C. Taylor's *German Warships of World War II* in 1966 and Erminio Bagnasco's *Submarines of World War Two*, published in 1977. A more recent compilation in 1989 was V. E. Tarrant's *The U-boat Offensive: 1914-1945*. In 1990 a translated English edition of the 1985 edition of Gröner's work *Die deutschen Kriegsschiffe 1815-1945* appeared, unfortunately without making necessary revisions to the loss register.

Compiling almost a decade's work on the subject of U-boat losses, this book now gives a detailed compilation of up-to-date information on the whereabouts of all German U-boats contracted or impressed by the German Kriegsmarine between 1935 and 1945. Fortunately, the great bulk of the wartime operational records is now being declassified. Previously, a critical review of the immediate postwar assessments of U-boat losses was greatly hampered by the lack of related records. The amount of revisions and corrections made will be seen quickly by comparison with the data published earlier on the subject. In cases of doubt or those still under consideration at the time of publication, the reader is referred to the information given in the footnotes to these losses.

In a number of cases where the previous loss assessment had been proven incorrect, no final explanation for the loss of these U-boats could be found in Allied records. Thus, the number of U-boats now recorded as lost to unknown cause has markedly increased. A certain proportion of these U-boats probably fell victim to mines. Other losses were probably the result of marine accidents, mechanical or technical failure, or sabotage acts committed by resistance members at the dockyards and U-boat bases. Owing to the usually unobserved occurrence of such sinkings, many of these losses will remain uncertain until positive proof can be found.

A total of 1,167 U-boats including 15 captured foreign submarines were commissioned for the German Kriegsmarine from 1935 to 1945. After the start of World War II, 1,110 entered service. During the war, 859 U-boats left from Germany or German-held bases for a front-line patrol. In addition, 63 U-boats detailed and equipped for front-line service had sailed from Germany. The majority of them were still undergoing final training or adjustments at Norwegian bases at the cessation of hostilities in May 1945.

A total of 757 U-boats was lost to Allied action or other causes, both at sea or in port. Of these, 648 were lost at sea during front-line service. The remarkable number of 215 U-boats, amounting to one-third of all front-line losses, was lost during their first war patrol. The mortality rate among German U-boat men can be surmised based on the fact that 429 U-boats lost in front-line service perished with their total crews. Presently more than 30,000 servicemen of the German U-boat arm are recorded as lost during World War II. The percentage-loss rate among the front-line U-boat personnel for the whole period of the war exceeded 60 percent. During some months between 1943 and 1945, one out of two boats sailing on patrol into the Atlantic did not return. In the end, the majority of German U-boat crews paid the utmost price for their failure to recognize the real face and intentions of their fanatic political and military leadership, leaving behind families, relatives, and friends in lasting sorrow over their loss.

Today the names of all personnel of the U-boat arm killed in World War II are shown together with the names of their comrades killed during World War I on bronze tablets in the U-boat Memorial at Möltenort near Kiel, Germany. I feel greatly relieved that through this work the final fate of thousands of U-boat crew members who perished on all seven oceans has now been determined. It is one of the fundamentals in our society to remember our ancestors. Remembrance to individuals, however, always needs a clear focal point, either in time or in space.

Explanation of Table and Index Formats

Loss register

In agreement with the normal wartime criteria to differ the total number of U-boats, the overall number has been grouped according to the individual U-boat types designed before and during World War II. Preceding the information on the individual boats, the main technical characteristics of the various U-boat types are given with tabular information on the building figures for each German U-boat type, arranged according to building yard and final building status. For detailed information on the development of the individual German U-boat types and their design features, see Eberhard Rössler's *The U-boat: The Evolution and Technical History of German Submarines* of 1981 and the various other publications by Köhl, Rössler, and Niestlé listed in the bibliography of this volume.

In order to present the information in a condensed form, the data in the pages ahead have been arranged in columns numbered 1 through 6 with the information in each column presented in abbreviated form as described in the following pages.

Column 1. Number or name of U-boat.

Column 2. Date of commission into the German Kriegsmarine or other Axis navies where applicable. In cases where U-boats have been commissioned more than once, the individual dates are arranged chronologically. A series of dashes (------) indicates that the U-boat was sunk or scuttled after launching but prior to commission.

Column 3. Date of last departure from a German controlled U-boat base or port prior to the loss of the boat. After the occupation of Norway, U-boats leaving a German port for their first war patrol usually made fast at Kristiansand South or other ports in southern Norway to top up fuel and provisions before leaving finally on patrol. In a number of cases when boats were lost on their first patrol, it has not yet been possible to ascertain the exact date when they left a Norwegian port. In these cases the date of departure from Kiel as the normal fitting out and departure base for front-line U-boats in Germany is given.

Column 4. Name of German controlled U-boat base or port from which the boat departed prior to its loss. Location names are given in abbreviated form as a two-letter code. The key to the abbreviation of departure ports follows:

Aa	Aalesund, Norway	Lo	Lorient, France
Be	Bergen, Norway	Lv	Larvik, Norway
Bl	Boulogne, France	Me	Messina, Italy
Bo	Bordeaux, France	Na	St. Nazaire, France
Br	Brest, France	Nv	Narvik, Norway
Cu	Cuxhaven, Germany	Pa	La Pallice, France
Dj	Jakarta, Dutch East Indies	Pe	Penang, British Malaya
Dr	Trondheim, Norway	Po	Pola, Yugoslavia
Eg	Egersund, Norway	Pp	St. Peter Port, Britain
Fa	Farsund, Norway	Re	Reval, Estonia
Fl	Flensburg, Germany	Sa	Salamis, Greece
Ge	Gelting Bay, Germany	Sh	Shonan/Singapore, Dutch East Indies
Ha	Harstad, Norway	Sm	Stormelö, Finland
He	Heligoland, Germany	So	Sonderburg, Denmark
Hf	Hammerfest, Norway	Sp	La Spezia, Italy
Ho	Horten, Norway	Sr	Surabaya, Dutch East Indies
Ki	Kiel, Germany	St	Stavanger, Norway
Kk	Kirkenes, Norway	To	Toulon, France
Ko	Constanza, Rumania	Tr	Tromsö, Norway
Kr	Kristiansand, Norway	Tv	Travemünde, Germany
Li	Libau, Latvia	Wi	Wilhelmshaven, Germany

Column 5. Rank and family name of U-boat commander at the time of its loss or final fate as described in column 6. Names put in parentheses indicate that the named officer was assigned as future commanding officer to the boat but did not commission it for reasons described in column 6. Abbreviation of ranks as follows:

German Kriegsmarine
LT	Leutnant zur See	Ensign
OL	Oberleutnant zur See	Lieutenant (junior grade)

KL	Kapitänleutnant	Lieutenant
KK	Korvettenkapitän	Lieutenant commander
FK	Fregattenkapitän	Commander
KzS	Kapitän zur See	Captain

Italian Navy

TV	Teniente di Vascello	Lieutenant
CC	Capitano di Corvetta	Lieutenant commander

Column 6. Final fate of the boat. For U-boats lost at sea or in port by sinking, the data are arranged in the following sequence: date and sometimes time of loss, geographical location and position (latitude/longitude) of loss, reason or weapons responsible for the loss, type, nationality and name(s) of ship(s) or designation of aircraft and airforce unit(s) involved in the loss together with rank, initials, and family name of commanding officer or pilot at the time of sinking action, total number of crew killed as the result of loss, and total number of crew rescued after loss.

Time according to the 24-hour clock in Central European Time (CET) or German Summer Time (GST), where applicable. Positions are given in latitude and longitude: n ≈ north, s ≈ south, w ≈ west, e ≈ east. Punctuation between degrees and minutes of latitude and longitude is by a degree symbol (°). Decimal fractions of a minute are separated by a comma. The accuracy of positions given in contemporary records varies dependent on the prevailing situation to fix the nautical position during or after the attack. Positions listed in the loss section therefore often indicate no wreck positions at any given time.

Explanatory numbers behind the U-boat number refer to explanatory notes in chapter notes.

The key to abbreviations follows.

Ship Types:

AM	Fleet Minesweeper	PE	Patrol Escort (Corvette)
CV	Carrier Vessel	PF	Patrol Frigate
CVE	Carrier Vessel Escort	PS	Patrol Sloop
DD	Destroyer	SS	Submarine
DE	Destroyer Escort	S/fi	Fishing Vessel
MTB	Motor Torpedo Boat	S/S	Steam Ship
M/V	Motor Ship	TB	Torpedo boat
PC	Patrol Craft (A/S)	TWL	A/S Trawler

Aircraft Types:

Alb   Albacore; single-engined biplane for carrier operation, designed by Fairey
      Aviation Co., U.K.

Ave   Avenger (TBF-1); single-engined monoplane for carrier operation, designed
      by Grumman Aircraft Corp., USA

Bar   Barracuda; single-engined monoplane for carrier operation, designed by
      Fairey Aviation Co., U.K.

Bft   Beaufighter; twin-engined monoplane for land-based operation, designed by
      Bristol Aeroplane Co., U.K.

Bis   Bisley; twin-engined monoplane for land-based operation, designed by
      Rootes Securities Ltd., U.K.

Ble   Blenheim; twin-engined monoplane for land-based operation, designed by
      Bristol Aeroplane Co., U.K.

Cat   Catalina (PBY); twin-engined monoplane, flying boat, designed by
      Consolidated Aircraft Corp., USA

Dig   Digby (B-18A), twin-engined monoplane for land-based operation, designed
      by Douglas Aircraft Corp., USA

Fir   Firefly; single-engined monoplane for carrier operation, designed by Fairey
      Aviation Co., U.K.

For   Fortress (B-17); four-engined monoplane for land-based operation, designed
      by Boeing Aircraft Corp., USA

Hal   Halifax; four-engined monoplane for land-based operation, designed by
      Handley Page Aircraft Ltd., U.K.

Ham   Hampden; twin-engined monoplane for land-based operation, designed by
      Handley Page Aircraft Ltd., U.K.

Hav   Havoc (A-20); twin-engined monoplane for land-based operation, designed
      by Douglas Aircraft Corp., USA

Hud   Hudson; twin-engined monoplane for land-based operation, designed by
      Lockheed Aircraft Corp., USA

Kin   Kingfisher (O2SU); single-engined monoplane, float plane, designed by
      Vought Aircraft Corp., USA

Lan   Lancaster; four-engined monoplane for land-based operation, designed by
      A.V. Roe Co. Ltd, U.K.

Lib   Liberator (B-24, PB4Y-1); four-engined monoplane for land-based operation,
      designed by Consolidated Aircraft Corp., USA

Mar   Mariner (PBM-1); twin-engined monoplane, flying boat, designed by Martin
      Aircraft Corp., USA

Mat   Martlet; single-engined monoplane for carrier operation, designed by
      Grumman Aircraft Corp., USA, British version of Wildcat

Mit   Mitchell (B-25, PBJ); twin-engined monoplane for land-based operation, designed by North American Aircraft Corp., USA

Mos   Mosquito; twin-engined monoplane for land-based operation, designed by De Havilland Aircraft Co., U.K.

Sun   Sunderland; four-engined monoplane, flying boat, designed by Short Bros. Ltd., U.K.

Swd   Swordfish; single-engined biplane for carrier operations, designed by Fairey Aviation Co., U.K.

Typ   Typhoon; single-engined monoplane for land-based operation, designed by Hawker Aircraft Co., U.K.

Ven   Ventura (PBV-1); twin-engined monoplane for land-based operation, designed by Lockheed Aircraft Corp., USA

War   Warwick; twin-engined monoplane for land-based operation, designed by Vickers Armstrong Ltd., U.K.

Wel   Wellington; twin-engined monoplane for land-based operation, designed by Vickers Armstrong Ltd., U.K.

Wes   Wellesley; single-engined monoplane for land-based operation, designed by Vickers Armstrong Ltd., U.K.

Wht   Whitley; twin-engined monoplane for land-based operation, designed by Armstrong Whitworth Ltd., U.K.

Wil   Wildcat (F4F-3); single-engined monoplane for carrier operation, designed by Grumman Aircraft Corp., USA

Miscellaneous:

≈	approximately, about	bomb	aerial bomb
↑	raised, salvaged	decomm.	decommissioned
→	transferred to, see	recomm.	recommissioned
✠	sunk	ULD	U-boat training division
(✠)	scuttled	HKT	Higher Command
✠	total loss of crew, no	KLA	Warship Instruction Department
	survivors	Sqn	Squadron
§	stricken	OTU	Operational Training Unit
br	broken up, scrapped	TAC	Tactical Air Command
D/Cs	depth charges	TAF	Tactical Air Force
VB	USN designation for bomber squadron	VP	USN designation for patrol aircraft squadron
VC	USN designation for composite squadron, i.e. A/S and fighter role	VPB	USN designation for bomber/ patrol aircraft squadron

Nationality:

HMS	His/Her Majesty's Ship	USN	United States Navy
HMS/m	His/Her Majesty's Submarine	FAA	Fleet Air Arm of British Royal Navy
HMCS	His/Her Majesty's Canadian Ship	RAF	Royal Air Force
KNM	His/Her Norwegian Majesty's Ship	RAFVR	Royal Air Force Volunteer Reserve
HMInS	His/Her Majesty's Indian Ship	RAAF	Royal Australian Air Force
USS	United States Ship	RAFO	Reserve Air Force Officer
FNFL	Forces Navales Françaises Libres (Free French Navy)	RCAF	Royal Canadian Air Force
HNeMS	His/Her Netherlands Majesty's Ship	RHN	Royal Hellenic Navy
HMSAS	His/Her Majesty's South African Ship	RNAF	Royal Norwegian Air Force
HHMS	His/Her Greek Majesty's Ship	USAAF	United States Army Air Force
IJN	Imperial Japanese Navy	FAB	Brazilian Air Force
ORP	Okret Rzeczypospolites Polskiej (Polish Navy)	FAFL	Free French Air Force
USCG	United States Coast Guard		

Allied naval ranks:

Capt.	Captain
Comdr.	Commander
Kpt. 3.Rg	Kapitän 3d Ranga (Soviet Navy only)
Lt. Comdr.	Lieutenant commander
Kl.	Kapitän leitenant (Soviet Navy only)
Lt.	Lieutenant
Ltn.	Leitenant (Soviet Navy only)
Sub-Lt.	Sub-lieutenant (Royal Navy only)
Lt.[jg]	Lieutenant (junior grade) (U.S. Navy/Coast Guard only)
Ens	Ensign (U.S. Navy/Coast Guard only)
PO	Petty Officer
CPO	Chief Petty Officer
A	Acting
T	Temporary
E.V.1	Enseigne de vaisseau de 1 ére classe (French Navy only)
L.V.	Lieutenant de vaisseau (French Navy only)

Allied air force ranks:

G/C	Group captain	F/L	Flight lieutenant
W/C	Wing commander	F/O	Flying officer
S/L	Squadron leader	P/O	Pilot officer
F/Sgt	Flight sergeant	1st Lt.	1st Lieutenant (USAAF only)
Sgt	Sergeant	2d Lt.	2d Lieutenant (USAAF only)
Capt.	Captain (USAAF only)	Maj.	Major (USAAF only)

For abbreviation of German ranks see p. 5 column 5.

Since World War II, several names of places or locations used in the register have been changed.

Dagö	now Hiiumaa	Memel	now Klaipeda
Danzig	now Gdansk	Odensholm	now Osmussaarr
Dievenow	now Dziwnow	Pillau	now Baltijsk
Galatz	now Galati	Pola	now Pula
Gotenhafen	now Gdynia	Reval	now Tallinn
Hela	now Hel	Stettin	now Szczecin
Kahlberg	now Krynica Morska	Stolpmünde	now Ustka
Königsberg	now Kaliningrad	Swinemünde	now Swinoujscie
Libau	now Liepaja	Wesermünde	now Bremerhaven

Index A: U-Boat Commanding Officers

All commanding officers of U-boats holding command at the time of its loss or final fate are listed in alphabetical order, along with the following information: family name, first name(s), number of officers crew (class) for active officers or time of entry for reserve officers or Kriegsoffiziere (D), rank at the time of loss or final fate, U-boat reference to the loss register in chapter 3. Abbreviations of ranks are given according to the official abbreviation instruction for the German Kriegsmarine. Two or more ranks given for one person indicate that rank changed between subsequent commands.
Abbreviations used follow:

Lt. z. S.	Leutnant zur See	Ensign
Oblt. z. S.	Oberleutnant zur See	Lieutenant (junior grade)
Kaptlt.	Kapitänleutnant	Lieutenant
K. Kapt.	Korvettenkapitän	Lieutenant commander
F. Kapt.	Fregattenkapitän	Commander
Kapt. z. S.	Kapitän zur See	Captain

d. Res.	der Reserve	Reserve status
z.V.	zur besonderen Verwendung	for special employment
(K.O.)	Kriegsoffizier	Chief petty officer promoted to officer rank
i.V.	in Vertretung	acting for
TV	Teniente di Vascello (Italian navy)	Lieutenant
CC	Capitano di Corvetta (Italian navy)	Lieutenant commander

Index B: Allied and Axis Commanding Officers or Pilots Involved in Sinking Action

All Allied or Axis commanding officers of ship or boats and aircraft pilots directly or indirectly involved in U-boat sinkings by enemy action or other causes are listed in alphabetical order, along with the following information: family name, first name(s) or initials, rank, and U-boat reference to the loss register in chapter 3. For abbreviation of ranks, see explanatory information for loss section, column 6, on p. 6.

Index C: Allied and Axis Ships

Allied and Axis naval and merchant ships or boats involved in U-boat sinkings by enemy action or other causes are listed in alphabetical order, along with the following information: ship's name, pennant number or hull number in parentheses, ship's class or type, former names where applicable, and U-boat reference to the loss register in chapter 3. Spelling of warships' names is based on spellings in the common naval handbooks or wartime records.

Index D: Allied Air Force Units

Allied air force units involved in U-boat sinkings by enemy action are listed in alphabetical order, along with the following information: nationality, unit designation, and U-boat reference to the loss register in chapter 3.

I

PRINCIPLES OF U-BOAT LOSS ASSESSMENT DURING WORLD WAR II

While the U-boat war against the merchant shipping of the Allied nations on the transoceanic communication lines became a centerpoint in the German naval strategy of World War II, the number of U-boats sunk in battle was an important measure of success in the worldwide Allied campaign against the German U-boats. Especially after the defeat of the German U-boat offensive against the transatlantic convoy traffic in May 1943, the destruction of the U-boats themselves more and more became the primary objective of the Allied antisubmarine forces. Although the German U-boat Command tried to get a maximum of information on the times and causes of individual U-boat losses during front-line operations, the actual results were often not satisfying. The reasons for the failure to achieve better intelligence on U-boat losses, however, were inherent to the U-boat warfare.

The extent of tactical command exercised by the German U-boat Command on the operations of individual boats at sea was limited. Commanding officers of U-boats ordered to patrol independently on the shipping lanes in distant areas off the American and African Atlantic coasts or in the Indian Ocean assumed a maximum of tactical freedom in the conduct of their patrols. The role of U-boat Command was limited to the allocation of general operational areas or focal points and the eventual supply of additional information on the enemy (shipping routes, sightings, etc.). Even during group operations against Allied Atlantic convoys, the control of individual boats mostly concentrated on the direction of search operations until contact with the enemy had been established.

Apart from boats engaged in running convoy operations, U-boats on patrol normally took great care to remain unobserved at least until the first attack. Out- and inbound boats were to send a short signal when certain lines along their passage routes had been passed in order to allow U-boat Command any further disposition of the boats at sea. Until the autumn of 1944, U-boats outbound from French bases into the Atlantic normally transmitted a passage report between the longitudes of 15° to 18° west, whereas boats from German or Norwegian bases directed into the Atlantic normally signalled after a successful break through the passages north of Britain. Inbound boats usually reported their appearance at the rendezvous points off the various bases between twenty-four and seventy-two hours in advance to make allowance for the preparation of harbor escorts.

Simultaneous with the introduction of the schnorkel and the beginning of continuous submerged patrols in the inshore billets around Britain and the North American coast from autumn 1944 onward, a major change compared with the previous German practice in the use of radio signals took place. Fearing the now-known dangers of being monitored by ship or shore-based Allied radio direction-finding systems, it became normal practice that a U-boat only reported twice during its entire patrol. Usually the first report consisted of a passage report sent to indicate the successful outbound trip around the north of Britain into the Atlantic. The second message was a situation report about the operational area and any successes, also indicating that the boat had left its operational area to return home. This practice resulted in long periods of strict radio silence that could last for many weeks.

In general, U-boat Command was often unaware of the state of the individual boats during their patrols. The presumed rough positions of the operational boats were plotted on a daily basis to allow for a limited overview of the U-boat disposition. Where possible, information drawn from monitoring enemy signals was related to individual U-boats. Therefore, it is not surprising that some U-boats were still believed to be operational by U-boat Command although they had been sunk weeks before. In the case of U 863, its loss was finally established four months after the actual date of loss.

Usually losses became apparent when a U-boat remained silent for a longer period or failed to signal upon direct orders from U-boat Command. Under these circumstances, it was advised to radio its position or to transmit a short weather report without delay to verify its existence. As atmospheric or tactical conditions might prevent boats from receiving or sending messages, U-boat Command repeated such radio orders at least three times over a period of several days. Even when no answer was received, U-boat Command often continued to plot overdue boats in the daily dislocation for up to several weeks because there was still the possibility of a radio station breakdown. In many cases, boats were plotted until they theoretically would have run out of fuel and provisions. However, despite the very careful procedure to establish losses, there were a few cases when U-boats were wrongly considered as lost but did make a report later or entered base afterward without prior notification. In each case, radio problems were identified as the reason for the failure to report after repeated orders from U-boat Command.

Sometimes U-boats were able to transmit a final radio message prior to their sinking or friendly forces were on the scene and could pick up survivors. The latter was a very rare case because German U-boats operated almost exclusively in distant, enemy-controlled waters without any assistance from their own surface forces or aircraft. Crew members surviving the loss of their boat were normally picked up by Allied forces and became prisoners of war.

When a loss became evident but had not yet been confirmed from other evidence, the boat in question was officially posted as missing. In German naval terminology, this meant the attribution of a "one star" mark indicating a probable loss. Almost each U-boat loss was discussed in some detail in the war diary of U-boat Command on the basis of the available evidence, trying to establish the probable date and cause of the loss. Starting from late 1941, summary lists of U-boats lost during individual months together with statistical information were appended to the U-boat Command war diary. Up to March 1944, the operational department of U-boat Command also prepared a summarized report on the final patrol of each U-boat lost during front-line service, based on orders and radio messages and information derived from sinking reports, interception of Allied ASW reports, and so on. Owing to a lack of proper intelligence sources, U-boat Command gained no exact information on the date or cause of loss in more than 60 percent of the front-line U-boat losses.

Positive confirmation for a U-boat loss sometimes became available via the International Red Cross, which, under the Geneva Convention, usually received the names of those taken as prisoners of war by the belligerent parties. Often the hull numbers of U-boats sunk together with the number or names of surviving crew members were broadcast in the Allied news propaganda. In addition, prisoners of war of a sunken U-boat were sometimes able to report details about its loss to German authorities by using coded words in private letters to their next of kin.

When the final fate of a missing U-boat had become known or no clue about its fate and its crew had been established after sufficient time, the boat was assigned a "two star" mark and the case was officially closed by the operations department of U-boat Command.

The Allies were in a much better position to gain information on the causes of U-boat losses. The British Admiralty had set up the special U-boat Assessment Committee immediately after the start of the war. Committee members represented the different armed services and Admiralty departments involved in the antisubmarine campaign. The main objective of the committee was to centralize the assessment of all antisubmarine actions performed by British naval ships and aircraft. After the entry of the United States into the war, the U.S. Navy had set up a similar committee under the authority of the commander in chief U.S. Navy (Cominch). By agreement with the British Admiralty, Cominch became the assessing authority for all antisubmarine attacks by U.S. forces and the Admiralty for British and Commonwealth forces.

Each attack against a submarine target had to be reported to the committees with all details and postattack observations on special forms together with any other available evidence to verify the presence of a submarine and to assess the damage inflicted by the attack. Additional evidence could include action photographs taken during or after the attack. Surface ships often provided oil samples or pieces of wreckage picked up after their attacks. Sometimes even more gruesome evidence was presented to confirm a successful attack against a submerged U-boat.

Every reported attack was discussed and assessed within a few weeks by the committees in their regular meetings. A letter was assigned to each case indicating its situation. Standard assessments adopted by the Admiralty and Cominch are listed below with the letters given to them:

1. Assessment of "A" (known sunk) was not awarded unless positive proof of destruction had been obtained. Submarines very rarely sink without a trace, and the collection of surface evidence, prisoners, wreckage, human remains, and such things, is the only reliable proof of a sinking.

2. Assessment of "B" (probably sunk) was awarded when the committee felt morally convinced that the submarine was destroyed, but lacked concrete evidence of a corpus delicti.

3. Assessment of "C" (probably damaged) was awarded to promising attacks that were believed to have damaged the submarine seriously, and that may have

proved fatal, but on which an assessment of "B" or "A" had not been given pending receipt of further intelligence justifying a higher assessment.

4. Assessment of "D" (probably damaged) was awarded to attacks that were believed to have damaged the submarine sufficiently seriously to force it to return to base.

5. Assessment of "E" (probably slightly damaged) was awarded to attacks that were believed to have caused material damage of such a character as to hamper the submarine in the further prosecution of its patrol.

6. Assessment of "F" (insufficient evidence of damage) was awarded to those attacks that gave insufficient evidence of damage to the submarine believed to have been present.

7. Assessment of "G" (no damage) was awarded to those attacks that could have caused no damage to the submarine believed to have been present.

8. Assessment of "H" (insufficient evidence of presence of submarine) was awarded to those attacks that gave insufficient evidence of the presence of a submarine.

9. Assessment of "I" (target attacked not a submarine) was awarded to those attacks where the target was definitely nonsubmarine.

10. Assessment of "J" (insufficient information to assess) was awarded to those attacks concerning which no letter reports had been received, and when the dispatches were too indefinite to evaluate.

The results from precision raids or area bombing attacks against German U-boat construction sites or base and harbor facilities were independently assessed from aerial photographs by the photo interpretation units of the RAF Bomber Command and the USAAF.

The assessment of the individual damage inflicted by antisubmarine attacks offered many possibilities for misinterpretation and error. The simple fact that submarines unlike surface ships can submerge below the water surface without necessarily being considered as sunk is one of them. Attacks against submarines staying submerged are even more problematic as all action is directed against an invisible target hidden in a medium almost impenetrable by the human eye. Additional difficulties arose from the numerous attacks on nonsub contacts. With the German policy of "Total Underwater War" adopted in autumn 1944 after the introduction of the schnorkel installation, the assessment committees were faced with the problem that many of the attacks reported were probably not directed against genuine U-boats. The schnorkel had reduced the silhouette of a patrolling U-boat at best to an elusive schnorkel head sticking out of the water from time to time. Especially among aircraft crews employed in AS-sweeps, this resulted in a kind of "schnorkelmania" during the final year of the anti-U-boat campaign. The actual extent of these "bogus" sightings and related attacks against nonsubmarine contacts by Allied aircraft was realized several years after the war. Many of the U-boat schnorkel contacts reported were actually meteorological phenomena such as whirlwinds (whillywaws) or spouting whales.

Top secret "Ultra"-information derived from the deciphering of German radio messages was often very helpful in the evaluation of the total number of German U-boat losses and their general loss areas. However, its use in the attribution of individual U-boat losses to individual Allied antisubmarine attacks was obviously less successful as shown by the large number of postwar reassessments. The same applies to information drawn from the interrogation of surviving U-boat crew members taken as prisoners of war.

Statistical information and details on numerous antisubmarine attacks together with the Admiralty or Cominch assessment were regularly published in classified monthly publications—the RAF *Coastal Command Review*, the U.S. *Antisubmarine Warfare Bulletin*, and the Admiralty *Anti-Submarine Report*. The reports of the assessment committees on damage to enemy submarines for the more than 10,000 U-boat incidents or Allied attacks on U-boats are now filed at the Naval Historical Center in Washington, D.C., the National Archives Records Administration in College Park, Maryland and the The National Archives in London.

2

GERMAN U-BOAT NUMBERS AND TYPES, 1935–1945

All U-boats contracted or impressed by the German Kriegsmarine between 1935 and 1945 are listed. Missing U-numbers indicate that for various reasons no building contract was placed for these U-boats.

U–No.	Design type	Ordered	Yard No.	Building yard
U 1–U 6	Type II A	02.02.35	236–241	Deutsche Werke Kiel AG
U 7–U 12	Type II B	20.07.34	541–546	Germaniawerft AG Kiel
U 13–U 16	Type II B	02.02.35	248–251	Deutsche Werke Kiel AG
U 17–U 24	Type II B	02.02.35	547–554	Germaniawerft AG Kiel
U 25–U 26	Type I A	17.12.34	903–904	Deschimag AG Weser Bremen
U 27–U 32	Type VII	01.04.35	908–913	Deschimag AG Weser Bremen
U 33–U 36	Type VII	25.03.35	556–559	Germaniawerft AG Kiel
U 37–U 40	Type IX	29.07.36	942–945	Deschimag AG Weser Bremen
U 41–U 44	Type IX	21.11.36	946–949	Deschimag AG Weser Bremen
U 45–U 51	Type VII B	21.11.36	580–583, 585, 587, 589	Germaniawerft AG Kiel
U 52–U 53	Type VII B	15.05.37	584, 586	Germaniawerf't AG Kiel
U 54–U 55	Type VII B	16.07.37	588, 590	Germaniawerft AG Kiel
U 56–U 59	Type II C	17.06.37	254–257	Deutsche Werke Kiel AG
U 60–U 63	Type II C	21.07.37	259–262	Deutsche Werke Kiel AG
U 64–U 65	Type IX B	16.07.37	952–953	Deschimag AG Weser Bremen
U 66–U 68	Type IX C	07.08.39	985–987	Deschimag AG Weser Bremen[1]
U 69–U 70	Type VII C	30.05.38	604–605	Germaniawerft AG Kiel[2]
U 71–U 72	Type VII C	25.01.39	618–619	Germaniawerft AG Kiel[3]
U 73–U 76	Type VII B	02.06.38	1–4	Bremer Vulkan Vegesacker Werft
U 77–U 82	Type VII C	25.01.39	5–10	Bremer Vulkan Vegesacker Werft
U 83	Type VII B	28.11.38	291	Lübecker Flender-Werke AG[4]
U 84–U 87	Type VII B	09.06.38	280–283	Lübecker Flender-Werke AG
U 88–U 92	Type VII C	25.01.39	292–296	Lübecker Flender-Werke AG

U–No.	Design type	Ordered	Yard No.	Building yard
U 93–U 98	Type VII C	30.05.38	598–603	Germaniawerft AG Kiel[5]
U 99–U 102	Type VII B	15.12.37	593–596	Germaniawerft AG Kiel[6]
U 103–U 110	Type IX B	24.05.38	966–973	Deschimag AG Weser Bremen
U 111	Type IX B	08.08.38	976	Deschimag AG Weser Bremen
U 112–U 115	Type XI	27.01.39	977–980	Deschimag AG Weser Bremen
U 116–U 118	Type X B	31.01.39	615–617	Germaniawerft AG Kiel
U 119	Type X B	07.08.39	624	Germaniawerft AG Kiel
U 120–U 121	Type II B	28.08.37	268–269	Lübecker Flender-Werke AG[7]
U 122–U 124	Type IX B	15.12.37	954–956	Deschimag AG Weser Bremen
U 125–U 131	Type IX C	07.08.39	988–994	Deschimag AG Weser Bremen
U 132–U 136	Type VII C	07.08.39	11–15	Bremer Vulkan Vegesacker Werft
U 137–U 152	Type II D	25.09.39	266–281	Deutsche Werke Kiel AG
U 153–U 158	Type IX C	25.09.39	995–1000	Deschimag AG Weser Bremen
U 159–U 160	Type IX C	23.12.39	1009–1010	Deschimag AG Weser Bremen
U 161–U 166	Type IX C	25.09.39	700–705	Deschimag Seebeck Werft AG Wesermünde
U 167–U 170	Type IX C/40	15.08.40	706–709	Deschimag Seebeck Werft AG Wesermünde
U 171–U 176	Type IX C	23.12.39	1011–1016	Deschimag AG Weser Bremen
U 177–U 179	Type IX D2	28.05.40	1017–1019	Deschimag AG Weser Bremen[8]
U 180	Type IX D1	28.05.40	1020	Deschimag AG Weser Bremen[9]
U 181–U 182	Type IX D2	15.08.40	1021–1022	Deschimag AG Weser Bremen
U 183–U 188	Type IX C/40	15.08.40	1023–1028	Deschimag AG Weser Bremen
U 189–U 194	Type IX C/40	04.11.40	1035–1040	Deschimag AG Weser Bremen
U 195	Type IX D1	04.11.40	1041	Deschimag AG Weser Bremen
U 196–U 200	Type IX D2	04.11.40	1042–1046	Deschimag AG Weser Bremen
U 201–U 204	Type VII C	23.09.39	630–633	Germaniawerft AG Kiel
U 205–U 212	Type VII C	16.10.39	634–641	Germaniawerft AG Kiel
U 213–U 218	Type VII D	16.02.40	645–650	Germaniawerft AG Kiel
U 219–U 220	Type X B	06.08.40	625–626	Germaniawerft AG Kiel
U 221–U 226	Type VII C	15.08.40	651–656	Germaniawerft AG Kiel
U 227–U 232	Type VII C	07.12.40	657–662	Germaniawerft AG Kiel
U 233–U 234	Type X B	07.12.40	663–664	Germaniawerft AG Kiel
U 235–U 240	Type VII C	20.01.41	665–670	Germaniawerft AG Kiel
U 241–U 246	Type VII C	10.04.41	675–680	Germaniawerft AG Kiel
U 247–U 250	Type VII C	05.06.41	681–684	Germaniawerft AG Kiel
U 251–U 255	Type VII C	23.09.39	16–20	Bremer Vulkan Vegesacker Werft
U 256–U 261	Type VII C	23.12.39	21–26	Bremer Vulkan Vegesacker Werft
U 262–U 267	Type VII C	15.08.40	27–32	Bremer Vulkan Vegesacker Werft
U 268–U 273	Type VII C	20.01.41	33–38	Bremer Vulkan Vegesacker Werft

U–No.	Design type	Ordered	Yard No.	Building yard
U 274–U 279	Type VII C	10.04.41	39–44	Bremer Vulkan Vegesacker Werft
U 280–U 291	Type VII C	05.06.41	45–56	Bremer Vulkan Vegesacker Werft
U 292–U 297	Type VII C/41	14.10.41	57–62	Bremer Vulkan Vegesacker Werft
U 298–U 300	Type VII C/41	23.03.42	63–65	Bremer Vulkan Vegesacker Werft
U 301–U 302	Type VII C	06.08.40	301–302	Lübecker Flender-Werke AG
U 303–U 304	Type VII C	07.12.40	303–304	Lübecker Flender-Werke AG
U 305–U 308	Type VII C	20.01.41	305–308	Lübecker Flender-Werke AG
U 309–U 312	Type VII C	05.06.41	309–312	Lübecker Flender-Werke AG
U 313–U 316	Type VII C	25.08.41	313–316	Lübecker Flender-Werke AG
U 317–U 322	Type VII C/41	14.10.41	317–322	Lübecker Flender-Werke AG
U 323–U 328	Type VII C/41	02.04.42	323–328	Lübecker Flender-Werke AG
U 329–U 330	Type VII C/41	16.07.42	349–350	Lübecker Flender-Werke AG
U 331–U 334	Type VII C	23.09.39	203–206	Nordseewerke Emden
U 335–U 336	Type VII C	15.08.40	207–208	Nordseewerke Emden
U 337–U 338	Type VII C	21.11.40	209–210	Nordseewerke Emden
U 339–U 340	Type VII C	17.12.40	211–212	Nordseewerke Emden
U 341–U 344	Type VII C	20.01.41	213–216	Nordseewerke Emden
U 345–U 348	Type VII C	10.04.41	217–220	Nordseewerke Emden
U 349–U 350	Type VII C	05.06.41	221–222	Nordseewerke Emden
U 351–U 354	Type VII C	23.09.39	470–473	Flensburger Schiffbaugesellschaft
U 355–U 358	Type VII C	26.10.39	474–477	Flensburger Schiffbaugesellschaft
U 359–U 360	Type VII C	06.08.40	480–481	Flensburger Schiffbaugesellschaft
U 361–U 362	Type VII C	07.12.40	482–483	Flensburger Schiffbaugesellschaft
U 363–U 366	Type VII C	20.01.41	484–487	Flensburger Schiffbaugesellschaft
U 367–U 370	Type VII C	25.08.41	490–493	Flensburger Schiffbaugesellschaft
U 371–U 374	Type VII C	23.09.39	2–5	Howaldtswerke AG Kiel
U 375–U 382	Type VII C	16.10.39	6–13	Howaldtswerke AG Kiel
U 383–U 386	Type VII C	15.08.40	14–17	Howaldtswerke AG Kiel
U 387–U 390	Type VII C	21.11.40	18–21	Howaldtswerke AG Kiel
U 391–U 394	Type VII C	20.01.41	23–26	Howaldtswerke AG Kiel
U 395–U 398	Type VII C	10.04.41	27–30	Howaldtswerke AG Kiel
U 399–U 400	Type VII C	25.08.41	31–32	Howaldtswerke AG Kiel
U 401–U 404	Type VII C	23.09.39	102–105	Danziger Werft AG
U 405–U 408	Type VII C	16.10.39	106–109	Danziger Werft AG
U 409–U 412	Type VII C	30.10.39	110–113	Danziger Werft AG
U 413–U 416	Type VII C	15.08.40	114–117	Danziger Werft AG
U 417–U 420	Type VII C	20.01.41	119–122	Danziger Werft AG
U 421–U 424	Type VII C	10.04.41	123–126	Danziger Werft AG
U 425–U 428	Type VII C	05.06.41	127–130	Danziger Werft AG

U–No.	Design type	Ordered	Yard No.	Building yard
U 429–U 430	Type VII C	25.08.41	131–132	Danziger Werft AG
U 431–U 434	Type VII C	23.09.39	1472–1475	F. Schichau GmbH Danzig
U 435–U 438	Type VII C	16.10.39	1477–1480	F. Schichau GmbH Danzig
U 439–U 442	Type VII C	05.01.40	1490–1493	F. Schichau GmbH Danzig
U 443–U 444	Type VII C	13.04.40	1498–1499	F. Schichau GmbH Danzig
U 445–U 448	Type VII C	06.08.40	1505–1508	F. Schichau GmbH Danzig
U 449–U 450	Type VII C	21.11.40	1520–1521	F. Schichau GmbH Danzig
U 451–U 454	Type VII C	30.10.39	282–285	Deutsche Werke Kiel AG
U 455–U 458	Type VII C	16.01.40	286–289	Deutsche Werke Kiel AG
U 459–U 462	Type XIV	14.05.40	290–293	Deutsche Werke Kiel AG
U 463–U 464	Type XIV	15.08.40	294–295	Deutsche Werke Kiel AG
U 465–U 468	Type VII C	15.08.40	296–299	Deutsche Werke Kiel AG
U 469–U 474	Type Vll C	20.01.41	300–305	Deutsche Werke Kiel AG
U 475–U 480	Type VIIC	10.04.41	306–311	Deutsche Werke Kiel AG
U 481–U 486	Type VII C	05.06.41	316–321	Deutsche Werke Kiel AG
U 487–U 490	Type XIV	17.07.41	312–315	Deutsche Werke Kiel AG
U 491–U 493	Type XIV	22.09.42	322–324	Deutsche Werke Kiel AG
U 494–U 498	Type XIV	14.12.43	744–748	Germaniawerft AG Kiel[2]
U 499–U 500	Type XIV	14.12.43	749–750	Germaniawerft AG Kiel[3]
U 501–U 506	Type IX C	25.09.39	291–296	Deutsche Werft AG Hamburg
U 507–U 512	Type IX C	12.10.39	303–308	Deutsche Werft AG Hamburg
U 513–U 524	Type IX C	14.02.40	309–314, 334–339	Deutsche Werft AG Hamburg
U 525–U 532	Type IX C/40	15.08.40	340–347	Deutsche Werft AG Hamburg
U 533–U 538	Type IX C/40	10.04.41	351–357	Deutsche Werft AG Hamburg
U 539–U 550	Type IX C/40	05.06.41	360–371	Deutsche Werft AG Hamburg
U 551–U 558	Type VII C	25.09.39	527–534	Blohm & Voss AG Hamburg
U 559–U 562	Type VII C	16.10.39	535–538	Blohm & Voss AG Hamburg
U 563–U 574	Type Vll C	24.10.39	539–550	Blohm & Voss AG Hamburg
U 575–U 586	Type VII C	08.01.40	73–86	Blohm & Voss AG Hamburg
U 587–U 598	Type VII C	16.01.40	87–98	Blohm & Voss AG Hamburg
U 599–U 610	Type VII C	22.05.40	99–110	Blohm & Voss AG Hamburg
U 611–U 634	Type VII C	15.08.40	111–134	Blohm & Voss AG Hamburg
U 635–U 646	Type VII C	20.01.41	135–146	Blohm & Voss AG Hamburg
U 647–U 650	Type VII C	10.04.41	147–150	Blohm & Voss AG Hamburg
U 651–U 662	Type VII C	09.10.39	800–811	Howaldtswerke AG Hamburg
U 663–U 668	Type VII C	15.08.40	812–817	Howaldtswerke AG Hamburg
U 669–U 674	Type VII C	20.01.41	818–823	Howaldtswerke AG Hamburg
U 675–U 680	Type VII C	05.06.41	824–829	Howaldtswerke AG Hamburg

U–No.	Design type	Ordered	Yard No.	Building yard
U 681–U 686	Type VII C	25.08.41	830–835	Howaldtswerke AG Hamburg
U 687–U 692	Type VII C/41	02.04.42	836–841	Howaldtswerke AG Hamburg
U 693–U 698	Type VII C/41	22.09.42	843–848	Howaldtswerke AG Hamburg
U 699–U 700	Type VII C/42St	17.04.43	849–850	Howaldtswerke AG Hamburg[4]
U 701–U 706	Type VII C	09.10.39	760–764, 766	Stülckens-Werft Hamburg
U 707–U 708	Type VII C	06.08.40	771–772	Stülckens-Werft Hamburg
U 709–U 710	Type VII C	15.08.40	773–774	Stülckens-Werft Hamburg
U 711–U 714	Type VII C	07.12.40	777–780	Stülckens-Werft Hamburg
U 715–U 718	Type VII C	10.04.41	781–784	Stülckens-Werft Hamburg
U 719–U 722	Type VII C	25.08.41	785–788	Stülckens-Werft Hamburg
U 723–U 726	Type VII C/41	14.10.41	793–796	Stülckens-Werft Hamburg
U 727–U 730	Type VII C/41	13.06.42	798–801	Stülckens-Werft Hamburg
U 731–U 734	Type VII C	21.11.40	1522–1525	F. Schichau GmbH Danzig
U 735–U 740	Type VII C	10.04.41	1532–1537	F. Schichau GmbH Danzig
U 741–U 746	Type VII C	05.06.41	1544–1549	F. Schichau GmbH Danzig
U 747–U 750	Type Vll C	25.08.41	1557–1560	F. Schichau GmbH Danzig
U 751–U 762	Type VII C	09.10.39	134–145	Kriegsmarinewerft Wilhelmshaven
U 763–U 770	Type VII C	15.08.40	146–153	Kriegsmarinewerft Wilhelmshaven
U 771–U 776	Type VII C	21.11.40	154 159	Kriegsmarinewerft Wilhelmshaven
U 777–U 782	Type Vll C	20.01.41	160–165	Kriegsmarinewerft Wilhelmshaven
U 783–U 788	Type VII C/42CM	22.02.43	168–173	Kriegsmarinewerft Wilhelmshaven[5]
U 789–U 790	Type VII C/42CM	17.04.43	174–175	Kriegsmarinewerft Wilhelmshaven
U 791	Type V 300	18.02.42	698	Germaniawerft AG Kiel
U 792–U 793	Type Wa 201	19.06.42	455–456	Blohm & Voss AG Hamburg
U 794–U 795	Type Wk 202	07.08.42	718–719	Germaniawerft AG Kiel
U 796–U 797	Type XVIII	14.12.43	755–756	Germaniawerft AG Kiel[6]
U 798	Type XVII K	15.02.44	787	Germaniawerft AG Kiel
U 801–U 804	Type IX C/40	07.12.40	710–713	Deschimag Seebeck Werft AG Wesermünde
U 805–U 808	Type IX C/40	10.04.41	714–717	Deschimag Seebeck Werft AG Wesermünde
U 809–U 812	Type IX C/40	25.08.41	722–725	Deschimag Seebeck Werft AG Wesermünde
U 813–U 816	Type IX C/40	17.04.43	759–742	Deschimag Seebeck Werft AG Wesermünde
U 821–U 824	Type VII C	20.01.41	821–824	Stettiner Oderwerke AG
U 825–U 826	Type VII C	06.08.42	1588–1589	F. Schichau GmbH Danzig[7]
U 827–U 828	Type VII C/41	06.08.42	1590–1591	F. Schichau GmbH Danzig[8]
U 829–U 832	Type VII C/41	06.08.42	1592–1595	F. Schichau GmbH Danzig[9]
U 833–U 838	Type VII C/41	22.09.42	1596–1601	F. Schichau GmbH Danzig

U–No.	Design type	Ordered	Yard No.	Building yard
U 839–U 840	Type VII C/41	22.02.43	1604–1605	F. Schichau GmbH Danzig
U 841–U 846	Type IX C/40	20.01.41	1047–1052	Deschimag AG Weser Bremen
U 847–U 852	Type IX D2	20.01.41	1053–1058	Deschimag AG Weser Bremen
U 853–U 858	Type IX C/40	05.06.41	1059–1064	Deschimag AG Weser Bremen
U 859–U 864	Type IX D2	05.06.41	1065–1070	Deschimag AG Weser Bremen
U 865–U 870	Type IX C/40	25.08.41	1073–1078	Deschimag AG Weser Bremen
U 871–U 876	Type IX D2	25.08.41	1079–1084	Deschimag AG Weser Bremen
U 877–U 882	Type IX C/40	02.04.42	1085–1090	Deschimag AG Weser Bremen
U 883–U 888	Type IX D42	02.04.42	1091–1096	Deschimag AG Weser Bremen
U 889–U 894	Type IX C/40	22.09.42	1097–1102	Deschimag AG Weser Bremen
U 895–U 900	Type IX D42	22.09.42	1103–1108	Deschimag AG Weser Bremen
U 901–U 902	Type VII C	10.04.41	14–15	Vulcan Stettiner Maschinenbau AG
U 903–U 904	Type VII C	18.09.42	329–330	Lübecker Flender-Werke AG[10]
U 905–U 908	Type VII C	06.08.42	802–805	Stülckens-Werft Hamburg[11]
U 909–U 912	Type VII C/41	22.09.42	806–809	Stülckens-Werft Hamburg
U 913–U 918	Type VII C/42St	17.04.43	810–815	Stülckens-Werft Hamburg
U 921–U 924	Type VII C	06.06.41	508–511	Neptunwerft Rostock
U 925–U 928	Type VII C	25.08.41	512–515	Neptunwerft Rostock
U 929–U 932	Type VII C/41	02.04.42	516–519	Neptunwerft Rostock
U 933–U 936	Type VII C/41	22.09.42	524–527	Neptunwerft Rostock
U 937–U 942	Type VII C/42St	17.04.43	529–534	Neptunwerft Rostock
U 951–U 958	Type VII C	10.04.41	151–158	Blohm & Voss AG Hamburg
U 959–U 982	Type VII C	05.06.41	159–182	Blohm & Voss AG Hamburg
U 983–U 994	Type VII C	25.08.41	183–194	Blohm & Voss AG Hamburg
U 995–U 1006	Type VII C/41	14.10.41	195–206	Blohm & Voss AG Hamburg
U 1007–U 1018	Type VII C/41	23.03.42	207–218	Blohm & Voss AG Hamburg
U 1019–U 1030	Type VII C/41	13.06.42	219–230	Blohm & Voss AG Hamburg
U 1031–U 1042	Type VII C/41	22.09.42	231–242	Blohm & Voss AG Hamburg
U 1043–U 1050	Type VII C/41	02.01.43	243–250	Blohm & Voss AG Hamburg
U 1051–U 1058	Type VII C	05.06.41	685–692	Germaniawerft AG Kiel
U 1059–U 1062	Type VII F	25.08.41	693–696	Germaniawerft AG Kiel
U 1063–U 1068	Type VII C/41	14.10.41	700–705	Germaniawerft AG Kiel
U 1069–U 1080	Type VII C/42St	16.07.42	706–717	Germaniawerft AG Kiel
U 1081–U 1092	Type XVII G	04.01.43	720–731	Germaniawerft AG Kiel
U 1093–U 1098	Type VII C/42St	17.04.43	732–737	Germaniawerft AG Kiel
U 1099–U 1100	Type VII C/42CM	17.04.43	738–739	Germaniawerft AG Kiel
U 1101–U 1102	Type VII C	05.06.41	223–224	Nordseewerke Emden
U 1103–U 1106	Type VII C	14.10.41	225–228	Nordseewerke Emden[12]
U 1107–U 1110	Type VII C/41	02.04.42	229–232	Nordseewerke Emden

U–No.	Design type	Ordered	Yard No.	Building yard
U 1111–U 1114	Type VII C/41	22.09.42	233–236	Nordseewerke Emden
U 1115–U 1120	Type VII C/42St	17.04.43	237–242	Nordseewerke Emden
U 1131–U 1132	Type VII C	25.08.41	33–34	Howaldtswerke AG Kiel
U 1133–U 1140	Type VII C/41	02.01.43	35–42	Howaldtswerke AG Kiel
U 1141–U 1146	Type VII C/41	22.02.43	43–48	Howaldtswerke AG Kiel
U 1147–U 1152	Type VII C/42St	17.04.43	49–54	Howaldtswerke AG Kiel
U 1153–U 1154	Type XXII	06.07.43	55–56	Howaldtswerke AG Kiel
U 1161–U 1162	Type VII C	25.08.41	133–134	Danziger Werft AG
U 1163–U 1166	Type VII C/41	14.10.41	135–138	Danziger Werft AG
U 1167–U 1170	Type VII C/41	02.04.42	139–142	Danziger Werft AG
U 1171–U 1176	Type VII C/41	16.07.42	143–148	Danziger Werft AG
U 1177–U 1182	Type VII C/41	22.09.42	149–154	Danziger Werft AG
U 1183–U 1188	Type VII C/41	13.01.43	155–160	Danziger Werft AG
U 1189–U 1190	Type VII C/41	22.03.43	161–162	Danziger Werft AG
U 1191–U 1198	Type VII C	25.08.41	1561–1568	F. Schichau GmbH Danzig
U 1199–U 1204	Type VII C	14.10.41	1573–1578	F. Schichau GmbH Danzig[13]
U 1205–U 1210	Type VII C	02.04.42	1582–1587	F. Schichau GmbH Danzig
U 1211–U 1214	Type VII C/41	22.02.43	1606–1609	F. Schichau GmbH Danzig
U 1215–U 1220	Type VII C/42St	22.02.43	1610–1615	F. Schichau GmbH Danzig
U 1221–U 1226	Type IX C/40	25.08.41	384–389	Deutsche Werft AG Hamburg
U 1227–U 1238	Type IX C/40	14.10.41	390–401	Deutsche Werft AG Hamburg
U 1239–U 1244	Type IX C/40	02.04.42	402–407	Deutsche Werft AG Hamburg
U 1245–U 1250	Type IX C/40	23.05.42	408–413	Deutsche Werft AG Hamburg
U 1251–U 1262	Type IX C/40	22.09.42	434–445	Deutsche Werft AG Hamburg
U 1271–U 1273	Type VII C/41	23.03.42	66–68	Bremer Vulkan Vegesacker Werft
U 1274–U 1279	Type VII C/41	13.06.42	69–74	Bremer Vulkan Vegesacker Werft
U 1280–U 1285	Type VII C/41	22.09.42	75–80	Bremer Vulkan Vegesacker Werft
U 1286–U 1291	Type VII C/42St	22.09.42	81–86	Bremer Vulkan Vegesacker Werft[14]
U 1292–U 1297	Type VII C/42St	02.01.43	87–92	Bremer Vulkan Vegesacker Werft
U 1301–U 1304	Type VII C/41	02.04.42	494–497	Flensburger Schiffbaugesellschaft
U 1305–U 1308	Type VII C/41	01.08.42	498–501	Flensburger Schiffbaugesellschaft
U 1309–U 1312	Type VII C/41	22.09.42	502–505	Flensburger Schiffbaugesellschaft
U 1313–U 1318	Type VII C/42St	17.04.43	509–514	Flensburger Schiffbaugesellschaft
U 1331–U 1334	Type VII C/41	16.07.42	351–354	Lübecker Flender-Werke AG
U 1335–U 1338	Type VII C/41	22.09.42	355–358	Lübecker Flender-Werke AG
U 1339–U 1344	Type VII C/42St	22.02.43	359–364	Lübecker Flender-Werke AG
U 1345–U 1350	Type VII C/42St	17.04.43	365–370	Lübecker Flender-Werke AG
U 1401–U 1404	Type VII C/41	02.01.43	251–254	Blohm & Voss AG Hamburg
U 1405–U 1416	Type XVII B	04.01.43	255–266	Blohm & Voss AG Hamburg

U–No.	Design type	Ordered	Yard No.	Building yard
U 1417–U 1422	Type VII C/41	22.02.43	267–272	Blohm & Voss AG Hamburg
U 1423–U 1434	Type VII C/42St	22.02.43	273–284	Blohm & Voss AG Hamburg
U 1435–U 1439	Type VII C/41	17.04.43	285–289	Blohm & Voss AG Hamburg
U 1440–U 1463	Type VII C/42CM	17.04.43	290–313	Blohm & Voss AG Hamburg
U 1501–U 1506	Type IX C/40	10.07.43		Deschimag Seebeck Werft AG Wesermünde[15]
U 1507–U 1512	Type IX C/40	22.02.43	1121–1126	Deschimag AG Weser Bremen
U 1513–U 1530	Type IX C/40	17.04.43	1127–1144	Deschimag AG Weser Bremen
U 1531–U 1542	Type IX D/42	17.04.43	1145–1156	Deschimag AG Weser Bremen
U 1601–U 1615	Type XX	14.12.43	760–762, 766–768, 772–774, 778–780, 784–786	Germaniawerft AG Kiel[16]
U 1701–U 1715	Type XX	14.12.43	757–759, 763–765, 769–771, 775–777, 781–783	Germaniawerft AG Kiel[17]
U 1801–U 1804	Type VII C/41	22.03.43	163–166	Danziger Werft AG
U 1805–U 1810	Type VII C/42St	22.03.43	167–172	Danziger Werft AG
U 1811–U 1822	Type VII C/42St	17.04.43	173–184	Danziger Werft AG
U 1823–U 1828	Type VII C/41	03.07.43		Danziger Werft AG
U 1901–U 1904	Type VII C/42CM	17.04.43	176–179	Kriegsmarinewerft Wilhelmshaven
U 2001–U 2004	Type VII C/42St	17.04.43	851–854	Howaldtswerke AG Hamburg
U 2101–U 2104	Type VII C/42CM	17.04.43	740–743	Germaniawerft AG Kiel
U 2201–U 2204	Type XIV	14.12.43	751–754	Germaniawerft AG Kiel[18]
U 2301–U 2318	Type VII C/42St	17.04.43	1616–1633	F. Schichau GmbH Danzig
U 2321–U 2331	Type XXIII	20.09.43	475–485	Deutsche Werft AG Hamburg
U 2332–U 2333	Type XXIII	07.07.44	941–942	Germaniawerft AG Kiel[19]
U 2334–U 2370	Type XXIII	20.09.43	488–524	Deutsche Werft AG Hamburg
U 2371–U 2400	Type XXIII	07.07.44	525–554	Deutsche Werft AG Hamburg[20]
U 2401–U 2430	Type XXIII	20.09.43	804–833	Ansaldo Genoa
U 2431–U 2445	Type XXIII	20.09.43	656–670	Cantiere Riuniti Del Adriatico Monfalcone
U 2446–U 2460	Type XXIII	01.05.44		Schiffswerft Linz AG[21]
U 2501–U 2631	Type XXI	06.11.43	2501–2631	Blohm & Voss AG Hamburg
U 2632–U 2762	Type XXI	06.05.44	2632–2762	Blohm & Voss AG Hamburg
U 3001–U 3088	Type XXI	06.11.43	1160–1241	Deschimag AG Weser Bremen
U 3089–U 3176	Type XXI	06.05.44	895–982	Bremer Vulkan "Valentin" pen yard
U 3177–U 3288	Type XXI	27.09.44	983–1100	Bremer Vulkan "Valentin" pen yard[22]
U 3501–U 3571	Type XXI	06.11.43	1646–1716	F. Schichau GmbH Danzig
U 3572–U 3642	Type XXI	06.05.44	1726–1796	F. Schichau GmbH Danzig

U–No.	Design type	Ordered	Yard No.	Building yard
U 3643–U 3684	Type XXI	27.09.44	1797–1838	F. Schichau GmbH Danzig[23]
U 4001–U 4070	Type XXIII	11.05.44		Deutsche Werft AG Hamburg[24]
U 4501–U 4600	Type XXVI W	28.09.44	4501–4600	Blohm & Voss AG Hamburg[25]
U 4701–U 4750	Type XXIII	12.07.44	943–990, 1081–1082	Germaniawerft AG Kiel
U 4751–U 4891	Type XXIII	23.11.44	1189–1329	Germaniawerft AG Kiel[26]
V 80	Experimental	06.03.39	597	Germaniawerft AG Kiel

Foreign submarines captured by German forces and designated for service in the Kriegsmarine

U–No.	Design type	Yard No.	Building yard
UA	*Saldiray*-class	575	Germaniawerft AG, Kiel
UB	*Porpoise*-class		Admiralty Dockyard, Chatham
UC 1–UC 2	B-class (Holland Type)	116–117	Marinens Hovedverft, Horten
UD 1	*O 8*-class, ex British *H-6* (Holland Type H-class)		Canadian Vickers & Co., Montreal
UD 2	*O 12*-class	186	K.M. De Schelde, Vlissingen
UD 3	*O 21*-class	667	Wilton-Fijenoord, Schiedam
UD 4–UD 5	*O 21*-class	209–210	Rotterdamsche Droogdokmaatschappij, Rotterdam
UF 1–UF 2	*Aurore*-class	196, 195	Atelier et Chant. Worms & Cie, Le Trait
UF 3	*Aurore*-class	200	Anciens Chantier Dubigeon, Nantes
UIT 1–UIT 3	*Romolo*-class	287–289	Odero Terni Orlando, Muggiano-I.a Spezia
UIT 4–UIT 6	*Romolo*-class	1471–1473	Cantiere Riuniti dell Adriatico, Monfalcone
UIT 7–UIT 8	*CM*-class	1513–1514	Cantiere Riuniti dell Adriatico, Monfalcone
UIT 21	*Calvi*-class		Odero Terni Orlando, Muggiano-La Spezia
UIT 22–UIT 23	*Liuzzi*-class		Franco Tosi, Taranto
UIT 24	*Marcello*-class		Odero Terni Orlando. Muggiano-La Spezia
UIT 25	*Marconi*-class		Odero Terni Orlando, Muggiano-La Spezia
ex *La Martinique*	*Roland Morillot*-class		Navy Yard Arsenal Cherbourg
ex *Sparide*	*Tritone*-class		Odero Terni Orlando, Muggiano-La Spezia
ex *Morena*	*Tritone*-class		Odero Terni Orlando, Muggiano-La Spezia
ex *Grongo*	*Tritone*-class		Odero Terni Orlando, Muggiano-La Spezia
cx *Nautilo*	*Tritone-class*		Cantiere Riuniti dell Adriatico, Monfalcone
cx *Beilul*	*Adua*-class		Odero Terni Orlando, Muggiano-La Spezia

3

LOSS REGISTER

The total number of German U-boats is arranged according to the official German design types. For cross-referencing of design types with U-boat hull numbers, see chapter 2.

Type I A

Oceangoing combat U-boat type of conventional design developed in 1933–34
Surface/submerged displacement: 862/983 t
Overall length/beam/draught: 72.39 m/6.21 m/4.30 m
Standard main armament: 6 torpedo tubes (4 bow, 2 stern) with up to 14 torpedoes

Building yard	Total no. ordered	Completed (comm.)	Under construction	Construction not started	Canceled after keel laying	Canceled prior to keel laying
Deschimag AG Weser Bremen	2	2	—	—	—	—
Total	2	2	—	—	—	—

1	2	3	4	5	6
U 25	6.4.36	1.8.40	Wi	KK H. Beduhn	≈2.8.40 ✠ North Sea N. of Terschelling: ≈54°14n/05°07e / missing – ≈sea mine British "Field No. 7" / 49 dead / ✠.[1]
U 26	11.5.36	20.6.40	Wi	KL H. Scheringer	1.7.40 ✠ N. Atlantic S.W. of Ireland: 48°03n/11°30w / D/Cs / PE HMS *Gladiolus* (Lt. Comdr. H. M. C. Sanders) and Sun H (F/L W. N. Gibson), 10 Sqn RAAF / 48 rescued.

Type II A

Coastal combat U-boat type of conventional design developed in 1933–34
Surface/submerged displacement: 254/302 t
Overall length/beam/draught: 40.90 m/4.08 m/3.38 m
Standard main armament: 3 torpedo tubes (3 bow) with up to 5 torpedoes

Building yard	Total no. ordered	Completed (comm.)	Under construction	Construction not started	Canceled after keel laying	Canceled prior to keel laying
Deschimag AG Weser Bremen	6	6	—	—	—	—
Total	6	6	—	—	—	—

1	2	3	4	5	6
U 1	29.6.35	6.4.40	Wi	KL J. Deecke	6.4.40 ✠ North Sea N. of Terschelling: ≈54°14n/05°07e / missing – sea mine British "Field No. 7" / 24 dead / ✠.[2]
U 2	25.7.35	20.6.40		OL W. Schwarzkopf	8.4.44 ✠ 07h45 Baltic W. of Pillau: 54°48n/19°55e / collision / German S/fi *Helmi Söhle* / 17 dead / 18 rescued/ ↑ 9.4.44, →Pillau Seekanal, decomm., cannibalized, hulk 25.4.45 captured by USSR forces at Pillau, br?
U 3	6.8.35			LT H. Neumeister	1.8.44 decomm. Neustadt; 1945 cannibalized, hulk 3.5.45 captured by British forces at Neustadt, br.
U 4	17.8.35			OL H. Rieger	1.8.44 decomm. Gotenhafen; 1945 cannibalized, →Stolpmünde, hulk 9.3.45 captured by USSR forces at Stolpmünde, br 1951.
U 5	31.8.35			LT H. Rahn	19.3.43 18h00 ✠ Baltic W. of Pillau: 54°50n/19°34e / diving accident during deep dive test / 21 dead / ✠
U 6	7.9.35			LT E. Jestel	7.8.44 decomm. Gotenhafen, 1945 cannibalized, →Stolpmünde, hulk 9.3.45 captured by USSR forces at Stolpmünde, br 1951.

Type II B

Coastal combat U-boat type of conventional design developed in 1935
Surface/submerged displacement: 279/328 t
Overall length/beam/draught: 42.70 m/4.08 m/3.90 m
Standard main armament: 3 torpedo tubes (3 bow) with up to 5 torpedoes

Building yard	Total no. ordered	Completed (comm.)	Under construction	Construction not started	Canceled after keel laying	Canceled prior to keel laying
Germaniawerft AG Kiel	14	14	—	—	—	—
Deutsche Werke Kiel AG	4	4	—	—	—	—
Lübecker Flender-Werke AG	2	2	—	—	—	—
Total	20	20	—	—	—	—

1	2	3	4	5	6
U 7	18.7.35			OL J. Loeschke	18.2.44 ✠ 09h30 Baltic W. of Pillau: 54°52n/19°29,8e / diving accident / 29 dead ✠.
U 8	5.8.35			OL J. Krieghammer	31.3.45 decomm. Wilhelmshaven, 5.5.45 (✠) Wilhelmshaven, western entrance to Raeder lock: 53°31n/08°10e / br.
U 9	21.8.35			KL H.-J. Schmidt-Weichert	30.4.42 decomm. Kiel, →Black Sea, recomm. Galati.
	28.10.42			OL H. Klapdor	20.8.44 ✠ 10h30 Constanza: 44°10n/28°41e / bomb / Soviet Naval Air Force / none dead / ↑ 22.10.44 by USSR, →Nikolaev, 19.4.45 Soviet *TS-16*, Black Sea Fleet, reconstruction planned but constructive total loss, § 12.12.46, br.
U 10	9.9.35			OL K. Ahlers	?.7.44 decomm. Danzig (?), instructional boat 1.ULD, cannibalized, →Stolpmünde, hulk 9.3.45 captured by USSR forces at Stolpmünde, 1951 br.
U 11	21.9.35			OL G. Dobenecker	14.12.44 decomm. Gotenhafen, 1.2.45 → Kiel; 3.5.45 (✠) Kiel, Arsenal, 1947 br.
U 12	30.9.35	23.9.39	Wi	KL D. von der Ropp	After 23.9.39 ✠ ≈ Western entrance English Channel S. of Dover; ≈51°10n/01°30e / missing – ≈sea mine / 27 dead / ✠.[3]
U 13	30.11.35	26.5.40	Ki	KL M. Schulte	31.5.40 ✠ North Sea E. of Lowestoft: 52°26n/02°02e / D/Cs / PS HMS *Weston* (Lt. Comdr. S. C. Tuke) / 26 rescued.

1	2	3	4	5	6
U 14	18.1.36			OL H.-J. Dierks	3.3.45 decomm. Wilhelmshaven, 5.5.45 (✝) Wilhelmshaven, western entrance to Raeder lock: 53°31n/08°10e / br.
U 15	7.3.36	29.1.40	Wi	KL P. Frahm	30.1.40 ✝ 03h05 North Sea N. of Heligoland: 54°24,7n/07°50,7e / collision / German TB *Iltis* (KL H. Schuur) / 25 dead / ✝.
U 16	16.5.36	18.10.39	Ki	KL H. Wellner	25.10.39 (✝) English Channel ≈Goodwin Sands E. of Dover: 51°09n/01°28e / ≈following sea mine damage / 28 dead / ✝.[4]
U 17	3.12.35			OL F. Baumgärtel	?.2.45 decomm. Wilhelmshaven, 5.5.45 (✝) Wilhelmshaven, western entrance to Raeder lock: 53°31n/08°10e / br.
U 18	4.1.36			KL H. Pauckstadt	20.11.36 ✝ 09h54 Baltic, Lübeck Bay: 54°07n/11°07e / collision / German TB *T 156* (OL Huber) / 8 dead / 12 rescued / ↑ 28.11.36, → Kiel, repaired.
	3.5.37			OL F.-W. Wißmann	25.9.42 decomm. Kiel, → Black Sea, recomm. Galati.
	6.5.43			OL K. Fleige	25.8.44 (✝) Constanza Roads S.E. Cape Tuzla: 43°52n/28°51e / following bomb damage Soviet air raid 20.8.44 / ↑ USSR late 1944, constructive total loss, 26.5.47 ✝ torpedo Soviet SS *M-120* off Sevastopol.
U 19	16.1.36			OL H.-L. Gaude	30.4.42 decomm. Kiel, → Black Sea, recomm. Galati.
	28.12.42	25.8.44	Ko	OL H. Verpoorten	11.9.44 22h30 (✝) Black Sea N. of Zonguldak: 41°34n/31°50e.
U 20	1.2.36			OL C. Schöler	26.9.42 decomm. Kiel, →Black Sea, recomm. Galati.
	27.5.43	19.8.44	Ko	OL K. Grafen	10.9.44 21h30 (✝) Black Sea N. of Karasu: 41°10n/30°47e.
U 21	6.8.36	21.3.40	Wi	KL W.-H. Stiebler	26.3.40 23h30 ✝ S.E. of Mandal, Oldknuppen I.: 57°57,5n/ 07°34,5e / grounded by navigational error / 28.3.40 refloated, interned Norway: → Kristiansand / 9.4.40 recaptured. 16.4.40 → Kiel, refit, recomm. Kiel.
	13.7.40			OL W. Schwarzkopf	?.7.44 decomm. Pillau, instructional boat 1.ULD, February 1945 cannibalized, hulk 25.4.45 captured by USSR forces at Pillau, br?
U 22	21.8.36	20.3.40	Wi	KL K.-H. Jenisch	after 20.3.40 ✝ ≈North Sea-Skagerrak / missing / 27 dead / ✝.[5]

1	2	3	4	5	6
U 23	24.9.36			KL R.-B. Wahlen	20.10.42 decomm. Kiel, → Black Sea, recomm. Galati.
	3.6.43	16.8.44	Ko	OL R. Arendt	10.9.44 22h10 (✞) Black Sea N. of Agra: 41°11n/30°00e.
U 24	10.10.36			OL H. Rodler von Roithberg	30.4.42 decomm. Kiel, → Black Sea, recomm. Galati.
	14.10.42			OL D. Lenzmann	25.8.44 (✞) Constanza Roads: 44°12n/28°41e / following bomb damage Soviet air raid 20.8.44 / ↑ USSR spring 1945, constructive total loss, 26.5.47 ✞ torpedo Soviet SS *M-120* off Sevastopol.
U 120	20.4.40			OL R. R. Bensel	5.5.45 (✞) Wesermünde / October 1949 to November 1950 br.
U 121	28.5.40			OL F. Horst	5.5.45 (✞) Wesermünde-Alten Hafen / ↑ 2.12.49, br.

Type II C

Coastal combat U-boat type of conventional design developed in 1937
Surface/submerged displacement: 291/341 t
Overall length/beam/draught: 43.90 m/4.08 m/3.82 m
Standard main armament: 3 torpedo tubes (3 bow) with up to 5 torpedoes

Building yard	Total no. ordered	Completed (comm.)	Under construction	Construction not started	Canceled after keel laying	Canceled prior to keel laying
Deutsche Werke Kiel AG	8	8	—	—	—	—
Total	8	8	—	—	—	—

1	2	3	4	5	6
U 56	26.11.38			OL J. Sauerbier	?.4.45 decomm. Kiel, 3.5.45 (✝) Kiel: 54°19n/10°10e, br.
U 57	29.12.38	31.8.40	Be	OL E. Topp	3.9.40 ✝ 00h15 Brunsbüttel Roads, 200m S. of mole 3: 53°53n/09°09e / collision / Norwegian S/S *Rona* / 6 dead / 19 rescued / ↑ 9.9.40, → Kiel, 16.9.40 decomm., repaired Deutsche Werke Kiel, recomm. Kiel.
	11.1.41			OL P. Kühl	?.4.45 decomm. Kiel, 3.5.45 (✝) Kiel: 54°19n/10°10e, br.
U 58	4.2.39			OL R. Schulz	?.4.45 decomm. Kiel, 3.5.45 (✝) Kiel: 54°19n/10°10e / br.
U 59	4.3.39			LT H. Walther	?.4.45 decomm. Kiel, 3.5.45 (✝) Kiel, Kriegsmarine dockyard. 1945 br.
U 60	22.7.39			OL H. Schmidt	28.2.45 decomm. Wilhelmshaven, 5.5.45 (✝) Wilhelmshaven, western entrance to Raeder lock: 53°31n/08°10e / br.
U 61	12.8.39			LT W. Zapf	27.3.45 decomm. Wilhelmshaven, 5.5.45 (✝) Wilhelmshaven, western entrance to Raeder lock: 53°31n/08°10e / br.
U 62	21.12.39			LT H. E. Augustin	20.3.45 decomm. Wilhelmshaven, 5.5.45 (✝) Wilhelmshaven, western entrance to Raeder lock: 53°31n/08°10e / br.
U 63	18.1.40	17.2.40	He	OL G. Lorentz	25.2.40 ✝ North Sea S. of Shetland Is.: 58°40n/00°10w / D/Cs / DD's HMS *Escort* (Lt. Comdr. J. Bostock), HMS *Inglefield* (Capt. P. Todd), HMS *Imogen* (Comdr. C. L. Firth) / 1 dead / 24 rescued.

Type II D

Coastal combat U-boat type of conventional design developed in 1939
Surface/submerged displacement: 314/364 t
Overall length/beam/draught: 43.97 m/4.92 m/3.93 m
Standard main armament: 3 torpedo tubes (3 bow) with up to 5 torpedoes

Building yard	Total no. ordered	Completed (comm.)	Under construction	Construction not started	Canceled after keel laying	Canceled prior to keel laying
Deutsche Werke Kiel AG	16	16	—	—	—	—
Total	16	16	—	—	—	—

1	2	3	4	5	6
U 137	15.6.40			OL H.-J. Dierks	5.5.45 (✝) Wilhelmshaven, western entrance to Raeder lock: 53°31n/08°10e / br.
U 138	27.6.40	12.6.41	Lo	OL F. Gramitzky	18.6.41 ✝ 11h00 N. Atlantic W. of Cadiz: 36°04n/07°29w / D/Cs / DD HMS *Faulknor* (Capt. A. F. de Salis) / 27 rescued.
U 139	24.7.40			OL W. Kimmelmann	5.5.45 (✝) Wilhelmshaven, western entrance to Raeder lock: 53°31n/08°10e / br.
U 140	7.8.40			OL W. Scherfling	5.5.45 (✝) Wilhelmshaven, western entrance to Raeder lock: 53°31n/08°10e / br.
U 141	21.8.40			OL H.-D. Hoffmann	5.5.45 (✝) Wilhelmshaven, U-boat base: 53°31n/08°10e / br.
U 142	4.9.40			OL F. Baumgärtel	5.5.45 (✝) Wilhelmshaven, western entrance to Raeder lock: 53°31n/08°10e / br.
U 143	18.9.40			OL W. Kasparek	Heligoland, →Wilhelmshaven, 30.6.45 sailed →Loch Ryan / 22.12.45 (✝) artillery DD HMS *Onslow* 55°58n/ 09°35w / Op. Deadlight.
U 144	2.10.40	28.7.41	Sm	KL G. von Mittelstaedt	10.8.41 ✝ 22h18 Baltic W. of Dagö Isl.: 58°58n/21°24,5e / torpedo / Soviet SS *Shch -307* (Kl. N. I. Petrov) / 28 dead / ✝.
U 145	16.10.40			OL F.-K. Görner	5.5.45 Surrender Heligoland, →Wilhelmshaven, 30.6.45 sailed →Loch Ryan / 22.12.45 ✝ artillery DD HMS *Onslow* 55°47n/ 09°56w / Op. Deadlight.

1	2	3	4	5	6
U 146	30.10.40			OL K. Schauroth	5.5.45 (✝) Wilhelmshaven, western entrance to Raeder lock: 53°31n/08°10e / br.
U 147	11.12.40	25.5.41	Be	OL E. Wetjen	2.6.41 ✝ N. Atlantic N.W. of Ireland: 56°38n/10°24w / D/Cs / DD HMS *Wanderer* (Comdr. A. F. St.G. Orpen), PE HMS *Periwinkle* (Lt. Comdr. P. G. Maclver) / 26 dead / ✝.
U 148	28.12.40			OL R. Tammen	5.5.45 (✝) Wilhelmshaven, western entrance to Raeder lock: 53°31n/08°10e / br.
U 149	13.11.40			OL H. Plohr	5.5.45 Surrender Heligoland, →Wilhelmshaven, 30.6.45 sailed →Loch Ryan / 21.12.45 ✝ artillery DD ORP *Piorun* 55°40,5n/ 08°00w / Op. Deadlight.
U 150	27.11.40			OL J. Kriegshammer	5.5.45 Surrender Heligoland, →Wilhelmshaven, 30.6.45 sailed →Loch Ryan / 21.12.45 ✝ artillery DD HMS *Onslaught*, PS HMS *Fowey* 56°04n/09°35w / Op. Deadlight.
U 151	15.1.41			OL F. Graf Arco	5.5.45 (✝) Wilhelmshaven, western entrance to Raeder lock: 53°31n/08°10e / br.
U 152	29.1.41			OL G. Thiel	5.5.45 (✝) Wilhelmshaven, western entrance to Raeder lock: 53°31n/08°10e / br.

Type VII

Seagoing combat U-boat type of conventional design developed in 1933–34
Surface/submerged displacement: 626/745 t
Overall length/beam/draught: 64.51 m/5.85 m/4.37 m
Standard main armament: 5 torpedo tubes (4 bow, 1 stern) with up to 11 torpedoes

Building yard	Total no. ordered	Completed (comm.)	Under construction	Construction not started	Canceled after keel laying	Canceled prior to keel laying
Deutsche Werke Kiel AG	6	6	—	—	—	—
Germaniawerft AG Kiel	4	4	—	—	—	—
Total	8	8	—	—	—	—

1	2	3	4	5	6
U 27	12.8.36	23.8.39	Wi	KL J. Franz	20.9.39 ✠ N. Atlantic W. of Hebrides: 58°35n/09°02w / D/Cs / DD's HMS *Fortune* (Comdr. E. A. Gibbs), HMS *Forester* (Lt. Comdr. E. B. Tancock) / 38 rescued.
U 28	12.9.36			OL D. Sachse	17.3.44 ✠ Neustadt U-boat quay: 54°07n/10°50e / accident, ↑ ?.3.44: ?.4.44 decomm., instructional boat 3.ULD Neustadt, final fate ?
U 29	16.11.36			OL U.-P. Graf von und zu Arco-Zinneberg	17.4.44 decomm., →instructional boat 4.ULD Memel, later 2.ULD Gotenhafen, →Flensburg. November 1944 conversion to floating torpedo firing station for HKT planned, but not executed: 5.5.45 (✠) Flensburg Fiord, Kupfermühlen Bay. June 1993 still present.
U 30	8.10.36			OL G. Schimmel	?.1.45 decomm. Kiel. →Flensburg, conversion to floating torpedo firing station for HKT planned, but not executed: 5.5.45 (✠) Flensburg Fiord. Kupfermühlen Bay / br.
U 31	28.12.36			KL J. Habekost	11.3.40 ✠ 12h North Sea, Jade Bay near buoy 12: ≈53°37n/08°10e / bomb / Ble O (S/L M. Delap), 82 Sqn RAF / 58 dead / ✠ / ↑ 24.3.40, decomm. Wilhelmshaven, repaired, recomm. Wilhelmshaven.
	30.7.40	19.10.40	Lo	KL W. Prellberg	2.11.40 ✠ N. Atlantic N.W. of Ireland: 56°26n/10°18w / D/Cs / DD HMS *Antelope* (Lt. Comdr. R. T. White) / 2 dead / 44 rescued.

1	2	3	4	5	6
U 32	15.4.37	24.10.40	Lo	OL H. Jenisch	30.10.40 ✠ N. Atlantic N.W. of Ireland: 55°37n/12°19w / D/Cs / DD's HMS *Harvester* (Lt. Comdr. M. Thornton), HMS *Highlander* (Comdr. W. A. Dallmeyer) / 9 dead / 33 rescued.
U 33	25.7.36	6.2.40	He	KL H.-W. von Dresky	12.2.40 ✠ North Channel, Firth of Clyde: 55°23,4n/05°08,2w / D/Cs / AM HMS *Gleaner* (Lt. Comdr. H. P. Price) / 25 dead / 17 rescued.
U 34	12.9.36			LT E. Aust	5.8.43 ✠ 21h55 Memel: 55°43,7n/21°06,5e / collision / U-boat tender *Lech* (KL W.-G. Schapler) / 4 dead / 39 rescued / ↑ 24.8.43, docked Lindenau-Werft; 8.9.43 decomm. Memel, → Schichauwerft Königsberg, May 1944 br.
U 35	3.11.36	18.11.39	Wi	KL W. Lott	29.11.39 ✠ North Sea N.W. of Bergen: 60°53n/02°47e / D/Cs / DD's HMS *Kashmir* (Comdr. H. A. King), HMS *Kingston* (Lt. Comdr. P. Somerville), HMS *Icarus* (Lt. Comdr. C. D. Maud) / 43 rescued.
U 36	16.12.36	3.12.39	Wi	KL W. Fröhlich	4.12.39 ✠ North Sea S.W. of Kristiansand: 57°00n/05°20e / torpedo / SS HMS/m *Salmon* (Lt. Comdr. E. O. Bickford) / 40 dead / ✠.

Type VII B

Seagoing combat U-boat type of conventional design developed in 1934–35
Surface/submerged displacement: 753/857 t
Overall length/beam/draught: 66.50 m/6.18 m/4.74 m
Standard main armament: 5 torpedo tubes (4 bow, 1 stern) with up to 14 torpedoes

Building yard	Total no. ordered	Completed (comm.)	Under construction	Construction not started	Canceled after keel laying	Canceled prior to keel laying
Bremer Vulkan Vegesacker Werft	4	4	—	—	—	—
Germaniawerft AG Kiel	15	15	—	—	—	—
Lübecker Flender-Werke AG	5	5	—	—	—	—
Total	24	24	—	—	—	—

1	2	3	4	S	6
U 45	25.6.38	5.10.39	Ki	KL A. Gelhaar	14.10.39 ✠ N. Atlantic S.W. of Ireland: 50°58n/12°57w / D/Cs / DD's HMS *Inglefield* (Capt. P. Todd), HMS *Ivanhoe* (Comdr. B. Jones), HMS *Intrepid* (Comdr. J. W. Josselyn), HMS *Icarus* (Lt. Comdr. C. D. Maud) / 38 dead / ✠.
U 46	2.11.38			OL E. Jewinski	?.11.43 decomm. Neustadt, →instructional boat 3.ULD, →Flensburg, November 1944 conversion to floating torpedo firing station for HKT planned, but not executed; 5.5.45 (✠) Flensburg Fiord, Kupfermühlen Bay: 54°50n/09°29e.
U 47	17.12.38	20.2.41	Lo	KK G. Prien	7.3.41 ✠ N. Atlantic S. of Iceland: ≈60°n/13°w / missing / 45 dead / ✠.[6]
U 48	22.4.39			OL D. Todenhagen	?.11.43 decomm. Neustadt, →instructional boat 3.ULD; 3.5.45 (✠) Neustadt: 54°07n/10°50e.
U 49	12.8.39	3.4.40	Wi	KL C. von Goßler	15.4.40 ✠ Arctic N.E. of Harstad: 68°53n/16°59e / D/Cs / DD's HMS *Fearless* (Comdr. K. L. Harkness), HMS *Brazen* (Lt. Comdr. Sir M. Culme-Seymour) / 1 dead / 41 rescued.
U 50	12.12.39	6.4.40	Wi	KL M.-H. Bauer	≈6.4.40 ✠ North Sea N. of Terschelling: ≈54°14n/05°07e / missing – ≈sea mine British "Field No. 7" / 44 dead / ✠.[7]

1	2	3	4	S	6
U 51	6.8.38	9.8.40	Ki	KL D. Knorr	20.8.40 ✝ Biscay W. of St. Nazaire: 47°06n/04°51w / torpedo / SS HMS/m *Cachalot* (Lt. Comdr. J.D. Luce) / 43 dead / ✝.
U 52	4.2.39			OL E.-A. Racky	22.10.43 decomm. Danzig, →Neustadt, →instructional boat 3.ULD: 3.5.45 ✝ Neustadt: 54°07n/10°50e / rockets / 4 Typhoons (led by F/L R. C. Nutter), 175 Sqn RAF / br 1946/47.
U 53	24.6.39	6.2.40	He	KK H. Grosse	24.2.40 ✝ N. Atlantic W. of Shetland Is.: 60°32n/06°14w / D/Cs / DD HMS *Gurkha* (Comdr. A. W. Buzzard) / 42 dead / ✝.
U 54	23.9.39	12.2.40	He	KL G. Kutschmann	≈13.2.40 ✝ North Sea: 54°58,3n/ 05°28,4e / sea mine British "Field No. 6" / 41 dead / ✝.[8]
U 55	21.11.39	16.1.40	Ki	KL W. Heidel	30.1.40 ✝ N. Atlantic S.W. of Scilly Is.: 48°37n/07°48w / D/Cs / DD HMS *Whitshed* (Comdr. E. R. Conder), PS HMS *Fowey* (Comdr. H. B. Ellison) and Sun Y (F/O K. J. Brooks), 228 Sqn RAF / 1 dead / 41 rescued.
U 73	30.9.40	4.12.43	To	OL H. Deckert	16.12.43 ✝ Mediterranean N. of Oran: 36°07n/00°50w / D/Cs, artillery / DD's USS *Woolsey* (Comdr. H. R. Wier), USS *Trippe* (Comdr. R. C. Williams) / 16 dead / 34 rescued.
U 74	31.10.40	23.4.42	Sp	OL K. Friederich	2.5.42 ✝ Mediterranean E. of Cartagena: 37°12n/00°01e / D/Cs / DD's HMS *Wishart* (Comdr. H. G.. Scott), HMS *Wrestler* (Lt. R. W. B. Lacon) / 47 dead / ✝.[9]
U 75	19.12.40	22.12.41	Sa	KL H. Ringelmann	28.12.41 ✝ Mediterranean N. of Mersa Matruh: 31°50n/26°40e / D/Cs / DD HMS *Kipling* (Comdr. A. St. Clair-Ford) / 14 dead / 30 rescued.
U 76	3.12.40	29.3.41	Be	OL F. von Hippel	5.4.41 ✝ N. Atlantic S. of Iceland: 58°35n/20°20w / D/Cs / DD HMS *Wolverine* (Lt. Comdr. J. M. Rowland), PS HMS *Scarborough* (Lt.. A. P. Northey) / 1 dead / 42 rescued.
U 83	8.2.41	1.3.43	Sp	OL U. Wörißhoffer	4.3.43 ✝ 12h05 Mediterranean S.E. of Cartagena: 37°10n/00°05e / D/Cs / Hud V (Sgt. G. Jakimov), 500 Sqn RAF / 50 dead / ✝.

1	2	3	4	S	6
U 84	29.4.41	10.6.43	Br	KL H. Uphoff	7.8.43 ✠ W. Atlantic: 27°55n/68°30w / D/C, homing torpedo / Lib B-4 (Lt. T. R. Evert), V PB-105 Sqn USN / 46 dead / ✠.[10]
U 85	7.6.41	21.3.42	Na	OL E. Greger	14.4.42 ✠ N. Atlantic N.E. of Cape Hatteras: 35°55n/75°13w / artillery / DD USS *Roper* (Lt. Comdr. H. W. Howe) / 46 dead / ✠.
U 86	8.7.41	11.11.43	Br	KL W. Schug	29.11.43 ✠ N. Atlantic E. of Azores: 40°42n/18°54w / D/Cs / DD's HMS *Tumult* (Lt Comdr. N. Lanyon), HMS *Rocket* (Lt. M.R.S. Smithwick) / 50 dead / ✠.[11]
U 87	19.8.41	9.1.43	Br	KL J. Berger	4.3.43 ✠ N. Atlantic W. of Leixoes: 41°36n/13°31w / D/Cs / DD HMCS *St. Croix* (A/Lt. Comdr. A. H. Dobson), PE HMCS *Shediac* (T/Lt. J. E. Clayton) / 49 dead / ✠.
U 99	18.4.40	22.2.41	Lo	KK O. Kretschmer	17.3.41 ✠ 03h43 N. Atlantic S.E. of Iceland: 61°n/11°48w / D/Cs / DD HMS *Walker* (Comdr. D. G. F. W. MacIntyre) / 3 dead / 40 rescued.
U 100	30.5.40	9.3.41	Ki	KL J. Schepke	17.3.41 ✠ 03h18 N. Atlantic S.E. of Iceland: 61°04n/11°30w / D/Cs, ramming / DD's HMS *Walker* (Comdr. D. G. F. W. MacIntyre), HMS *Vanoc* (Lt. Comdr. J. G. W. Deneys) / 38 dead / 6 rescued.
U 101	11.3.40			OL H. Münster	22.10.43 decomm. Neustadt, →instructional boat 3.ULD; 3.5.45 ✠ Neustadt: 54°07n/10°50e / rockets / 4 Typhoons (led by F/L R. C. Nutter), 175 Sqn RAF / br.
U 102	27.4.40	22.6.40	Ki	KL H. von Klot	1.7.40 ✠ N. Atlantic S.W. of Ireland: 48°33n/10°26w / D/Cs / DD HMS *Vansittart* (Lt. Comdr. W. Evershed) / 43 dead / ✠.[12]

Type VII C

Seagoing combat U-boat type of conventional design developed in 1937–38
Surface/submerged displacement: 769/871 t
Overall length/beam/draught: 67.10 m/6.18 m/4.74 m
Standard main armament: 5 torpedo tubes (4 bow, 1 stern) with up to 14 torpedoes

Building yard	Total no. ordered	Completed (comm.)	Under construction	Construction not started	Canceled after keel laying	Canceled prior to keel laying
Nordseewerke Emden	26	26	—	—	—	—
Kriegsmarine-werft Wilhelms-haven	32	27	—	—	3	2
Bremer Vulkan Vegesacker Werft	52	52	—	—	—	—
Stülckens-Werft Hamburg	26	24	—	—	2	—
Blohm & Voss AG Hamburg	144	144	—	—	—	—
Howaldts-werke AG Hamburg	36	33	—	—	3	—
Flensburger Schiffbauge-sellschaft	20	20	—	—	—	—
Germaniawerft AG Kiel	58	58	—	—	—	—
Deutsche Werke Kiel AG	30	29	—	—	1	—
Howaldts-werke AG Kiel	32	31	—	—	1	—
Lübecker Flender-Werke AG	23	23	—	—	—	—
Neptunwerft Rostock	8	8	—	—	—	—
Stettiner Oder-werke AG	4	2	—	—	2	—
Vulcan Stettiner Maschinen-bau AG	2	1	—	—	1	—

Building yard	Total no. ordered	Completed (comm.)	Under construction	Construction not started	Canceled after keel laying	Canceled prior to keel laying
Danziger Werft AG	32	32	—	—	—	—
F. Schichau GmbH Danzig	62	62	—	—	—	—
Total	587	572	—	—	13	2

1	2	3	4	5	6
U 69	2.11.40	2.1.43	Lo	KL U. Gräf	17.2.43 ✠ N. Atlantic E. of Newfoundland: 50°36n/41°07w / D/Cs / DD HMS *Fame* (Comdr. R. Heathcote) / 46 dead / ✠.[13]
U 70	23.11.40	22.2.41	He	KL J. Matz	7.3.41 ✠ N. Atlantic S.E. of Iceland: 60°15n/14°00w / D/Cs / PE's HMS *Camellia* (Lt. Comdr. A. E. Willmott), HMS *Arbutus* (Lt. Comdr. H. Lloyd-Williams) / 20 dead / 25 rescued.
U 71	14.12.40			OL E. Ranzau	27.2.45 decomm. Wilhelmshaven; 5.5.45 (✠) Wilhelmshaven, western entrance to Raeder lock: 53°31n/08°10e / br.
U 72	4.1.41			OL K.-T. Mayer	30.3.45 ✠ Bremen, Deschimag-AG Weser, Industriehafen: 53°08n/08°46e / bomb / air raid 8. USAAF / none dead / ↑ until 2.7.47, br.
U 77	18.1.41	3.3.43	Sp	OL O. Hartmann	29.3.43 ✠ 01h15 Mediterranean E. of Cartagena: 38°33n/00°14e / following D/Cs / Hud C (P/O F. J. Clerke), 500 Sqn RAF, Hud L (F/O E. F. Castell), 233 Sqn RAF 28.3.43 / 38 dead / 9 rescued.[14]
U 78	15.2.41			OL H. D. Hübsch	16.4.45 ✠ 21h50 Pillau, Seedienst-Bahnhof quay: 54°38n/19°54e / artillery / Soviet Army / none dead / while operating as generating plant.
U 79	13.3.41	21.12.41	Sa	KL W. Kaufmann	23.12.41 ✠ Mediterranean N. of Sollum: 32°15n/25°19e / D/Cs / DD's HMS *Hasty* (Lt. N. H. G. Austen), HMS *Hotspur* (Lt. T. D. Herrick) / 44 rescued.
U 80	8.4.41			KL H. Keerl	28.11.44 ✠ Baltic W. of Pillau: 54°40n/19°30e / diving accident / 50 dead / ✠.
U 81	26.4.41			OL J. O. Krieg	9.1.44 ✠ 11h30 Pola: 44°52n/13°51 e / bomb / air raid 15. USAAF / 2 dead / ↑ 22.4.44, docked, constructive total loss, br.

1	2	3	4	5	6
U 82	14.5.41	11.1.42	Pa	KL S. Rollmann	6.2.42 ✠ N. Atlantic N.E. of Azores: 44°10n/23°52w / D/Cs / PS HMS *Rochester* (Comdr. C. B. Allen), PE HMS *Tamarisk* (Lt. S. Ayles) / 45 dead / ✠.
U 88	15.10.41	25.8.42	Nv	KL H. Bohmann	12.9.42 ✠ Arctic S.W. of Spitzbergen: 75°04n/04°49e / D/Cs / DD HMS *Faulknor* (Capt. A. K. Scott-Moncrieff) / 46 dead / ✠.
U 89	19.11.41	25.4.43	Pa	KK D. Lohmann	12.5.43 ✠ N. Atlantic N. of Azores: 46°30n/25°40w / D/Cs / Swd B, 811 Sqn FAA CVE HMS *Biter* (Capt. E. M. C. Abel-Smith) and DD HMS *Broadway* (Comdr. E. H. Chevasse), PF HMS *Lagan* (Lt. Comdr. A. Ayre) / 48 dead / ✠.
U 90	20.12.41	2.7.42	Kr	KL H.-J. Oldörp	24.7.42 ✠ N. Atlantic E. of Newfoundland: 48°12n/40°56w / D/Cs / DD HMCS *St. Croix* (A/Lt. Comdr. A. H. Dobson) / 44 dead / ✠.
U 91	28.1.42	25.1.44	Br	KL H. Hungershausen	26.2.44 ✠ N. Atlantic: 49°45n/26°20w / D/Cs / DE's HMS *Affleck* (A/Comdr. C. Gwinner), HMS *Gore* (Lt. J. V. Reeves-Brown), HMS *Gould* (Lt. D. W. Ungoed) / 36 dead / 16 rescued.
U 92	3.3.42			OL W. Brauel	12.10.44 decomm. Trondheim, cannibalized, hulk →Hoplafiord, 7.3.45 ✠ there accidentally, May 45 wreck captured by British forces, br.
U 93	30.7.40	23.12.41	Na	OL H. Elfe	15.1.42 ✠ N. Atlantic N.E. of Madeira: 36°40n/15°52w / D/Cs / DD HMS *Hesperus* (Lt. Comdr. A. A. Tait) / 6 dead / 40 rescued.
U 94	10.8.40	3.8.42	Na	OL O. Ites	28.8.42 ✠ Caribbean E. of Jamaica: 17°40n/74°30w / D/Cs, ramming / PE HMCS *Oakville* (T/A Lt. Comdr. C. A. King) and Cat (Lt. G. R. Fiss), VP-92 Sqn USN / 19 dead / 26 rescued.
U 95	31.8.40	19.11.41	Lo	KL G. Schreiber	28.11.41 ✠ 01h50 Mediterranean S.W. of Almeria: 36°24n/03°20w / torpedo / SS HNetMS/m *0 21* (Lt. Comdr. J. F. van Dulm) / 35 dead / 12 rescued.
U 96	14.9.40			OL R. Rix	15.2.45 decomm. Wilhelmshaven; 30.3.45 ✠ Wilhelmshaven, Hipper Basin: 53°31n/08°10e / bomb / air raid 8. USAAF / br.

1	2	3	4	5	6
U 97	28.9.40	5.6.43	Po	KL H.-G. Trox	16.6.43 ✠ 16h40 Mediterranean W. of Haifa: 33°00n/34°00e / D/Cs / Hud T (F/Sgt D. T. Barnard), 459 Sqn RAAF / 27 dead / 21 rescued.
U 98	12.10.40	22.10.42	Na	OL K. Eichmann	15.11.42 ✠ N. Atlantic W. of Gibraltar: 36°09n/07°42w / D/Cs / DD HMS *Wrestler* (Lt. R. W. B. Lacon) / 46 dead / ✠.[15]
U 132	29.5.41	6.10.42	Pa	KL E. Vogelsang	≈4.11.42 ✠ ≈00h44 N. Atlantic S.E. of Cape Farewell: ≈55°38n/39°52w / missing – ≈explosion British S/S *Hatimura* (Capt. W. F. Putt) / 47 dead / ✠.[16]
U 133	5.7.41	14.3.42	Sa	OL E. Mohr	14.3.42 ✠ 19h00 Mediterranean S. of Salamis: 37°50n/23°35e / German sea mine / 45 dead / ✠.
U 134	26.7.41	10.6.43	Pa	KL H.-G. Brosin	27.8.43 ✠ 00h39 Biscay N of Cape Ortegal: 40°44n/08°05w / D/Cs / PF HMS *Rother* (Lt. Comdr. R. V. E. Case) / 48 dead / ✠.[17]
U 135	16.8.41	7.6.43	Lo	OL O. Luther	15.7.43 ✠ 13h06 mid-Atlantic E. of Canary Is.: 28°20n/13°17w / D/Cs / PS HMS *Rochester* (Comdr. H. V. King), PE's HMS *Mignonette* (Lt. H. H. Brown), HMS *Balsam* (Lt. J. E. L. Peters) and D/Cs Cat P-6 (Lt.[jg] R. J. Finnie), VP-92 Sqn USN / 5 dead / 41 rescued.
U 136	30.8.41	29.6.42	Na	KL H. Zimmermann	11.7.42 ✠ mid-Atlantic W. of Madeira: 33°30n/22°52w / D/Cs / PF HMS *Spey* (Comdr. H. G. Boys-Smith), PS HMS *Pelican* (Comdr. G. V. Gladstone), DD FNFL *Leopard* (Capt. de frégate J. Evenou) / 45 dead / ✠.
U 201	25.1.41	3.1.43	Br	OL G. Rosenberg	17.2.43 ✠ N. Atlantic E. of Newfoundland: 50°50n/40°50w / D/Cs / DD HMS *Viscount* (Lt. Comdr. J. V. Waterhouse) / 49 dead / ✠.[18]
U 202	22.3.41	29.4.43	Br	KL G. Poser	2.6.43 ✠ 00h30 N. Atlantic S.E. of Cape Farewell: 56°12n/39°52w / D/Cs, artillery / PS HMS *Starling* (Comdr. F. J. Walker) / 18 dead / 30 rescued.
U 203	18.2.41	3.4.43	Br	KL H. Kottmann	25.4.43 ✠ N. Atlantic S. of Cape Farewell: 55°05n/42°25w / D/Cs / Swd L, 811 Sqn FAA CVE HMS *Biter* (Capt. E. M. C. Abel-Smith) and DD HMS *Pathfinder* (Comdr. E. A. Gibbs) / 10 dead / 38 rescued.

1	2	3	4	5	6
U 204	8.3.41	20.9.41	Br	KL W. Kell	19.10.41 ✠ N. Atlantic N.W. of Tangier: 35°46n/06°02w / D/Cs / PE HMS *Mallow* (Lt. W. R. B. Noall), PS HMS *Rochester* (Comdr. C. B. Allen) / 46 dead / ✠.
U 205	3.5.41	11.2.43	Sa	OL F. Bürgel	17.2.43 ✠ 17h37 Mediterranean, N.W. of Derna: 32°56n/22°01e / foundered while under tow by PE HMS *Gloxinia* (Lt. A. F. Harkness) following D/Cs HMS *Paladin* (Lt. Comdr. L. St. G. Rich) and Bis W (Capt. C. R. Brinton), 15 Sqn SAAF / 8 dead / 42 rescued.
U 206	17.5.41	29.11.41	Na	KL H. Opitz	≈29.11.41 ✠ Biscay S.W. of St. Nazaire: ≈47°05n/02°40w / missing – ≈British air-laid mine, field "Beech" / 46 dead / ✠.[19]
U 207	7.6.41	24.8.41	Dr	OL F. Meyer	11.9.41 ✠ N. Atlantic S.E. of Angmagsalik: 63°59n/34°48w / D/Cs / DD's HMS *Leamington* (Lt. Comdr. H. G. Bowermann), HMS *Veteran* (Comdr. W. E. J. Eames) / 41 dead / ✠.
U 208	5.7.41	3.12.41	Br	OL A. Schlieper	7.12.41 ✠ N. Atlantic W. of Gibraltar: 35°51n/07°45w / D/Cs / DD's HMS *Harvester* (Lt. Comdr. M. Thornton), HMS *Hesperus* (Lt. Comdr. A. A. Tait) / 45 dead / ✠.[20]
U 209	11.10.41	9.4.43	Kr	KL H. Brodda	≈7.5.43 ✠ N. Atlantic: ≈52° n/38° w / missing – ≈diving accident following D/Cs damage Canso W (S/L B. H. Moffit), 5(BR) Sqn RCAF 4.5.43 / 46 dead / ✠.[21]
U 210	21.2.42	20.7.42	Kr	KK R. Lemcke	6.8.42 ✠ N. Atlantic S. of Cape Farewell: 54°24n/39°37w / D/Cs, artillery, ramming / DD HMCS *Assiniboine* (A/Lt. Comdr. J. H. Stubbs) / 6 dead / 37 rescued.
U 211	7.3.42	14.10.43	Br	KL K. Hause	19.11.43 ✠ 03h45 N. Atlantic E. of Azores: 40°15n/19°18w / D/Cs / Wel F (F/O D. F. McRae), 179 Sqn RAF / 54 dead / ✠.
U 212	25.4.42	5.7.44	Br	KL H. Vogler	21.7.44 ✠ English Channel S. of Brighton: 50°27n/00°13w / D/Cs / DE HMS *Curzon* (A/Lt. Comdr. A. A. Diggens), *Ekins* (T/Lt. G. G. Bonner-Davis) / 49 dead / ✠.
U 221	9.5.42	20.9.43	Na	KL H. Trojer	27.9.43 ✠ N. Atlantic S.W. of Ireland: ≈47°n/18°w / D/Cs / Hal B (F/O E. L. Hartley), 58 Sqn RAF / 50 dead / ✠.
U 222	22.5.42			KL R. von Jessen	2.9.42 ✠ 21h50 Baltic S. of Bornholm: ≈54°33n/15°35e / collision / U 626 (LT H.-B. Bade) / 42 dead / 3 rescued.

1	2	3	4	5	6
U 223	6.6.42	16.3.44	To	OL P. Gerlach	30.3.44 ✠ Mediterranean N.E. of Palermo: 38°48n/14°10e / D/Cs / DD's HMS *Laforey* (Capt. H. T. Armstrong), HMS *Tumult* (Lt. Comdr. N. Lanyon), DE's HMS *Hambledon* (Lt. L. G. Toone), HMS *Blencathra* (Lt. Comdr. E. G. Warren) / 23 dead / 27 rescued.
U 224	20.6.42	3.1.43	Na	OL H.-C. Kosbadt	13.1.43 ✠ Mediterranean W. of Algiers: 36°28n/00°49e / D/Cs, ramming / PE HMCS *Ville de Quebec* (Lt. Comdr. A. R. E. Coleman) / 45 dead / 1 rescued.
U 225	11.7.42	2.2.43	Br	OL W. Leimkühler	22.2.43 ✠ 08h47 N. Atlantic: 48°37n/30°35w / D/Cs / PE HMS *Dianthus* (Lt. N. F. Israel) / 46 dead / ✠.[22]
U 226	1.8.42	5.10.43	Na	OL A. Gänge	6.11.43 ✠ 07h N. Atlantic E. of Newfoundland: 44°49n/41°13w / D/Cs / PS's HMS *Starling* (Comdr. F. J. Walker), HMS *Woodcock* (Lt. Comdr. C. Gwinner), HMS *Kite* (Lt. Comdr. W. F. R. Segrave) / 51 dead / ✠.
U 227	22.8.42	26.4.43	Kr	KL J. Kuntze	30.4.43 ✠ 11h55 Arctic N. of Faeroe Is.: 64°05n/06°40w / D/Cs / Ham X (F/Sgt J. S. Freeth), 455 Sqn RAAF / 49 dead / ✠.
U 228	12.9.42			KL H. Engel	4.10.44 ✠ Bergen, Laksevaag Yard: 60°23n/05°18e / bomb / air raid 6 (RCAF) and 8 Groups RAF Bomber Command / capsized and sank with floating dock ↑ ?.11.44, 26.1.45 decomm. cannibalized. May 45 Bergen captured by British forces, br 1946 by Stavanger Skibs-Ophugnings Co. A/S.
U 229	3.10.42	31.8.43	Pa	OL R. Schetelig	22.9.43 ✠ 08h20 N. Atlantic S.E. of Cape Farewell: 54°36n/36°25w / artillery, ramming and D/Cs / DD HMS *Keppel* (Comdr. M. J. Evans) / 50 dead / ✠.
U 230	24.10.42	17.8.44	To	OL H.-E. Eberbach	21.8.44 (✠) Toulon Roads off St. Mandrier Peninsula: 43°04n/05°54e / blown up after grounding / 50 rescued / 1945 partly br, 1953 completely br.
U 231	14.11.42	26.12.43	Pa	KL W. Wenzel	13.1.44 ✠ N. Atlantic N.E. of Azores: 44°15n/20°38w / D/Cs / Wel L (P/O W. N. Armstrong), 172 Sqn RAF / 7 dead / 43 rescued.
U 232	28.11.42	10.5.43	Kr	KL E. Ziehm	9.7.43 ✠ 18h12 N. Atlantic N.W. of Lisbon: 39°48n/14°22w / D/Cs / Wel R (F/O E. J. Fisher), 179 Sqn RAF / 46 dead / ✠.[23]

1	2	3	4	5	6
U 235	19.12.42			OL K. Becker	14.5.43 ✠ Kiel, Germaniawerft fitting out quay / bomb / air raid 8. USAAF / 2 dead / ↑ 31.5.43, decomm., repaired, recomm. Kiel.
	29.10.43	10.4.45	Ki	KL F. Huisgen	14.4.45 ✠ 07h00 North Sea N. of Skagens Horn: 58°09n/10°48e / erroneous D/Cs / German TB *T 17* (KL H. Liermann) / 46 dead / ✠.
U 236	9.1.43			OL R. Ziesmer	14.5.43 ✠ Kiel, Germaniawerft inside pontoon No. 5 / bomb / air raid 8. USAAF / none dead / ↑ 22.5.43, 25.5.43 decomm., repaired Germaniawerft Kiel, recomm. Kiel.
	29.9.43	4.5.45	Ge	OL H. Mumm	5.5.45 (✠) Baltic, W. of Schleimünde: 54°37n/10°03e / following damage air strike Typhoons, 184 Sqn RAF and 245 Sqn RAF 4.5.45 / all rescued.
U 237	30.1.43			KL H. Nordheimer	14.5.43 ✠ Kiel, Germaniawerft inside pontoon No. 5 / bomb / air raid 8. USAAF / none dead / ↑ 26.5.43. decomm., repaired, recomm. Kiel.
	8.10.43			KL K.-H. Menard	4.4.45 ✠ Kiel, Germaniawerft fitting out quay / bomb / air raid 8. USAAF / 1 dead / br.
U 238	20.2.43	27.1.44	Br	KL H. Hepp	9.2.44 ✠ N. Atlantic S.W. of Ireland: 49°45n/16°07w / D/Cs / PS's HMS *Kite* (Lt. Comdr. W. F. R. Segrave), HMS *Magpie* (Lt. Comdr. R. S. Abram), HMS *Starling* (Capt. F. J. Walker) / 50 dead / ✠.
U 239	13.3.43			OL U. Vöge	24.7.44 ✠ Kiel, Howaldtswerke AG / bomb / air raid RAF Bomber Command / 5.8.44 decomm., br 1944.
U 240	3.4.43	14.5.44	Be	OL G. Link	after 14.5.44 ✠ Arctic W. of Norway / missing / 50 dead / ✠.[24]
U 241	24.7.43	15.5.44	Be	OL A. Werr	18.5.44 ✠ Arctic N.E. of Shetland Is.: 63°36n/01°42e / D/Cs / Cat S (F/O B. Bastable), 210 Sqn RAF / 51 dead / ✠.
U 242	14.8.43	3.3.45	Kr	OL H. Riedel	5.4.45 ✠ 07h15 St.-George-Channel: 52°02,9n/05°46,8w / British sea mine, field "QZX" / 44 dead / ✠.[25]
U 243	2.10.43	15.6.44	Be	KL H. Märtens	8.7.44 ✠ Biscay W. of St. Nazaire: 47°06n/06°40w / D/Cs / Sun H (F/O W. B. Tilley), 10 Sqn RAAF / 11 dead / 38 rescued.

1	2	3	4	5	6
U 244	9.10.43	15.4.45	Be	OL H.-P. Mackeprang	14.5.45 Surrender Loch Foyle, →Lisahally / 30.12.45 ✝ artillery DD ORP *Piorun* 55°46n/08°32w / Op. Deadlight.
U 245	18.12.43	9.4.45	He	KK F. Schumann-Hindenberg	10.5.45 Surrender Bergen, 30.5.45 sailed →Loch Ryan / 7.12.45 ✝ foundered while under tow 55°25n/06°19w / Op. Deadlight.
U 246	11.1.44	21.2.45	Be	KL E. Raabe	17.3.45 ✝ 16h10 Irish Sea S. of Isle of Man: 53°40n/04°53,5w / D/Cs / TWL HMT *Lady Madeleine* (T/Lt. J. D. W. Lewis) / 48 dead / ✝.[26]
U 247	23.10.43	26.8.44	Br	OL G. Matschulat	1.9.44 ✝ English Channel S. of Landsend: 49°54n/05°49w / D/Cs / PF's HMCS *Saint John* (A/Lt. Comdr. W. R. Stacey), HMCS *Swansea* (Comdr. A. F. C. Layard) / 52 dead / ✝.
U 248	6.11.43	3.12.44	Dr	OL J.-F. Loos	16.1.45 ✝ N. Atlantic: 47°43n/26°37w / D/Cs / DE's USS *Hayter* (Lt. Comdr. F. Huey), USS *Otter* (Lt. Comdr. J. M. Irvine), USS *Varian* (Lt. Comdr. L. A. Myhre), USS *Joseph C. Hubbard* (Lt. Comdr. L. C. Mabley) / 47 dead / ✝.
U 249	20.11.43	3.4.45	Be	KL U. Kock	10.5.45 Surrender Portland: HMS/m *N 85*, tests, →Loch Ryan / 13.12.45 ✝ torpedo SS HMS/m *Tantivy* 56°10n/10°05w / Op. Deadlight.
U 250	12.12.43	25.7.44	Re	KL W.-K. Schmidt	30.7.44 ✝ 19h25 Baltic, Gulf of Finland, Koivisto Strait: 60°27,9n/28°24,9e / D/Cs / Soviet PC *MO 103* (Obltn. A. P. Kolenko) / 46 dead / 6 rescued / ↑ 14.9.44 USSR, 25.9.44 →Kronstadt, 12.4.45 Soviet *TS-14*, constructive total loss, § 20.8.45, br.
U 251	20.9.41	16.4.45	Ki	OL F. Säck	19.4.45 ✝ 17h04 Baltic, Kattegat S. of Göteborg: 56°37n/11°51e / rockets, machine-gun fire / Mos R, P, Z, T, 235 Sqn RAF, Mos J, 143 Sqn RAF, Mos S, T, ?, 248 Sqn RAF / 39 dead / 4 rescued.
U 252	4.10.41	29.3.42	He	KL K. Lerchen	14.4.42 ✝ 22h30 N. Atlantic S.W. of Ireland: 47°00n/18°14w / D/Cs / PS HMS *Stork* (Comdr. F. J. Walker), PE HMS *Vetch* (T/Lt. Comdr. H. J. Beverley) / 44 dead / ✝.
U 253	21.10.41	14.9.42	Kr	KL A. Friedrichs	≈25.9.42 ✝ N. Atlantic, Denmark Straits: ≈67° n/23° w / missing – ≈British sea mine / 45 dead / ✝.[27]
U 254	8.11.41	21.11.42	Br	KL H. Gilardone	8.12.42 ✝ 21h54 N. Atlantic S.E. of Cape Farewell: 58°45n/33°02w / collision / U 221 (OL H. Trojer) / 41 dead / 4 rescued.

1	2	3	4	5	6
U 255	29.11.41	8.5.45	Na	OL H. Heinrich	17.5.45 Surrender Loch Eriboll, →Lisahally, →Loch Ryan / 13.12.45 ✝ rockets / Bft, 254 Sqn RAF 55°50n/10°05w / Op. Deadlight.
U 256	18.12.41			KL O. Loewe	30.11.42 decomm. Brest following D/C damage Wel Z, 77 Sqn RAF 2.9.42 / repaired, recomm. Brest.
	16.8.43			OL W. Brauel	?.6.44 decomm. Brest following D/C damage Lib M (F/O E. E. Allen), 224 Sqn RAF 7.6.44, August 1944 emergency repair, recomm. Brest.
	16.8.44			KK H. Lehmann-Willenbrock	23.10.44 decomm. Bergen, cannibalized; May 45 Bergen captured by British forces, br.
U 257	14.1.42	2.1.44	Na	KL H. Rahe	24.2.44 ✝ N. Atlantic: 47°19n/26°00w / D/Cs / PF's HMCS *Waskesiu* (Lt. Comdr. J. P. Fraser), HMS *Nene* (Comdr. J. D. Birch) / 30 dead / 19 rescued.
U 258	4.2.42	1.4.43	Pa	KL W. von Mäßenhausen	20.5.43 ✝ 18h12 N. Atlantic: 55°18n/27°49w / D/Cs / Lib P (S/L J. R. E. Proctor), 120 Sqn RAF / 49 dead / ✝.
U 259	18.2.42	5.11.42	Pa	KL K. Köpke	15.11.42 ✝ 11h00 Mediterranean N. of Algiers: 37°20n/03°05e / D/Cs / Hud S (F/O M. A. Ensor), 500 Sqn RAF / 48 dead / ✝.
U 260	14.3.42	20.2.45	Kr	OL K. Becker	12.3.45 (✝) 22h30 N. Atlantic S. of Ireland: ≈51°29n/09°06w / following sea mine damage British field "CF A" 12.3.45 / 48 rescued.
U 261	28.3.42	10.9.42	Kr	KL H. Lange	15.9.42 ✝ 16h04 N. Atlantic N.W. of Hebrides: 59°50n/09°28w / D/Cs / Wht Q (Sgt B. F. Snell), 58 Sun RAF / 43 dead / ✝.
U 262	15.4.42			KL K.-H. Laudahn	2.4.45 decomm. Kiel / May 45 captured by British forces, 1947 br.
U 263	6.5.42	19.1.44	Pa	KL K. Nölke	20.1.44 ✝ Biscay S.W. of La Rochelle: ≈45°40n/03°00w / missing – ≈diving accident / 51 dead/ ✝.[28]
U 264	22.5.42	5.2.44	Na	KL H. Looks	19.2.44 ✝ 17h07 N. Atlantic: 48°31n/22°05w / D/Cs / PS's HMS *Woodpecker* (Comdr. H. L. Pryse), HMS *Starling* (Capt. F. J. Walker) / 52 rescued.
U 265	6.6.42	26.1.43	Be	OL L. Auffhammer	3.2.43 ✝ N. Atlantic S. of Iceland: 56°35n/22°49w / D/Cs / For N (P/O K. Ramsden), 220 Sqn RAF / 46 dead / ✝.
U 266	24.6.42	14.4.43	Na	KL R. von Jessen	15.5.43 ✝ N. Atlantic N.W. of Spain: 45°28n/10°20w / D/Cs / Hal M (W/C W. E. Oulton), 58 Sqn RAF / 47 dead / ✝.[29]

1	2	3	4	5	6
U 267	11.7.42			KL O. Tinschert	6.7.44 decomm. St. Nazaire, laid up U-boat pen St. Nazaire; later emergency repair, recomm. St. Nazaire.
	23.9.44 (?)			OL B. Knieper	5.5.45 (✝) Gelting Bay: 54°48n/09°49e / br.
U 268	29.7.42	10.1.43	Be	OL E. Heydemann	19.2.43 ✝ Biscay W. of St. Nazaire: 47°03n/05°56w / D/Cs / Wel B (F/O G. D. Lundon), 172 Sqn RAF / 44 dead / ✝.
U 269	19.8.42	18.6.44	Pp	OL G. Uhl	25.6.44 ✝ English Channel S.E. of Torquay: 49°56n/02°46w / D/Cs / DE HMS *Bickerton* (Comdr. D. G. F. W. MacIntyre) / 13 dead / 39 rescued.
U 270	5.9.42			KL P.-F.Otto	?.6.44 decomm. Lorient, laid up U-boat pen Lorient; later recomm. Lorient.
	?.8.44	10.8.44	Lo	OL H. Schreiber	13.8.44 ✝ 00h10 Biscay N.W. of La Rochelle: 46°19n/02°56w / D/Cs / Sun A (F/O D. A. Little), 461 Sqn RAAF / 71 rescued.
U 271	23.9.42	12.1.44	Br	KL C. Barleben	28.1.44 ✝ N. Atlantic W. of Ireland: 53°15n/15°52w / D/Cs / Lib E (Lt. C. A. Enloe), VB-103 Sqn USN / 51 dead / ✝.
U 272	7.10.42			OL H. Hepp	12.11.42 ✝ 19h15 Baltic off Hela: 54°37,6n/18°50,7e / collision / U 634 (OL H.-G. Brosin) / 29 dead / 19 rescued.
U 273	21.10.42	13.5.43	Be	OL H. Roßmann	19.5.43 ✝ N. Atlantic S.W. of Iceland: 59°25n/24°33w / D/Cs / Hud M (F/O J. N. P. Bell), 269 Sqn RAF / 46 dead / ✝.
U 274	7.11.42	13.10.43	Dr	OL G. Jordan	23.10.43 ✝ N. Atlantic: 57°14n/27°50w / D/Cs / DD's HMS *Duncan* (Comdr. P. W. Gretton), HMS *Vidette* (Lt. Comdr. R. Hart) and Lib Z (A/S/L E. J. Wicht), 224 Sqn RAF / 48 dead / ✝.
U 275	25.11.42	25.2.45	Na	OL H.Wehrkamp	10.3.45 ✝ English Channel S. of Newhaven: 50°36n/00°04e / British sea mine, field "Brazier E" / 48 dead / ✝.
U 276	9.12.42			KL H. Zwarg	29.9.44 decomm. Lübeck; →Neustadt, floating power plant, 3.5.45 ✝ Neustadt: 54°07n/10°50e / rockets / 4 Typhoons (led by F/L R. C. Nutter), 175 Sqn RAF / br ≈1947.
U 277	21.12.42	11.4.44	Hf	KL R. Lübsen	1.5.44 ✝ 02h47 Arctic S.W. of Bear I.: 73°24n/15°32e / D/Cs / Swd C (Sub-Lt. L. G. Cooper), 842 Sqn FAA CVE HMS *Fencer* (A/Capt. W. W. R. Bentinck) / 50 dead / ✝.
U 278	16.1.43			KL J. Franze	9.5.45 Surrender Narvik, →Loch Eriboll, →Lisahally / 31.12.45 ✝ artillery DD ORP *Blyskawica* 55°44n/08°21w / Op. Deadlight.

1	2	3	4	5	6
U 279	3.2.43	8.9.43	Be	KL O. Finke	4.10.43 16h56 ✠ N. Atlantic S.W. of Iceland: 60°40n/26°30w / D/Cs / Ven B (Comdr. C. L. Westhofen), VB-128 Sqn USN / 48 dead / ✠.[30]
U 280	13.2.43	16.10.43	Be	OL W. Hungershausen	16.11.43 ✠ N. Atlantic: 49°11n/27°32w / D/Cs / Lib M (F/O J. H. Bookless), 86 Sqn RAF / 49 dead / ✠.
U 281	27.2.43			KL H. von Davidson	9.5.45 Surrender Kristiansand. 29.5.45 sailed →Loch Ryan / 30.11.45 ✠ foundered while under tow 55°32,8n/ 07°38,2w / Op. Deadlight.
U 282	13.3.43	16.10.43	Be	OL R. Müller	29.10.43 ✠ N. Atlantic: 55°28n/31°57w / D/Cs / DD's HMS *Vidette* (Lt. Comdr. R. Hart), HMS *Duncan* (Comdr. P. W. Gretton), PE HMS *Sunflower* (Lt. Comdr. J. Plomer) / 48 dead / ✠.
U 283	31.3.43	15.1.44	Kr	OL G. Ney	11.2.44 ✠ N. Atlantic S.E. of Iceland: 60°45n/12°50w / D/Cs / Wel D (F/O P. W. Heron), 407 Sqn RCAF / 49 dead / ✠.
U 284	14.4.43	28.11.43	Kr	OL G. Scholz	21.12.43 (✠) 16h55 N. Atlantic: 55°04n/30°23w / following failure of electric motors 17.12.43 / 49 rescued.
U 285	15.5.43	26.3.45	Be	KL K. Bomhaupt	15.4.45 ✠ N. Atlantic S.W. of Ireland: 50°13n/12°48w / D/Cs / DE's HMS *Grindall* (T/A/Lt. Comdr. D. Turquand-Young), HMS *Keats* (T/A/Lt. Comdr. N. F. Israel) / 44 dead / ✠.
U 286	5.6.43	17.4.45	Ha	OL W. Dietrich	29.4.45 ✠ Barents Sea off Kola Inlet: 69°29n/33°37e / D/Cs / PF's HMS *Loch Shin* (Comdr. J. P. de W. Kitcat), HMS *Anguilla* (T/A/Lt. Comdr. C. Morrison-Payne), DE HMS *Cotton* (Lt. Comdr. I. W. T. Beloe) / 51 dead / ✠.
U 287	22.9.43	29.4.45	Kr	OL H. Meyer	16.5.45 (✠) Elbe estuary ≈Altenbruch Roads: ≈53°50n/08°50e / all rescued / br.
U 288	26.6.43	23.3.44	Nv	OL W. Meyer	3.4.44 ✠ 04h43 Barents Sea E. of Bear I.: 73°44n/27°12e / D/Cs, rockets / Ave G (Lt. J. S. Toner), Wil Y (Sub-Lt. G. W. McCabe), 846 Sqn FAA CVE HMS *Tracker* (A/Capt. J. H. Huntley), Swd C (Lt. S. Brilliant), 819 Sqn FAA CVE HMS *Activity* (A/Capt. G. Willoughby) / 49 dead / ✠.
U 289	10.7.43	7.5.44	Nv	KL A. Hellwig	31.5.44 ✠ Arctic S.W. of Bear I.: 73°32n/00°28e / D/Cs / DD HMS *Milne* (Capt. M. Richmond) / 51 dead / ✠.
U 290	24.7.43			OL H. Baum	5.5.45 (✠) Flensburg Fiord, Kupfermühlen Bay / br.

1	2	3	4	5	6
U 291	4.8.43			OL H. Neumeister	5.5.45 Surrender Cuxhaven, →Wilhelmshaven, 24.6.45 sailed →Loch Ryan / 21.12.45 ✝ artillery DD HMS *Onslaught* 55°50,5n/09°08w / Op. Deadlight.
U 301	9.5.42	20.1.43	Sp	KL W.-R. Körner	21.1.43 ✝ 08h48 Mediterranean W. of Corsica: 41°27n/07°04e / torpedo / SS HMS/m *Sahib* (Lt. J. H. Bromage) / 45 dead / 1 rescued.
U 302	16.6.42	11.3.44	Pa	KL H. Sickel	6.4.44 ✝ N. Atlantic N.W. of Azores: 45°05n/35°11w / D/Cs / PF HMS *Swale* (Lt. Comdr. J. Jackson) / 51 dead / ✝.
U 303	7.7.42	21.5.43	To	KL K.-F. Heine	21.5.43 ✝ 16h15 Mediterranean S. of Toulon: 42°50n/06°00e / torpedo / SS HMS/m *Sickle* (Lt. J. R. Drummond) / 20 dead / 28 rescued.
U 304	5.8.42	29.4.43	Kr	OL H. Koch	28.5.43 ✝ N. Atlantic S.E. of Cape Farewell: 54°50n/37°20w / D/Cs / Lib E (F/O D. C. Fleming-Williams), 120 Sqn RAF / 46 dead / ✝.
U 305	17.9.42	8.12.43	Br	KL R. Bahr	16.1.44 ✝ 05h39 N. Atlantic N.E. of Azores: ≈49° n/18° w / missing – ≈own torpedo / 50 dead / ✝.[31]
U 306	21.10.42	14.10.43	Br	KL C. von Trotha	31.10.43 ✝ N. Atlantic: 46°19n/20°44w / D/Cs / DD HMS *Whitehall* (Lt. Comdr. C. L. de H. Bell), PE HMS *Geranium* (T/ Lt. A. R. J. Tilston) / 51 dead / ✝.
U 307	18.11.42	17.4.45	Ha	OL E. Krüger	29.4.45 ✝ Barents Sea N. of Kola Inlet: 69°24n/33°44e / D/Cs / PF HMS *Loch Insh* (T/A/Lt. Comdr. E. W. C. Dempster) / 37 dead / 14 rescued.
U 308	23.12.42	31.5.43	Kr	OL K. Mühlenpfordt	4.6.43 ✝ Arctic N.E. of Faeroe Is.: 64°28n/03°09w / torpedoes / SS HMS/m *Truculent* (Lt. Comdr. R. L. Alexander) / 44 dead / ✝.
U 309	27.1.43	8.2.45	Kr	OL H. Loeder	16.2.45 ✝ North Sea E. of Moray Firth: 58°09n/02°23w / D/Cs / PF HMCS *Saint John* (Comdr. A. F. C. Layard) / 47 dead / ✝.
U 310	24.2.43			OL W. Ley	9.5.45 Surrender Trondheim, unserviceable, not sailed to U.K., br March 1947.
U 311	23.3.43	9.3.44	Br	KL. J. Zander	22.4.44 ✝ N. Atlantic S.W. of Ireland: 52°09n/19°07w / D/Cs / PF's HMCS *Matane* (Comdr. A. F. C. Layard), HMCS *Swansea* (A/Comdr. C. A. King) / 51 dead / ✝.[32]

1	2	3	4	5	6
U 312	21.4.43			OL J. von Gaza	9.5.45 Surrender Narvik, →Loch Eriboll, →Lisahally, →Loch Ryan / 29.11.45 ✝ artillery DD HMS *Onslow* 55°35n/07°54w / Op. Deadlight.
U 313	20.5.43			KL F. Schweiger	9.5.45 Surrender Narvik, →Loch Eriboll, →Lisahally, →Loch Ryan / 21.12.45 ✝ foundered while under tow 55°40n/08°24w / Op. Deadlight.
U 314	10.6.43	25.1.44	Hf	KL G.-W. Basse	30.1.44 ✝ Barents Sea S.E. of Bear I.: 73°40n/27°20e / D/Cs / DD HMS *Inconstant* (Lt. Comdr. J. H. Eaden) / 49 dead / ✝.[33]
U 315	10.7.43			OL H. Zoller	9.5.45 Surrender Trondheim, unserviceable, not sailed to U.K., br March 1947.
U 316	5.8.43			OL G. König	2.5.45 (✝) Travemünde: 53°59n/10°56e / br.
U 331	31.3.41	7.11.42	Sp	KL H.-D. Frhr. von Tiesenhausen	17.11.42 ✝ Mediterranean N.W. of Algiers: 37°05n/02°27e / D/Cs, aerial torpedo / Hud C (F/Sgt W. M. Young), Hud Z (S/L I. C. Patterson), Hud L (F/L A. W. Barwood), 500 Sqn RAF, Alb (Sub-Lt. J. Bridge), 820 Sqn FAA, Mat (Lt. R. B. Pearson), Mat (Sub-Lt. J. Myerscough), 893 Sqn FAA CV HMS *Formidable* (Capt. A. G. Talbot) / 32 dead / 17 rescued.
U 332	7.6.41	26.4.43	Pa	OL E. Hüttemann	29.4.43 ✝ Biscay N. of Spain: 45°08n/09°33w / D/Cs / Lib D (F/L A. R. Laughland), 224 Sqn RAF / 45 dead / ✝.[34]
U 333	25.8.41	23.7.44	Lo	KL H. Fiedler	31.7.44 ✝ N. Atlantic W. of Scilly Is.: 49°39n/07°28w / D/Cs / PS HMS *Starling* (Comdr. N. W. Duck), PF HMS *Loch Killin* (Lt. Comdr. S. Darling) / 45 dead / ✝.
U 334	9.10.41	5.6.43	Be	OL H. Ehrich	14.6.43 ✝ N. Atlantic S.W. of Iceland: 58°16n/28°20w / D/Cs / PF HMS *Jed* (Lt. Comdr. R. C. Freaker), PS HMS *Pelican* (Comdr. G. N. Brewer) / 47 dead / ✝.
U 335	17.12.41	1.8.42	Kr	KL H.-H. Pelkner	3.8.42 ✝ Arctic N. of Shetland Is.: 62°48n/00°12w / torpedo / SS HMS/m *Saracen* (Lt. M. G. R. Lumby) / 43 dead / 1 rescued.
U 336	14.2.42	14.9.43	Br	KL H. Hunger	5.10.43 09h00 ✝ N. Atlantic S.W. of Iceland: 62°43n/27°17w / rockets / Hud F (F/Sgt G. C. Allsop), 269 Sqn RAF / 50 dead / ✝.[35]

1	2	3	4	5	6
U 337	6.5.42	27.12.42	Kr	OL K. Ruwiedel	after 3.1.43 ✠ N. Atlantic / missing / 47 dead / ✠.[36]
U 338	25.6.42	25.8.43	Na	KL M. Kinzel	≈20.9.43 ✠ N. Atlantic S.W. of Iceland: ≈57°n/30°w / missing / 51 dead / ✠.[37]
U 339	25.8.42			OL W. Remus	23.2.45 decomm. Wilhelmshaven; 5.5.45 (✠) Wilhelmshaven, western entrance to Raeder lock: 53°31n/08°10e / br.
U 340	16.10.42	17.10.43	Na	OL H.-J. Klaus	2.11.43 (✠) 04h30 Mediterranean S.W. of Punta Almina: 35°49n/05°14w / following D/Cs PS HMS *Fleetwood* (Comdr. W. B. Piggott), DD's HMS *Active* (Lt. Comdr. P. G. Merriman), HMS *Witherington* (Lt. Comdr. R. B. S. Tennant) and Wel R (F/O A. H. Ellis), 179 Sqn RAF / 1 dead / 48 rescued.
U 341	28.11.42	31.8.43	Pa	OL D. Epp	19.9.43 ✠ N. Atlantic S.W. of Iceland: 58°34n/25°30w / D/Cs / Lib A (F/L R. F. Fisher), 10(BR) Sqn RCAF / 50 dead / ✠.
U 342	12.1.43	3.4.44	Be	OL A. Hossenfelder	17.4.44 ✠ N. Atlantic S.W. of Iceland: 60°23n/29°20w / D/Cs / Cat S (F/O T. C. Cooke), 162 Sqn RCAF / 51 dead / ✠.
U 343	18.2.43	6.3.44	To	OL W. Rahn	10.3.44 ✠ Mediterranean S. of Sardinia: 38°07n/09°41e / D/Cs / TWL HMT *Mull* (T/Lt. R. R. Simpson) / 51 dead / ✠.
U 344	26.3.43	3.8.44	Nv	KL U. Pietsch	22.8.44 ✠ 08h34 Arctic N.W. of Bear I.: 74°54n/15°26e / D/Cs / Swd X (Lt. G. Bennett), 825 Sqn FAA CVE HMS *Vindex* (Capt. H. T. T. Bayliss) / 50 dead / ✠.[38]
U 345	4.5.43			OL U. Knackfuss	23.12.43 decomm. Kiel following bomb damage air raid 8. USAAF at Howaldtswerke Kiel 13.12.43 / 2.2.44 ✠ 01h25 Baltic N. of Warnemünde: 54°20,5n/12°04,5e / foundered while under tow / ↑ April 1953, →Stralsund, Volkswerft, pulled on slip, br.
U 346	7.6.43			OL A. Leisten	20.9.43 ✠ Baltic off Hela: 54°25n/18°50e / diving accident / 37 dead / 6 rescued.
U 347	7.7.43	3.7.44	Nv	OL J. de Buhr	17.7.44 ✠ Arctic W. of Narvik: 68°36n/08°33e / D/Cs / Lib U (P/O M. G. Moseley), 86 Sqn RAF / 49 dead / ✠.[39]
U 348	10.8.43			OL H.-N. Schunck	30.3.45 ✠ Hamburg-Finkenwerder off U-boat pen Fink II inside pontoon dock: 53°32,5n/09°51,4e / bomb / air raid 8. USAAF / 2 dead.
U 349	8.9.43			OL U.-W. Dähne	5.5.45 (✠) Gelting Bay: 54°48n/09°49e / 1 dead / 1948 br.

1	2	3	4	5	6
U 350	7.10.43			OL E. Niester	30.3.45 ✞ Hamburg-Finkenwerder off U-boat pen Fink II inside pontoon dock: 53°32,5n/09°51,4e / bomb / air raid 8. USAAF / none dead / br.
U 351	20.6.41			OL H. Strehl	5.5.45 (✞) Hörup Haff: 54°53n/09°52e / 1948 br.
U 352	28.8.41	7.4.42	Na	KL H. Rathke	9.5.42 ✞ N. Atlantic S. of Cape Hatteras: 34°13n/76°34w / D/Cs / USCGC *Icarus* (Lt. Comdr. M. D. Jester) / 15 dead / 33 rescued.
U 353	31.3.42	25.9.42	Kr	OL W. Römer	16.10.42 ✞ N. Atlantic: 53°54n/29°30w / D/Cs / DD HMS *Fame* (Comdr. R. Heathcote) / 6 dead / 39 rescued.
U 354	22.4.42	21.8.44	Nv	OL H.-J. Sthamer	24.8.44 ✞ 08h02 Barents Sea N.E. of North Cape: 72°49n/30°41e / D/Cs / PS's HMS *Mermaid* (Lt. Comdr. J. P. Mosse), PF HMS *Loch Dunvegan* (Comdr. E. Wheeler) / 51 dead / ✞.[40]
U 355	29.10.41	25.3.44	Nv	KK G. La Baume	1.4.44 ✞ Arctic S.W. of Bear I.: ≈73°00n/13°00e / missing / 52 dead / ✞.[41]
U 356	20.12.41	5.12.42	Na	OL G. Ruppelt	27.12.42 ✞ N. Atlantic N. of Azores: 45°30n/25°40w / D/Cs / DD HMCS *St. Laurent* (Lt. Comdr. G. S. Windeyer), PE's HMCS *Chilliwack* (T/A/Lt. Comdr. L. L. Foxall), HMCS *Battleford* (T/Lt. F. A. Beck), HMCS *Napanee* (Lt. S. Henderson) / 46 dead / ✞.
U 357	18.6.42	18.12.42	Eg	KL A. Kellner	26.12.42 ✞ N. Atlantic N.W. of Ireland: 57°10n/15°40w / D/Cs / DD's HMS *Hesperus* (Comdr. D. G. F. W. MacIntyre), HMS *Vanessa* (Lt. C. E. Sheen) / 36 dead / 6 rescued.
U 358	15.8.42	14.2.44	Na	KL R. Manke	1.3.44 ✞ N. Atlantic N.E. of Azores: 45°46n/23°16w / D/Cs / DE's HMS *Gould* (Lt. D. W. Ungoed), HMS *Affleck* (A/Comdr. C. Gwinner), HMS *Gore* (Lt. J. V. Reeves-Brown), HMS *Garlies* (Lt. R. L. Caple) / 50 dead / 1 rescued.
U 359	5.10.42	29.6.43	Na	OL H. Förster	26.7.43 ✞ Caribbean E. of Jamaica: 18°06n/75°00w / D/Cs / Mar P-12 (Lt. R. W. Rawson), VP-32 Sqn USN / 47 dead / ✞.[42]
U 360	12.11.42	29.3.44	Dr	KL K. Becker	2.4.44 ✞ Arctic N.W. of Hammerfest: 73°28n/13°04e / D/Cs / DD HMS *Keppel* (Comdr. I. J. Tyson) / 51 dead / ✞.
U 361	18.12.42	27.6.44	Ha	KL H. Seidel	17.7.44 ✞ Arctic W. of Narvik: 68°35n/06°00e / D/Cs / Cat Y (F/O J. A. Cruickshank), 210 Sqn RAF / 52 dead / ✞.[43]

1	2	3	4	5	6
U 362	4.2.43	2.8.44	Hf	OL L. Franz	5.9.44 ✠ 08h32 Kara Sea N.E. of Krawkowa I.: 75°51n/89°27e / D/Cs / Soviet AM *T-116* (KL. W. A. Babanov) / 51 dead / ✠.
U 363	18.3.43			KL W. Nees	9.5.45 Surrender Narvik, →Loch Eriboll, →Lisahally / 31.12.45 ✠ artillery DD ORP *Blyskawica* 55°45n/08°18w / Op. Deadlight.
U 364	3.5.43	28.11.43	Kr	OL P.-H. Sass	29.1.44 ✠ 22h07 Biscay W. of Bordeaux: 45°33n/06°05w / D/Cs / Hal U (F/L W. Hunter), 502 Sqn RAF / 49 dead / ✠.[44]
U 365	8.6.43	25.11.44	Ha	OL D. Todenhagen	13.12.44 ✠ Arctic E. of Jan Mayen I.: 70°43n/08°07e / D/Cs / Swd L (Sub-Lt. W. J. Hutchison), Swd Q (Sub-Lt. M. W. Henley), 813 Sqn FAA CVE HMS *Campania* (A/Capt. K. A. Short) / 50 dead / ✠.
U 366	16.7.43	4.3.44	Hf	OL B. Langenberg	5.3.44 ✠ Arctic N.W. of Hammerfest: 72°10n/14°45e / rockets / Swd F (Sub-Lt. J. F. Mason), 816 Sqn FAA CVE HMS *Chaser* (Capt. H. V. P. McClintock) / 50 dead / ✠.
U 367	27.8.43			OL H. Stegemann	15.3.45 ✠ Baltic off Hela: 54°34n/18°52,8e / sea mine / Soviet SS *L-21* (Kpt. 3.Rg S. S. Mogilevskij) / 43 dead / ✠.[45]
U 368	7.1.44			OL G. Roth	5.5.45 Surrender Heligoland, →Wilhelmshaven. 23.6.45 sailed →Loch Ryan / 17.12.45 ✠ artillery DD ORP *Blyskawica* 56°14n/10°37,6w / Op. Deadlight.
U 369	15.10.43			OL H.-N. Schunck	9.5.45 Surrender Kristiansand, 29.5.45 sailed →Loch Ryan / 30.11.45 ✠ artillery DD HMS *Onslaught* 55°31,7n/07°27,7w / Op. Deadlight.
U 370	19.11.43			OL K. Nielsen	5.5.45 (✠) Gelting Bay: 54°48n/09°49e / 1948 br.
U 371	15.3.41	23.4.44	To	OL H.-A. Fenski	4.5,44 ✠ 04h09 Mediterranean N.E. of Bougie: 37°49n/05°39e / D/Cs / DE's USS *Pride* (Comdr. R. R. Curry), USS *Joseph E. Campbell* (Lt. J. M. Robertson), FNFL *Sénégalais* (Capt. de corvette P. M. A. Poncet), HMS *Blankney* (Lt. B. H. Brown) / 3 dead / 49 rescued.
U 372	19.4.41	27.7.42	Sa	KL H.-J. Neumann	4.8.42 ✠ Mediterranean W. of Yaffa: 32°28n/34°37e / D/Cs / DD's HMS *Sikh* (Capt. St. J. A. Micklethwait), HMS *Zulu* (Comdr. R. T. White), DE's HMS *Croome* (Lt. Comdr. R. C. Egan), HMS *Tetcott* (Lt. H. R. Rycroft) and Wel M (F/O D. N. Cochrane), 221 Sqn RAF / 48 rescued.

1	2	3	4	5	6
U 373	22.5.41	7.6.44	Br	OL D. von Lehsten	8.6.44 ✝ 02h40 Biscay W. of Brest: 48°10n/05°31w / D/Cs / Lib G (F/O K. O. Moore), 224 Sqn RAF / 4 dead / 47 rescued.
U 374	21.6.41	18.12.41	Sp	OL U. von Fischel	12.1.42 ✝ Mediterranean N.E. of Catania: 37°50n/16°00e / torpedoes / SS HMS/m *Unbeaten* (Lt. Comdr. E. A. Woodward) / 42 dead / 1 rescued.
U 375	19.7.41	10.7.43	To	KL J. Könenkamp	after 25.7.43 ✝ Mediterranean S. of Sicily / missing / 46 dead / ✝.[46]
U 376	21.8.41	6.4.43	Pa	KL F.-K. Marks	after 6.4.43 ✝ Biscay / missing / 47 dead / ✝.[47]
U 377	2.10.41	15.12.43	Br	OL G. Kluth	17.1.44 ✝ 20h56 N. Atlantic S.W. of Ireland: 49°39n/20°10w / D/Cs / DD HMS *Wanderer* (Lt. Comdr. R. F. Whinney), PF HMS *Glenarm* (Lt. Comdr. W. R. B. Noal) / 52 dead / ✝.[48]
U 378	30.10.41	6.9.43	Pa	KL E. Mäder	20.10.43 ✝ N. Atlantic: 47°40n/28°27w / D/Cs / Ave T-2 (Lt.[jg] R. W. Hayman). Wil (Lt. Comdr. C. W. Brewer), VC-13 Sqn USN CVE USS *Core* (Capt. J. R. Dudley) / 48 dead / ✝.
U 379	29.11.41	27.6.42	Kr	KL P.-H. Kettner	8.8.42 ✝ N. Atlantic S.E. of Cape Farewell: 57°11n/30°57w / D/Cs, ramming / PE HMS *Dianthus* (Lt. Comdr. C. E. Bridgman) / 40 dead / 5 rescued.
U 380	22.12.41			KL A. Brandi	11.3.44 ✝ Toulon, Missiessy Docks: 43°07n/05°55e / bomb / air raid 15. USAAF / 1 dead / ↑ 1944 br.
U 381	25.2.42	31.3.43	Na	KL W.-H. Graf von Pückler und Limpurg	after 9.5.43 ✝ N. Atlantic / missing / 47 dead / ✝.[49]
U 382	25.4.42			OL E.-A. Gerke	30.6.44 decomm. La Pallice, laid up U-boat pen La Pallice.
	25.8.44			OL G. Schimmel	20.3.45 decomm. Wilhelmshaven; 5.5.45 (✝) Wilhelmshaven, western entrance to Raeder lock 53°31n/08°10e / br.
U 383	6.6.42	29.7.43	Br	KL H. Kremser	≈1.8.43 ✝ N. Atlantic S.W. of Ireland: ≈47°00n/10°30w / following D/Cs damage / Sun V (F/O S. White), 228 Sqn RAF 1.8.43 / 52 dead / ✝.[50]
U 384	18.7.42	6.3.43	Pa	OL H.-A. von Rosenberg Gruszczynski	19.3.43 ✝ N. Atlantic: 54°18n/26°15w / D/Cs / For B (P/O L. G. Clark), 206 Sqn RAF / 47 dead / ✝.[51]
U 385	29.8.42	9.8.44	Na	KL H. G. Valentiner	11.8.44 ✝ Biscay N.W. of La Rochelle: 46°16n/02°45w / D/Cs / PS HMS *Starling* (Comdr. N. W. Duck) and Sun P (P/O I. F. Southall), 461 Sqn RAAF / 1 dead / 42 rescued.

1	2	3	4	5	6
U 386	10.10.42	29.12.43	Na	OL F. Albrecht	19.2.44 ✠ N. Atlantic: 48°51n/22°44w / D/Cs / PF HMS *Spey* (Lt. Comdr. G. A. G. Ormsby) / 33 dead / 16 rescued.
U 387	24.11.42	22.11.44	Ha	KK R. Büchler	9.12.44 ✠ Barents Sea off Kola Inlet: 69°41n/33°12e / D/Cs / PE HMS *Bamborough Castle* (T/Lt. M. S. Work) / 51 dead / ✠.
U 388	31.12.42	10.6.43	Kr	OL P. Sues	20.6.43 ✠ N. Atlantic S.E. of Cape Farewell: 57°36n/31°20w / homing torpedo / Cat P-1 (Lt. E. W. Wood), VP-84 Sqn USN / 47 dead / ✠.
U 389	6.2.43	19.9.43	Dr	KL S. Heilmann	4.10.43 19h12 ✠ N. Atlantic S.W. of Iceland: 60°51n/28°26w / D/Cs / Lib X (F/L J. F. McEwen), 120 Sqn RAF / 50 dead / ✠.[52]
U 390	13.3.43	27.6.44	Br	OL H. Geissler	5.7.44 ✠ 15h English Channel, Seine Bay: 49°52n/00°48w / D/Cs / DD HMS *Wanderer* (Lt. Comdr. R. F. Whinney), PF HMS *Tavy* (T/A/Lt. Comdr. F. Ardern) / 48 dead / 1 rescued.
U 391	24.4.43	30.10.43	Dr	OL G. Dültgen	13.12.43 ✠ Biscay N.W. of Spain: 45°45n/09°38w / D/Cs / Lib B (S/L G. Crawford), 53 Sqn RAF / 51 dead / ✠.
U 392	29.5.43	29.2.44	Br	OL H. Schümann	16.3.44 ✠ Strait of Gibraltar: 35°55n/05°41w / D/Cs / DE HMS *Affleck* (A/Comdr. C. Gwinner), DD HMS *Vanoc* (Lt. Comdr. P. R. Ward) and Cat P-8 (Lt. R. C. Spears), Cat P-7 (Lt. M. J. Vopatek), Cat P-l (Lt. V. A. T. Lingle), VP-63 Sqn USN / 52 dead / ✠.
U 393	3.7.43	4.5.45	Ge	OL F.-G. Herrle	5.5.45 (✠) Gelting Bay off Holnis: 54°53n/09°37e / following bomb damage air strike 9. USAAF XXIX TAC 4.5.45 / br.[53]
U 394	7.8.43	6.8.44	Hf	KL W. Borger	2.9.44 ✠ Arctic W. of Harstad: 69°47n/04°10e / rockets, D/Cs / Swd V (Lt. Comdr. F. G. B. Sheffield), 825 Sqn FAA CVE HMS *Vindex* (Capt. H. T. T. Bayliss), DD's HMS *Keppel* (Comdr. I. J. Tyson). HMS *Whitehall* (Lt. Comdr. P. J. Cowell), PS's HMS *Mermaid* (Lt. Comdr. J. P. Mosse), HMS *Peacock* (Lt. Comdr. R. B. Stannard) / 50 dead / ✠.
U 395				(OL E.-G. Unterhorst)	29.7.43 bomb damage air raid 8. USAAF Howaldtswerke Kiel, fitting out quay, planned completion for first quarter 1944 delayed, construction abandoned spring 1944, 22.7.44 contract canceled, 3.5.45 (✠) Kiel-Dietrichsdorf, Kriegsmarine artillery dockyard jetty IIIa, br.

1	2	3	4	5	6
U 396	16.10.43	13.3.45	Dr	KL H. Siemon	after 11.4.45 ✝ N. Atlantic or Arctic N.W. of Britain / missing – ≈diving accident? / 45 dead / ✝.[54]
U 397	20.11.43			KL G. Groth	5.5.45 (✝) Gelting Bay: 54°48n/09°49e / br.
U 398	18.12.43	17.4.45	Kr	OL W. Cranz	after 17.4.45 North Sea or Arctic N. of Britain / missing / 43 dead / ✝.[55]
U 399	22.1.44	8.2.45	Kr	OL H. Buhse	26.3.45 ✝ English Channel S. of Lizard Point: 49°56n/05°22w / D/Cs / DE HMS *Duckworth* (Comdr. R. G. Mills) / 46 dead / 1 rescued.
U 400	18.3.44	18.11.44	Kr	KL H. Creutz	after 14.12.44 ✝ N. Atlantic N.W. of Newquay: 50°33,16n/05°11,37w / sea mine British field "HW A3" / 50 dead / ✝.[56]
U 401	10.4.41	9.7.41	Dr	KL G. Zimmermann	3.8.41 ✝ N. Atlantic S.W. of Ireland: 50°30n/19°35w / D/Cs / PE HMS *Hydrangea* (Lt. J. E. Woolfenden) / 45 dead / ✝.[57]
U 402	21.5.41	4.9.43	Pa	KK S. Frhr. von Forstner	13.10.43 ✝ N. Atlantic: 48°56n/29°41w / homing torpedo / Ave T-9 (Lt. Comdr. H. M. Avery), Ave (Ens. B. C. Sheela), VC-9 Sqn USN CVE USS *Card* (Capt. A. J. Isbell) / 50 dead / ✝.
U 403	25.6.41	13.7.43	Br	KL K.-F. Heine	18.8.43 ✝ mid-Atlantic W. of Dakar: 13°42n/17°36w / D/Cs / Wel 26 – HZ 697, (E.V.1st E.H.P. Bigo), Free-French 2nd Bomb Sdn / 49 dead / ✝.[58]
U 404	6.8.41	24.7.43	Na	OL A. Schönberg	28.7.43 ✝ Biscay N.W. of Spain: 45°53n/09°25w / D/Cs / Lib N (Lt. A. J. Hammer), 4th A/S Sqn USAAF, Lib W (F/O R. V. Sweeny), 224 Sqn RAF / 51 dead / ✝.
U 405	17.9.41	10.10.43	Na	KK R.-H. Hopmann	1.11.43 ✝ N. Atlantic: 49°00n/31°14w / D/Cs, ramming, artillery, fire arms / DD USS *Borie* (Lt. C. H. Hutchins) / 49 dead / ✝.
U 406	22.10.41	5.1.44	Na	KL H. Dieterichs	18.2.44 ✝ 14h30 N. Atlantic: 48°32n/23°36w / D/Cs / PF HMS *Spey* (Lt. Comdr. G. A. G. Ormsby) / 12 dead / 45 rescued.
U 407	18.12.41	9.9.44	Sa	OL H. Kolbus	19.9.44 ✝ Mediterranean S. of Milos: 36°27n/24°33e / D/Cs / DD's HMS *Troubridge* (Capt. C. L. Firth), HMS *Terpsichore* (Comdr. A. C. Behague), ORP *Garland* (Comdr. B. Biskupski) / 5 dead / 48 rescued.
U 408	19.11.41	31.10.42	Nv	KL R. von Hymmen	5.11.42 ✝ N. Atlantic, Denmark Straits: 67°40n/18°32w / D/Cs / Cat H (Lt. R. C. Millard), VP-84 Sqn USN / 45 dead / ✝.

1	2	3	4	5	6
U 409	21.1.42	29.6.43	To	OL H. F. Maßmann	12.7.43 ✠ Mediterranean N.E. of Algiers: 37°12n/04°00e / D/Cs / DD HMS *Inconstant* (Lt. Comdr. J. H. Eaden) / 11 dead / 37 rescued.
U 410	23.2.42			OL H.-A. Fenski	11.3.44 ✠ Toulon, Missiessy Docks: 43°07n/05°55e / bomb damage air raid 15. USAAF / none dead / 28.3.44 decomm., cannibalized / August 1944 captured by Allied forces Toulon, Quay Noel, berth 11. 1946 br.
U 411	18.3.42	7.11.42	Na	KL J. Spindlegger	13.11.42 ✠ N. Atlantic W. of Gibraltar: 36°00n/09°35w / D/Cs / Hud D (S/L J. B. Ensor), 500 Sqn RAF / 46 dead / ✠.[59]
U 412	29.4.42	19.10.42	Kr	KL W. Jahrmärker	22.10.42 ✠ Arctic N.E. of Faeroe Is.: 63°55n/00°24e / D/Cs / Wel B (F/Sgt A. D. S. Martin), 179 Sqn RAF / 47 dead / ✠.
U 413	3.6.42	2.8.44	Br	OL D. Sachse	20.8.44 ✠ English Channel S. of Brighton: 50°21n/00°01w / D/Cs / DD's HMS *Forester* (Lt. D. C. Beatty), HMS *Vidette* (T/A/Lt. Comdr. G. S. Woolley), DE HMS *Wensleydale* (Lt. Comdr. W. P. Goodfellow) / 45 dead / 1 rescued.
U 414	1.7.42	13.5.43	Sp	OL W. Huth	25.5.43 ✠ Mediterranean N.W. of Tenes: 36°31n/00°40e / D/Cs / PE HMS *Vetch* (Lt. Comdr. H. J. Beverley) / 47 dead / ✠.
U 415	5.8.42			OL H. Werner	14.7.44 ✠ 09h15 Brest W. of torpedo net barrier: 48°22n/04°29w / British air-laid mine, field "Jellyfish No. 5", capsized / 2 dead; ↑ 21.7.44, →Clemenceau dock, cannibalized, August 1944 (✠) inside dock, 1946 br.
U 416	4.11.42			OL C. Reich	8.4.43 17h30 decomm. Stettin following damage 30.3.43 Baltic W. of Bornholm: 54°51n/14°35e / British air-laid mine, field "Pollock" / repaired Schichau-Werft Königsberg, recomm. Königsberg.
	4.10.43			OL E. Rieger	12.12.44 ✠ 05h18 Baltic N.W. of Pillau: 54°51n/19°39,5e / collision / German AM *M 203* (OL E. von Caemmerer) / 36 dead / 5 rescued.
U 417	26.9.42	5.6.43	Kr	OL W. Schreiner	11.6.43 ✠ N. Atlantic S.E. of Iceland: 63°20n/10°30w / D/Cs / For R (W/C R. B. Thompson), 206 Sqn RAF / 46 dead / ✠.
U 418	21.10.42	26.4.43	Kr	OL G. Lange	30.5.43 ✠ Biscay S.W. of Brest: 47°00n/14°00w / D/Cs / Cat G (F/L D. W. Eadie), 210 Sqn RAF / 48 dead / ✠.[60]

1	2	3	4	5	6
U 419	18.11.42	13.9.43	Be	OL D. Giersberg	8.10.43 ✠ N. Atlantic: 56°31n/27°05w / D/Cs / Lib R (F/L J. Wright), 86 Sqn RAF / 48 dead / 1 rescued.
U 420	16.12.42	9.10.43	Br	OL H.-J. Reese	after 20.10.43 ✠ N. Atlantic / missing / 49 dead / ✠.[61]
U 421	13.1.43			OL H. Kolbus	29.4.44 ✠ 11h30 Toulon, Missiessy Quay: 43°07n/05°55e / bomb / air raid 15. USAAF / none dead / ↑, →Missiessy Dock No. 2 / 1946 br.
U 422	10.2.43	8.9.43	Be	OL H.-W. Poeschel	4.10.43 ✠ N. Atlantic N. of Azores: 43°13n/28°58w / homing torpedo / Ave T-3 (Lt.[jg] R. L. Stearns), Wil F-16 (Lt.[jg] E. S. Heim), Wil F-19 (Lt.|jg] D. O. Puckett), VC-9 Sqn USN CVE USS *Card* (Capt. A. J. Isbell) / 49 dead / ✠.[62]
U 423	3.3.43	14.6.44	Be	OL K Hackländer	17.6.44 ✠ Arctic N.E. of Shetland Is.: 63°06n/02°05e / D/Cs / Cat D (Lt. C. F. Krafft), 333 Sqn (Norwegian) RAF / 53 dead / ✠.
U 424	7.4.43	29.1.44	Br	OL G. Lüders	11.2.44 ✠ N. Atlantic S.W. of Ireland: 50°00n/18°14w / D/Cs / PS's HMS *Woodpecker* (Comdr. H. L. Pryse), HMS *Wild Goose* (Comdr. D. E. G. Wemyss) / 50 dead / ✠.
U 425	21.4.43	7.2.45	Ha	KL H. Bentzien	17.2.45 ✠ Barents Sea off Kola Inlet: 69°39n/35°50e / D/Cs / PS HMS *Lark* (Comdr. H. Lambton), PE HMS *Alnwick Castle* (A/Lt. Comdr. H. A. Stonehouse) / 52 dead / 1 rescued.
U 426	12.5.43	3.1.44	Br	KL C. Reich	8.1.44 ✠ N. Atlantic N.W. of Spain: 46°47n/10°42w / D/Cs / Sun U (F/O J. P. Roberts), 10 Sqn RAAF / 51 dead / ✠.
U 427	2.6.43			OL C.-G. Gudenus	9.5.45 Surrender Narvik, →Loch Eriboll, →Lisahally, →Loch Ryan / 21.12.45 ✠ artillery DD's HMS *Onslaught*, ORP *Piorun*, DE HMS *Zetland*, PS HMS *Fowey* 56°04n/ 09°35w / Op. Deadlight.
U 428	26.6.43			CC A. Fraternale	comm. as *S 1* for Italian Navy, 10.9.43 taken over by the Kriegsmarine at Gotenhafen.
	26.10.43			OL H.-U. Hanitsch	5.5.45 (✠) Obereider near Audorf, Kaiser-Wilhelm-Canal km 64: 54°19n/09°40e / 1946 br.
U 429	14.7.43			TV A. Amendolia	comm. as *S 4* for Italian Navy, 10.9.43 taken over by the Kriegsmarine at Gotenhafen.
	27.10.43			OL M. Kuttkat	30.3.45 ✠ Wilhelmshaven, Bauhafen Quay: 53°31n/08°08e / bomb / air raid 8. USAAF / none dead / br.

1	2	3	4	5	6
U 430	4.8.43			TV M. Rosetto	comm. as S 6 for Italian Navy, 10.9.43 taken over by the Kriegsmarine at Gotenhafen.
	29.9.43			OL U. Hammer	30.3.45 ✞ Bremen, Deschimag-AG Weser, Werfthafen-Bollwerk: 53°07n/08°45e / bomb / air raid 8. USAAF / 2 dead.
U 431	5.4.41	26.9.43	To	OL D. Schöneboom	21.10.4.3 ✞ Mediterranean E. of Cartagena: 37°23n/00°35e / D/Cs / Wel Z (Sgt. D. M. Cornish), 179 Sqn RAF / 52 dead / ✞.[63]
U 432	26.4.41	14.2.43	Pa	KL H. Eckhardt	11.3.43 ✞ N. Atlantic: 51°35n/28°20w / D/Cs, artillery / PE FNFL *Aconit* (Capt. de frègate J. Levasseur) / 26 dead / 20 rescued.
U 433	24.5.41	8.11.41	Na	OL H. Ey	16.11.41 ✞ 21h55 Mediterranean S. of Malaga: 36°13n/04°42w / D/Cs, artillery / PE HMS *Marigold* (T/Lt. J. Renwick) / 6 dead / 38 rescued.
U 434	21.6.41	2.11.41	Kr	KL W. Heyda	18.12.41 ✞ N. Atlantic N. of Madeira: 36°15n/15°48w / D/Cs / DD HMS *Stanley* (Lt. Comdr. D. B. Shaw), DE HMS *Blankney* (Lt. Comdr. P. F. Powlett) / 2 dead / 42 rescued.
U 435	30.8.41	20.5.43	Br	KK S. Strelow	9.7.43 ✞ 12h43 N. Atlantic N.W. of Lisbon: 39°20n/13°00w / D/Cs / Lib B (Lt. T. E. Kuenning), 1st A/S Sqn USAAF / 48 dead / ✞.[64]
U 436	27.9.41	25.4.43	Na	KL G. Seibicke	26.5.43 ✞ N. Atlantic N.W. of Cape Finisterre: 43°49n/15°56w / D/Cs / PF HMS *Test* (Lt. Comdr. F. B. Collinson), PE HMS *Hyderabad* (T/Lt. T. Cooper) / 47 dead / ✞.
U 437	25.10.41			KL H. Lamby	4.10.44 ✞ 09h30 Bergen, Laksevaag Yard, capsized in floating dock: 60°23n/05°18e / bomb / air raid 6 (RCAF) and 8 Groups RAF Bomber Command / 5.10.44 decomm. Bergen, cannibalized: May 45 captured by British forces, br.
U 438	22.11.41	31.3.43	Br	KL H. Heinsohn	6.5.43 ✞ N. Atlantic N.E. of Newfoundland: 52°00n/45°10w / D/Cs / PS HMS *Pelican* (Comdr. G. N. Brewer) / 48 dead / ✞.
U 439	20.12.41	27.4.43	Br	OL H. von Tippelskirch	4.5.4.3 ✞ 00h30 N. Atlantic N.W. of Spain: 43°32n/13°20w / collision / U 659 (KL H. Stock) / 40 dead / 9 rescued.
U 440	24.1.42	26.5.43	Na	OL W. Schwaff	31.5.43 ✞ N. Atlantic N.W. of Spain: 45°38n/13°04w / D/Cs / Sun R (F/L D. M. Gall), 201 Sqn RAF / 46 dead / ✞.

1	2	3	4	5	6
U 441	21.2.42	6.6.44	Br	KL K. Hartmann	30.6.44 ✠ English Channel W. of Guernsey: 49°37n/03°41w / D/Cs / Lib L (F/L J. W. Barling), 224 Sqn RAF and DE's HMS *Essington* (A/Lt. Comdr. W. Lambert), HMS *Duckworth* (Comdr. R. G. Mills), HMS *Dommett* (Lt. Comdr. S. Gordon), HMS *Cooke* (Lt. Comdr. L. C. Hill) / 51 dead / ✠.[65]
U 442	21.3.42	20.12.42	Na	KK H.-J. Hesse	12.2.43 ✠ N. Atlantic S.W. of Lisbon: 37°32n/11°56w / D/Cs / Hud F (F/O G. R. Mayhew), 48 Sqn RAF / 48 dead / ✠.
U 443	18.4.42	16.2.43	Sp	OL K. von Puttkamer	23.2.43 ✠ Mediterranean N. of Algiers: 36°55n/02°25e / D/Cs / DE's HMS *Bicester* (Lt. Comdr. S. W. F. Bennets), HMS *Lamerton* (Lt. Comdr. C. R. Purse), HMS *Wheatland* (Lt. Comdr. R. de L. Brooke) / 48 dead / ✠.
U 444	9.5.42	1.3.43	Pa	OL A. Langfeld	11.3.43 ✠ N. Atlantic: 51°14n/29°18w / D/Cs, ramming / DD HMS *Harvester* (Comdr. A. A. Tait), PE FNFL *Aconit* (Capt. de frègate J. Levasseur) / 41 dead / 4 rescued.
U 445	30.5.42	22.8.44	Lo	OL R. Fischler Graf von Treuberg	24.8.44 ✠ Biscay S.W. of Brest: 47°21 n/05°50w / D/Cs / DE HMS *Louis* (Comdr. L. B. A. Majendie) / 52 dead / ✠.
U 446	20.6.42			OL H. Richard	21.9.42 ✠ 13h10 Baltic, Danzig Bay off Kahlberg: 54°27n/18°55e / British air-laid mine, field "Privet II" / 23 dead / 18 rescued / ↑ 1.11.42; → Gotenhafen, 12.11.42 decomm., test hulk; 2.5.45 (✠) Lübeck-Petroleumhafen: 53°54,3n/10°42,2e / br 1947.
U 447	11.7.42	27.4.43	Br	KL F. Bothe	7.5.43 ✠ N. Atlantic S.W. of Gibraltar: 35°30n/11°55w / D/Cs / Hud X (Sgt J. V. Holland), 233 Sqn RAF, Hud I (Sgt J. W. McQueen), 48 Sqn RAF / 48 dead / ✠.
U 448	1.8.42	14.2.44	Na	OL H. Dauter	14.4.44 ✠ N. Atlantic: 46°22n/19°35w / D/Cs / PF HMCS *Swansea* (A/Comdr. C. A. King), PS HMS *Pelican* (Comdr. J. S. Dalison) / 9 dead / 42 rescued.
U 449	22.8.42	3.6.43	Kr	OL H. Otto	24.6.43 ✠ 16h N. Atlantic N.W. of Spain: 45°00n/11°59w / D/Cs / PS's HMS *Wren* (Lt. Comdr. R. M. Aubrey), HMS *Woodpecker* (Lt. Comdr. R. E. S. Hugonin), HMS *Kite* (Lt. Comdr. W. F. R. Segrave), HMS *Wild Goose* (Comdr. F. J. Walker) / 48 dead / ✠.

1	2	3	4	5	6
U 450	12.9.42	14.2.44	To	OL K. Böhme	10.3.44 ✠ Mediterranean N.W. of Naples: 41°11n/12°27e / D/Cs / DE's HMS *Blankney* (Lt. Comdr. D. H. R. Bromley), HMS *Blencathra* (Lt. Comdr. E. G. Warren), HMS *Brecon* (A/Lt. Comdr. N. R. H. Rodney), HMS *Exmoor* (Comdr. R. N. J. Jefferies), DD USS *Madison* (Comdr. D. A. Stuart) / 51 rescued.
U 451	3.5.41	15.12.41	Lo	KK E. Hoffmann	21.12.41 ✠ N. Atlantic N.W. of Tangier: 35°55n/06°08w / D/Cs / Swd A (Sub-Lt. P. McQ. Wilkinson), 812 Sqn FAA / 44 dead / 1 rescued.
U 452	29.5.41	19.8.41	Dr	KL J. March	25.8.41 ✠ N. Atlantic S. of Iceland: 61°30n/15°30w / D/Cs / TWL HMT *Vascama* (Lt. R. Walgate) and Cat J (F/O E. A. Jewiss), 209 Sqn RAF / 42 dead / ✠.
U 453	26.6.41	30.4.44	Po	OL D. Lührs	21.5.44 ✠ Mediterranean N.E. of Cape Spartivento: 38°13n/16°36e / D/Cs / DD's HMS *Termagant* (Lt. Comdr. J. P. Scatchard), HMS *Tenacious* (Lt. Comdr. D. F. Townsend), DE HMS *Liddesdale* (Lt. C. J. Bateman) / 1 dead / 51 rescued.
U 454	24.7.41	29.7.43	Pa	KL B. Hackländer	1.8.43 ✠ 14h N. Atlantic N.W. of Spain: 45°36n/10°23w / D/Cs / Sun B (F/L K. G. Fry), 10 Sqn RAAF / 32 dead / 14 rescued.
U 455	21.8.41	22.2.44	To	KL H.-M. Scheibe	5.4.44 ✠ Mediterranean S.W. of Genoa: 44°18,6′n/09°02,9′e / sea mine, German field "Fuß-Ball-Klub" / 51 dead / ✠.[66]
U 456	18.9.41	24.4.43	Br	KL M.-M. Teichert	12.5.43 ✠ N. Atlantic: 46°39n/26°54w / missing – ≈diving accident facing approaching DD HMS *Opportune* (Comdr. J. Lee-Barber) following homing torpedo damage Lib B (F/L J. Wright), 86 Sqn RAF / 49 dead / ✠.[67]
U 457	5.11.41	10.9.42	Nv	KK K. Brandenburg	16.9.42 ✠ Barents Sea N.E. of Kola Inlet: 75°05n/43°15e / D/Cs / DD HMS *Impulsive* (Lt. Comdr. E. G. Roper) / 45 dead / ✠.
U 458	12.12.41	14.8.43	To	KL K. Diggins	22.8.43 ✠ Mediterranean S.E. of Pantelleria: 36°25n/12°39e / D/Cs / DE's HMS *Easton* (Lt. Comdr. C. W. Malins), RHN *Pindos* (Lt. Comdr. D. Fifas) / 8 dead / 39 rescued.
U 465	20.5.42	29.4.43	Na	KL H. Wolf	2.5.43 ✠ Biscay N.W. of Cape Ortegal: 44°48n/08°58w / D/Cs / Sun M (A/F/L E. C. Smith), 461 Sqn RAAF / 48 dead / ✠.[68]

1	2	3	4	5	6
U 466	17.6.42			KL G. Thäter	19.8.44 (✠) 20h30 Toulon off St. Mandrier: 43°05n/05°56e / 1946 br.
U 467	15.7.42	20.5.43	Be	KL H. Kummer	25.5.43 ✠ N. Atlantic S. of Iceland: 62°25n/14°52w / homing torpedo / Cat F (Lt. R. C. Millard), VP-84 Sqn USN / 46 dead / ✠.
U 468	12.8.42	7.7.43	Pa	OL K. Schamong	11.8.43 ✠ mid-Atlantic S.W. of Dakar: 12°20n/20°07w / D/Cs / Lib D (F/O L. A. Trigg), 200 Sqn RAF / 44 dead / 7 rescued.
U 469	7.10.42	19.3.43	Kr	OL E. Claussen	25.3.43 ✠ N. Atlantic S. of Iceland: 62°12n/16°40w / D/Cs / For L (F/L W. Roxburgh), 206 Sqn RAF / 47 dead / ✠.
U 470	7.1.43	28.9.43	Be	OL G. Grave	16.10.43 ✠ N. Atlantic S.E. of Cape Farewell: 58°20n/29°20w / D/Cs / Lib C (P/O W. G. Loney), 59 Sqn RAF, Lib Z (F/L B. E. Peck), Lib E (F/L H. F. Kerrigan), 120 Sqn RAF / 46 dead / 2 rescued.
U 471	5.5.43			KL F. Kloevekorn	6.8.44 ✠ Toulon, Missiessy Dock No. 1: 43°07n/05°55e / bomb / air raid 15. USAAF / none dead / ↑ 20.5.1945, French war prize, 1946 French *Mille* (S 609), decomm. 9.7.63, Q 339, br.
U 472	26.5.43	24.2.44	Nv	OL W.-F. Frhr. von Forstner	4.3.44 ✠ Barents Sea S.E. of Bear I.: 73°05n/26°40e / rockets, artillery / Swd B (T/Sub-Lt. P. J. Beresford), 816 Sqn FAA CVE HMS *Chaser* (Capt. H. V. P. McClintock), DD HMS *Onslaught* (Comdr. Hon. A. Pleydell-Bouverie) / 23 dead / 30 rescued.
U 473	16.6.43	24.4.44	Lo	KL H. Sternberg	6.5.44 ✠ 00h33 N. Atlantic S.W. of Ireland: 49°29n/21°22w / D/Cs, artillery / PS's HMS *Starling* (Capt. F. J. Walker), HMS *Wild Goose* (A/Lt. Comdr. D. E. G. Wemyss), HMS *Wren* (Lt. Comdr. S. R. J. Woods) / 23 dead / 30 rescued.
U 474	-------				14.5.43 ✠ Kiel, Deutsche Werke fitting out quay / bomb / air raid 8. USAAF / ↑ ?.5.43, →slip No. 3 Deutsche Werke Kiel for reconstruction of stern section, completion planned for March 1944, delayed, contract suspended following new bomb damage, 11.10.44 afloat, construction November 1944 briefly resumed, 3.5.45 (✠) Kiel, Deutsche Werke No. 4 berth / 1946 br.
U 475	7.7.43			KL O. Stoeffler	3.5.45 (✠) Kiel, Tirpitz basin No. 36 berth / 1947 br.

1	2	3	4	5	6
U 476	28.7.43	20.5.44	Be	OL O. Niethmann	25.5.44 (✝) 01h02 Arctic N.W. of Trondheim: 65°08n/04°53e / torpedo / *U 990* (KL H. Nordheimer) / following D/Cs damage Cat V (Capt. F. W. L. Maxwell), 210 Sqn RAF 24.5.44 / 34 dead / 21 rescued.
U 477	18.8.43	28.5.44	Kr	OL K.-J. Jenssen	3.6.44 ✝ Arctic W. of Trondheim: 63°59n/01°37e / D/Cs / Cat T (F/L R. E. MacBride), 162 Sqn RCAF / 51 dead / ✝.
U 478	8.9.43	26.6.44	Be	OL R. Rademacher	30.6.44 ✝ Arctic N.E. of Faeroe Is.: 63°27n/00°50w / D/Cs / Lib E (F/O N. E. M. Smith), 86 Sqn RAF, Cat A (F/L R. E. MacBride), 162 Sqn RCAF / 52 dead / ✝.
U 479	27.10.43	27.10.44	Li	OL F. Sons	after 27.11.44 ✝ Baltic, Gulf of Finland N.W. of Odensholm I.: 59°20n/23°10e / Soviet sea mine / 51 dead / ✝.[69]
U 480	6.10.43	6.1.45	Dr	OL H.-J. Förster	after 29.1.45 ✝ English Channel S.W. of Portsmouth: 50°22n/01°44w / sea mine, British field "Brazier D2" / 48 dead / ✝.[70]
U 481	10.11.43			KL K. Andersen	9.5.45 Surrender Narvik, →Loch Eriboll, →Lisahally, →Loch Ryan / 30.11.45 ✝ artillery DD ORP *Blyskawica* 56°11n/10°00w / Op. Deadlight.
U 482	1.12.43	18.11.44	Be	KL H. Graf von Matuschka	25.11.44 ✝ N. Atlantic W. of Shetland Is.: 60°18n/04°52w / D/Cs / PF HMS *Ascension* (Comdr. W. J. Moore) following sighting by Sun G (Lt. J. Buer), 330 Sqn (Norwegian) RAF 24.11.44 / 48 dead / ✝.[71]
U 483	22.12.43			KL H.-J. von Morstein	9.5.45 Surrender Trondheim, 29.5.45 sailed →Loch Ryan / 16.12.45 ✝ bomb British aircraft 55°50n/10°05w / Op. Deadlight.
U 484	19.1.44	16.8.44	Kr	KK W.-A. Schaefer	9.9.44 ✝ N. Atlantic N.W. of Ireland: 55°45n/11°41w / D/Cs / PE HMS *Portchester Castle* (Lt. A. G. Scott), PF HMS *Helmsdale* (Comdr. C. W. McCullen) / 52 dead / ✝.[72]
U 485	23.2.44	29.4.45	Pa	KL F. Lutz	12.5.45 Surrender Gibraltar, →Lisahally, →Loch Ryan / 8.12.45 ✝ torpedo SS HMS/m *Tantivy* 56°10n/10°05 / Op. Deadlight.
U 486	22.3.44	7.4.45	Be	OL G. Meyer	12.4.45 ✝ 07h57 North Sea N.W. of Bergen: 60°44n/04°39e / torpedo / SS HMS/m *Tapir* (Lt. J. C. Y. Roxbourgh) / 48 dead / ✝.
U 551	7.11.40	18.3.41	Be	KL K. Schrott	23.3.41 ✝ N. Atlantic S. of Iceland: 62°37n/16°47w / D/Cs / TWL HMT *Visenda* (Lt. R. S. Winder) / 45 dead / ✝.

1	2	3	4	5	6
U 552	4.12.40			OL G. Lube	?.2.45 decomm. Wilhelmshaven, 5.5.45 (✠) 07h00 Wilhelmshaven, western entrance to Raeder lock: 53°31n/08°10e / br.
U 553	23.12.40	16.1.43	Pa	KK K. Thurmann	after 20.1.43 ✠ N. Atlantic / missing / 47 dead / ✠.[73]
U 554	15.1.41			OL W. Remus	5.5.45 (✠) Wilhelmshaven, western entrance to Raeder lock: 53°31n/08°10e / br.
U 555	30.1.41			OL D. Fritz	?.3.45 decomm. Hamburg-Finkenwerder. May 45 3.5.45 (✠) Hamburg, Neßkanal: 53°32,5n/09°50,7e.
U 556	6.2.41	19.6.41	Lo	KL H. Wohlfarth	27.6.41 ✠ N. Atlantic S.W. of Iceland: 60°24n/29°00w / D/Cs / PE's HMS *Nasturtium* (Lt. Comdr. R. C. Freaker), HMS *Celandine* (T/Lt. Comdr. A. Harrison), HMS *Gladiolus* (Lt. Comdr. H. M. C. Sanders) / 5 dead / 41 rescued.
U 557	13.2.41	9.12.41	Me	KL O. Paulshen	16.12.41 ✠ 21h44 Mediterranean W. of Crete: 35°31n/23°19e / erroneous ramming / Italian TB *Orione* (TV M. Gambetta) / 43 dead / ✠.
U 558	20.2.41	8.5.43	Br	KL G. Krech	20.7.43 ✠ Biscay N.W. of Spain: 45°10n/09°42w / D/Cs / Hal E (F/L G. A. Sawtell), 58 Sqn RAF, Lib F (Lt. C. F. Gallmeier), 19th A/S Sqn USAAF / 45 dead / 5 rescued.
U 559	27.2.41	29.9.42	Me	KL H. Heidtmann	30.10.42 ✠ 23h13 Mediterranean N.E. of Port Said: 32°30n/33°00e / D/Cs / DD's HMS *Pakenham* (Capt. E. B. K. Stevens), HMS *Petard* (Lt. Comdr. M. Thornton), HMS *Hero* (Lt. W. Scott), DE's HMS *Dulverton* (Lt. Comdr. W. N. Petch), HMS *Hurworth* (Lt. Comdr. D. A. Shaw) and Wes F (F/Sgt. R. J. Moore), 47 Sqn RAF / 7 dead / 38 rescued.
U 560	6.3.41			OL P. Jacobs	3.5.45 (✠) Kiel: 54°19n/10°10e / 1946 br.
U 561	13.3.41	10.7.43	To	OL F. Henning	12.7.43 ✠ Mediterranean, Strait of Messina: 38°16n/15°39e / torpedo / HM *MTB 81* (T/Lt. L. V. Strong) / 42 dead / 5 rescued.
U 562	20.3.41	9.2.43	Me	KL H. Hamm	19.2.43 ✠ 18h42 Mediterranean N.E. of Bengazi: 32°57n/20°54e / D/Cs / DD HMS *Isis* (Lt. Comdr. D. R. Mitchell), DE HMS *Hursley* (Lt. Comdr. W. J. P. Church) following sighting by Wel S (F/O I. B. Butler), 38 Sqn RAF / 49 dead / ✠.

1	2	3	4	5	6
U 563	27.3.41	29.5.43	Br	OL G. Borchardt	31.5.43 ✠ N. Atlantic N.W. of Spain: 46°35n/10°40w / D/Cs / Hal R (W/C W. E. Oulton), 58 Sqn RAF, Sun X (F/O W. M. French), 228 Sqn RAF, Sun E (F/L M. S. Mainprize), 10 Sqn RAAF / 49 dead / ✠.
U 564	3.4.41	9.6.43	Bo	OL H. Fiedler	14.6.43 ✠ 17h30 N. Atlantic N.W. of Cape Ortegal: 44°17n/10°25w / D/Cs / Wht G (Sgt A. J. Benson), 10 OTU RAF / 28 dead / 18 rescued.
U 565	10.4.41			KL F. Henning	30.9.44 (✠) Salamis, Skaramanga Bay: 37°57n/23°34e / following bomb damage air raid 15. USAAF 15.9.44 and 24.9.44.
U 566	17.4.41	18.10.43	Br	KL H. Hornkohl	24.10.43 (✠) 04h30 N. Atlantic W. of Porto: 41°12n/09°31w / following D/Cs damage Wel A (Sgt D. M. Cornish), 179 Sqn RAF / 49 rescued.
U 567	24.4.41	18.12.41	Na	KL E. Endrass	21.12.41 ✠ N. Atlantic N.E. of Azores: 44°02n/20°10w / D/Cs / PS HMS *Deptford* (Lt. Comdr. H. R. White) / 47 dead / ✠.
U 568	1.5.41	24.5.42	Me	KL J. Preuss	28.5.42 ✠ 05h00 Mediterranean N.E. of Tobruk: 32°42n/24°53e / D/Cs / DD HMS *Hero* (Lt. W. Scott), DE's HMS *Eridge* (Lt. Comdr. W. F. N. Gregory-Smith), HMS *Hurworth* (Lt. Comdr. J. T. B. Birch) and Ble S (F/Sgt Nash), 203 Sqn RAF / 47 rescued.
U 569	8.5.41	19.4.43	Pa	OL H. Johannsen	22.5.43 ✠ N. Atlantic: 50°40n/35°21w / D/Cs / Ave T-6 (Lt.[jg] W. F. Chamberlain), Ave T-7 (Lt. H. S. Roberts), VC-9 Sqn USN CVE USS *Bogue* (Capt. G. E. Short) / 21 dead / 25 rescued.
U 570	15.5.41	23.8.41	Dr	KL H.-J. Rahmlow	27.8.41 N. Atlantic S. of Iceland: 62°15n/18°35w / captured by Hud S (S/L J. H. Thompson), 269 Sqn RAF, 44 rescued, → 29.8.41 beached Thorlakshafn by TWL HMT *Westwater*, HMT *Windermere*, 29.9.41 comm. HMS/m *Graph*, *P 715*, later *N 46*; 7.2.44 decomm., 20.3.44 grounded Islay I.: 55°48,8n/06°27w, 1961 br.
U 571	22.5.41	8.1.44	Pa	OL G. Lüssow	28.1.44 ✠ N. Atlantic W. of Ireland: 52°41n/14°27w / D/Cs / Sun D (F/L R. D. Lucas), 461 Sqn RAAF / 52 dead / ✠.
U 572	29.5.41	2.6.43	Pa	OL H. Kummetat	3.8.43 ✠ mid-Atlantic N.E. of Trinidad: 11°35n/54°05w / D/Cs / Mar P-6 (Lt.[jg] C. C. Cox), VP-205 Sqn USN / 47 dead / ✠.

1	2	3	4	5	6
U 573	5.6.41	23.4.42	Me	KL H. Heinsohn	2.5.42 entered Cartagena, Spain, following D/Cs damage Hud M (Sgt. T. M. Brent), 233 Sqn RAF N.W. of Algiers 1.5.42 / 1 dead / 43 rescued / interned / 2.8.42 decomm. Cartagena, 19.8.42 sold →Spain, 15.11.47 comm. Spanish SS *G 7*, 15.6.60 *S 01*, 2.5.70 decomm., br.
U 574	12.6.41	10.11.41	Kr	OL D. Gengelbach	19.12.41 ✞ N. Atlantic S.W. of Lisbon: 38°12n/17°23w / D/Cs / PS HMS *Stork* (Comdr. F. J. Walker) / 28 dead / 16 rescued.
U 575	19.6.41	29.2.44	Na	OL W. Boehmer	13.3.44 ✞ N. Atlantic N. of Azores: 46°18n/27°34w / D/Cs, artillery, rockets / PF HMCS *Prince Rupert* (Lt. Comdr. R. W. Draney), DD USS *Hobson* (Lt. Comdr. K. Loveland), DE USS *Haverfield* (Lt. Comdr. J. A. Mathews) and Ave T-3 (Lt. Comdr. J. F. Adams), VC-95 Sqn USN CVE USS *Bogue* (Capt. J. B. Dunn), For J (F/O W. R. Travell), 220 Sqn RAF, For R (F/L A. D. Beaty), 206 Sqn RAF, Wel B (F/O J. P. Finnessy), 172 Sqn RAF / 18 dead / 37 rescued.
U 576	26.6.41	16.6.42	Na	KL H.-D. Heinicke	15.7.42 ✞ 20h23 N. Atlantic E. of Cape Hatteras: 34°51n/75°22w / D/Cs, artillery / Kin (Ens. C. D. Webb), Kin (Ens. F. C. Lewis), VS-9 Sqn USN and US M/V *Unicoi* (Capt. J. Muhle) / 45 dead / ✞.
U 577	3.7.41	7.1.42	Me	KL H. Schauenburg	15.1.42 ✞ Mediterranean N.W. of Mersa Matruh: 32°40n/25°48e / D/Cs / Swd G (Sub-Lt. E. D. Dunkerley), 815 Sqn FAA / 43 dead / ✞.[74]
U 578	10.7.41	6.8.42	Na	KK E.-A. Rehwinkel	after 6.8.42 ✞ Biscay / missing / 49 dead / ✞.[75]
U 579	17.7.41			KL D. Lohmann	12.10.41 decomm. Danzig following fire in forward torpedo compartment 29.9.41 Danzig Bay, repaired Holmwerft Danzig, recomm. Danzig.
	27.5.42	5.5.45	So	OL H.-D. Schwarzenberg	5.5.45 ✞ 16h42 Baltic, Kattegat E. of Aarhus: 56°10,7n/11°04e / D/Cs / Lib K (F/O A. A. Bruneau), 547 Sqn RAF / at least 24 dead / ✞.[76]
U 580	24.7.41			OL H.-G. Kuhlmann	11.11.41 ✞ 20h30 Baltic W. of Memel: 55°39,6n/20°38,5e / collision / German target ship *Angelburg* (Kapitän K. Kabbe) / 12 dead / 32 rescued.
U 581	31.7.41	11.1.42	Na	KL W. Pfeifer	2.2.42 ✞ N. Atlantic W. of Azores: 38°24n/28°30w / D/Cs / DD HMS *Westcott* (Comdr. I. H. Bockett-Pugh) / 4 dead / 41 rescued.

1	2	3	4	5	6
U 582	7.8.41	14.9.42	Br	KL W. Schulte	5.10.42 ✞ 10h25 N. Atlantic S.W. of Iceland: 58°52n/21°42w / D/Cs / Cat I (Chief Aviation Pilot M. Luke), VP-73 Sqn USN / 46 dead / ✞.[77]
U 583	14.8.41			KL H. Ratsch	15.11.41 ✞ 21h48 Baltic N. of Stolpmünde: 55°18,5n/16°53,5e / collision / U 153 (KK W. Reichmann) / 45 dead / ✞.
U 584	21.8.41	2.9.43	Br	KL J. Deecke	31.10.43 ✞ N. Atlantic: 49°14n/31°55w / homing torpedo / Ave T-7 (Lt.[jg] W. S. Fowler), Ave T-1 (Lt.[jg] L. S. Balliett), Ave T-8 (Lt.[jg] A. McAuslan), VC-9 Sqn USN CVE USS *Card* (Capt. A. J. Isbell) / 53 dead / ✞.
U 585	28.8.41	28.3.42	Kk	KL B. Lohse	≈30.3.42 ✞ Barents Sea N. of Kola Inlet: ≈70° n/34° e / missing – ≈floating German sea mine, field "Bantos-A" / 44 dead / ✞.[78]
U 586	4.9.41			OL H. Götze	5.7.44 ✞ 12h30 Toulon, Missiessy East Quay: 43°07n/05°55e / bomb / air raid 15. USAAF / none dead / 12.7.44 decomm. / 1947 br.
U 587	11.9.41	12.2.42	Na	KL U. Borcherdt	27.3.42 ✞ N. Atlantic: 47°21n/21°39w / D/Cs / DD's HMS *Volunteer* (Lt. A. S. Pomeroy), HMS *Leamington* (Lt. Comdr. H. G. Bowerman), DE's HMS *Grove* (Lt. Comdr. J. W. Rylands), HMS *Aldenham* (Lt. H. A. Stuart-Menteth) / 42 dead / ✞.
U 588	18.9.41	19.7.42	Na	KL V. Vogel	31.7.42 ✞ N. Atlantic: 49°59n/36°36w / D/Cs / DD HMCS *Skeena* (Lt. Comdr. K. L. Dyer), PE HMCS *Wetaskiwin* (Lt. Comdr. G. S. Windeyer) / 46 dead / ✞.
U 589	25.9.41	9.9.42	Nv	KL H.-J. Horrer	14.9.42 ✞ Barents Sea S. of Spitzbergen: 75°40n/20°32e / D/Cs / DD HMS *Onslow* (Capt. H. T. Armstrong) and Swd, 825 Sqn FAA CVE HMS *Avenger* (Comdr. A. P. Colthurst) / 44 dead / ✞.
U 590	2.10.41	8.6.43	Na	OL W. Krüer	9.7.43 ✞ mid-Atlantic E. of Amazon estuary: 03°22n/48°38w / D/Cs / Cat P-l (Lt.[jg] S. E. Auslander), VP-94 Sqn USN / 45 dead / ✞.
U 591	9.10.41	26.6.43	Na	OL R. Ziesmer	30.7.43 ✞ S. Atlantic E. of Recife: 08°36s/34°34w / D/Cs / Ven B-10 (Lt. [jg] W. C. Young), VB-127 Sqn USN / 19 dead / 28 rescued.
U 592	16.10.41	10.1.44	Na	OL H. Jaschke	31.1.44 ✞ 10h N. Atlantic S.W. of Ireland: 50°20n/17°29w / D/Cs / PS's HMS *Starling* (Capt. F. J. Walker), HMS *Wild Goose* (Comdr. D. E. G. Wemyss), HMS *Magpie* (Lt. Comdr. R. S. Abram) / 49 dead / ✞.

1	2	3	4	5	6
U 593	23.10.41	1.12.43	To	KL G. Kelbling	13.12.43 ✝ Mediterranean N. of Constantine: 37°38n/05°58e / D/Cs / DD USS *Wainwright* (Comdr. W. W. Strohbehn), DE HMS *Calpe* (Lt. Comdr. H. Kirkwood) / 51 rescued.
U 594	30.10.41	23.5.43	Na	KL F. Mumm	5.6.43 ✝ N. Atlantic W. of Gibraltar: 36°02n/10°28w / D/Cs / Hud M (F/O H. W. B. Wright), 48 Sqn RAF / 50 dead / ✝.[79]
U 595	6.11.41	31.10.42	Br	KL H. Quaet-Faslem	14.11.42 ✝ Mediterranean, Algerian coast W. of Tenes: 36°38n/00°30e / deliberately beached following severe damage by D/Cs Hud C (F/O G. Williams), Hud D (P/O C. A. Livingstone), 608 Sqn RAF and subsequent D/Cs by Hud F (F/O H. M. S. Green), Hud K (F/O G. A. B. Lord), Hud W (P/O J.H. Simpson), Hud X (A/W/C D. F. Spotswood), 500 Sqn RAF / 45 rescued.
U 596	13.11.41			OL H. Kolbus	24.9.44 ✝ Piraeus, yard basin: 37°59n/23°39e / bomb / air raid 15. USAAF / 1 dead.
U 597	20.11.41	16.9.42	Br	KL E. Bopst	12.10.42 ✝ N. Atlantic: 56°50n/28°05w / D/Cs / Lib H (S/L T. M. Bulloch), 120 Sqn RAF / 49 dead / ✝.
U 598	27.11.41	26.6.43	Na	KL G. Holtorf	23.7.43 ✝ S. Atlantic E. of Natal: 04°05s/33°23w / D/Cs / Lib B-12 (Lt.[jg] C. A. Baldwin), Lib B-8 (Lt. W. R. Ford), Lib B-6 (Lt.[jg] G. E. Waugh), VB-107 Sqn USN / 43 dead / 2 rescued.
U 599	4.12.41	30.8.42	Kr	KL W. Breithaupt	24.10.42 ✝ N. Atlantic: 46°07n/17°40w / D/Cs / Lib G (P/O B. P. Liddington), 224 Sqn RAF/ 44 dead /✝.
U 600	11.12.41	7.11.43	Br	KL B. Zurmühlen	25.11.43 ✝ N. Atlantic E. of Azores: 40°31n/22°07w / D/Cs / DE's HMS *Bazely* (Lt. Comdr. J. V. Brock), HMS *Blackwood* (Lt. Comdr. L. T. Sly) / 54 dead / ✝.
U 601	18.12.41	17.2.44	Nv	KL O. Hansen	25.2.44 ✝ Arctic N.W. of Harstad: 70°26n/12°40e / D/Cs / Cat M (S/L F. J. French), 210 Sqn RAF / 51 dead / ✝.
U 602	29.12.41	11.4.43	To	KL P. Schüler	after 19.4.43 ✝ Mediterranean ≈N. of Oran / missing / 48 dead / ✝.[80]
U 603	2.1.42	5.2.44	Br	KL H.-J. Bertelsmann	after 18.2.44 ✝ N. Atlantic / missing / 51 dead / ✝.[81]
U 604	8.1.42	24.6.43	Hi	KL H. Höltring	11.8.43 (✝) S. Atlantic N.W. of Ascension: 04°15s/21°20w / following D/Cs damage Ven B-9 (Lt. Comdr. T. D. Davies), VB-129 Sqn USN 30.7.43 / 14 dead in ✝ U 185 / 31 rescued.[82]

1	2	3	4	5	6
U 605	15.1.42	21.10.42	Sp	KL H.-V. Schütze	14.11.42 ✠ Mediterranean N.W. of Tenes: 36°20n/01°01w / D/Cs / Hud B (P/O J. W. Barling), 233 Sqn RAF / 46 dead / ✠.[83]
U 606	22.1.42	4.1.43	Br	OL H. Döhler	22.2.43 ✠ N. Atlantic: 47°44n/33°43w / D/Cs / USCGC *Campbell* (Comdr. J. A. Hirschfield), DD ORP *Burza* (Lt. Comdr. F. Pitulko) / 36 dead / 11 rescued.
U 607	29.1.42	10.7.43	Br	OL W. Jeschonnek	13.7.43 ✠ 08h Biscay N.W. of Spain: 45°02n/09°14w / D/Cs / Sun N (F/O R. D. Hanbury), 228 Sqn RAF / 45 dead / 7 rescued.
U 608	5.2.42	7.8.44	Lo	OL W. Reisener	10.8.44 ✠ Biscay N.W. of La Rochelle: 46°30n/03°08w / D/Cs / PS HMS *Wren* (Lt. Comdr. S. R. J. Woods) and Lib C (W/C R. T. F. Gates), 53 Sqn RAF / 52 rescued.
U 609	12.2.42	16.1.43	Na	KL K. Rudloff	6.2.43 ✠ 22h04 N. Atlantic: 54°56n/28°11w / D/Cs / PE FNFL *Lobelia* (Capt. de frégate P. de Morsier) / 47 dead / ✠.[84]
U 610	19.2.42	12.9.43	Na	KL W. Frhr. von Freyberg-Eisenberg-Allmendingen	8.10.43 ✠ N. Atlantic: 55°45n/24°33w / D/Cs / Sun J (F/O A. H. Russell), 423 Sqn RCAF / 51 dead / ✠.
U 611	26.2.42	4.11.42	Ha	KL N. von Jacobs	8.12.42 ✠ 11h28 N. Atlantic S.E. of Cape Farewell: 57°25n/35°19w / D/Cs / Lib B (S/L T. M. Bulloch), 120 Sqn RAF / 45 dead / ✠.[85]
U 612	5.3.42			KL P. Siegmann	6.8.42 ✠ Baltic, Danzig Bay: 54°24,1n/19°00,9e / collision / U 444 (OL A. Langfeld) / 2 dead / 57 rescued / ↑ 18.8.42, 24.8.42 Danzig decomm., repaired Holmwerft Danzig, recomm. Danzig.
	31.5.43			OL H.-P. Dick	1.5.45 (✠) Warnemünde U-boat base: 54°10,3n/12°05,7e / ↑ ?.7.45, br.
U 613	12.3.42	10.7.43	Pa	KL H. Köppe	23.7.43 ✠ N. Atlantic S. of Azores: 35°32n/28°36w / D/Cs / DD USS *George E. Badger* (Lt. T. H. Byrd) / 48 dead / ✠.
U 614	19.3.42	25.7.43	Na	KL W. Sträter	29.7.43 ✠ N. Atlantic N.W. of Spain: 46°42n/11°03w / D/Cs / Wel G (W/C R. G. Musson), 172 Sqn RAF / 49 dead / ✠.
U 615	26.3.42	12.6.43	Pa	KL R. Kapitzky	7.8.43 ✠ Caribbean N.E. of Curacao: 12°38n/64°15w / D/Cs / Mar P-6 (Lt. [jg] J. M. Erskine), Mar P-8 (Lt.[jg] J. W. Dresbach),VP-204 Sqn USN, Mar P-2 (Lt. Comdr. R. S. Null), Mar P-4 (Lt. A. R. Matuski), Mar P-l 1 (Lt. L. D. Crockett), VP-205 Sqn USN, Ven B-5 (Lt.[jg] T. M. Holmes), VB-130 USN / 4 dead / 43 rescued.

1	2	3	4	5	6
U 616	2.4.42	4.5.44	To	OL S. Koitschka	17.5.44 ✠ Mediterranean E. of Cartagena: 36°46n/00°52e / D/Cs / DD's USS *Nields* (Comdr. A. R. Heckey), USS *Hambleton* (Comdr. H. A. Renken), USS *Gleaves* (Comdr. B. L. Gurnette), USS *Ellyson* (Comdr. E. W. Longton), DM's USS *Macomb* (Lt. Comdr. G. Hutchinson), USS *Rodman* (Comdr. J. F. Foley), USS *Emmons* (Comdr. E. B. Billingsley), USS *Hilary P. Jones* (Lt. Comdr. F. M. Stiesberg) following D/Cs Wel K (W/O J. M. Cooke), 36 Sqn RAF 15.5.44 / 53 rescued.
U 617	9.4.42	29.8.43	To	KL A. Brandi	12.9.43 (✠) Mediterranean W. of Cape Tres Forcas: 35°13n/03°13w / beached following D/Cs Wel J (P/O W. H. Brunini), Wel P (S/L D. B. Hodgkinson), 179 Sqn RAF 11.9.43 / wreck destroyed by artillery / TWL HMS *Haarlem* (T/ Lt. J. R. T. Broom), PE HMS *Hyacinth* (Lt. Comdr. J. D. Hayes), AM HMAS *Wollongong* (Lt. T. H. Smith) / 49 rescued.
U 618	16.4.42	11.8.44	Br	OL E. Faust	15.8.44 ✠ Biscay S.W. of Lorient: 47°22n/04°39w / D/Cs / DE's HMS *Duckworth* (Comdr. R. G. Mills), HMS *Essington* (A/Lt. Comdr. W. Lambert) following D/Cs Lib G (F/L G. G. Potier), 53 Sqn RAF / 61 dead / ✠.
U 619	23.4.42	12.9.42	Kr	OL K. Makowski	5.10.42 ✠ 11h53 N. Atlantic S.W. of Iceland: 58°41n/22°58w / D/Cs / Hud N (F/O J. Markham), 269 Sqn RAF / 44 dead / ✠.[86]
U 620	30.4.42	19.12.42	Pa	KL H. Stein	13.2.43 ✠ N. Atlantic N.W. of Lisbon: 39°18n/11°17w / D/Cs / Cat J (F/L H. R. Sheardown), 202 Sqn RAF / 47 dead / ✠.[87]
U 621	7.5.42	13.8.44	Br	OL H. Stuckmann	18.8.44 ✠ Biscay W. of La Rochelle: 45°52n/02°36w / D/Cs / DD's HMCS *Ottawa* (Comdr. J. D. Prentice), HMCS *Kootenay* (Lt. Comdr. W. H. Willson), HMCS *Chaudière* (Lt. Comdr. C. P. Nixon) / 56 dead / ✠.
U 622	14.5.42			KL H.-T. Queck	24.7.43 ✠ 13h53 Trondheim, harbor basin No. IV, Strandveis quay: 63°26n/10°25e / bomb / air raid 8. USAAF / none dead / ↑ 20.4.44, 12.5.44 docked, May 45 wreck captured by British forces, br.
U 623	21.5.42	2.2.43	Na	OL H. Schröder	21.2.43 ✠ N. Atlantic: 48°08n/29°37w / D/Cs / Lib T (S/L D. J. Isted), 120 Sqn RAF / 46 dead / ✠.

1	2	3	4	5	6
U 624	28.5.42	7.1.43	Na	KL U. Graf von Soden-Fraunhofen	7.2.43 ✠ N. Atlantic: 55°42n/26°17w / D/Cs / For J (P/O G. P. Roberson), 220 Sqn RAF / 45 dead / ✠.
U 625	4.6.42	29.2.44	Br	OL S. Straub	10.3.44 ✠ N. Atlantic W. of Ireland: 52°35n/20°19w / D/Cs / Sun U (F/L S. W. Butler), 422 Sqn RCAF / 53 dead / ✠.
U 626	11.6.42	8.12.42	Be	LT H.-B. Bade	After 14.12.42 ✠ N. Atlantic S.E. of Greenland / missing / 47 dead / ✠.[88]
U 627	18.6.42	18.10.42	Kr	KL R. Kindelbacher	27.10.42 ✠ N. Atlantic S. of Iceland: 59°14n/22°49w / D/Cs / For F (P/O R. L. Cowey), 206 Sqn RAF / 44 dead / ✠.
U 628	25.6.42	1.7.43	Br	KL H. Hasenschar	3.7.43 ✠ Biscay N.W. of Cape Ortegal: 44°11n/08°45w / D/Cs / Lib J (S/L P. J. Cundy), 224 Sqn RAF / 49 dead / ✠.
U 629	2.7.42	6.6.44	Br	OL H.-H. Bugs	7.6.44 ✠ 05h13 Biscay W. of Brest: 48°34n/05°23w / D/Cs / Lib L (F/L J. W. Carmichael), 53 Sqn RAF / 51 dead / ✠.[89]
U 630	9.7.42	21.3.43	Kr	OL W. Winkler	6.5.43 ✠ N. Atlantic N.E. of Newfoundland: 52°31n/44°50w / D/Cs / DD HMS *Vidette* (Lt. R. Hart) / 47 dead / ✠.[90]
U 631	16.7.42	18.9.43	Br	OL J. Krüger	17.10.43 ✠ N. Atlantic S.E. of Cape Farewell: 58°13n/32°29w / D/Cs / PE HMS *Sunflower* (Lt. Comdr. J. Plomer) / 54 dead / ✠.
U 632	23.7.42	15.3.43	Br	KL H. Karpf	6.4.43 ✠ N. Atlantic S.W. of Iceland: 58°02n/28°42w / D/Cs / Lib R (F/L C. W. Burcher), 86 Sqn RAF / 48 dead / ✠.
U 633	30.7.42	23.2.43	Kr	OL B. Müller	8.3.43 ✠ N. Atlantic S.E. of Greenland: 58°21n/31°00w / D/Cs / USCGC *John C. Spencer* (Comdr. H. S. Berdine) / 43 dead / ✠.[91]
U 634	6.8.42	12.6.43	Br	OL E. Dahlhaus	30.8.43 ✠ N. Atlantic E. of Azores: 40°13n/19°24w / D/Cs / PS HMS *Stork* (Comdr. G. W. E. Castens), PE HMS *Stonecrop* (Lt. Comdr. J. P. Smythe) / 47 dead / ✠.
U 635	13.8.42	18.3.43	Kr	OL H. Eckelmann	5.4.43 ✠ N. Atlantic S.W. of Iceland: 58°20n/31°52w / D/Cs / Lib N (F/L G. L. Hatherly), 120 Sqn RAF / 47 dead / ✠.[92]
U 636	20.8.42	1.4.45	Dr	OL E. Schendel	21.4.45 ✠ N. Atlantic N.W. of Ireland: 55°50n/10°31w / D/Cs / DE's HMS *Bazely* (A/Lt. Comdr. J. W. Cooper), HMS *Drury* (Lt. Comdr. N. J. Parker), HMS *Bentinck* (A/Lt. Comdr. P. R. G. Worth) / 42 dead / ✠.

1	2	3	4	5	6
U 637	27.8.42			OL(Ing) K. Weber i.V.	9.5.45 Surrender Stavanger, 27.5.45 sailed →Lisahally, →Loch Ryan / 21.12.45 ✝ foundered while under tow 55°35n/07°46w / Op. Deadlight.
U 638	3.9.42	20.4.43	Pa	KL O. Staudinger	5.5.43 ✝ N. Atlantic N.E. of Newfoundland: 54°12n/44°05w / D/Cs / PE HMS *Sunflower* (Lt. Comdr. J. Plomer) / 44 dead / ✝.[93]
U 639	10.9.42	12.8.43	Tr	OL W. Wichmann	28.8.43 ✝ 10h51 Kara Sea N.E. of Mys Zelanija: 76°40n/69°40e / torpedo / Soviet SS *S 101* (KL. J. N. Trofimov) / 47 dead / ✝.
U 640	17.9.42	4.5.43	Kr	OL K.-H. Nagel	14.5.43 ✝ N. Atlantic E. of Cape Farewell: 60°32n/31°05w / D/Cs / Cat K (Lt.[jg] P. A. Bodinet), VP-84 Sqn USN / 49 dead / ✝.[94]
U 641	24.9.42	11.12.43	Na	KL H. Rendtel	19.1.44 ✝ N. Atlantic S.W. of Ireland: 50°25n/18°49w / D/Cs / PE HMS *Violet* (Lt. C. N. Stewart) / 50 dead / ✝.
U 642	1.10.42			KL H. Brünning	5.7.44 ✝ Toulon, Missiessy Dock No. 2: 43°07n/05°55e / bomb damage air raid 15. USAAF / none dead / 12.7.44 10h00 decomm., ↑ 12.4.45, 1946 br.
U 643	8.10.42	14.9.43	Be	KL H. H. Speidel	8.10.43 ✝ N. Atlantic: 56°14n/26°55w / D/Cs / Lib T (F/O D. C. L. Webber), 120 Sqn RAF, Lib Z (F/O C. W. Burcher), 86 Sqn RAF / 30 dead / 18 rescued.
U 644	15.10.42	18.3.43	Be	OL K. Jensen	7.4.43 ✝ Arctic S.W. of Jan Mayen I.: 69°38n/05°40w / torpedoes / SS HMS/m *Tuna* (Lt. D. S. R. Martin) / 45 dead / ✝.
U 645	22.10.42	2.12.43	Pa	OL O. Ferro	after 12.12.43 ✝ Biscay or N. Atlantic W. of Spain / missing / 55 dead / ✝.[95]
U 646	29.10.42	12.5.43	Dr	OL H. Wulff	17.5.43 ✝ N. Atlantic S.E. of Iceland: 62°10n/14°30w / D/Cs / Hud J (F/Sgt F. H. W. James), 269 Sqn RAF / 46 dead / ✝.
U 647	5.11.42	25.7.43	Kr	KL W. Hertin	after 28.7.43 ✝ Arctic ≈N. of Shetland Is. / missing / 48 dead / ✝.[96]
U 648	12.11.42	9.10.43	Na	OL P. Stahl	after 22.11.43 ✝ N. Atlantic ≈W. of Spain / missing / 50 dead / ✝.[97]
U 649	19.11.42			OL R. Tiesler	24.2.43 ✝ 05h30 Baltic N. of Leba: 55°15n/17°15e / collision / U 232 (KL E. Ziehm) / 35 dead /11 rescued.
U 650	26.11.42	9.12.44	Be	OL R. Zorn	after 1.1.45 ✝ English Channel S. of Penzance: 49°51n/05°30w / D/Cs / unknown vessel / 47 dead / ✝.[98]

1	2	3	4	5	6
U 651	12.2.41	12.6.41	Be	KL P. Lohmeyer	29.6.41 ✝ 07h37 N. Atlantic S. of Iceland: 59°52n/18°36w / D/Cs / DD's HMS *Malcolm* (Comdr. C. D. Howard-Johnston), HMS *Scimitar* (Lt. R. D. Franks), PE's HMS *Arabis* (Lt. Comdr. J. P. Stewart), HMS *Violet* (Lt. Comdr. K. M. Nicolson), AM HMS *Speedwell* (Lt. Comdr. J. J. Youngs) / 45 rescued.
U 652	3.4.41	26.5.42	Po	OL G.-W. Fraatz	2.6.42 (✝) 10h50 Mediterranean, Gulf of Sollum: 31⁰55n/25°13e / torpedo U 81 / (KL F. Guggenberger) / following D/Cs damage Swd L (Lt. G.H. Bates), 815 Sqn FAA / 46 rescued.
U 653	25.5.41	2.3.44	Br	OL H.-A. Kandler	15.3.44 ✝ N. Atlantic: 53°46n/24°35w / D/Cs / Swd A (Sub-Lt. P. Cumberland), 825 Sqn FAA CVE HMS *Vindex* (Capt. H. T. T. Bayliss), PS's HMS *Starling* (Capt. F. J. Walker), HMS *Wild Goose* (Lt. Comdr. D. E. G. Wemyss) / 51 dead / ✝.
U 654	5.7.41	11.7.42	Lo	OL L. Forster	22.8.42 ✝ 20h58 Caribbean N. of Colon: 12°00n/79°56w / D/Cs / Dig (Lt. P. A. Koenig), 45 Bomb Sqn USAAF / 44 dead / ✝.
U 655	11.8.41	15.3.42	He	KL A. Dumrese	24.3.42 ✝ Barents Sea S.E. of Bear I.: 73°00n/21°00e / ramming / AM HMS *Sharpshooter* (Lt. Comdr. D. Lampen) / 45 dead / ✝.
U 656	17.9.41	4.2.42	Br	KL E. Kröning	1.3.42 ✝ 18h00 N. Atlantic S. of Cape Race: 46⁰15n/53°15w / D/Cs / Hud P-8 (Ens. W. Tepuni), VP-82 Sqn USN / 45 dead / ✝.
U 657	8.10.41	4.5.43	Dr	KL H. Göllnitz	17.5.43 ✝ N. Atlantic S. of Cape Farewell: 58°54n/42°33w / D/Cs / PF HMS *Swale* (Lt. Comdr. J. Jackson) / 47 dead / ✝.⁹⁹
U 658	5.11.41	6.10.42	Na	KL H. Senkel	30.10.42 ✝ N. Atlantic E. of Newfoundland: 50°32n/46°32w / D/Cs / Hud Y (F/O E. L. Robinson), 145(BR) Sqn RCAF / 48 dead / ✝.
U 659	9.12.41	25.4.43	Br	KL H. Stock	4.5.43 ✝ 00h30 N. Atlantic W. of Cape Finisterre: 43°32n/13°20w / collision / U 439 (OL H. von Tippelskirch) / 44 dead / 3 rescued.
U 660	8.1.42	24.10.42	Sp	KL G. Baur	12.11.42 ✝ Mediterranean N. of Oran: 36°07n/01°00w / D/Cs / PE's HMS *Lotus* (Lt. H. J. Hall), HMS *Starwort* (Lt. A. H. Kent) / 2 dead / 45 rescued.

1	2	3	4	5	6
U 661	12.2.42	7.9.42	Kr	OL E. von Lilienfeld	15.10.42 ✠ N. Atlantic: 53°42n/35°56w / ramming / DD HMS *Viscount* (Lt. Comdr. J. V. Waterhouse) / 44 dead / ✠.[100]
U 662	9.4.42	26.6.43	Na	KL H.-E. Müller	21.7.43 ✠ mid-Atlantic E. of Amazon estuary: 03°56n/48°46w / D/Cs / Cat P-4 (Lt.[jg] R. H. Rowland), VP-94 Sqn USN / 44 dead / 3 rescued.
U 663	14.5.42	5.5.43	Br	KL H. Schmid	8.5.43 ✠ Biscay S.W. of Brest: ≈46°50n/10°00w / missing – ≈diving accident following D/Cs damage Sun W (F/L G. G. Rossiter), 10 Sqn RAAF 7.5.43 / 49 dead / ✠.[101]
U 664	17.6.42	21.7.43	Br	KL A. Graef	9.8.43 ✠ N. Atlantic W. of Azores: 40°12n/37°29w / D/Cs / Ave (Lt.[jg] J. C. Forney), Ave (Lt.[jg] G. G. Hogan), Wil (Lt.[jg] N. D. Hodson), VC-1 Sqn USN CVE USS *Card* (Capt. A. J. Isbell) / 7 dead / 44 rescued.
U 665	22.7.42	23.2.43	Kr	OL H.-J. Haupt	after 21.3.43 ✠ Biscay W. of La Pallice / missing / 46 dead / ✠.[102]
U 666	26.8.42	25.12.43	Na	OL E.-A. Wilberg	10.2.44 ✠ 14h38 N. Atlantic W. of Ireland: 53°56n/17°16w / D/Cs / Swd A (T/Sub-Lt. W. H. Thompson), 842 Sqn FAA CVE HMS *Fencer* (Capt. W. W. R. Bentinck) / 51 dead / ✠.[103]
U 667	21.10.42	22.7.44	Na	KL K.-H. Lange	≈26.8.44 ✠ Biscay W. of La Rochelle: ≈46°00n/01°35w / British air-laid mine, field "Cinnamon" / 45 dead / ✠.[104]
U 668	16.11.42			KL F. Henning	9.5.45 Surrender Narvik, →Loch Eriboll, →Lisahally / 1.1.46 ✠ artillery DD HMS *Onslaught* 56°03n/09°24w / Op. Deadlight.
U 669	16.12.42	29.8.43	Na	OL K. Köhl	30.8.43 ✠ Biscay W. of La Rochelle: ≈45°33n/03°50w / missing – possibly marine cause during deep-diving trial / 52 dead / ✠.[105]
U 670	26.1.43			OL G. Hyronimus	20.8.43 ✠ 23h30 Baltic, Danzig Bay: 54°51,2n/19°16,8e / collision / German target ship *Bolkoburg* (Kapitän J. Salz) / 21 dead / 22 rescued.
U 671	3.3.43	26.7.44	Bl	KL W. Hegewald	4.8.44 ✠ 02h30 English Channel S. of Newhaven: 50°23n/00°06e / D/Cs / DE's HMS *Stayner* (Lt. Comdr. H. J. Hall), HMS *Wensleydale* (Lt. Comdr. W. P. Goodfellow) / 47 dead / 5 rescued.
U 672	6.4.43	6.7.44	Na	OL U. Lawaetz	18.7.44 (✠) English Channel N. of Guernsey: 50°03n/02°30w / following D/Cs damage / DE HMS *Balfour* (Lt. Comdr. C. D. B. Coventry) / 52 rescued.

1	2	3	4	5	6
U 673	8.5.43	22.10.44	Be	OL E.-A. Gerke	24.10.44 ✠ 01h15 North Sea, entrance to Felsafiord: 59°17n/05°57e / beached on Smaskjer reef following collision / U 382 (OL H.-D. Wilke) / ↑ 9.11.44, →Stavanger, decomm., hulk May 45 captured by British forces, br.
U 674	15.6.43	17.4.44	Nv	OL H. Muhs	2.5.44 ✠ 06h25 Arctic W. of Tromsö: 70°32n/04°37e / rockets / Swd B (Sub-Lt. B. F. Vibert), 842 Sqn FAA CVE HMS *Fencer* (A/Capt. W. W. R. Bentinck) / 49 dead / ✠.
U 675	14.7.43	20.5.44	Kr	OL K.-H. Sammler	24.5.44 ✠ Arctic W. of Aalesund: 62°27n/03°04e / D/Cs / Sun R (F/O T. F. P. Frizell), 4 (C)OTU RAF / 51 dead / ✠.
U 676	6.8.43	22.1.45	Li	KL W. Sass	after 12.2.45 ✠ Baltic, Gulf of Finland S. of Hangö: 59°30n/23°00e / sea mine, Soviet field "Vantaa 3" / 57 dead / ✠.[106]
U 677	20.9.43			OL G. Ady	9.4.45 ✠ Hamburg-Finkenwerder, U-boat pen Fink II box No. 5: 53°32,6n/09°51,3e / bomb / air raid RAF Bomber Command / none dead / br.
U 678	25.10.43	8.6.44	Kr	OL G. Hyronimus	6.7.44 ✠ English Channel S.W. of Brighton: 50°32n/00°23w / D/Cs / DD's HMCS *Ottawa* (Comdr. J. D. Prentice), HMCS *Kootenay* (Lt. Comdr. W. H. Willson), PE HMS *Statice* (Lt. R. Wolfendon) / 52 dead / ✠.
U 679	29.11.43	4.11.44	Li	OL E. Aust	After 26.12.44 ✠ Baltic, Gulf of Finland N.E. of Osmussaar: ≈59°26n/23°37e / Soviet sea mine / 51 dead / ✠.[107]
U 680	23.12.43			OL M. Ulber	5.5.45 Surrender Fredericia, →Wilhelmshaven, 24.6.45 sailed →Loch Ryan / 28.12.45 ✠ artillery DD HMS *Onslaught* 55°24n/06°29w / Op. Deadlight.
U 681	3.2.44	15.2.45	Kr	OL W. Gebauer	11.3.45 ✠ 09h30 English Channel W. of Bishop Rock: 49°53n/06°31w / D/Cs / Lib N (Lt. N. R. Field), VPB-103 Sqn USN following damage from grounding on Bishop Rock / 11 dead / 38 rescued.
U 682	17.4.44			OL S. Thienemann	11.3.45 ✠ 01h15 Hamburg, Howaldtswerke repair quay: 53°32n/09°57e / bomb / air raid 8. USAAF / none dead / ↑ July–August 1945, →Blankenese, br.
U 683	30.5.44	5.2.45	Kr	KL G. Keller	after 20.2.45 ✠ ≈N. Atlantic S.W. of Ireland or English Channel / missing / 49 dead / ✠.[108]

1	2	3	4	5	6
U 684	--------				delivery planned July 1944, but construction abandoned spring 1944, 23.9.44 contract canceled; incomplete hull 3.5.45 (✞) Hamburg, Howaldtswerke entrance to western box of U-boat pen Elbe II: 53°32n/ 09°57e / br.
U 685	--------				delivery planned September 1944, but construction abandoned spring 1944, 23.9.44 contract canceled; incomplete hull 3.5.45 (✞) Hamburg, Howaldtswerke Vulkan basin off U-boat pen Elbe II: 53°32n/ 09°57e / br.
U 686					delivery planned November 1944, but construction abandoned spring 1944, 23.9.44 contract canceled, incomplete pressure hull 3.5.45 still on slip No. 1 Howaldtswerke Hamburg, captured by British forces, br.
U 701	16.7.41	20.5.42	Lo	KL H. Degen	7.7.42 ✞ mid-Atlantic E. of Cape Hatteras: 34°50n/74°55w / D/Cs / Hud 9-29 (Lt. H. J. Kane, Jr.), 396 Bomb Sqn USAAF / 39 dead / 7 rescued.
U 702	3.9.41	30.3.42	He	KL W.-R. von Rabenau	≈31.3.42 ✞ North Sea W. of Denmark: ≈56°34n/06°16e / missing – probably sea mine British field "FD 37" / SS FNFL *Rubis* (Lt. H. L. G. Rousselot) / 44 dead / ✞.[109]
U 703	16.10.41	16.9.44	Nv	OL J. Brünner	after 16.9.44 ✞ Arctic ≈East coast of Iceland / missing / 54 dead / ✞.[110]
U 704	18.11.41			OL G. Nolte	24.3.45 decomm. Bremen-Vegesack, ≈30.4.45 (✞) Vegesack: 53°10n/08°38e / blown up 4.4.46, 1947 br.
U 705	30.12.41	4.8.42	Be	KL K.-H. Horn	3.9.42 ✞ 17h52 N. Atlantic N.W. of Spain: 46°42n/11°07w / D/Cs / Wht P (F/ Sgt A. A. MacInnes), 77 Sqn RAF / 45 dead / ✞.[111]
U 706	16.3.42	29.7.43	Pa	KL A. von Zitzewitz	2.8.43 ✞ 06h30 N. Atlantic N.W. of Spain: 46°15n/10°25w / D/Cs / Lib T (Capt. J. L. Hamilton), 4th A/S Sqn USAAF, Ham A (S/L C. G. Ruttan), 415 Sqn RCAF / 42 dead / 4 rescued.
U 707	1.7.42	19.10.43	Pa	OL G. Gretschel	9.11.43 ✞ N. Atlantic E. of Azores: 40°31n/20°17w / D/Cs / For J (F/L R. P. Drummond), 220 Sqn RAF / 51 dead / ✞.
U 708	24.7.42			OL H. Kühn	5.5.45 (✞) Wilhelmshaven, western entrance to Raeder lock: 53°31n/08°10e / 1947 br.

1	2	3	4	5	6
U 709	12.8.42	25.1.44	Lo	OL R. Ites	after 19.2.44 ♱ N. Atlantic / missing / 52 dead / ♱.[112]
U 710	2.9.42	17.4.43	Kr	OL D. von Carlowitz	24.4.43 ♱ N. Atlantic S. of Iceland: 61°25n/19°48w / D/Cs / For D (F/O R. L. Cowey), 206 Sqn RAF / 49 dead / ♱.
U 711	26.9.42			KL H.-G. Lange	4.5.45 ♱ Harstad, Kilbotn U-boat base: 68°43,7n/16°34,6e / D/Cs / Ave, Wil, 846, 853, 882 Sqn FAA CVE's HMS *Trumpeter* (A/Capt. K. S. Colquhoun), HMS *Queen* (A/Capt. K. J. D'Arcy), HMS *Searcher* (Capt. J. W. Grant) / 32 dead / 18 rescued.
U 712	5.11.42			OL E. Frhr. von Ketelhodt	9.5.45 Surrender Kristiansand, 31.5.45 sailed →Loch Ryan. August 1945 British war prize, tests, 31.12.45 laid up Lisahally, 26.6.49 →Messrs T. W. Ward Ltd, Hayle, br.
U 713	29.12.42	5.2.44	Nv	OL H. Gosejacob	after 24.2.44 ♱ Arctic N.W. of Narvik / missing / 50 dead / ♱.[113]
U 714	10.2.43	3.3.45	Kr	KL H.-J. Schwebcke	14.3.45 ♱ North Sea, Firth of Forth: 55°57n/01°57w / D/Cs / PF HMSAS *Natal* (Lt. Comdr. D. A. Hall), DD HMS *Wivern* (Lt. C. C. Anderson) / 50 dead / ♱.
U 715	17.3.43	8.6.44	St	KL H. Röttger	13.6.44 ♱ 10h30 Arctic N.E. of Faeroe Is.: 62°55n/02°59w / D/Cs / Cat T (W/C C. G. W. Chapman), 162 Sqn RAF / 36 dead / 16 rescued.
U 716	15.4.43			OL J. Thimme	9.5.45 Surrender Narvik, →Loch Eriboll, →Lisahally, →Loch Ryan / 11.12.45 ♱ rockets / Mos, 248 Sqn RAF 55°50n/10°05w / Op. Deadlight.
U 717	19.5.43			OL S. von Rothkirch und Panthen	5.5.45 (♱) Flensburg Fiord, Wassersleben Bay: 54°49n/09°27e / br.
U 718	25.6.43			OL H. Wieduwilt	18.11.43 ♱ Baltic N.E. of Bornholm: 55°21n/15°24e / collision / U 476 (OL O. Niethmann) / 43 dead / 7 rescued.
U 719	27.7.43	22.5.44	St	OL K.-D. Steffens	26.6.44 ♱ N. Atlantic N.W. of Ireland: 55°33n/11°02w / D/Cs / DD HMS *Bulldog* (Lt. J. H. Pennell) / 52 dead / ♱.
U 720	17.9.43			OL E. Wendelberger	5.5.45 Surrender Heligoland. →Wilhelmshaven, 24.6.45 sailed →Loch Ryan / 21.12.45 ♱ artillery DD's HMS *Onslaught*, ORP *Piorun*, DE HMS *Zetland*, PS HMS *Fowey* 56°04n/09°35w / Op. Deadlight.
U 721	8.11.43			OL L. Fabricius	5.5.45 (♱) Gelting Bay: 54°48n/09°49e / br.

1	2	3	4	5	6
U 722	15.12.43	21.2.45	Dr	OL H. Reimers	27.3.45 ✠ N. Atlantic, Sea of the Hebrides: 57°09n/06°55w / D/Cs / DE's HMS *Fitzroy* (Lt. Comdr. O. G. Stuart), HMS *Redmill* (Lt. J. R. A. Denne), HMS *Byron* (Lt. J. B. Burfield) / 44 dead / ✠.
U 731	3.10.42	18.4.44	Lo	OL A. Graf Keller	15.5.44 ✠ Strait of Gibraltar N. of Tangier: 35°54n/05°45w / D/Cs / PE HMS *Kilmarnock* (T/A/Lt. Comdr. K. B. Brown), TWL HMT *Blackfly* (T/A/Lt. Comdr. A. P. Hughes) and Cat P-1 (Lt. H. L. Worrell), Cat P-14 (Lt.[jg] M. J. Vopatek), VP-63 Sqn USN / 54 dead / ✠.
U 732	24.10.42	17.10.43	Br	OL C.-P. Carlsen	31.10.43 ✠ Strait of Gibraltar N. of Tangier: 35°54n/05°52w / D/Cs / TWL HMT *Imperialist* (T/A/Lt. Comdr. B. H. C. Rodgers), DD HMS *Douglas* (Lt. Comdr. K. H. J. L. Phibbs) / 31 dead / 18 rescued.
U 733	14.11.42			OL W. von Trotha	8.4.43 ✠ Gotenhafen, harbour entrance / collision / German patrol ship *Vp 313* / none dead / ↑ 9.4.43, 16h00 docked Deutsche Werke Gotenhafen, 16.4.43 decomm., repaired Schichau-Werft Königsberg, recomm. Königsberg.
	3.2.44	4.5.45	Ge	OL U. Hammer	5.5.45 (✠) Flensburg Fiord: 54°48n/09°49e / following bomb damage air strike 9. USAAF XXIX TAC 4.5.45 / none dead / br 1948.
U 734	5.12.42	31.1.44	Lo	OL H.-J. Blauert	9.2.44 ✠ N. Atlantic S.W. of Ireland: 49°43n/16°23w / D/Cs / PS's HMS *Wild Goose* (Comdr. D. E. G. Wemyss), HMS *Starling* (Capt. F. J. Walker) / 49 dead / ✠.
U 735	28.12.42			OL H.-J. Börner	28.12.44 ✠ 23h59 Horten: 59°28n/10°29e / bomb / air raid 5 Group RAF Bomber Command / 42 dead / 1 rescued.
U 736	16.1.43	5.8.44	Lo	OL R. Reff	6.8.44 ✠ Biscay W. of St. Nazaire: 47°19n/04°16w / D/Cs / PF HMS *Loch Killin* (Lt. Comdr. S. Darling) / 28 dead / 19 rescued.
U 737	30.1.43	14.12.44	Dr	OL F.-A. Gréus	19.12.44 ✠ 00h18 Arctic, Vest-Fjord: 68°10n/15°28e / collision / German *MRS 25* (KK K. Kamlah) / 31 dead / 20 rescued.
U 738	20.2.43			OL E.-M. Hoffmann	14.2.44 ✠ 18h00 Baltic 2 sm off Gotenhafen: 54°31n/18°33e / collision / German S/S *Erna* / 22 dead / 24 rescued / ↑ 29.2.44, → Gotenhafen, 3.3.44 decomm., from November 1944 training hulk 3.ULD Neustadt, final fate ?

1	2	3	4	5	6
U 739	6.3.43	1.4.45	Nv	OL F. Kosnick	11.5.45 Surrender Borkum, 13.5.45 →Emden, →Wilhelmshaven, 30.6.45 sailed →Loch Ryan / 16.12.45 ✝ torpedo SS HMS/m *Tantivy* 56°10n/10°05w / Op. Deadlight.
U 740	27.3.43	6.6.44	Br	KL G. Stark	8.6.44 ✝ 02h15 Biscay W. of Brest / 48°27n/05°47w / DCs / Lib G (F/O K.O. Moore), 224 Sdn RAF / 51 dead / ✝.[114]
U 741	10.4.43	3.8.44	Hv	OL G. Palmgren	15.8.44 ✝ English Channel S.W. of Brighton: 50°02n/00°36w / D/Cs / PE HMS *Orchis* (T/A/Lt. Comdr. B. W. Harris) / 48 dead / 1 rescued.
U 742	1.5.43	4.7.44	Ha	KL H. Schwaßmann	18.7.44 ✝ Arctic W. of Narvik: 68°24n/09°51e / D/Cs / Cat Z (F/O R. W. G. Vaughan), 210 Sqn RAF / 52 dead / ✝.
U 743	15.5.43	21.8.44	Dr	OL H. Kandzior	after 21.8.44 ✝ ≈Arctic or N. Atlantic N.W. of Britain / missing / 50 dead / ✝.[115]
U 744	5.6.43	24.2.44	Br	OL H. Blischke	6.3.44 ✝ 18h30 N. Atlantic: 52°01n/22°37w / torpedo / DD HMS *Icarus* (Lt. Comdr. R. Dyer) following D/Cs PF HMCS *St. Catharines* (T/ Lt. Comdr. A. F. Pickard), PE's HMCS *Fennel* (Lt. Comdr. W. P. Moffat), HMCS *Chilliwack* (Lt. Comdr. C. R. Coughlin), HMS *Kenilworth Castle* (Lt. J. J. Alton), DD's HMCS *Chaudière* (Lt. Comdr. C. P. Nixon), HMCS *Gatineau* (A/Lt. Comdr. H. V. W. Groos), HMS *Icarus* (Lt. Comdr. R. Dyer) and unsuccessful towing attempt / 12 dead / 40 rescued.
U 745	19.6.43	24.12.44	Li	KL W. von Trotha	31.1.45 ✝ Baltic, Gulf of Finland S. of Hangö: 59°30n/23°00e / sea mine, Soviet field "Vantaa 3" / 48 dead / ✝.[116]
U 746	4.7.43			TV A. Biagini	comm. as *S 2* for Italian Navy, 10.9.43 taken over by the Kriegsmarine at Gotenhafen.
	30.9.43	4.5.45	Ge	OL E. Lottner	5.5.45 (✝) Gelting Bay: 54°48n/09°49e / following bomb damage air strike 9. USAAF XXIX TAC 4.5.45 / none dead / 1948 br.
U 747	17.7.43			TV R. Rigoli	comm. as *S 3* for Italian Navy, 10.9.43 taken over by the Kriegsmarine at Gotenhafen.
	?.11.43			OL G. Zahnow	3.5.45 (✝) Hamburg-Finkenwerder, U-boat pen Fink II, box No. 3: 53°32,6n/09°51,3e / br.
U 748	31.7.43			CC M. Arillo	comm. as *S 5* for Italian Navy, 10.9.43 taken over by the Kriegsmarine at Gotenhafen.

1	2	3	4	5	6
	6.10.43			OL G. Dingler	5.5.45 (✝) Rendsburg, Kaiser Wilhelm-Canal km 71: 54°21n/09°46e / ↑ ?.6.45, br.
U 749	14.8.43			TV A. Longhi	comm. as *S 7* for Italian Navy, 10.9.43 taken over by the Kriegsmarine at Gotenhafen.
	29.9.43			KL F. Huisgen	4.4.45 ✝ Kiel, Germaniawerft fitting out quay No. 11 berth: 54°19n/10°08e / bomb / air raid 8. USAAF / 2 dead / br.
U 750	26.8.43			TV E. Siriani	comm. as *S 9* for Italian Navy, 10.9.43 taken over by the Kriegsmarine at Gotenhafen.
	7.9.43			OL J. Grawert	5.5.45 (✝) Flensburg Fiord: 54°50n/09°30e / br.
U 751	31.1.41	14.7.42	Na	KL G. Bigalk	17.7.42 ✝ N. Atlantic N.W. of Spain: 45°14n/12°22w / D/Cs / Wht H (P/O A. R. A. Hunt), 502 Sqn RAF, Lan F (F/L P. R. Casement), 61 Sqn RAF / 48 dead / ✝.
U 752	24.5.41	22.4.43	Na	KL K.-E. Schroeter	23.5.43 ✝ N. Atlantic: 51°40n/29°49w / rockets / Swd G (A/T/Sub-Lt. H. Horrocks), 819 Sqn FAA, Mat B (Sub-Lt. W. G. Bowles), 892 Sqn FAA CVE HMS *Archer* (Capt. J. I. Robertson) / 29 dead / 17 rescued.
U 753	18.6.41	5.5.43	Pa	KK A. Manhardt von Mannstein	13.5.43 ✝ N. Atlantic: 48°37n/22°39w / D/Cs / PF's HMCS *Drumheller* (Lt. L. P. Denny), HMS *Lagan* (Lt. Comdr. A. Ayre) and Sun G (F/L J. Musgrave), 423 Sqn RCAF / 47 dead / ✝.[117]
U 754	28.8.41	19.6.42	Br	KL J. Oestermann	31.7.42 ✝ N. Atlantic N.E. of Boston: 43°02n/64°52w / D/Cs / Hud 625 (S/L N. E. Small), 113(BR) Sqn RCAF / 43 dead / ✝.
U 755	3.11.41	18.5.43	To	KL W. Göing	28.5.43 ✝ Mediterranean N.W. of Mallorca: 39°58n/01°41e / rockets / Hud M (F/O G. A. K. Ogilvie), 608 Sqn RAF / 40 dead / 9 rescued.
U 756	30.12.41	17.8.42	Kr	KL K. Harney	1.9.42 ✝ N. Atlantic S.E. of Cape Farewell: 57°41n/31°30w / D/Cs / PE HMCS *Morden* (T/Lt. J. J. Hodgkinson) / 43 dead / ✝.[118]
U 757	28.2.42	29.12.43	Na	KL F. Deetz	8.1.44 ✝ N. Atlantic S.W. of Ireland: 50°33n/18°03w / D/Cs / DE HMS *Bayntun* (Lt. Comdr. L. P. Bourke), PE HMCS *Camrose* (Lt. Comdr. L. R. Pavillard) / 49 dead / ✝.
U 758	5.5.42			OL H.-A. Feindt	16.3.45 decomm. Kiel following bomb damage air raid 8. USAAF 11.3.45; May 45 captured by British forces / 1946/47 br.

1	2	3	4	5	6
U 759	15.8.42	7.6.4.3	Lo	KL R. Friedrich	15.7.43 ✠ Caribbean S. of Haiti: 15°58n/73°44w / D/Cs / Mar P-10 (Lt. R. C. Mayo), VP-32 Sqn USN / 47 dead / ✠.[119]
U 760	15.10.42	24.7.43	Pa	KL O.-U. Blum	8.9.43 entered Vigo, Spain following engine damage / interned El Ferrol / 23.7.45 sailed →Loch Ryan / 13.12.45 ✠ rockets / Bft, 254 Sqn RAF 55°50n/10°05w / Op. Deadlight.
U 761	3.12.42	12.2.44	Br	OL H. Geider	24.2.44 ✠ Strait of Gibraltar N. of Tangier: 35°55n/05°45w / D/Cs / DD's HMS *Anthony* (Lt. Comdr. J. H. Wallace), HMS *Wishart* (Lt. J. A. Holdsworth) and Cat G (F/L J. Finch), 202 Sqn RAF, Cat P-14 (Lt.[jg] H. J. Baker), Cat P-15 (Lt.[jg] T. R. Woolley), VP-63 Sqn USN / 9 dead / 48 rescued.
U 762	30.1.43	28.12.43	Br	OL W. Pietschmann	8.2.44 ✠ N. Atlantic S.W. of Ireland: 49°02n/16°58w / D/Cs / PS's HMS *Woodpecker* (Comdr. H. L. Pryse), HMS *Wild Goose* (Comdr. D. E. G. Wemyss) / 51 dead / ✠.
U 763	13.3.43			OL K.-H. Schröter	29.1.45 (✠) Königsberg, Schichau-Werft: 54°42n/20°32e / unable to move.[120]
U 764	6.5.43	26.4.45	Be	OL H. von Bremen	14.5.45 Surrender Loch Eriboll, →Lisahally / 3.1.46 ✠ artillery DD ORP *Piorun* 56°06n/09°00w / Op. Deadlight.
U 765	19.6.43	3.4.44	Be	OL W. Wendt	6.5.44 ✠ N. Atlantic: 52°30n/28°28w / D/Cs / Swd V (Lt. Comdr. F. G. B. Sheffield), 825 Sqn FAA CVE HMS *Vindex* (Capt. H. T. T. Bayliss) and DE's HMS *Bickerton* (Comdr. D. G. F. W. MacIntyre), HMS *Bligh* (A/Lt. Comdr. R. E. Blyth), HMS *Aylmer* (Lt. A. D. P. Campbell) / 37 dead / 11 rescued.
U 766	30.7.43			OL H.-D. Wilke	24.8.44 decomm. La Pallice, laid up U-boat pen La Pallice / May 45 captured by French forces; 1947 French *Laubie* (S 610); decomm. 11.3.63, Q 335, br.
U 767	11.9.43	22.5.44	Lv	OL W. Dankleff	18.6.44 ✠ English Channel S.W. of Guernsey: 49°03n/03°13w / D/Cs / DD's HMS *Fame* (Comdr. R. A. Currie), HMS *Inconstant* (Lt. Comdr. J. H. Eaden), HMS *Havelock* (Lt. Comdr. R. Hart) / 49 dead / 1 rescued.
U 768	14.10.43			OL J. Buttjer	20.11.43 ✠ Baltic, Danzig Bay: 54°25,5n/19°09,9e / collision / U 745 (KL W. von Trotha) / 44 rescued.

1	2	3	4	5	6
U 769					all construction parts delivered to →Oderwerke Stettin 1941 before keel laying →U 821, replacement yard number allocated after U 782; 30.9.43 suspension announced, 6.11.43 construction suspended, 22.7.44 contract canceled.
U 770					all construction parts delivered to →Neptun Werft Rostock 1941 before keel laying →U 921, replacement yard number allocated after U 782; 30.9.43 suspension announced, 6.11.43 construction suspended, 22.7.44 contract canceled.
U 771	18.11.43	23.10.44	Hf	OL H. Block	11.11.44 ✝ Arctic, Andfiord: 69°17n/16°28e / torpedo / SS HMS/m *Venturer* (Lt J. S. Launders) / 51 dead / ✝.
U 772	23.12.43	19.11.44	Dr	KL E. Rademacher	17.12.44 ✝ N. Atlantic S. of Cork: 51°16n/08°05w / D/Cs / PF HMS *Nyasaland* (T/A/Lt. Comdr. J. Scott) / 48 dead / ✝.[121]
U 773	20.1.44			OL H. Baldus	9.5.45 Surrender Trondheim, Lofiord, 29.5.45 sailed →Loch Ryan / 8.12.45 ✝ torpedo SS HMS/m *Tantivy* 56°10n/10°05w / Op. Deadlight.
U 774	17.2.44	14.3.45	Be	KL W. Sausmikat	8.4.45 ✝ N. Atlantic S.W. of Ireland: 49°58n/11°51w / D/Cs / DE's HMS *Calder* (A/T/Lt. Comdr. E. Playne), HMS *Bentinck* (A/Lt. Comdr. P. R. G. Worth) / 44 dead / ✝.
U 775	23.3.44			OL E. Taschenmacher	9.5.45 Surrender Trondheim, 29.5.45 sailed →Loch Ryan / 8.12.45 ✝ artillery DD HMS *Onslow* 55°40n/08°25w / Op. Deadlight.
U 776	13.4.44	23.3.45	Kr	KL L. Martin	16.5.45 Surrender Portland, HMS/m *N 65* / exhibition tour British East Coast, →Loch Ryan / 3.12.45 ✝ foundered while under tow 55°08,1n/05°30w / Op. Deadlight.
U 777	9.5.44			OL G. Ruperti	15.10.44 ✝ 20h02 Wilhelmshaven, Bauhafen berth B 5: 53°51n/08°08e / bomb / air raid 1, 3, 4, 6 (RCAF), 8, 100 Groups RAP Bomber Command / none dead / ↑, 22.11.44 decomm., wreck 5.5.45 (✝) western entrance to Raeder lock: 53°31n/08°10e, br.
U 778	7.7.44			KL R. Jürs	9.5.45 Surrender Bergen, 2.6.45 sailed →Loch Ryan / 1.12.45 ✝ foundered while under tow 55°32,5n/07°3w / Op. Deadlight.

1	2	3	4	5	6
U 779	24.8.44			OL J. Stegmann	5.5.45 Surrender Cuxhaven, —>Wilhelmshaven, 24.6.45 sailed →Loch Ryan/ 17.12.45 ✠ artillery DD HMS *Onslow*, DE HMS *Cubitt* 55°50n/10°05w / Op. Deadlight.
U 780					30.9.43 suspension announced, 6.11.43 contract suspended. 22.7.44 contract canceled; incomplete pressure hull broken up early 1945 on slip No. 1 Kriegsmarinewerft Wilhelmshaven.
U 781					30.9.43 suspension announced, 6.11.43 contract suspended, 22.7.44 contract canceled; incomplete pressure hull broken up early 1945 on slip No. 1 Kriegsmarinewerft Wilhelmshaven.
U 782					30.9.43 suspension announced, 6.11.43 contract suspended, 22.7.44 contract canceled; construction abandoned immediately after keel laying, broken up late 1943 slip No. 1 Kriegsmarinewerft Wilhelmshaven.
U 821	11.10.43	6.6.44	Br	OL U. Knackfuss	10.6.44 ✠ 11h45 Biscay W. of Brest: 48°31n/05°11w / D/Cs, MG-fire / Lib K (F/L A. D. S. Dundas), 206 Sqn RAF, Mos S (F/O G. N. E. Yeates), Mos T (F/L S. G. Nunn), Mos V (F/Sgt W. W. Scott), Mos W (F/O K. Norrie), 248 Sqn RAF / 50 dead / 1 rescued.
U 822	1.7.44			OL J. Elsinghorst	5.5.45 (✠) W. of Wesermünde: 53°32n/08°35e / 1948 br.
U 823					construction abandoned after keel laying owing to lack of labour, until March 1943 only keel plates completed; 30.9.43 suspension announced, 6.11.43 contract suspended, 22.7.44 contract canceled, incomplete keel broken up April 1944 on slip No. 1 of Oderwerke Stettin.
U 824					laid down possibly 24.11.41, construction abandoned immediately thereafter owing to lack of labour; 30.9.43 suspension announced, 6.11.43 contract suspended, 22.7.44 contract canceled.
U 825	4.5.44	1.4.45	Be	OL G. Stoelker	13.5.45 Surrender Loch Eriboll, →Lisahally / 3.1.46 ✠ artillery DD ORP *Blyskawica* 55°31n/07°30w / Op. Deadlight.
U 826	11.5.44	10.3.45	Kr	KL O. Lübcke	11.5.45 Surrender Loch Eriboll, →Lisahally, →Loch Ryan / 1.12.45 ✠ artillery DD's HMS *Onslaught*, ORP *Piorun* 56°10n/10°05w / Op. Deadlight.

1	2	3	4	5	6
U 901	29.4.44	14.4.45	St	KL H. Schrenk	15.5.45 Surrender Stavanger, 27.5.45 sailed →Lisahally / 6.1.46 ✠ artillery DD HMS *Onslaught* 55°50n/08°30w / Op. Deadlight.
U 902	-------				11.4.44 ✠ Stettin, Vulcan Stettiner Maschinenbau AG fitting out quay: 53°26,9n/14°35e / bomb / air raid 8. USAAF / constructive total loss, 22.7.44 contract canceled, ↑ , wreck ≈24.4.45 (✠) Oder River N. of Stettin, ↑ USSR summer 1946, →Stettin, final fate?
U 903	4.9.43			KL O. Tinschert	5.5.45 (✠) Gelting Bay: 55°48n/09°49e / br 1947.
U 904	25.9.43			OL G. Stührmann	4.5.45 (✠) Eckernförde, U-boat base: 54°28n/09°51e / br.[122]
U 905	8.3.44	13.3.45	Dr	OL B. Schwarting	27.3.45 ✠ N. Atlantic, Minch Canal: 58°34n/05°46w / D/Cs / DE HMS *Conn* (Lt. Comdr. R. Hart) / 45 dead / ✠.[123]
U 906	-------			(OL E. Pick)	31.12.44 ✠ Hamburg, Stülckens-Werft fitting out quay: 53°33n/ 09°58e / bomb / air raid 8. USAAF / while under repair and fitting out following bomb damage during air raid 8. USAAF 18.6.44, br.
U 907	18.5.44			OL S. Cabolet	9.5.45 Surrender Bergen, 2.6.45 sailed →Loch Ryan / 7.12.45 ✠ foundered while under tow 55°17n/05°59w / Op. Deadlight.
U 908					18.6.44 bomb damage air raid 8. USAAF on slip No. 3 Stülckens-Werft Hamburg, constructive total loss, 22.7.44 contract canceled, wreck 3.5.45 still on slip, captured by British forces, br.
U 921	30.5.43	5.9.44	Nv	OL A. Werner	after 24.9.44 ✠ Arctic N.W. of Narvik / missing / 51 dead / ✠.[124]
U 922	1.8.43			OL E. Käselau	3.5.45 (✠) Kiel: 54°21n/10°09e / br 1947.
U 923	4.10.43			OL H. Frömmer	9.2.45 ✠ Baltic, N. E. of Kiel: 54°31n/10°18e / British air-laid mine field "Forgetmenot" / 48 dead / ✠ / ↑ .12.52., 1.53 br.[125]
U 924	20.11.43			OL H.-J. Schild	3.5.45 (✠) Kiel, Deutsche Werke, berth #6: 54°21n/10°09e / br 1947.
U 925	30.12.43	24.8.44	Kr	OL H. Knoke	after 24.8.44 ✠ ≈North Sea or Arctic N. of Britain / missing / 51 dead / ✠.[126]
U 926	29.2.44			OL H. Rehren	5.5.45 decomm. Bergen following structural damage during diving test, May 45 captured by British forces, →Norway, 10.1.49 KNM *Kya* (S 307), 4.4.64 decomm., 5.65 sold to Andreas Stoltenberg, Oslo, br.

1	2	3	4	5	6
U 927	27.6.44	31.1.45	Kr	KL J. Ebert	24.2.45 ✝ English Channel S.E. of Falmouth: 49°54n/04°45w / D/Cs / War K (F/L A. G. Brownsill), 179 Sqn RAF / 47 dead / ✝.[127]
U 928	11.7.44			KL H. Stähler	9.5.45 Surrender Bergen, 30.5.45 sailed →Lisahally / 16.12.45 ✝ artillery DD HMS *Onslaught* 55°50n/10°05w / Op. Deadlight.
U 951	3.12.42	15.5.43	Kr	KL K. Pressel	7.7.43 ✝ N. Atlantic N.W. of Cape St. Vincent: 37°40n/15°30w / D/Cs / Lib K (Lt. W. S. McDonell), 1st A/S Sqn USAAF / 46 dead / ✝.
U 952	10.12.42			KL O. Curio	5.7.44 ✝ Toulon, Missiessy Dock No. 3: 43°07n/05°55e / bomb damage air raid 15. USAAF / none dead / 12.7.44 decomm., 1946 br.
U 953	17.12.42			OL E. Steinbrink	9.5.45 Surrender Trondheim, 29.5.45 sailed →Loch Ryan, August 1945 British war prize, HMS/m *N* ... tests, 31.12.45 laid up Lisahally, 4.6.49 →Clayton & Davie Ltd., Dunston-on-Tyne, br.
U 954	23.12.42	10.4.43	Kr	KL O. Loewe	19.5.43 ✝ N. Atlantic S.E. of Cape Farewell: 54°54n/34°19w / D/Cs / PF HMS *Jed* (Lt. Comdr. R. C. Freaker), CGC HMS *Sennen* (Lt. Comdr. F. H. Thornton) / 47 dead / ✝.[128]
U 955	31.12.42	15.4.44	Be	OL H. H. Baden	7.6.44 ✝ Biscay N. of Spain: 45°13n/08°30w / D/Cs / Sun S (F/O L. H. Baveystock), 201 Sqn RAF / 50 dead / ✝.
U 956	6.1.43	2.4.45	Dr	KL H.-D. Mohs	13.5.45 Surrender Loch Eriboll, →Lisahally, →Loch Ryan / 17.12.45 ✝ foundered while under tow 55°50n/10°05w / Op. Deadlight.
U 957	7.1.43			OL G. Schaar	21.10.44 decomm. Narvik following damage from pack ice 19.9.44, cannibalized, hulk probably (✝) 5.45 Skjömenfiord.
U 958	14.1.43			OL F. Stege	3.5.45 (✝) Kiel: 54°21n/10°10e / 1947 br.
U 959	21.1.43	22.4.44	Nv	OL F. Weitz	2.5.44 ✝ 16h45 Arctic S.E. of Jan Mayen I.: 69°20n/00°20w / D/Cs / Swd K (Sub-Lt. L. G. Cooper), 842 Sqn FAA CVE HMS *Fencer* (A/Capt. W. W. R. Bentinck) / 53 dead / ✝.
U 960	28.1.43	29.4.44	Pa	OL G. Heinrich	19.5.44 ✝ Mediterranean N.W. of Algiers: 37°20n/01°35e / D/Cs / DD's USS *Niblack* (Comdr. R. R. Conner), USS *Ludlow* (Lt. Comdr. W. R. Barnes) and Wel M (F/O B. G. H. Robinson), Wel U (P/O K.H.N. Bulmer), 36 Sqn RAF, Ven V (W/O E. A. K. Mundy), 500 Sqn RAF / 31 dead / 20 rescued.

1	2	3	4	5	6
U 961	4.2.43	25.3.44	Be	OL K. Fischer	29.3.44 ✠ Arctic N.E. of Faeroe Is.: 64°31n/03°19w / D/Cs / PS HMS *Starling* (Capt. F. J. Walker) / 49 dead / ✠.
U 962	11.2.43	14.2.44	Na	OL E. Liesberg	8.4.44 ✠ N. Atlantic N.W. of Cape Finisterre: 45°43n/19°57w / D/Cs / PS's HMS *Crane* (Lt. Comdr. R. G. Jenkins), HMS *Cygnet* (Comdr. A. H. Thorold) / 50 dead / ✠.
U 963	17.2.43	23.4.45	Dr	OL R.-W. Wentz	20.5.45 (✠) 10h00 N. Atlantic off Nazaré: 39°36n/09°05w / 48 rescued.
U 964	18.2.43	5.10.43	Be	OL E. Hummerjohann	16.10.43 ✠ 19h30 N. Atlantic: 57°27n/28°17w / D/Cs / Lib Y (F/O G. D. Gamble), 86 Sqn RAF / 47 dead / 3 rescued.
U 965	25.2.43	5.3.45	Dr	OL G. Unverzagt	30.3.45 ✠ N. Atlantic, North Minch: 58°19n/05°31w / D/Cs / DE's HMS *Rupert* (Lt. P. C. S. Black), HMS *Conn* (Lt. Comdr. R. Hart) / 51 dead / ✠.[129]
U 966	4.3.43	5.10.43	Dr	OL E. Wolf	10.11.43 ✠ 08h Biscay S.E. of Punta Estaca: 43°46,8n/07°38w / beached 2 sm off the coast following D/Cs Wel B (W/O I. D. Gunn), 612 Sqn RAF, Lib E (Lt. K. L. Wright), VB-103 Sqn USN, Lib E (Lt. W. W. Parish), VB-110 Sqn USN, Lib D (F/Sgt O. Zanta), 311 Sqn (Czech) RAF / 8 dead / 42 rescued.
U 967	11.3.43			OL H.-E. Eberbach	19.8.44 (✠) 20h30 Toulon off St. Mandrier: 43°05n/05°56e / following bomb damage air raid 8. USAAF 5.7.44 and 11.7.44 / 2 dead / ↑ 1945, br.
U 968	18.3.43			OL O. Westphalen	9.5.45 Surrender Narvik, →Loch Eriboll, →Lisahally, →Loch Ryan / 29.11.45 ✠ foundered while under tow 55°24,2n/06°22,7 / Op. Deadlight.
U 969	24.3.43			OL M. Dobbert	6.8.44 ✠ Toulon, Castigneau Dock No. 2: 43°07n/05°55e / bomb / air raid 15. USAAF / none dead / br 1947.
U 970	25.3.43	6.6.44	Pa	KL H.-H. Ketels	8.6.44 ✠ 01h35 Biscay W. of Bordeaux: 45°15n/04°10w / D/Cs / Sun R (F/L J. Quinn), 228 Sqn RAF / 38 dead / 14 rescued.
U 971	1.4.43	8.6.44	Kr	OL W. Zeplien	24.6.44 ✠ 19h17 English Channel S. of Landsend: 49°01n/05°35w / D/Cs / DD's HMCS *Haida* (Comdr. H. G. DeWolf). HMS *Eskimo* (Lt. Comdr. E. N. Sinclair) and Lib O (F/O J. Vella), 311 Sqn (Czech) RAF / 1 dead / 51 rescued.

1	2	3	4	5	6
U 972	8.4.43	2.12.43	Kr	OL K.-D. König	after 15.12.43 ✝ N. Atlantic / missing / 49 dead / ✝.[130]
U 973	15.4.43	4.3.44	Nv	OL K. Paepenmöller	6.3.44 ✝ Arctic N.W. of Narvik: 70°04n/05°48e / rockets / Swd X (Sub-Lt. E. B. Bennett), 816 Sqn FAA CVE HMS *Chaser* (Capt. H. V. P. McClintock) / 51 dead / 2 rescued.
U 974	22.4.43	18.4.44	Kr	OL H.Wolff	19.4.44 ✝ 07h10 North Sea, Karmsund: 59°08n/05°23e / torpedoes / SS KNM *Ula* (Lt. S. Valvatne) / 42 dead / 8 rescued.
U 975	29.4.43			KL W. Brauel	9.5.45 Surrender Horten, 27.5.45 sailed →Lisahally / 10.2.46 ✝ artillery PF HMS *Loch Arkaig* 55°42n/09°01w / Op. Deadlight.
U 976	5.5.43	20.3.44	Na	OL R. Tiesler	25.3.44 ✝ 09h46 Biscay S.W. of St. Nazaire: 46°50n/02°41,5w / artillery / Mos L (F/O D. J. Turner), Mos I (F/O A. H. Hilliard), 248 Sqn RAF / 4 dead / 49 rescued.
U 977	6.5.43	2.5.45	Kr	OL H. Schäffer	17.8.45 Surrender Mar del Plata: 38°01s/57°32w / 25.8.45 sailed →United States, U.S. war prize; 13.11.46 ✝ N. Atlantic off Cape Cod: 42°33n/69°43w / torpedo SS USS *Atule*.
U 978	12.5.43			KL G. Pulst	9.5.45 Surrender Trondheim, Lofiord, 29.5.45 sailed →Loch Ryan / 11.12.45 ✝ torpedo SS HMS/m *Tantivy* 56°10n/10°05w / Op. Deadlight.
U 979	20.5.43	29.3.45	Be	KL J. Meermeier	24.5.45 (✝) North Sea S.W. of Amrum: 54°36,5n/08°21,7e / following grounding on sand bank / wreck July 1991 still present.
U 980	27.5.43	3.6.44	Be	KL H. Dahms	11.6.44 ✝ Arctic N.W. of Bergen: 63°07n/00°26e / D/Cs / Cat B (F/O L. Sherman), 162 Sqn RCAF / 52 dead / ✝.
U 981	3.6.43	7.8.44	Lo	OL G. Keller	12.8.44 ✝ 06h43 Biscay off La Rochelle: 46°06,4n/01°35,3w / British air-laid mine, field "Cinnamon" and D/Cs / Hal F (F/O J. Capey), 502 Sqn RAF / 12 dead / 40 rescued.
U 982	10.6.43			OL C. Hartmann	9.4.45 ✝ 14h00 Hamburg-Finkenwerder, U-boat pen Fink II box No. 5: 53°32,6n/09°51,3e / bomb / air raid RAF Bomber Command / none dead / br.
U 983	16.6.43			LT H. Reimers	8.9.43 ✝ 19h27 Baltic N. of Leba: 54°56n/17°14e / collision / U 988 (OL E. Dobberstein) / 5 dead / 38 rescued.

1	2	3	4	5	6
U 984	17.6.43	26.7.44	Br	OL H. Sieder	after 2.8.44 ✠ English Channel S.W. of Brighton: 50°04n/00°32e / unknown cause / 45 dead / ✠.[131]
U 985	24.6.43			KL H. Wolff	15.11.44 decomm. Kristiansand following damage German sea mine 22.10.44 off Lister: 58°08n/06°22e / cannibalized / May 45 captured by British forces, br.
U 986	1.7.43	10.2.44	Kr	OL K.-E. Kaiser	after 10.4.44 ✠ N. Atlantic or Bay of Biscay / missing / 50 dead / ✠.[132]
U 987	8.7.43	29.5.44	Be	OL H. Schreyer	15.6.44 ✠ Arctic W. of Narvik: 68°01n/05°08e / torpedoes / SS HMS/m *Satyr* (Lt. T. S. Weston) / 53 dead / ✠.
U 988	15.7.43	23.5.44	Be	OL E. Dobberstein	22.6.44 ✠ English Channel N.W. of Cherbourg: 50°02,7n/02°01,4e / D/Cs / Lib K (Lt. R. D. Spalding, Jr.), VB-110 Sqn USN / 50 dead / ✠.[133]
U 989	22.7.43	8.2.45	Kr	KL H. Rodler von Roithberg	14.2.45 ✠ Arctic N. of Shetland Is.: 61°36n/01°35w / D/Cs / DE's HMS *Bayntun* (Lt. Comdr. L. P. Bourke), HMS *Braithwaite* (Lt. Comdr. P. J. Stoner), PF's HMS *Loch Eck* (Lt. Comdr. R. C. Freaker), HMS *Loch Dunvegan* (Comdr. E.Wheeler) / 47 dead / ✠.
U 990	28.7.43	22.5.44	Be	KL H. Nordheimer	25.5.44 ✠ 07h35 Arctic W. of Bodö: 65°05n/07°28e / D/Cs / Lib S (S/L B. A. Sisson), 59 Sqn RAF / 20 dead / 33 rescued.
U 991	29.7.43			KL D. Balke	9.5.45 Surrender Bergen, 2.6.45 sailed →Loch Ryan / 11.12.45 ✠ torpedo SS HMS/m *Tantivy* 56°10n/10°05w / Op. Deadlight.
U 992	2.8.43			OL H. Falke	9.5.45 Surrender Narvik, →Loch Eriboll, →Lisahally, →Loch Ryan / 16.12.45 ✠ torpedo SS HMS/m *Tantivy* 56°10n/10°05w / Op. Deadlight.
U 993	19.8.43			OL K.-H. Steinmetz	4.10.44 ✠ 09h30 Bergen, Laksevaag Yard, capzised in floating dock: 60°23n/05°18e / bomb / air raid 6 (RCAF) and 8 Groups RAF Bomber Command / 2 dead / decomm., May 45 captured by British forces, br.
U 994	2.9.43			OL V. Melzer	9.5.45 Surrender Trondheim, 29.5.45 sailed →Loch Ryan / 5.12.45 ✠ foundered while under tow 55°43n/08°21w / Op. Deadlight.

1	2	3	4	5	6
U 1051	4.3.44	29.12.44	Kr	OL H. von Holleben	26.1.45 ✠ Irish Sea S. of Isle of Man: 53°39n/05°23w / D/Cs, ramming / DE's HMS *Aylmer* (Lt. A. D. P. Campbell), HMS *Calder* (A/T/Lt. Comdr. E. Playne), HMS *Bentinck* (Comdr. R. C. S. Garwood), HMS *Manners* (A/Comdr. J. V. Waterhouse) / 47 dead / ✠.[134]
U 1052	20.1.44			OL G.Scholz	9.5.45 Surrender Bergen, 30.5.45 sailed →Loch Ryan / 9.12.45 ✠ rockets Fir, 816 Sqn FAA CVE HMS *Nairana* 55°50n/10°05w / Op. Deadlight.
U 1053	12.2.44			OL H. Lange	15.2.45 ✠ North Sea, Byfjord N.W. of Bergen: 60°26n/05°16e / diving accident during deep diving trial / 45 dead / ✠.
U 1054	25.3.44			KL W. Riekeberg	15.9.44 16h30 decomm. Kiel, Kriegsmarine dockyard following collision Norwegian M/F *Peter Wessel* 18.8.44 Hela buoy 1; 5.5.45 (✠) Flensburg Fiord, br.
U 1055	8.4.44	5.4.45	Be	OL R. Meyer	after 23.4.45 ✠ ≈N. Atlantic or English Channel / missing / 49 dead / ✠.[135]
U 1056	29.4.44			OL G. Schröder	5.5.45 (✠) Gelting Bay: 54°48n/09°49e / br.
U 1057	20.5.44			OL G. Lüth	9.5.45 Surrender Bergen, 2.6.45 sailed →Loch Ryan; HMS/m *N 22*, USSR war prize, 6.12.45 at Libau →USSR, 13.2.46 Soviet *N-22*, South Baltic-Fleet, 9.6.49 *S-81*, 30.12.55 Reserve, test hulk Northern Fleet 21.9.57 ✠ Barents Sea off Novaja Zemlja during atomic test, § 16.10.57, br.
U 1058	10.6.44	28.4.45	Be	OL H. Bruder	10.5.45 Surrender Loch Eriboll, →Lisahally; HMS/m *N 23*, USSR war prize. 6.12.45 at Libau →USSR, 13.2.46 Soviet *N-23*, South Baltic Fleet, 9.6.49 *S-82*, 29.12.55 Reserve, 18.1.56 floating torpedo fire station *PZS-32*, § 25.3.58, br.
U 1101	10.11.43			OL R. Dübler	5.5.45 (✠) Gelting Bay: 54°48n/09°49e / br.
U 1102	22.2.44			OL B. Schwarting	24.3.44 ✠ Pillau, quay U-boat base, diving accident, ↑, 12.5.44 decomm., repaired Danzig, recomm. Danzig.
	?.9.44			OL E. Sell	13.5.45 Surrender Hohwacht Bay, →Kiel, →Wilhelmshaven, 23.6.45 sailed →Loch Ryan / 21.12.45 ✠ artillery DD's HMS *Onslaught*, ORP *Piorun*, DE HMS *Zetland*, PS HMS *Fowey* 56°04n/09°35w / Op. Deadlight.

1	2	3	4	5	6
U 1103	8.1.44			KL W. Eisele	5.5.45 Surrender Cuxhaven, →Wilhelmshaven, 23.6.45 sailed →Loch Ryan / 30.12.45 ✠ artillery DD HMS *Onslaught* 56°03n/10°05w / Op. Deadlight.
U 1104	15.3.44			OL R. Perleberg	9.5.45 Surrender Bergen, 30.5.45 sailed →Loch Ryan / 15.12.45 ✠ demolition charge 55°35n/07°57w / Op. Deadlight.
U 1105	3.6.44	12.4.45	Kr	OL H.-J. Schwarz	10.5.45 Surrender Loch Eriboll, →Lisahally, HMS/m *N16*, tests; U.S. war prize, 15.12.45 →United States, tests, 11.2.46 decomm., laid up, 18.11.48 ✠ Chesapeake Bay / demolition trials. ↑ ?.8.49, 19.9.49 ✠ Chesapeake Bay: 38°08,1n/76°33,1w / demolition trials.
U 1106	5.7.44	22.3.45	Kr	OL E. Bartke	After 22.03.45 ✠ North Sea or Arctic N. of Britain / missing / 46 dead / ✠.[136]
U 1131	20.5.44			OL G. Fiebig	30.3.45 ✠ Hamburg-Finkenwerder. Rüschkanal, inside pontoon dock S.E. of U-boat pen Fink II: 53°33,5n/09°51,3e / bomb / air raid 8. USAAF / none dead / br.
U 1132	24.6.44			OL W. Koch	5.5.45 (✠) Flensburg Fiord, Kupfermühlen Bay / br.
U 1161	25.8.43			TV F. de Siervo	comm. as *S 8* for Italian Navy, 10.9.43 taken over by the Kriegsmarine at Gotenhafen.
	27.9.43			KL B. Schwalbach	5.5.45 (✠) Flensburg Fiord, Kupfermühlen Bay / br.
U 1162	15.9.43			KL H.-H. Ketels	5.5.45 (✠) Gelting Bay: 54°48n/09°49e / br.
U 1191	9.9.43	22.5.44	St	OL P. Grau	3.7.44 ✠ English Channel S.W. of Brighton: 50°09n/00°15w / D/Cs / DD's HMS *Onslaught* (Comdr. Hon. A. Pleydell-Bouverie), HMS *Oribi* (Lt. Comdr. J. C. A. Ingram), DE's HMS *Brissenden* (Lt. Hon. D. D. E. Vivian), HMS *Wensleydale* (Lt. Comdr. W. P. Goodfellow), HMS *Talybont* (Lt. E. F. Baines), PF HMS *Seymour* (Lt. G. J. Parry) / ✠.[137]
U 1192	23.9.43			OL K. Meenen	3.5.45 (✠) Kiel: 54°19n/10°10e / br.
U 1193	7.10.43			OL J. Guse	5.5.45 (✠) Gelting Bay: 54°48n/09°49e / br.
U 1194	21.10.43	4.5.45	Cu	OL H. Zeissler	9.5.45 Surrender Cuxhaven, →Wilhelmshaven, 23.6.45 sailed →Loch Ryan / 22.12.45 ✠ artillery DD HMS *Onslow* 55°59n/09°55w / Op. Deadlight.

1	2	3	4	5	6
U 1195	4.11.43	24.2.45	Be	KL E. Cordes	6.4.45 ✠ English Channel S. of Spithead Roads: 50°33n/00°55w / D/Cs / DD HMS *Watchman* (T/A/Lt. Comdr. J. R. Clarke) / 32 dead / 18 rescued / April 1945 British salvage attempt, given up.
U 1196	18. 11.43			OL R. Ballert	2.5.45 (✠) Travemünde: 53°59n/10°56e / br.
U 1197	2.12.43			OL K. Lau	25.4.45 decomm. Wesermünde following bomb damage air raid 8. USAAF 30.3.45 Bremen, Deschimag-AG Weser / captured by British forces, 7.2.46 ✠ North Sea by US Navy.
U 1198	9.12.43	4.5.45	Cu	OL G. Peters	8.5.45 Surrender Cuxhaven, → Wilhelmshaven, 24.6.45 sailed →Loch Ryan / 17.12.45 ✠ artillery DD ORP *Blyskawica* 56°14n/10°37,5w / Op. Deadlight.
U 1199	23.12.43	1.1.45	Be	KL R. Nollmann	21.1.45 ✠ English Channel E. of Scilly Is.: 49°57n/05°42w / D/Cs / DD HMS *Icarus* (Lt. Comdr. D. D. Bone), PE HMS *Mignonette* (Lt. H. H. Brown) / 48 dead / 1 rescued.
U 1200	5.1.44	19.10.44	Be	OL H. Mangels	After 12.11.44 ✠ English Channel S.E. of Start Point: 50°01,3n/02°59,7w / unknown cause / 53 dead / ✠.[138]
U 1201	13.1.44			OL R. Merkle	3.5.45 (✠) Hamburg, Neßkanal: 53°32,5n/09°50,7e following bomb damage air raid 8. USAAF 11.3.45 / br.
U 1202	27.1.44			KL R. Thomsen	9.5.45 Surrender Bergen, unserviceable, not sailed to U.K., →Norway, 1.7.51 KNM *Kinn* (S 308), decomm. 1.6.61, 1963 for br →Hamburg.
U 1203	10.2.44			OL S. Seeger	9.5.45 Surrender Trondheim, Lofiord, 29.5.45 sailed →Loch Ryan / 8.12.45 ✠ aerial torpedo / Bar, 816 Sqn FAA CVE HMS *Nairana* 55°50n/10°05w / Op. Deadlight.
U 1204	17.2.44			OL E. Jestel	5.5.45 (✠) Gelting Bay: 54°48n/09°49e / br.
U 1205	2.3.44			KL H. Zander	3.5.45 (✠) Kiel, Deutsche Werke: 54°21n/10°09e / br.
U 1206	16.3.44	7.4.45	Kr	KL K.-A. Schlitt	14.4.45 (✠) North Sea E. of Peterhead: 57°22n/01°46,7w / following diving accident / 4 dead / 46 rescued.
U 1207	23.3.44			OL K. Lindemann	5.5.45 (✠) Gelting Bay: 54°48n/09°49e / br.

1	2	3	4	5	6
U 1208	6.4.44	14.1.45	Kr	KK G. Hagene	24.2.45 ✝ English Channel S.W. of Landsend: 49°55n/06°08w / D/Cs / DE's HMS *Duckworth* (Comdr. R. G. Mills), HMS *Rowley* (Lt. Comdr. F. J. G. Jones) / 49 dead / ✝.[139]
U 1209	13.4.44	24.11.44	Kr	OL E. Hülsenbeck	18.12.44 (✝) English Channel E. of Scilly Is.: 49°57n/05°47w / following grounding damage Wolf Rock / 9 dead / 44 rescued.
U 1210	22.4.44			KL P. Gabert	3(?).5.45 ✝ Eckernförde, off U-boat base: 54°28n/09°51e / bomb? / air strike 9. USAAF XXIX TAC ? / 1 dead.

Type VII C/41

Seagoing combat U-boat type of conventional design developed in 1941
Surface/submerged displacement: 769/871 t
Overall length/beam/draught: 67.23 m/6.18 m/4.74 m
Standard main armament: 5 torpedo tubes (4 bow, 1 stern) with up to 12 torpedoes

Building yard	Total no. ordered	Completed (comm.)	Under construction	Construction not started	Canceled after keel laying	Canceled prior to keel laying
Nordseewerke Emden	8	4	—	—	—	4
Bremer Vulkan Vegesacker Werft	24	18	—	—	3	3
Stülckens-Werft Hamburg	12	—	—	—	2	10
Blohm & Voss AG Hamburg	71	28	5	—	5	33
Howaldtswerke AG Hamburg	12	—	—	—	—	12
Flensburger Schiffbauge-sellschaft	12	8	—	—	—	4
Germaniawerft AG Kiel	6	3	—	—	—	3
Howaldts-werke AG Kiel	14	—	—	—	4	10
Lübecker Flender-Werke AG	22	12	—	—	2	8
Neptunwerft Rostock	8	2	—	—	2	4
Danziger Werft AG	38	10	—	—	7	21
F. Schichau GmbH Danzig	18	2	—	—	2	14
Total	245	87	5	—	27	126

1	2	3	4	5	6
U 292	25.8.43	24.5.44	Be	OL W. Schmidt	27.5.44 ♱ Arctic W. of Trondheim: 62°37n/00°57e / D/Cs / Lib S (F/L V. E. Camacho), 59 Sqn RAF / 51 dead / ♱.
U 293	8.9.43	1.4.45	Dr	KL L. Klingspor	11.5.45 Surrender Loch Eriboll, →Lisahally, →Loch Ryan / 13.12.45 ♱ bomb British aircraft and artillery DD HMS *Orwell* 55°50n/10°05w / Op. Deadlight.
U 294	6.10.43			OL H. Schütt	9.5.45 Surrender Narvik, →Loch Eriboll, →Lisahally / 31.12.45 ♱ artillery DD HMS *Offa* 55°44n/08°40w / Op. Deadlight.
U 295	20.10.43			KL G. Wieboldt	9.5.45 Surrender Narvik, →Loch Eriboll. →Lisahally, →Loch Ryan / 17.12.45 ♱ artillery DD ORP *Blyskawica* 56°14n/10°37,5w / Op. Deadlight.
U 296	3.11.43	27.2.45	Be	KL K.-H. Rasch	≈12.3.45 ♱ ≈N.W. Approaches to North Channel: ≈55°30n/07°w / missing – ≈British sea mine, field "T1" or "T2" / 42 dead / ♱.[140]
U 297	17.11.43	26.11.44	Kr	OL W. Aldegarmann	after 6.12.44 ♱ N. Atlantic E. of Orkney Is.: 59°00,9n/03°54w / unknown cause / 50 dead / ♱.[141]
U 298	1.12.43			OL H. Gehrken	9.5.45 Surrender Bergen, 30.5.45 sailed →Loch Ryan / 29.11.45 ♱ artillery DD HMS *Onslow*, DE HMS *Cubitt* 55°35n/07°54w / Op. Deadlight.
U 299	15.12.43			OL B. Emde	9.5.45 Surrender Kristiansand, 29.5.45 sailed →Loch Ryan / 4.12.45 ♱ foundered while under tow 55°38,7n/07°54w / Op. Deadlight.
U 300	29.12.43	20.1.45	Dr	OL F. Hein	22.2.45 ♱ N. Atlantic W. of Cadiz: 36°29n/08°20w / D/Cs / AM's HMS *Recruit* (A/Comdr. A. E. Doran), HMS *Pincher* (T/A/Lt. Comdr. C. B. Blake) / 8 dead / 41 rescued.
U 317	23.10.43	21.6.44	Eg	OL P. Rahlf	26.6.44 ♱ Arctic N.E. of Shetland Is.: 62°03n/01°45e / D/Cs / Lib N (F/L G. W. T. Parker), 86 Sqn RAF / 50 dead / ♱.
U 318	13.11.43			OL J. Will	9.5.45 Surrender Narvik, →Loch Eriboll, →Lisahally, →Loch Ryan / 21.12.45 ♱ artillery DD ORP *Piorun* 55°47n/08°30w / Op. Deadlight.
U 319	4.12.43	4.7.44	St	OL J. Clemens	15.7.44 ♱ North Sea S.W. of Lindesnes: 57°40,6n/04°26,4e / D/Cs / Lib E (F/O B. W. Thynne), 206 Sqn RAF / 51 dead / ♱.

1	2	3	4	5	6
U 320	30.12.43	29.4.45	Kr	OL H. Emmrich	8.5.45 (✝) 03h40 Arctic N.W. of Bergen: 61°32n/01°53e / following D/Cs Cat X (F/L K. M. Murray), 210 Sqn RAF 7.5.45 / all rescued.
U 321	20.1.44	16.3.45	Kr	OL F. Berends	2.4.45 ✝ N. Atlantic S.W. of Ireland: 50°00n/12°57w / D/Cs / Wel Y (W/O R. Marczak), 304 Sqn (Polish) RAF / 41 dead / ✝.
U 322	5.2.44	16.11.44	Kr	OL G. Wysk	29.12.44 ✝ 15h01 English Channel S. of Weymouth: 50°24,9n/02°26,3w / D/Cs / PE HMCS *Calgary* (Lt. Comdr. A. Wilkinson) / 52 dead / ✝.[142]
U 323	2.3.44			OL H.-J. Dobinski	5.5.45 (✝) Nordenham: 53°30n/08°30e / br.
U 324	5.4.44			OL E. Edelhoff	9.5.45 Surrender Bergen, not serviceable, not sailed to U.K., br March 1947.
U 325	6.5.44	20.3.45	Dr	OL E. Dohrn	after 30.4.45 ✝ English Channel S. of Lizard Pt.: 49°48n/05°12w / sea mine, British field "Artizan B3, part 1" / 52 dead / ✝.[143]
U 326	6.6.44	28.3.45	Be	KL P. Matthes	30.4.45 ✝ Biscay W. of Brest: 47°51n/06°46w / Retro bombs / Cat R (Lt. F. G. Lake), VP-63 Sqn USN / 43 dead / ✝.[144]
U 327	18.7.44	30.1.45	Kr	KL H. Lemcke	3.2.45 ✝ Arctic N.W. of Bergen: 61°21n/02°00e / D/Cs / DE's HMS *Bayntun* (Lt. Comdr. L. P. Bourke), HMS *Braithwaite* (Lt. Comdr. P. J. Stoner), PF HMS *Loch Eck* (Lt. Comdr. R. C. Freaker) / 46 dead / ✝.[145]
U 328	19.9.44			OL H.-U. Scholle	9.5.45 Surrender Bergen, 30.5.45 sailed →Loch Ryan / 30.11.45 ✝ bomb Ave, ? Sqn FAA / 55°50n/10°05w / Op. Deadlight.
U 329					30.9.43 suspension announced, 6.11.43 contract suspended. 22.7.44 contract canceled, incomplete pressure hull May 45 captured by British forces on slip No. 5 Flender-Werft Lübeck, br.
U 330					30.9.43 suspension announced, 6.11.43 contract suspended, 22.7.44 contract canceled, incomplete pressure hull broken up early 1944 on slip No. 2 Flender-Werft Lübeck.
U 687–U 688					30.9.43 suspension announced, 6.11.43 contract suspended, 22.7.44 contract canceled, incomplete pressure hull 3.5.45 captured by British forces on slip No. 1 Howaldtswerke Hamburg, br.

1	2	3	4	5	6
U 689– U 698					30.9.43 suspension announced, 6.11.43 contract suspended, 22.7.44 contract canceled.
U 723					30.9.43 suspension announced, 6.11.43 contract suspended, 18.6.44 bomb damage air raid 8. USAAF, 22.7.44 contract canceled, incomplete pressure hull broken up 8./9.44 on slip No. 3 Stülckens-Werft Hamburg.
U 724					30.9.43 suspension announced, 6.11.43 contract suspended, 18.6.44 bomb damage air raid 8. USAAF, 22.7.44 contract canceled, incomplete pressure hull broken up 9./10.44 on slip No. 3 Stülckens-Werft Hamburg.
U 725– U 730					30.9.43 suspension announced, 6.11.43 contract suspended, 22.7.44 contract canceled.
U 827	25.5.44			KL K. Baberg	5.5.45 (✠) Flensburg Fiord / 1948 br.
U 828	17.6.44			OL A. John	5.5.45 (✠) W. of Wesermünde: 53°32n/08°35e / 1948 br.
U 829– U 830					30.9.43 suspension announced, 6.11.43 contract suspended, 22.7.44 contract canceled, incomplete pressure hull broken up February 1944 on slip No. 4 Schichau-Werft Danzig.
U 831– U 840					30.9.43 suspension announced, 6.11.43 contract suspended, 22.7.44 contract canceled.
U 909– U 912					30.9.43 suspension announced, 6.11.43 contract suspended, 22.7.44 contract canceled.
U 929	6.9.44			OL W. Schulz	1.5.45 (✠) Baltic N. of Warnemünde: 54°15n/12°04e / ↑ 1956, br.
U 930	6.12.44			OL K. Mohr	9.5.45 Surrender Bergen, 30.5.45 sailed →Lisahally / 29.12.45 ✠ artillery DD HMS *Onslow* 55°22n/07°35w / Op. Deadlight.
U 931					delivery planned December 1944, but construction abandoned after July 1944, 23.9.44 contract canceled, pressure hull broken up October 1944 on slip No. 3 Neptun-Werft Rostock br.
U 932					delivery planned November 1944, but construction abandoned after April 1944, 23.9.44 contract canceled, pressure hull broken up October 1944 on slip No. 2 Neptun-Werft Rostock br.

1	2	3	4	5	6
U 933–U 936					30.9.43 suspension announced, 6.11.43 contract suspended, 22.7.44 contract canceled.
U 995	16.9.43			OL H.-G. Hess	9.5.45 Surrender Trondheim, not serviceable, not sailed to U.K., →Norway, 6.12.52 KNM *Kaura* (S 309); decomm. 15.12.62, October 1965 →German Federal Republic, 2.10.71 museum ship at Naval Memorial Laboe / Kiel Fiord.
U 996				(OL D. von Lehsten)	25.7.43 ✠ Hamburg, Blohm & Voss yard basin: 53°32n/09°57w / bomb / air raid 8. USAAF / ↑ ?.8.43, constructive total loss, →Schichauwerft Königsberg, May 1944 br, 22.7.44 contract canceled.
U 997	23.9.43			OL H. Lehmann	9.5.45 Surrender Narvik, →Lisahally, →Loch Ryan / 11.12.45 ✠ rockets Mos, 248 Sqn RAF 55°50n/10°05w / Op. Deadlight.
U 998	7.10.43			KL H. Fiedler	27.6.44 decomm. Bergen following D/Cs damage Mos H (Lt. E. U. Johansen), 333 Sqn (Norwegian) RAF 16.6.44 / cannibalized, 1944 br.
U 999	21.10.43			OL W. Heibges	5.5.45 (✠) Flensburg Fiord / 1948 br.
U 1000	4.11.43			OL W. Müller	29.9.44 decomm. Königsberg following damage British air-laid mine, field "Tangerine" 31.8.44 08h53 Baltic off Pillau: 54°41,6n/19°49e, cannibalized after 1.10.1944 at Schichau-Werft Königsberg, hulk 25.01.45 towed →Neustadt, but stranded 28.01.45 off Rixhöft: 54°50n/18°20e, blown up March 1945
U 1001	18.11.43	11.3.45	Kr	KL E.-U. Blaudow	8.4.45 ✠ N. Atlantic S.W. of Ireland: 49°19n/10°23w / D/Cs / DE's HMS *Fitzroy* (Lt. Comdr. O. G. Stuart), HMS *Byron* (Lt. J. B. Burfield) / 46 dead / ✠.
U 1002	30.11.43			OL H.-H. Boos	9.5.45 Surrender Bergen, 30.5.45 sailed →Lisahally / 13.12.45 ✠ torpedo SS HMS/m *Tantivy* 56°10n/10°05w / Op. Deadlight.
U 1003	9.12.43	19.2.45	Be	OL W. Strübing	23.3.45 (✠) North Channel E. of Malin Head: 55°38n/07°26w / following collision with PF HMCS *New Glasgow* (Lt. Comdr. R. M. Hanbury) 20.3.45 / 17 dead / 30 rescued.

1	2	3	4	5	6
U 1004	16.12.43			OL R. Hinz	9.5.45 Surrender Bergen, 2.6.45 sailed →Loch Ryan / 1.12.45 ✝ artillery DD's HMS *Onslaught*, ORP *Piorun* 56°10n/10°05w / Op. Deadlight.
U 1005	30.12.43	3.5.45	Be	OL H. Lauth	14.5.45 Surrender Bergen, 2.6.45 sailed →Loch Ryan / 5.12.45 ✝ foundered while under tow 55°33n/08°27w / Op. Deadlight.
U 1006	11.1.44	9.10.44	Be	OL H. Voigt	16.10.44 ✝ N. Atlantic S.E. of Faeroe Is.: 60°59n/04°49w / D/Cs, artillery / PF HMCS *Annan* (A/Lt. Comdr. C. P. Balfrey) / 6 dead / 44 rescued.
U 1007	18.1.44			OL K.-H. Raabe	2.5.45 ✝ Trave River N. of Lübeck: 53°54,4n/10°50,9e / rockets / Typ (F/L F. S. Murphy), Typ (F/O F. J. Pearson), Typ (W/O K. D. Bodden). Typ (F/Sgt C. M. Brocklehurst), 245 Sqn RAF / 2 dead / ↑ ?.5.46, br.
U 1008	1.2.44	5.5.45	So	OL H. Gessner	6.5.45 (✝) 22h30 Baltic, Kattegat N. of Hjelm Isl.: 56°14,2n/10°51,2e / following D/Cs damage Lib Z (F/L J. T. Lawrence). 86 Sqn RAF 5.5.45 / 44 rescued.[146]
U 1009	10.2.44	30.3.45	Dr	OL K. Hilgendorf	10.5.45 Surrender Loch Eriboll, →Lisahally, →Loch Ryan / 16.12.45 ✝ artillery DD HMS *Onslow* 55°31,5n/07°24w / Op. Deadlight.
U 1010	22.2.44	14.4.45	St	KL G. Strauch	14.5.45 Surrender Loch Eriboll, →Lisahally / 7.1.46 ✝ artillery DD ORP *Garland* 55°37,1n/07°49,1w / Op. Deadlight.
U 1011– U 1012					25.7.43 bomb damage air raid 8. USAAF on slip No. 3 Blohm & Voss Hamburg, construction abandoned March 1944, 22.7.44 contract canceled, after makeshift launching March 1944 incomplete hulls handed over to Kriegsmarine dockyard Hamburg, May 45 captured by British forces, br.
U 1013	2.3.44			OL G. Linck	17.3.44 ✝ 20h40 Baltic E. of Rügen: 54°2,2n/13°56e / collision / U 286 (OL W. Dietrich) / 25 dead / 26 rescued / ↑ 16.7.44, →Sassnitz, 23.7.44 decomm, final fate ?
U 1014	14.3.44	18.1.45	Be	OL W. Glaser	4.2.45 ✝ North Channel E. of Malin Head: 55°17n/06°44w / D/Cs / PF's HMS *Loch Scavaig* (A/T/Lt. Comdr. C. W. Hancock), HMS *Loch Shin* (Comdr. J. P. de W. Kitcat), HMS *Papua* (A/Lt. Comdr. C. W. Leadbetter), HMS *Nyasaland* (T/A/ Lt. Comdr. J. Scott) / 48 dead / ✝.

1	2	3	4	5	6
U 1015	23.3.44			OL H.-H. Boos	19.5.44 ✠ Baltic W. of Pillau: 55°09,6n/19°11,6e / collision / U 1014 (OL W. Glaser) / 36 dead / 14 rescued.
U 1016	4.4.44			OL W. Ehrhardt	5.5.45 (✠) Gelting Bay: 54°48n/09°49e / br.
U 1017	13.4.44	14.4.45	Dr	OL W. Riecken	29.4.45 ✠ N. Atlantic N.W. of Ireland: 56°04n/11°06w / D/Cs / Lib Q (F/O H. J. Oliver), 120 Sqn RAF / at least 34 dead / ✠.[147]
U 1018	25.4.44	21.1.45	Kr	KL W. Burmeister	27.2.45 ✠ English Channel S. of Lizard Point: 49°56n/05°20w / D/Cs / PF HMS *Loch Fada* (Comdr. B. A. Rogers) / 51 dead / 2 rescued.
U 1019	4.5.44			OL H. Rinck	9.5.45 Surrender Trondheim, 29.5.45 sailed →Loch Ryan / 7.12.45 ✠ artillery DD HMS *Onslaught* 55°37n/07°56w / Op. Deadlight.
U 1020	16.5.44	24.11.44	Kr	OL O. Eberlein	after 9.1.45 ✠ North Sea E. of Dundee: 56°32,7n/01°18,9w / British sea mine, field "SN 17" / 52 dead / ✠.[148]
U 1021	24.5.44	20.2.45	Be	OL W. Holpert	≈14.3.45 ✠ N. Atlantic S. of Bristol Channel: 59°39,8n/05°05,1w / British sea mine, field "HY A1" / 43 dead / ✠.[149]
U 1022	7.6.44			KL H.-J. Ernst	9.5.45 Surrender Bergen, 30.5.45 sailed →Lisahally / 29.12.45 ✠ artillery DD ORP *Piorun* 55°40n/08°15w / Op. Deadlight.
U 1023	15.6.44	25.3.45	Be	KL H. Schroeteler	10.5.45 Surrender Weymouth, HMS/m *N 83*, exhibition tour British West Coast, →Loch Ryan, →Lisahally / 8.1.46 ✠ foundered while under tow 55°49n/08°24w / Op. Deadlight.
U 1024	28.6.44	3.3.45	Kr	KL H.-J. Gutteck	13.4.45 ✠ Irish Sea S. of Isle of Man: 53°43,5n/04°57,5w / in tow PF HMS *Loch More* (Lt. Comdr. R. A. D. Cambridge) following D/Cs PF HMS *Loch Glendhu* (Lt. Comdr. E. G. P. B. Knapton) and capture 12.4.45 / 9 dead / 37 rescued.
U 1025	12.4.45			OL E. Pick	planned delivery in June 1944 at Blohm & Voss Hamburg suspended in May 1944, 23.9.44 completion shifted to Flensburger Schiffsbau Ges., 30.9.44 →Flensburg; 5.5.45 (✠) Flensburg Fiord, br.
U 1026	-------			(OL H. J. Hansen)	planned delivery in July 1944 at Blohm & Voss Hamburg suspended in May 1944, 23.9.44 completion shifted to Flensburger Schiffsbau Ges., late 1944 →Flensburg; 5.5.45 (✠) Flensburg Fiord, Kupfermühlen Bay, br.

1	2	3	4	5	6
U 1027	-------			(OL E.-G. Steinbeck)	delivery planned July 1944, but suspended May 1944, 23.9.44 contract canceled, 19.10.44 cancelation revoked, but planned transfer and completion at Flensburgcr Schiffsbau Ges. not executed, 24.1.45 →Kiel: 3.5.45 (✝) Kiel, Germaniawerft fitting out quay No. 10 berth / ↑ ?.8.47, br.
U 1028	-------			(OL F. Fabricius)	delivery planned July 1944, but suspended May 1944, 23.9.44 contract canceled, 19.10.44 cancelation revoked, but planned transfer and completion at Flensburger Schiffsbau Ges. not executed, ≈January 1945 →Kiel; 3.5.45 captured incomplete by British forces at Kiel, Kriegsmarine dockyard, br.
U 1029	-------				delivery planned August 1944, but suspended May 1944, 23.9.44 contract suspended, 27.10.44 suspension revoked, 1.11.44 transfer and completion at Flensburger Schiffsbau Ges. ordered, but not executed, 25.10.44 →Kiel; 3.5.45 captured incomplete by British forces at Kiel, Kriegsmarine dockyard, br.
U 1030	-------				delivery planned August 1944, but suspended May 1944, 23.9.44 contract suspended, 27.10.44 suspension revoked, 1.11.44 transfer and completion at Flensburger Schiffsbau Ges. ordered, but not executed, ≈November 1944 →Kiel: 3.5.45 (✝) Kiel, Germaniawerft fitting out quay No. 9 berth / ↑ 7.8.47, br.
U 1031– U 1032					30.9.43 suspension announced, 6.11.43 contract suspended, 22.7.44 contract canceled, incomplete pressure hull broken up February 1944 on slip No. 10 Blohm & Voss Hamburg.
U 1033– U 1050					30.9.43 suspension announced, 6.11.43 contract suspended, 22.7.44 contract canceled.
U 1063	8.7.44	12.3.45	Kr	KL K.-H. Stephan	15.4.45 ✝ English Channel W. of Landsend: 50°08n/03°53w / D/Cs / PF HMS *Loch Killin* (Lt. Comdr. S. Darling) / 29 dead / 17 rescued.
U 1064	29.7.44			KK H. Schneidewind	9.5.45 Surrender Trondheim, 29.5.45 sailed →Loch Ryan, HMS/m *N 24*, USSR war prize, 6.12.45 at Libau →USSR, 13.2.46 Soviet *N-24*, North Baltic Fleet, 9.6.49 *S-83*, 29.12.55 Reserve, 18.1.56 floating torpedo fire station *PZS-33*, 1.6.57 training hulk *UTS-49*, § 12.3.74, br.

1	2	3	4	5	6
U 1065	23.9.44	4.4.45	Ki	OL J. Panitz	9.4.45 ✠ North Sea N.W. of Göteborg: 57°58n/11°15e / rockets, machine gunfire / Mos H, D, K, A, I, G, Z, RAF Sqn 143, Mos P, W, N, RAF Sqn 235 / 45 dead / ✠.
U 1066– U 1068					30.9.43 suspension announced, 6.11.43 contract suspended, 22.7.44 contract canceled.
U 1107	8.8.44	30.3.45	Kr	KL F. Parduhn	25.4.45 ✠ Biscay W. of Brest: 48°12n/05°42w / homing torpedo / Lib K (Lt. D. D. Nott), VPB-103 Sqn USN / at least 37 dead / ✠.[150]
U 1108	18.11.44			OL W. Wigand	9.5.45 Surrender Horten, 27.5.45 sailed →Lisahally; August 1945 British war prize, HMS/m *N. . .*, tests, 12.5.49 →Messrs. T. W. Ward Ltd., Briton Ferry, br.
U 1109	31.8.44	17.4.45	Be	OL F. van Riesen	12.5.45 Surrender Loch Eriboll, →Lisahally / 6.1.46 ✠ torpedo SS HMS/m *Templar* 55°49n/08°31w / Op. Deadlight.
U 1110	24.9.44	4.5.45	Cu	OL J.-W. Bach	14.5.45 Surrender List, →Wilhelmshaven, 23.6.45 sailed →Loch Ryan / 21.12.45 ✠ artillery DD HMS *Onslow* 55°45n/08°19w / Op. Deadlight.
U 1111– U 1114					30.9.43 suspension announced, 6.11.43 contract suspended, 22.7.44 contract canceled.
U 1133					30.9.43 suspension announced, 6.11.43 contract suspended, 22.7.44 contract canceled, pressure hull May 45 captured by British forces on slip No. 4 Howaldswerke Kiel, br.
U 1134					30.9.43 suspension announced, 6.11.43 contract suspended, 22.7.44 contract canceled, pressure hull May 45 captured by British forces on slip No. 4 Howaldswerke Kiel, br.
U 1135					30.9.43 suspension announced, 6.11.43 contract suspended, 22.7.44 contract canceled, incomplete pressure hull May 45 captured by British forces on slip No. 6 Howaldswerke Kiel, br.
U 1136					30.9.43 suspension announced, 6.11.43 contract suspended, 22.7.44 contract canceled, incomplete pressure hull broken up early 1945 on slip No. 6 Howaldswerke Kiel.

1	2	3	4	5	6
U 1137– U 1140					30.9.43 suspension announced, 6.11.43 contract suspended, 22.7.44 contract canceled.
U 1141– U 1146					30.9.43 cancelation announced, 6.11.43 contract canceled.
U 1163	6.10.43			OL E.-L. Balduhn	9.5.45 Surrender Kristiansand, 29.5.45 sailed →Loch Ryan / 11.12.45 ✝ D/Cs Lib, 224 Sqn RAF, Sun, 201 Sqn RAF and War, 179 Sqn RAF 55°50n/10°05w / Op. Deadlight.
U 1164	27.10.43			KL H. Wengel	24.7.44 ✝ Kiel, Howaldtswerke AG: 54°19n/10°10e / bomb / air raid RAF Bomber Command / decomm., br.
U 1165	17.11.43			OL H. Homann	9.5.45 Surrender Narvik, →Loch Eriboll, →Lisahally / 31.12.45 ✝ artillery DD HMS *Offa* 55°44n/08°40w / Op. Deadlight.
U 1166	8.12.43			OL S. Ballert	28.8.44 decomm. Kiel following torpedo explosion 28.7.44 Eckernförde / floating power station, hulk May 45 (✝) Kiel, Deutsche Werke, off dry-dock No. 2, br.
U 1167	29.12.43			OL K.-H. Bortfeldt	30.3.45 ✝ Hamburg-Finkenwerder, inside pontoon dock S.E. of U-boat pen Fink II: 53°32,5n/09°51,3e / bomb / air raid 8. USAAF / 1 dead / br.
U 1168	19.1.44			KL H. Umlauf	4.5.45 (✝) Flensburg Fiord off Holnis: 54°53n/09°37,5e / after running aground, br.
U 1169	9.2.44	20.2.45	Kr	OL H. Goldbeck	After 16.3.45 ✝ N. Atlantic off Lands End or English Channel / missing / 49 dead / ✝.[151]
U 1170	1.3.44			KL F. Justi	2.5.45 (✝) Travemünde roads: 53°59n/10°56e / br.
U 1171	22.3.44			OL H. Koopmann	9.5.45 Surrender Stavanger, 27.5.45 sailed →Lisahally, British war prize. HMS/m *N 19*, tests, 3.2.46 laid up Lisahally, 13.6.49 →Thomas Young & Co, Sunderland.
U 1172	20.4.44	23.12.44	Kr	OL J. Kuhlmann	27.1.45 ✝ St. George's Channel: 52°24n/05°42w / D/Cs / DE's HMS *Tyler* (Lt. C. H. Rankin), HMS *Keats* (T/A/Lt. Comdr. N. F. Israel), HMS *Bligh* (Comdr. B. W. Taylor) / 52 dead / ✝.[152]
U 1173	-------			(OL R. Bressler)	construction abandoned 1944, 23.9.44 contract suspended, laid up incomplete Danzig, final fate ?[153]

1	2	3	4	5	6
U 1174	-------			(OL H. Knollmann)	construction abandoned 1944, 23.9.44 contract suspended, laid up incomplete Danzig; 30.3.45 captured by USSR forces, 1945 →Libau, final fate ?
U 1175	-------				construction abandoned 1944, 23.9.44 contract canceled, laid up incomplete Danzig, final fate ?
U 1176	-------				construction abandoned 1944, 23.9.44 contract canceled, laid up incomplete Danzig; 30.3.45 captured by USSR forces, 1945 →Libau, final fate ?
U 1177	-------				30.9.43 suspension announced, 6.11.43 contract suspended, but completed until launching, 22.7.44 contract canceled, laid up incomplete Kaiser basin, Danzig; 30.3.45 captured by USSR forces, 1945 →Libau, final fate ?
U 1178– U 1179					30.9.43 suspension announced, 6.11.43 contract suspended, 22.7.44 contract canceled, incomplete pressure hull broken up late 1943 on slip No. 3 Danziger Werft at Danzig.
U 1180– U 1190					30.9.43 suspension announced, 6.11.43 contract suspended, 22.7.44 contract canceled.
U 1211– U 1214					30.9.43 suspension announced, 6.11.43 contract suspended, 22.7.44 contract canceled.
U 1271	12.1.44			OL S. Thienemann	9.5.45 Surrender Bergen, 2.6.45 sailed →Loch Ryan / 8.12.45 ✠ foundered while under tow 55°28,8n/07°20,7w / Op. Deadlight.
U 1272	29.1.44	29.4.45	Kr	OL H. Schatteburg	10.5.45 Surrender Bergen, 30.5.45 sailed →Loch Ryan / 8.12.45 ✠ aerial torpedo / Bar, 816 Sqn FAA CVE HMS *Nairana* 55°50n/10°05w / Op. Deadlight.
U 1273	16.2.44			KL H. Knollmann	17.2.45 ✠ 08h30 Oslofiord off Horten: 59°24n/10°28e / British air-laid mine, field "Onions IV" / 43 dead / 8 rescued / partly br.
U 1274	1.3.44	5.4.45	Kr	OL H.-H. Fitting	16.4.45 ✠ North Sea N. of Newcastle: 55°36n/01°24w / D/Cs / DD HMS *Viceroy* (Lt. J. E. Manners) / 44 dead / ✠.
U 1275	22.3.44			OL G. Frohberg	3.5.45 (✠) Kiel, Deutsche Werke No. 5 berth / br.
U 1276	6.4.44	27.1.45	Be	OL K.-H. Wendt	20.2.45 ✠ N. Atlantic S. of Waterford: 51 °48n/07°07w / D/Cs / PS HMS *Amethyst* (Lt. Comdr. N. Scott-Elliott) / 49 dead / ✠.[154]

1	2	3	4	5	6
U 1277	3.5.44	22.4.45	Be	KL E. Stever	3.6.45 (✝) N. Atlantic N.W. of Porto: 41°13n/08°43w / 47 rescued.
U 1278	31.5.44	11.2.45	Kr	KL E. Müller-Bethke	17.2.45 ✝ Arctic N.W. of Bergen: 61°32n/01°36e / D/Cs / DE HMS *Bayntun* (Lt. Comdr. L. P. Bourke), PF HMS *Loch Eck* (Lt. Comdr. R. C. Freaker) / 48 dead / ✝.
U 1279	5.7.44	30.1.45	Fa	OL H. Falke	27.2.45 ✝ English Channel E. of Scilly Is.: 49°46n/05°47w / D/Cs / PF's HMS *Labuan* (T/A/Lt. Comdr. V. D. H. Bidwell), HMS *Loch Fada* (Comdr. B. A. Rogers), PS HMS *Wild Goose* (Lt. Comdr. D. E. G. Wemyss) and Lib H (Lt. O. B. Denison), VPB-112 Sqn USN / 48 dead / ✝.[155]
U 1280				(OL K. Mehne)	delivery planned July 1944, but construction abandoned June 1944, 23.9.44 contract canceled, incomplete hull 30.4.45 captured by British forces on slip No. 2 Vegesacker Werft Bremen, br.
U 1281				(OL H. Günther)	delivery planned August 1944, but construction abandoned June 1944, 23.9.44 contract canceled, incomplete hull 30.4.45 captured by British forces on slip No. 6 Vegesacker Werft Bremen, br.
U 1282				(OL K.-H. Menard)	delivery planned September 1944, but construction abandoned June 1944, 23.9.44 contract canceled, incomplete hull 30.4.45 captured by British forces on slip No. 6 Vegesacker Werft Bremen, br.
U 1283–U 1285					30.9.43 suspension announced, 6.11.43 contract suspended, 22.7.44 contract canceled.
U 1301	11.2.44			KL P. E. Lenkeit	9.5.45 Surrender Bergen, 2.6.45 sailed →Loch Ryan / 16.12.45 ✝ bomb British aircraft 55°50n/10°05w / Op. Deadlight.
U 1302	25.5.44	5.2.45	Kr	KL W. Herwartz	7.3.45 ✝ St. George's Channel: 52°19n/05°23w / D/Cs / PF's HMCS *La Hulloise* (Lt. Comdr. J. Brock), HMCS *Strathadam* (Lt. Comdr. H. L. Quinn), HMCS *Thetford Mines* (Lt. Comdr. J. A. R. Allan) / 48 dead / ✝.
U 1303	5.4.44			OL H. Herglotz	5.5.45 (✝) Flensburg Fiord, Kupfermühlen Bay / br.
U 1304	6.9.44			OL W. Süß	5.5.45 (✝) Flensburg Fiord. Kupfermühlen Bay / br.

1	2	3	4	5	6
U 1305	13.9.44	4.4.45	St	OL H. Christiansen	10.5.45 Surrender Loch Eriboll, →Lisahally; HMS/m *N 25*, USSR war prize, 6.12.1945 at Libau →USSR, 13.2.46 Soviet *N-25*, North Baltic Fleet, 9.6.49 *S-84*, 30.12.55 Reserve, test hulk Northern Fleet, 10.10.57 ✝ Barents Sea off Novaja Zemlja during atomic bomb test, § 1.3.58.
U 1306	20.12.44			OL U. Kiessling	5.5.45 (✝) Gelting Bay: 54°48n/09°49e / br.
U 1307	17.11.44			OL H. Buscher	9.5.45 Surrender Bergen, 2.6.45 sailed →Loch Ryan / 9.12.45 ✝ rockets Fir, 816 Sqn FAA CVE HMS *Nairana* 55°50n/10°05w / Op. Deadlight.
U 1308	17.1.45			OL H. Besold	1.5.45 (✝) Warnemünde, U-boat base: 54°10,3n/12°05,7e / ↑ 7.7.45, br.
U 1309– U 1312					30.9.43 suspension announced, 6.11.43 contract suspended, 22.7.44 contract canceled.
U 1331– U 1338					30.9.43 suspension announced, 6.11.43 contract suspended, 22.7.44 contract canceled.
U 1401– U 1404					30.9.43 suspension announced, 6.11.43 contract suspended, 22.7.44 contract canceled.
U 1417– U 1422					30.9.43 suspension announced, 6.11.43 contract suspended, 22.7.44 contract canceled.
U 1435– U 1439					30.9.43 suspension announced, 6.11.43 contract suspended, 22.7.44 contract canceled.
U 1801– U 1804					30.9.43 suspension announced, 6.11.43 contract suspended, 22.7.44 contract canceled.
U 1823– U 1828					30.9.43 cancelation announced, 6.11.43 contract canceled.

Type VII C/42

Seagoing combat U-boat type of conventional design developed in 1942–43
Surface/submerged displacement: 999/1099 t
Overall length/beam/draught: 68.70 m/6.85 m/5.00 m
Standard main armament: 5 torpedo tubes (4 bow, 1 stern) with up to 16 torpedoes

Building yard	Total no. ordered	Completed (comm.)	Under construction	Construction not started	Canceled after keel laying	Canceled prior to keel laying
Nordseewerke Emden	6	—	—	—	—	6
Kriegsmarine-werft Wilhelms-haven	12	—	—	—	—	12
Bremer Vulkan Vegesacker Werft	12	—	—	—	—	12
Stülckens-Werft Hamburg	6	—	—	—	—	6
Blohm & Voss AG Hamburg	36	—	—	—	—	36
Howaldtswerke AG Hamburg	6	—	—	—	—	6
Flensburger Schiffbauge-sellschaft	6	—	—	—	—	6
Germaniawerft AG Kiel	24	—	—	—	—	24
Howaldtswerke AG Kiel	6	—	—	—	—	6
Lübecker Flender-Werke AG	12	—	—	—	—	12
Neptunwerft Rostock	6	—	—	—	—	6
Danziger Werft AG	18	—	—	—	—	18
F. Schichau GmbH Danzig	24	—	—	—	—	24
Total	174	—	—	—	—	174

1	2	3	4	5	6
U 699– U 700					30.9.43 cancelation announced, 6.11.43 contract canceled.
U 783– U 790					30.9.43 cancelation announced, 6.11.43 contract canceled.
U 913– U 918					30.9.43 cancelation announced, 6.11.43 contract canceled.
U 937– U 942					30.9.43 cancelation announced, 6.11.43 contract canceled.
U 1069– U 1080					30.9.43 cancelation announced, 6.11.43 contract canceled.
U 1093– U 1100					30.9.43 cancelation announced, 6.11.43 contract canceled.
U 1115– U 1120					30.9.43 cancelation announced, 6.11.43 contract canceled.
U 1147– U 1152					30.9.43 cancelation announced, 6.11.43 contract canceled.
U 1215– U 1220					30.9.43 cancelation announced, 6.11.43 contract canceled.
U 1286– U 1291					30.9.43 cancelation announced, 6.11.43 contract canceled.
U 1292– U 1297					30.9.43 cancelation announced, 6.11.43 contract canceled.
U 1313– U 1318					30.9.43 cancelation announced, 6.11.43 contract canceled.
U 1339– U 1350					30.9.43 cancelation announced, 6.11.43 contract canceled.
U 1423– U 1434					30.9.43 cancelation announced, 6.11.43 contract canceled.
U 1440– U 1463					30.9.43 cancelation announced, 6.11.43 contract canceled.
U 1805– U 1822					30.9.43 cancelation announced, 6.11.43 contract canceled.
U 1901– U 1904					30.9.43 cancelation announced, 6.11.43 contract canceled.
U 2001– U 2004					30.9.43 cancelation announced, 6.11.43 contract canceled.
U 2101– U 2104					30.9.43 cancelation announced, 6.11.43 contract canceled.
U 2301– U 2318					30.9.43 cancelation announced, 6.11.43 contract canceled.

Type VII D

Seagoing combat/minelaying U-boat type of conventional design developed in 1939–40

Surface/submerged displacement:	965/1080 t
Overall length/beam/draught:	76.90 m/6.38 m/5.01 m
Standard main armament:	5 torpedo tubes (4 bow, 1 stern) with up to 14 torpedoes and 5 vertical mine tubes with 15 mines (SMA type)

Building yard	Total no. ordered	Completed (comm.)	Under construction	Construction not started	Canceled after keel laying	Canceled prior to keel laying
Germaniawerft AG Kiel	6	6	—	—	—	—
Total	6	6	—	—	—	—

1	2	3	4	5	6
U 213	30.8.41	23.7.42	Br	OL A. von Varendorff	31.7.42 ✠ N. Atlantic S.W. of Azores: 36°45n/22°50w / D/Cs / PS's HMS *Erne* (Lt. Comdr. E. D. J. Abbot), HMS *Rochester* (Comdr. C. B. Allen), HMS *Sandwich* (Lt. Comdr. H. Hill) / 50 dead / ✠.
U 214	1.11.41	22.7.44	Br	OL G. Conrad	26.7.44 ✠ English Channel S. of Start Point: 49°58n/03°30w / D/Cs / DE HMS *Cooke* (Lt. Comdr. L. C. Hill) / 48 dead / ✠.
U 215	22.11.41	11.6.42	Kr	KL F. Hoeckner	3.7.42 ✠ N. Atlantic E. of Boston: 41°48n/66°38w / D/Cs / TWL HMT *Le Tiger* (T/Lt. C.A. Hoodless) / 48 dead / ✠.
U 216	15.12.41	31.8.42	Kr	KL K.-O. Schultz	20.10.42 ✠ N. Atlantic S.W. of Ireland: 48°21n/19°25w / D/Cs / Lib H (F/O D. M. Sleep), 224 Sqn RAF / 45 dead / ✠.
U 217	31.1.42	19.4.43	Br	KL K. Reichenbach-Klinke	5.6.43 ✠ mid-Atlantic: 30°18n/42°50w / D/Cs / Ave T-11 (Lt.[jg] A. C. McAuslan), Wil F-13 (Lt. R. S. Rogers), VC-9 Sqn USN CVE USS *Bogue* (Capt. G. E. Short) / 50 dead / ✠.
U 218	24.1.42	22.3.45	Kr	KL R. Stock	8.5.45 entered Bergen, 2.6.45 sailed →Loch Ryan / 4.12.45 ✠ foundered while under tow 308° 11,2 sm Inishtrahull LT / Op. Deadlight.

Type VII F

Seagoing combat/torpedo supply U-boat type of conventional design developed in 1941
Surface/submerged displacement: 1084/1181 t
Overall length/beam/draught: 77.63 m/7.30 m/4.91 m
Standard main armament: 5 torpedo tubes (4 bow, 1 stern) with up to 14 torpedoes, up to
25 spare torpedoes in a stowage room for supply mission

Building yard	Total no. ordered	Completed (comm.)	Under construction	Construction not started	Canceled after keel laying	Canceled prior to keel laying
Germaniawerft AG Kiel	4	4	—	—	—	—
Total	4	4	—	—	—	—

1	2	3	4	5	6
U 1059	1.5.43	12.2.44	Be	OL G. Leupold	19.3.44 ✠ 09h29 mid-Atlantic S.W. of Cape Verde Is.: 13°10n/33°44w / D/Cs / Ave T-3 (Lt.[jg] N. T. Dowty), Wil (Lt. [jg] W. H. Cole), VC-6 Sqn USN CVE USS *Block Island* (Capt. F. M. Hughes) / 47 dead / 8 rescued.
U 1060	15.5.43	26.10.44	Nv	OL H. Brammer	27.10.44 ✠ Arctic S. of Vega fiord, northern tip of Fleina I.: 65°24,3n/11°59,5e / deliberately grounded following rocket damage air strike / Fir B (Lt. A. V. Donaghy), Fir L (Sub-Lt. R. J. Blackburn) and Fir J (Sub-Lt. H. R. L. Johns), 1771 Sqn FAA CV HMS *Implacable* (Capt. L. D. Mackintosh); later destroyed by D/Cs Hal D (F/L W. G. Powell), Hal T (S/L H. H. C. Holdemess), 502 Sqn RAF, Lib Y (F/O J. Pavelka), Lib H (S/L A. Sedivy). 311 Sqn (Czech) RAF / 14 dead / 43 rescued, br.
U 1061	25.8.43			OL W. Jäger	9.5.45 Surrender Bergen, 2.6.45 sailed →Loch Ryan / 1.12.45 ✠ artillery DD's HMS *Onslaught*, ORP *Piorun* 56°10n/10°05w / Op. Deadlight.
U 1062	19.6.43	15.7.44	Pe	OL K. Albrecht	30.9.44 ✠ mid-Atlantic S.W. of Cape Verde Is.: 11°36n/34°44w / D/Cs / DE USS *Fessenden* (Lt. Comdr. W. A. Dobbs) / 55 dead / ✠.

Type IX

Oceangoing combat U-boat type of conventional design developed in 1935–36
Surface/submerged displacement: 1032/1153 t
Overall length/beam/draught: 76.50 m/6.51 m/4.70 m
Standard main armament: 6 torpedo tubes (4 bow, 2 stern) with up to 22 torpedoes

Building yard	Total no. ordered	Completed (comm.)	Under construction	Construction not started	Canceled after keel laying	Canceled prior to keel laying
Deschimag AG Weser Bremen	8	8	—	—	—	—
Total	8	8	—	—	—	—

1	2	3	4	5	6
U 37	4.8.38			KL E. von Wenden	5.5.45 (✠) Hörup Haff: 54°53n/09°52e / br.
U 38	24.10.38			KK G. Peters	5.5.45 (✠) W. of Wesermünde: 53°34n/08°32e / br 1948.
U 39	10.12.38	19.8.39	Wi	KL G. Glattes	14.9.39 ✠ N. Atlantic W. of Hebrides: 58°32n/11°49w / D/Cs / DD's HMS *Faulknor* (Capt. C. S. Daniel), HMS *Foxhound* (Lt. Comdr. P. H. Hadow), HMS *Firedrake* (Lt. Comdr. S. H. Norris) / 44 rescued.
U 40	11.2.39	10.10.39	Wi	KK W. Barten	13.10.39 ✠ English Channel E. of Dover: 51°07,5n/01°48e / sea mine, British field "C3" / 45 dead / 3 rescued.
U 41	22.4.39	27.1.40	He	KL G.-A. Mugler	5.2.40 ✠ N. Atlantic S.W. of Ireland: 49°20n/10°04w / D/Cs / DD HMS *Antelope* (Lt. Comdr. R. T. White) / 49 dead / ✠.
U 42	15.7.39	2.10.39	Wi	KL R. Dau	13.10.39 ✠ N. Atlantic S.W. of Ireland: 49°12n/16°00w / D/Cs / DD's HMS *Imogen* (Comdr. E. B. K. Stevens), HMS *Ilex* (Lt. Comdr. P. L. Saumarez) / 26 dead / 20 rescued.
U 43	26.8.39	13.7.43	Lo	OL H.-J. Schwantke	30.7.43 ✠ mid-Atlantic: 34°57n/35°11w / homing torpedo / Ave T-13 (Lt.[jg] R. F. Richmond), Wil F-2 (Lt.[jg] E. van Vranken), VC-29 Sqn USN CVE USS *Santee* (Capt. H. F. Fick) / 55 dead / ✠.
U 44	4.11.39	13.3.40	Wi	KL L. Mathes	≈ 13.3.40 ✠ North Sea N. of Terschelling: ≈54°14n/05°07e / missing – ≈British sea mine, "Field No. 7" / 47 dead / ✠.[156]

Type IX B

Oceangoing combat U-boat type of conventional design developed in 1936
Surface/submerged displacement: 1051/1178 t
Overall length/beam/draught: 76.50 m/6.76 m/4.70 m
Standard main armament: 6 torpedo tubes (4 bow, 2 stern) with up to 22 torpedoes

Building yard	Total no. ordered	Completed (comm.)	Under construction	Construction not started	Canceled after keel laying	Canceled prior to keel laying
Deschimag AG Weser Bremen	14	14	—	—	—	—
Total	14	14	—	—	—	—

1	2	3	4	5	6
U 64	16.12.39	6.4.40	Wi	KL W. Schulz	13.4.40 ♱ Herjangs-Fiord N.E. of Narvik: 68°29n/17°30e / D/Cs / Swd (PO F. C. Rice), 700 Sqn FAA ship-borne aircraft BB HMS *Warspite* (Capt. V. A. C. Crutchley) / 8 dead / 38 rescued / ↑ 7.8.57, →Sandnessjoen, br.
U 65	15.2.40	12.4.41	Lo	KL J. Hoppe	28.4.41 ♱ N. Atlantic S.E. of Iceland: 59°51n/15°30w / D/Cs / DD HMS *Douglas* (Comdr. W. E. Banks) / 50 dead / ♱.[157]
U 103	5.7.40			KL G.-A. Janssen	13.3.44 decomm. Memel, → training boat 4.ULD Memel, later 2.ULD Gotenhafen, 29.1.45 →Hamburg-Finkenwerder, generating plant, April 45 →Kiel; ≈3.5.45 (♱) Kiel: 54°19n/10°10e / br.
U 104	19.8.40	18.11.40	Be	KL H. Jürst	≈28.11.40 ♱ N.W. of Ireland: ≈55°30n/08°00w / missing – ≈sea mine British field "SN 44" / 49 dead / ♱.[158]
U 105	10.9.40	16.3.43	Lo	KL J. Nissen	2.6.43 ♱ mid-Atlantic W. of Dakar: 14°15n/17°35w / D/Cs / CAMS flying boat *141-Antares* (L.V. P. Vauchez), 4.E Sqn FAFL / 53 dead / ♱.
U 106	24.9.40	28.7.43	Lo	OL W.-D. Damerow	2.8.43 ♱ N. Atlantic N.W. of Spain: 46°35n/11°55w / D/Cs / Sun N (F/O R. D. Hanbury), 228 Sqn RAF, Sun M (F/L I. A. F. Clarke), 461 Sqn RAF / 22 dead / 36 rescued.
U 107	8.10.40	16.8.44	Lo	LT K.-H. Fritz	18.8.44 ♱ Biscay S.W. of St. Nazaire: 46°46n/03°49w / D/Cs / Sun W (F/L L. H. Baveystock), 201 Sqn RAF / 58 dead / ♱.

1	2	3	4	5	6
U 108	22.10.40			OL M. Brünig	11.4.44 ✠ Stettin, U-boat base inside pontoon dock / bomb / air raid 8. USAAF / ↑ , 17.7.44 decomm. Stettin, 24.4.45 (✠) River Oder near Swinemünde(?), ↑ USSR summer 1946, →Stettin, final fate ?
U 109	5.12.40	28.4.43	Lo	OL J. Schramm	4.5.43 ✠ 16h36 N. Atlantic: 47°22n/22°40w / D/Cs / Lib P (P/O J. C. Green), 86 Sqn RAF / 52 dead / ✠.
U 110	21.11.40	15.4.41	Lo	KL F.-J. Lemp	10.5.41 ✠ 11h00 N. Atlantic E. of Cape Farewell: 60°22n/33°12w / in tow DD HMS *Bulldog* following D/Cs / PE HMS *Aubretia* (Lt. Comdr. V. F. Smith), DD's HMS *Bulldog* (Comdr. A. J. Baker-Cresswell), HMS *Broadway* (Lt. Comdr. T. Taylor) and capture 9.5.41 / 15 dead / 32 rescued.
U 111	19.12.40	14.8.41	Lo	KL W. Kleinschmidt	4.10.41 ✠ mid-Atlantic, Canary Is.: 27°15n/20°27w / D/Cs, artillery / TWL HMT *Lady Shirley* (Lt. Comdr. A. H. Callaway) / 8 dead / 44 rescued.
U 122	30.3.40	13.6.40	Ki	KK H.-G. Looff	after 21.6.40 ✠ N. Atlantic S.W. of Ireland-Biscay / missing / 49 dead / ✠.[159]
U 123	30.5.40			OL H. von Schroeter	?.8.44 decomm. Lorient, laid up U-boat pen Lorient box K3 / May 1945 captured by U.S. forces, French war prize, French *Blaison* (S 611). decomm. 15.8.59, Q 165, br.
U 124	11.6.40	27.3.43	Lo	KK J. Mohr	2.4.43 ✠ N. Atlantic W. of Porto: 41°02n/15°39w / D/Cs / PE HMS *Stonecrop* (Lt. Comdr. J. P. Smythe), PS HMS *Black Swan* (Lt. Comdr. R. C. V. Thomson) / 53 dead / ✠.

Type IX C

Oceangoing combat U-boat type of conventional design developed in 1938
Surface/submerged displacement: 1120/1232 t
Overall length/beam/draught: 76.76 m/6.76 m/4.70 m
Standard main armament: 6 torpedo tubes (4 bow, 2 stern) with up to 25 torpedoes

Building yard	Total no. ordered	Completed (comm.)	Under construction	Construction not started	Canceled after keel laying	Canceled prior to keel laying
Deschimag AG Weser Bremen	24	24	—	—	—	—
Deschimag Seebeck Werft Wesermünde	6	6	—	—	—	—
Deutsche Werft AG Hamburg	24	24	—	—	—	—
Total	54	54	—	—	—	—

1	2	3	4	5	6
U 66	2.1.41	16.1.44	Lo	OL G. Seehausen	6.5.44 ✟ mid-Atlantic W. of Cape Verde Is.: 17°17n/32°29w / D/Cs, artillery, ramming / Ave T-21 (Lt.[jg] J. J. Sellars), VC-55 Sqn USN CVE USS *Block Island* (Capt. F. M. Hughes), DE USS *Buckley* (Lt. Comdr. B. M. Abel) / 24 dead / 36 rescued.
U 67	22.1.41	10.5.43	Lo	KK G. Müller-Stöckheim	16.7.43 ✟ mid-Atlantic: 30°05n/44°17w / D/Cs / Ave (Lt. R. P. Williams), VC-13 Sqn USN CVE USS *Core* (Capt. M. R. Greer) / 48 dead / 3 rescued.
U 68	11.2.41	27.3.44	Lo	OL A. Lauzemis	10.4.44 ✟ mid-Atlantic N.W. of Madeira: 33°24n/18°59w / D/Cs, rockets / Ave T-22 (Lt. S. G. Parsons), Ave T-24 (Lt. H. E. Hoerner), Wil F-4 (Lt. Comdr. R. K. Gould), VC-58 Sqn USN CVE USS *Guadalcanal* (Capt. D. V. Gallery) / 56 dead / 1 rescued.
U 125	3.3.41	13.4.43	Lo	KL U. Folkers	6.5.43 ✟ N. Atlantic N.E. of Newfoundland: 52°30n/45°20w / ramming, artillery / DD HMS *Oribi* (Lt. Comdr. J. C. A. Ingram), PE HMS *Snowflake* (Lt. H. G. Chesterman) / 54 dead / ✟.
U 126	22.3.41	20.3.43	Lo	OL S. Kietz	3.7.43 ✟ N. Atlantic N.W. of Spain: 46°02n/11°23w / D/Cs / Wel R (F/Sgt A. Coumbis), 172 Sqn RAF / 55 dead / ✟.

1	2	3	4	5	6
U 127	24.4.41	1.12.41	Kr	KL B. Hansmann	15.12.41 ✠ N. Atlantic W. of Gibraltar: 36°28n/09°12w / D/Cs / DD HMAS *Nestor* (Comdr. A. S. Rosenthal) / 51 dead / ✠.
U 128	12.5.41	6.4.43	Lo	KL H. Steinert	17.5.43 ✠ S. Atlantic S. of Recife: 10°00s/35°35w / D/Cs, artillery / Mar P-5 (Lt.[jg.] H. C. Carey), Mar P-6 (Lt. H. S. Davis), VP-74 Sqn USN and DD's USS *Moffett* (Comdr. J. C. Sowell), USS *Jouett* (Comdr. F. L. Tedder) / 7 dead / 47 rescued.
U 129	21.5.41			OL R. von Harpe	?.8.44 decomm. Lorient, 18.8.44 (✠) S.W. of U-boat pen Keroman 1. May 1945 captured by U.S. forces, French war prize, br.
U 130	11.6.41	28.2.43	Lo	OL S. Keller	12.3.43 ✠ N. Atlantic W. of Azores: 37°10n/40°21w / D/Cs / DD USS *Champlin* (Lt. Comdr. C. L. Melson) / 53 dead / ✠.
U 131	1.7.41	29.11.41	Kr	KK A. Baumann	17.12.41 ✠ mid-Atlantic N.E. of Madeira: 34°12n/13°35w / D/Cs, artillery / DE's HMS *Exmoor* (Lt. Comdr. L. St. G. Rich), HMS *Blankney* (Lt. Comdr. P. F. Powlett), DD HMS *Stanley* (Lt. Comdr. D. B. Shaw), PE HMS *Pentstemon* (Lt. Comdr. J. Byron), PS HMS *Stork* (Comdr. F. J. Walker) and Mat (Sub-Lt. G. R. P. Fletcher), 802 Sqn FAA CVE HMS *Audacity* (Comdr. D. W. MacKendrick) / 47 rescued.
U 153	19.7.41	6.6.42	Lo	KK W. Reichmann	6.7.42 ✠ Caribbean N. W. of Aruba: 12°50n/72°20w / D/Cs / Hav 40-106 (1st Lt. M. E. Groover), 59 Bomb Sqn USAAF / 52 dead / ✠.[160]
U 154	2.8.41	20.6.44	Lo	OL G. Gemeiner	3.7.44 ✠ mid-Atlantic N.W. of Madeira: 34°00n/19°30w / D/Cs / DE's USS *Inch* (Lt. Comdr. D. A. Tufts), USS *Frost* (Lt. Comdr. J. H. McWhorter) / 57 dead / ✠.
U 155	23.8.41			OL F. Altmeier	5.5.45 Surrender Fredericia, →Wilhelmshaven. 22.6.45 →Loch Ryan / 21.12.45 ✠ artillery DD ORP *Blyskawica* 55°35n/07°39w / Op. Deadlight.
U 156	4.9.41	16.1.43	Lo	KK W. Hartenstein	8.3.43 ✠ 13h15 mid-Atlantic E. of Barbados: 12°38n/54°39w / D/Cs / Cat P-l (Lt. J. E. Dryden), VP-53 Sqn USN / 53 dead / ✠.
U 157	15.9.41	18.5.42	Lo	KK W. Henne	13.6.42 ✠ 21h50 Gulf of Mexico N.E. of Habana: 24°13n/82°03w / D/Cs / USCGC *Thetis* (Lt.[jg] N. C. McCormick) / 52 dead / ✠.

1	2	3	4	5	6
U 158	25.9.41	4.5.42	Lo	KL E. Rostin	30.6.42 ✞ mid-Atlantic W. of Bermuda: 32°50n/67°28w / D/Cs / Mar P-1 (Lt. R. E. Schreder), VP-74 Sqn USN / 54 dead / ✞.
U 159	4.10.41	12.6.43	Lo	OL H. Beckmann	28.7.43 ✞ Caribbean S.E. of Haiti: 15°57n/68°30w / D/Cs / Mar P-l (Lt.[jg] D. C. Pinholster), VP-32 Sqn USN / 53 dead / ✞.[161]
U 160	16.10.41	28.6.43	Bo	OL G. von Pommer-Esche	14.7.43 ✞ mid-Atlantic S. of Azores: 33°54n/27°13w / homing torpedo / Ave T-7 (Lt.[jg] J. H. Ballantine), Wil F-1 (Lt. H. B. Bass), VC-29 Sqn USN CVE USS *Santee* (Capt. H. F. Fick) / 50 dead / ✞.
U 161	8.7.41	8.8.43	Lo	KL A. Achilles	27.9.43 ✞ S. Atlantic E. of Salvador Bahia: 12°30s/35°35w / D/Cs / Mar P-2 (Lt.[jg] H. B. Patterson), VP-74 Sqn USN / 53 dead / ✞.
U 162	9.9.41	7.7.42	Lo	FK J. Wattenberg	3.9.42 ✞ mid-Atlantic N.E. of Trinidad: 12°21n/59°29w / D/Cs / DD's HMS *Vimy* (Lt. Comdr. H. G. D. de Chair), HMS *Pathfinder* (Comdr. E. A. Gibbs), HMS *Quentin* (Lt. Comdr. A. H. P. Noble) / 2 dead / 49 rescued.
U 163	21.10.41	10.3.43	Lo	KK K.-E. Engelmann	13.3.43 ✞ N. Atlantic N.W. of Cape Finisterre: 45°05n/15°00w / D/Cs / PE HMCS *Prescott* (Lt. W. Mclssac) / 57 dead / ✞.[162]
U 164	28.11.41	29.11.42	Lo	KK O. Fechner	6.1.43 ✞ S. Atlantic N.W. of Fortaleza: 01°58s/39°22w / D/Cs / Cat P-2 (Lt. W. R. Ford), VP-83 Sqn USN / 54 dead / 2 rescued.
U 165	3.2.42	9.8.42	Kr	KK E. Hoffmann	27.9.42 ✞ Biscay S.W. of Lorient: 47°00n/05°30w / D/Cs / Wel Q (F/O V. Student), 311 Sqn (Czech) RAF / 51 dead / ✞.[163]
U 166	24.3.42	17.6.42	Br	OL H.-G. Kuhlmann	30.7.42 ✞ Gulf of Mexico S. of Mobile: 28°40n/88°30w / D/Cs / USS *PC-566* (Lt. Comdr. H. G. Claudius) / 52 dead / ✞.[164]
U 171	25.10.41	19.6.42	Kr	KL G. Pfeffer	9.10.42 ✞ 13h45 Biscay S.W. of Lorient: 47°39n/03°34w / British air-laid mine, field "Artichokes" / 22 dead / 30 rescued.
U 172	5.11.41	22.11.43	Na	OL H. Hoffmann	13.12.43 18h20 ✞ mid-Atlantic S.W. of Canary Is.: 26°29n/29°58w / homing torpedo, D/Cs / Ave T-13 (Lt.[jg] E. C. Gaylord), VC-19 Sqn USN CVE USS *Bogue* (Capt. J. B. Dunn) and DD's USS *George E. Badger* (Lt. E. M. Higgins), USS *Clemson* (Lt. W. F. Moran), USS *Osmond Ingram* (Lt. Comdr. R. F. Miller), USS *DuPont* (Comdr. J. G. Marshall) / 13 dead / 46 rescued.

1	2	3	4	5	6
U 173	15.11.41	1.11.42	Lo	OL H.-A. Schweichel	16.11.42 ✠ mid-Atlantic W. of Casablanca: 33°40n/07°35w / D/Cs / DD's USS *Woolsey* (Comdr. B. L. Austin), USS *Swanson* (Lt. Comdr. L. M. Markham), USS *Quick* (Lt. Comdr. R. B. Nickerson) / 57 dead / ✠.
U 174	26.11.41	18.3.43	Lo	OL W. Grandefeld	27.4.43 ✠ N. Atlantic S. of Newfoundland: 43°35n/56°18w / D/Cs / Ven B-6 (Lt.[jg] T. Kinaszczuk), VB-125 Sqn USN / 53 dead / ✠.
U 175	5.12.41	10.4.43	Lo	KL H. Bruns	17.4.43 ✠ 15h N. Atlantic: 47°53n/22°04w / D/Cs, artillery / USCGC *John C. Spencer* (Comdr. H. S. Berdine) / 13 dead / 41 rescued.
U 176	15.12.41	6.4.43	Lo	KK R. Dierksen	15.5.43 ✠ mid-Atlantic N. of Cuba: 23°21n/80°18w / D/Cs / Cuban patrol craft *CS 13* (Alférez de Fregata M. R. Delgado) and Kin S-1, VS-62 Sqn USN / 53 dead / ✠.
U 501	30.4.41	7.8.41	Dr	KK H. Förster	10.9.41 ✠ 23h30 N. Atlantic S. of Angmagsalik: 62°50n/37°50w / D/Cs / PE's HMCS *Chambly* (Comdr. J. D. Prentice), HMCS *Moosejaw* (Lt. F. E. Grubb) / 11 dead / 37 rescued.
U 502	31.5.41	22.4.42	Lo	KL J. von Rosenstiel	6.7.42 ✠ Biscay W. of La Rochelle: 46°10n/06°40w / D/Cs / Wel H (P/O W. B. Howell), 172 Sqn RAF / 52 dead / ✠.
U 503	10.7.41	28.2.42	Be	KL O. Gericke	15.3.42 ✠ N. Atlantic S.E. of Newfoundland: 45°50n/48°50w / D/Cs / Hud (CPO D. F. Mason), VP-82 Sqn USN / 51 dead / ✠.
U 504	30.7.41	27.7.43	Lo	KL W. Luis	30.7.43 ✠ 15h43 N. Atlantic N.W. of Spain: 45°33n/10°56w / D/Cs / PS's HMS *Kite* (Comdr. F. J. Walker), HMS *Wild Goose* (Lt. Comdr. D. E. G. Wemyss), HMS *Wren* (Lt. Comdr. R. M. Aubrey), HMS *Woodpecker* (Lt. Comdr. R. E. S. Hugonin) / 53 dead / ✠.
U 505	26.8.41	16.3.44	Br	OL H. Lange	4.6.44 ✠ 11h20 mid-Atlantic N.W. of Dakar: 21°30n/19°20w / captured by DE USS *Pillsbury* (Lt. G. W. Cassleman) following D/Cs damage DE USS *Chatelain* (Lt. Comdr. D. S. Knox) and MG-fire Wil F-1 (Ens. J. W. Cadle, Jr.), Wil F-7 (Lt. W. W. Roberts), VC-8 Sqn USN CVE USS *Guadalcanal* (Capt. D. V. Gallery) / 1 dead / 59 rescued / towed in →Bermuda, Port Royal Bay: comm. as USS *Nemo*, 25.9.55 →Museum of Science & Industry, Chicago.

1	2	3	4	5	6
U 506	15.9.41	6.7.43	Lo	KL E. Würdemann	12.7.43 ✝ 15h50 N. Atlantic W. of Vigo: 42°30n/16°30w / D/Cs / Lib C (Lt. E. Salm), 1st A/S Sqn USAAF / 48 dead / 6 rescued.
U 507	8.10.41	28.11.42	Lo	KK H. Schacht	13.1.43 ✝ S. Atlantic N.W. of Fortaleza: 01°38s/39°52w / D/Cs / Cat P-10 (Lt. [jg] L. Ludwig), VP-83 Sqn USN / 54 dead / ✝.
U 508	20.10.41	9.11.43	Na	KL G. Staats	12.11.43 ✝ Biscay N. of Spain: 46°00n/07°30w / D/Cs / Lib C (Lt.[jg] R. B. Brownell), VB-103 Sqn USN / 57 dead / ✝.
U 509	4.11.41	3.7.43	Lo	KL W. Witte	15.7.43 ✝ mid-Atlantic S.E. of Azores: 34°02n/26°01w / homing torpedo / Ave T-12 (Lt.[jg] C. N. Barton), Wil F-7 (Ens. J. D. Anderson), VC-29 Sqn USN CVE USS *Santee* (Capt. H. F. Fick) / 54 dead / ✝.
U 510	25.11.41			KL A. Eick	9.5.45 Surrender St. Nazaire, French war prize, 1946 French *Bouan* (S 612), decomm. 1.5.59, 23.11.59 Q 176, 1960 br.
U 511	8.12.41			KL F. Schneewind	16.9.43 decomm. Kure →Japan, donation of Germany to the Emperor of Japan.
	16.9.43				comm. as *RO 500* for IJN; ?.8.45 Surrender Maizuru, 30.4.46 ✝ Gulf of Maizuru by US Navy.
U 512	20.12.41	17.8.42	Kr	KL W. Schultze	2.10.42 ✝ mid-Atlantic N.E. off Paramaribo: 06°50n/52°25w / D/Cs / Dig 71 (Capt. H. Burhanna, Jr.), 99 Bomb Sqn USAAF / 51 dead / 1 rescued.
U 513	10.1.42	18.5.43	Lo	KL F. Guggenberger	19.7.43 ✝ S. Atlantic S.E. of Sao Francisco do Sul: 27°17s/47°32w / D/Cs / Mar P-3 (Lt.[jg] R. S. Whitcomb), VP-74 Sqn USN / 46 dead / 7 rescued.
U 514	24.1.42	3.7.43	Lo	KL H.-J. Auffermann	8.7.43 ✝ Biscay N.W. of La Coruna: 43°37n/08°59w / rockets / Lib R (S/L T. M. Bulloch), 224 Sqn RAF / 54 dead / ✝.
U 515	21.2.42	30.3.44	Lo	KL W. Henke	9.4.44 ✝ 15h10 mid-Atlantic N.W. of Madeira: 34°35n/19°18w / D/Cs, rockets / Ave (Lt. Comdr. R. K. Gould), Ave, 2 Wil, VC-58 Sqn USN CVE USS *Guadalcanal* (Capt. D. V. Gallery) and DE's USS *Pope* (Lt. Comdr. E. H. Headland), USS *Pillsbury* (Lt. G. W. Casslemann), USS *Chatelain* (Lt. Comdr. J. L. Foley), USS *Flaherty* (Lt. Comdr. M. Johnston, Jr.) / 16 dead / 44 rescued.

1	2	3	4	5	6
U 516	10.3.42	5.4.45	Kr	OL F. Petran	14.5.45 Surrender Loch Eriboll, →Lisahally / 3.1.46 ✠ foundered while under tow 56°06n/09°00w / Op. Deadlight.
U 517	21.3.42	17.11.42	Lo	KL P. Hartwig	21.11.42 ✠ N. Atlantic S.W. of Ireland: 46°16n/17°09w / D/Cs / Alb I (T/Sub-Lt. T. H. Hands), 817 Sqn FAA CV HMS *Victorious* (Capt. L. D. Mackintosh) / 1 dead / 52 rescued.
U 518	25.4.42	12.3.45	Kr	OL H. Offermann	22.4.45 ✠ N. Atlantic N.W. of Azores: 43°26n/38°23w / D/Cs / DE's USS *Carter* (Lt. Comdr. F. J. T. Baker), USS *Neal A. Scott* (Lt. Comdr. P. D. Holden) / 56 dead / ✠.[165]
U 519	7.5.42	30.1.43	Lo	KL G. Eppen	after 30.1.43 ✠ ≈Biscay / missing / 50 dead / ✠.[166]
U 520	19.5.42	5.10.42	Kr	KL V. Schwartzkopff	30.10.42 ✠ N. Atlantic E. of Newfoundland: 47°47n/49°50w / D/Cs / Dig X (F/O D. F. Raymes), 10(BR) Sqn RCAF / 53 dead / ✠.
U 521	3.6.42	5.5.43	Lo	KL K. Bargsten	2.6.43 ✠ N. Atlantic N.E. of Norfolk: 37°43n/73°16w / D/Cs / PC USS *PC 565* (Lt. W. T. Flynn) / 51 dead / 1 rescued.
U 522	11.6.42	31.12.42	Lo	KL H. Schneider	23.2.43 ✠ mid-Atlantic S. of Azores: 31 °27n/26°22w / D/Cs / CGC HMS *Totland* (Lt. Comdr. L. E. Woodhouse) / 51 dead / ✠.
U 523	25.6.42	16.8.43	Lo	KL W. Pietzsch	25.8.43 ✠ N. Atlantic W. of Vigo: 42°03n/18°02w / D/Cs / DD HMS *Wanderer* (Lt. Comdr. R. F. Whinney), PE HMS *Wallflower* (Lt. Comdr. I. J. Tyson) / 17 dead / 37 rescued.
U 524	8.7.42	3.3.43	Lo	KL W. Frhr. von Steinaecker	22.3.43 ✠ mid-Atlantic S. of Madeira: 30°15n/18°13w / D/Cs / Lib T (Lt. W. L. Sanford), 2st A/S Sqn USAAF / 52 dead / ✠.

Type IX C/40

Oceangoing combat U-boat type of conventional design developed in 1939-40
Surface/submerged displacement: 1144/1257 t
Overall length/beam/draught: 76.76 m/6.86 m/4.67 m
Standard main armament: 6 torpedo tubes (4 bow, 2 stern) with up to 25 torpedoes

Building yard	Total no. ordered	Completed (comm.)	Under construction	Construction not started	Canceled after keel laying	Canceled prior to keel laying
Deschimag AG Weser Bremen	72	36	—	—	4	32
Deschimag Seebeck Werft Wesermünde	20	10	—	—	2	8
Deutsche Werft AG Hamburg	68	41	—	—	7	20
Total	160	87	—	—	13	60

1	2	3	4	5	6
U 167	4.7.42	27.2.43	Lo	KK K. Sturm	6.4.43 (✝) mid-Atlantic off Canary Is.: 27°47n/15°00w / following D/Cs damage / Hud W (F/Sgt K. R. Dalton), Hud L (A/F/L W. E. Willits), 233 Sqn RAF 5.4.43 / 50 rescued / ↑ 1951, →Spain, br.
U 168	9.9.42	5.10.44	Dj	KL H. Pich	6.10.44 ✝ 01h30 Pacific, Java Sea: 06°20s/111°28e / torpedo / SS HNetMS/m Zwaardvisch (Lt. Comdr. H. A. W. Goossens) / 23 dead / 27 rescued.
U 169	16.11.42	21.3.43	Kr	OL H. Bauer	27.3.43 ✝ N. Atlantic S. of Iceland: 60°54n/15°25w / D/Cs / For L (F/O A. C. I. Samuel), 206 Sqn RAF / 54 dead / ✝.
U 170	19.1.43			OL H. G. Hauber	9.5.45 Surrender Horten, 27.5.45 sailed →Loch Ryan / 30.11.45 ✝ artillery DD's ORP Piroun, HMS Onslaught 55°44n/07°53w / Op. Deadlight.
U 183	1.4.42	21.4.45	Dj	KL F. Schneewind	23.4.45 ✝ 07h29 Pacific, Java Sea: 04°56s/112°55e / torpedo / SS USS Besugo (Lt. Comdr. H. E. Miller) / 54 dead / 1 rescued.
U 184	29.5.42	9.11.42	Be	KL G. Dangschat	≈20.-21.11.42 ✝ N. Atlantic E. of Newfoundland: ≈49° n/45° w / missing / 50 dead / ✝.[167]

1	2	3	4	5	6
U 185	13.6.42	9.6.43	Bo	KL A. Maus	24.8.43 ✠ mid-Atlantic: 27°00n/37°06w / D/Cs / Ave T-5 (Lt. R. P. Williams), Wil (Lt.[jg] M. G. O'Neill), Wil (Lt. Comdr. C. W. Brewer), VC-13 Sqn USN CVE USS *Core* (Capt. M. R. Greer) / 29 dead + 14 dead of crew U 604 / 22 (23?) rescued.
U 186	10.7.42	17.4.43	Lo	KL S. Hesemann	12.5.43 ✠ N. Atlantic N. of Azores: 41°54n/31°49w / D/Cs / DD HMS *Hesperus* (Comdr. D. G. F. W. MacIntyre) / 53 dead / ✠.
U 187	23.7.42	14.1.43	Kr	KL R. Münnich	4.2.43 ✠ N. Atlantic: 50°12n/36°35w / D/Cs / DD's HMS *Vimy* (Lt. Comdr. R. B. Stannard), HMS *Beverley* (Lt. Comdr. R. A. Price) / 9 dead / 45 rescued.
U 188	5.8.42			KL S. Lüdden	20.8.44 decomm. Bordeaux, unserviceable, laid up, 25.8.44 (✠) Bordeaux, inside U-boat pen: 44°52n/00°34w /1947 br.
U 189	15.8.42	6.4.43	Kr	KL H. Kurrer	23.4.43 ✠ N. Atlantic E. of Cape Farewell: 59°50n/34°43w / D/Cs / Lib V (F/O J. K. Moffat), 120 Sqn RAF / 54 dead / ✠.
U 190	24.9.42	21.2.45	Kr	OL H.-E. Reith	12.5.45 Surrender at sea, →Bay Bulls, →Halifax, 25.5.45 →Canada, comm. Canadian *U 190*, tests, 24.7.47 decomm.; 21.10.47 ✠ S.W. of Newfoundland: 43°55n/63°00w / bomb aircraft 826 and 883 Sqn RCAF and artillery DD HMCS *Nootka*, AM HMCS *New Liskeard*.
U 191	20.10.42	17.3.43	Be	KL H. Fiehn	23.4.43 ✠ N. Atlantic S.E. of Cape Farewell: 56°45n/34°25w / D/Cs / DD HMS *Hesperus* (Comdr. D. G. F. W. MacIntyre) / 55 dead / ✠.
U 192	16.11.42	15.4.43	Kr	OL W. Happe	6.5.43 ✠ N. Atlantic S. of Cape Farewell: 53°06n/45°02w / D/Cs / PE HMS *Loosestrife* (A/Lt. Comdr. H. A. Stonehouse) / 55 dead / ✠.[168]
U 193	10.12.42	23.4.44	Lo	OL Dr. U. Abel	after 23.4.44 ✠ Biscay / missing / 59 dead / ✠.[169]
U 194	8.1.43	15.6.43	Kr	KL H. Hesse	24.6.43 ✠ N. Atlantic S.W. of Iceland: 59°00n/26°18w / homing torpedo / Cat G (Lt. J. F. Beach), VP-84 Sqn USN / 54 dead / ✠.[170]

1	2	3	4	5	6
U 525	30.7.42	27.7.43	Lo	KL H.-J. Drewitz	11.8.43 ✠ N. Atlantic N.W. of Azores: 41°29n/38°55w / D/Cs, homing torpedo / Ave (Lt.[jg] C. G. Hewitt), Wil F-18 (Ens. J. H. Stewart), VC-1 Sqn CVE USS *Card* (Capt. A. J. Isbell) / 54 dead / ✠.
U 526	12.8.42	11.2.43	Be	KL H. Möglich	14.4.43 ✠ 10h36 off Lorient near Trois pierre: 47°41,5n/03°22,5w / British air-laid mine / 42 dead / 12 rescued / ↑ 1943, br.
U 527	2.9.42	10.5.43	Lo	KL H. Uhlig	23.7.43 ✠ mid-Atlantic S. of Azores: 35°25n/27°56w / D/Cs / Ave (Lt.[jg] R. L. Stearns), VC-9 Sqn USN CVE USS *Bogue* (Capt. J. B. Dunn) / 40 dead / 13 rescued.
U 528	16.9.42	17.4.43	Kr	OL G. von Rabenau	11.5.43 ✠ N. Atlantic N.W. of Cape Finisterre: 46°55n/14°44w / D/Cs / PS HMS *Fleetwood* (Comdr. W. B. Piggott) following D/Cs damage Hal D (P/O J. B. Stark), 58 Sqn RAF/ 11 dead / 45 rescued.
U 529	30.9.42	2.2.43	Kr	KL G.-W. Fraatz	15.2.43 ✠ 12h04 N. Atlantic: 55°45n/31°09w / D/Cs / Lib S (F/O R. T. F. Turner), 120 Sqn RAF / 48 dead / ✠.[171]
U 530	14.10.42	4.3.45	Kr	OL O. Wermuth	10.7.45 Surrender Mar del Plata, Argentina; U.S. war prize, →United States; tests, 21.11.47 ✠ N. Atlantic N.E. of Cape Cod: 42°39n/69°32w / torpedo SS USS *Toro*.
U 531	28.10.42	15.4.43	Kr	KL H. Neckel	6.5.43 ✠ N. Atlantic N.E. of Newfoundland: 52°48n/45°18w / D/Cs / DD HMS *Vidette* (Lt. R. Hart) / 54 dead / ✠.[172]
U 532	11.11.42	13.1.45	Dj	FK O. Junker	13.5.45 Surrender Loch Eriboll. →Liverpool, →Loch Ryan / 9.12.45 ✠ torpedo SS HMS/m *Tantivy* 56°08n/10°07w / Op. Deadlight.
U 533	25.11.42	6.7.43	Lo	KL H. Hennig	16.10.43 ✠ Arabian Sea, Gulf of Oman: 25°28n/56°50e / D/Cs / Bis O (Sgt L. Chapman), 244 Sqn RAF / 52 dead / 1 rescued.
U 534	23.12.42	1.5.45	Ki	KL H. Nollau	5.5.45 ✠ 12h43 Baltic, Kattegat E. of Anholt: 56°45n/11°52e / D/Cs / Lib G (W/O J. D. Nicol), 86 Sqn RAF / 3 dead / 49 rescued / ↑ 23.8.93, →Hirtshals, 1995 →Liverpool, 30.5.96 arrived Birkenhead for display as museum boat.[173]

1	2	3	4	5	6
U 535	23.12.42	27.5.43	Kr	KL H. Ellmenreich	5.7.43 ✞ Biscay W. of Cape Ortegal: 43°38n/09°13w / D/Cs / Lib G (F/Sgt W. Anderson), 53 Sqn RAF / 55 dead / ✞.
U 536	13.1.43	29.8.43	Lo	KL R. Schauenburg	20.11.43 ✞ N. Atlantic N.E. of Azores: 43°50n/19°39w / D/Cs / PF HMS *Nene* (Comdr. J. D. Birch), PE's HMCS *Snowberry* (Lt. J. A. Dunn), HMCS *Calgary* (Lt. Comdr. H. K. Hill) / 38 dead / 17 rescued.
U 537	27.1.43	9.11.44	Sr	KL P. Schrewe	10.11.44 ✞ 00h26 Pacific, Java Sea E. of Soerabaja: 07°13s/115°17e / torpedoes / SS USS *Flounder* (Comdr. J. E. Stevens) / 58 dead / ✞.
U 538	10.2.43	24.10.43	Be	KL J.-E. Gossler	21.11.43 ✞ N. Atlantic: 45°40n/19°35w / D/Cs / DE HMS *Foley* (Lt. Comdr. D. E. Mansfield), PS HMS *Crane* (Lt. Comdr. R. G. Jenkins) / 55 dead / ✞.
U 539	24.2.43			KL H.-J. Lauterbach-Emden	9.5.45 Surrender Bergen, 2.6.45 sailed →Loch Ryan / 4.12.45 ✞ foundered while under tow 55°38,5n/07°57w / Op. Deadlight.
U 540	10.3.43	4.10.43	Be	KL L. Kasch	17.10.43 ✞ N. Atlantic S.E. of Cape Farewell: 58°38n/31°56w / D/Cs / Lib H (A/W/O B. W. Tumbull), 120 Sqn RAF, Lib D (F/L E. Knowles), 59 Sqn RAF / 55 dead / ✞.
U 541	24.3.43	10.4.45	Kr	KL K. Petersen	12.5.45 Surrender Gibraltar, →Lisahally / 5.1.46 ✞ artillery DD HMS *Onslaught* 55°38n/07°35,6 / Op. Deadlight.
U 542	7.4.43	23.10.43	Kr	OL C.-B. Coester	26.11.43 ✞ 05h25 N. Atlantic N. of Madeira: 39°35n/19°51w / D/Cs / Wel H (F/Sgt. D. M. Cornish), 179 Sqn RAF / 56 dead / ✞.[174]
U 543	21.4.43	28.3.44	Lo	KL H.-J. Hellriegel	2.7.44 ✞ mid-Atlantic S.W. of Canary Is.: 25°34n/21°36w / D/Cs, homing torpedo / Ave T-30 (Ens. F. L. Moore), VC-58 Sqn USN CVE USS *Wake Island* (Capt. J. R. Tague) / 58 dead / ✞.
U 544	5.5.43	13.11.43	Be	KL W. Mattke	16.1.44 ✞ N. Atlantic N.W. of Azores: 40°30n/37°20w / D/Cs, rockets / Ave T-12 (Ens. W. M. McLane), VC-13 Sqn USN CVE USS *Guadalcanal* (Capt. D. V. Gallery) / 57 dead / ✞.
U 545	19.5.43	11.12.43	Kr	KL Dr. G. Mannesmann	11.2.44 (✞) 13h00 N. Atlantic W. of Hebrides: 58°17n/13°22w / following D/Cs damage Wel O (P/O M. H. Paynter), 612 Sqn RAF 10.2.44 / 1 dead / 56 rescued.

1	2	3	4	5	6
U 546	2.6.43	21.3.45	Kr	KL P. Just	24.4.45 ✠ N. Atlantic N.W. of Azores: 43°53n/40°07w / D/Cs / DE's USS *Flaherty* (Lt. Comdr. H. C. Duff), USS *Neunzer* (Lt. Comdr. V. E. Gex), USS *Chatelain* (Lt. Comdr. D. S. Knox), USS *Varian* (Lt. Comdr. L. A. Myhre), USS *Janssen* (Lt. Comdr. S. G. Rubinow, Jr.), USS *Joseph C. Hubbard* (Comdr. L. C. Mabley), USS *Pillsbury* (Lt. Comdr. G. W. Cassleman), USS *Keith* (Lt. Comdr. W. W. Patrick) / 26 dead / 33 rescued.
U 547	16.6.43			OL H. Niemeyer	31.12.44 decomm. Stettin following damage British air-laid mine, field "Deodar" 11.8.44 Gironde off Pauillac; 1945 planned as floating torpedo fire station at HKT, final fate ?
U 548	30.6.43	7.3.45	Kr	OL E. Krempl	19.4.45 ✠ N. Atlantic S.E. of Halifax: 42°19n/61°45w / D/Cs / DE's USS *Buckley* (Lt. R. R. Crutchfield), USS *Reuben James* (Lt. Comdr. G. Cowherd) / 58 dead / ✠.[175]
U 549	14.7.43	14.5.44	Lo	KL D. Krankenhagen	29.5.44 ✠ mid-Atlantic S.W. of Madeira: 31°13n/23°03w / D/Cs / DE's USS *Eugene E. Elmore* (Lt. Comdr. G. L. Conkey), USS *Ahrens* (Comdr. M. H. Harris) / 57 dead / ✠.
U 550	28.7.43	9.2.44	Kr	KL K. Hänert	16.4.44 ✠ N. Atlantic E. of New York: 40°09n/69°44w / D/Cs, artillery / DE's USS *Gandy* (Lt. Comdr. W. A. Sessions), USS *Joyce* (Lt. Comdr. R. Wilcox), USS *Peterson* (Lt. Comdr. S. M. Hay) / 44 dead / 12 rescued.
U 801	24.3.43	26.2.44	Lo	KL H.-J. Brans	17.3.44 ✠ mid-Atlantic W. of Cape Verde Is.: 16°42n/30°28w / homing torpedo, D/Cs, artillery / Ave (Lt.[jg] C. A. Wooddell), Wil (Lt.[jg] P. Sorenson), Ave (Lt.[jg] N. T. Dowty), VC-6 Sqn USN CVE USS *Block Island* (Capt. F. M. Hughes) and DD USS *Corry* (Lt. Comdr. G. D. Hoffman), DE USS *Bronstein* (Lt. S. H. Kinney) / 9 dead / 47 rescued.
U 802	12.6.43	3.5.45	Be	KL H. Schmoeckel	11.5.45 Surrender Loch Eriboll. →Lisahally / 31.12.45 ✠ foundered while under tow 55°30n/08°25w / Op. Deadlight.

1	2	3	4	5	6
U 803	7.9.43			KL K. Schimpf	27.4.44 ✠ 07h00 Baltic N. of Swinemünde: 54°06,7n/14°35,5e / British air-laid mine, field "Geranium" / 9 dead / 49 rescued / ↑8.8.44, →Swinemünde, wreck April 45 captured by USSR forces, August 1946 still at Swinemünde, final fate ?
U 804	4.12.43	4.4.45	Ki	OL H. Meyer	9.4.45 ✠ North Sea N.W. of Göteborg: 57°58n/11°15e / rockets / Mos Z, X, W. N, Q, J, RAF Sqn 143, Mos H, S, R, D, RAF Sqn 235, Mos N, Z, L, RAF Sqn 248 / 55 dead / ✠.
U 805	12.2.44	17.3.45	Dr	KK R. Bernardelli	15.5.45 Surrender Portsmouth (N.H.), Victory Visits US East Coast, 8.2.46 ✠ N. Atlantic N.E. of Cape Cod: 42°32n/69°27w / torpedo SS USS *Sirago*.
U 806	29.4.44			KL K. Hornbostel	6.5.45 Surrender Aarhus, →Wilhelmshaven, 22.6.45 →Loch Ryan / 21.12.45 ✠ artillery DD ORP *Blyskawica* 55°44n/08°18w / Op. Deadlight.
U 807– U 812					30.9.43 suspension announced, 6.11.43 contract suspended, 22.7.44 contract canceled.
U 813– U 816					30.9.43 cancelation announced, 6.11.43 contract canceled.
U 841	6.2.43	4.10.43	Dr	KL W. Bender	17.10.43 ✠ N. Atlantic E. of Cape Farewell: 59°57n/31°06w / D/Cs / DE HMS *Byard* (Lt. Comdr. L. H. Phillips) / 27 dead / 27 rescued.
U 842	1.3.43	5.10.43	Be	KK W. Heller	6.11.43 ✠ 14h N. Atlantic W. of Newfoundland: 43°42n/42°08w / D/Cs / PS's HMS *Starling* (Comdr. F. J. Walker), HMS *Wild Goose* (Lt. Comdr. D. E. G. Wemyss) / 56 dead / ✠.
U 843	24.3.43	8.4.45	Kr	KL O. Herwartz	9.4.45 ✠ Baltic, Kattegat W. of Göteborg: 57°32,6n/11°23,6e / rockets / Mos A (F/O A. J. Rendell), 235 Sqn RAF / 44 dead / 12 rescued / ↑ 22.8.58, br 1958/59 Göteborg.
U 844	7.4.43	6.10.43	Be	OL G. Möller	16.10.43 ✠ N. Atlantic S.W. of Iceland: 58°30n/27°16w / D/Cs / Lib L (F/L E. A. Bland), 86 Sqn RAF, Lib S (F/O W. J. Thomas), 59 Sqn RAF / 53 dead / ✠.

1	2	3	4	5	6
U 845	1.5.43	8.1.44	Be	KK W. Weber	10.3.44 ✠ N. Atlantic: 48°20n/20°33w / D/Cs / DD's HMS *Forester* (Lt. Comdr. J. A. Burnett), HMCS *St Laurent* (Lt. Comdr, G. H. Stephen), PE HMCS *Owen Sound* (Lt. J. M. Watson), PF HMCS *Swansea* (Comdr. C. A. King) / 10 dead / 45 rescued.
U 846	29.5.43	29.4.44	Lo	OL B. Hashagen	4.5.44 ✠ Biscay N. of Spain: 46°04n/09°20w / D/Cs / Wel M (F/O L. J. Bateman), 407 Sqn RCAF / 57 dead / ✠.
U 853	25.6.43	23.2.45	St	OL H. Frömsdorf	6.5.45 ✠ N. Atlantic E. of Long Island: 41°13n/71°27w / D/Cs / DE USS *Atherton* (Lt. Comdr. L. Iselin), PF USS *Moberly* (Lt. Comdr. L. B. Tollaksen) / 55 dead / ✠.
U 854	19.7.43			KL H. Weiher	4.2.44 ✠ 11h57 Baltic N. of Swinemünde: 54°01,8n/14°16,3e / British air-laid mine, field "Geranium" / 51 dead / 7 rescued, ↑18.8.44, →Swinemünde, wreck April 45 captured by USSR forces, final fate ?
U 855	2.8.43	5.7.44	Aa	OL P. Ohlsen	after 11.9.44 ✠ N. Atlantic or Arctic N. of Britain / missing / 56 dead / ✠.[176]
U 856	19.8.43	26.2.44	St	OL F. Wittenberg	7.4.44 ✠ N. Atlantic S.E. of Boston: 40°18n/62°22w / D/Cs / DD USS *Champlin* (Comdr. J. J. Shaffer III), DE USS *Huse* (Lt. Comdr. R. H. Wanless) / 27 dead / 28 rescued.
U 857	16.9.43	8.2.45	Kr	KL R. Premauer	≈?.4.45 ✠ N. Atlantic ≈US East Coast / missing / 59 dead / ✠.[177]
U 858	30.9.43	13.3.45	Kr	KL T. Bode	14.5.45 Surrender Portsmouth (N.H.), August 1945 U.S. war prize, 21.11.47 ✠ N. Atlantic N.E. of Cape Cod: ≈42°41n/69°34w / torpedo SS USS *Sirago*.
U 865	25.10.43	8.9.44	Dr	OL D. Stellmacher	after 8.9.44 ✠ ≈Arctic or N. Atlantic N.W. of Britain / missing / 59 dead / ✠.[178]
U 866	17.11.43	5.2.45	Be	OL P. Rogowsky	18.3.45 ✠ N. Atlantic S.E. of Halifax: 43°18n/61°08w / D/Cs / DE's USS *Lowe* (Lt. Comdr. H. Feldman), USS *Menges* (Lt. Comdr. F. M. McCabe), USS *Pride* (Lt. Comdr. W. H. Buxton), USS *Mosley* (Lt. Comdr. E. P. MacBryde) / 55 dead / ✠.

1	2	3	4	5	6
U 867	12.12.43	12.9.44	Kr	KzS A. von Mühlendahl	19.9.44 (✝) Arctic N.W. of Bergen: 61°57n/02°22,5e / following Diesel damage and D/Cs Lib Q (F/L G. J. Rayner), 224 Sqn RAF / 60 dead / ✝.
U 868	23.12.43			OL E. Turre	9.5.45 Surrender Bergen, 30.5.45 sailed →Loch Ryan / 30.11.45 ✝ foundered while under tow 55°48n/08°33w / Op. Deadlight.
U 869	26.1.44	8.12.44	Kr	KL H. Neuerburg	11.2.45 ✝ 20h53 N. Atlantic S.E. of New York: 39°33n/73°02w / D/Cs / DE's USS *Howard D. Crow* (Lt. J. Nixon), USS *Koiner* (Lt. Comdr. C. Judson) / 56 dead / ✝.[179]
U 870	3.2.44			KK E. Hechler	30.3.45 ✝ Bremen, Deschimag-AG Weser, Industriehafen: 53°08n/08°46e / bomb / air raid 8. USAAF / none dead / ↑ until 7.8.46, br.
U 877	24.3.44	26.11.44	Kr	KL E. Findeisen	27.12.44 ✝ N. Atlantic: 46°25n/36°38w / D/Cs / PE HMCS *St. Thomas* (Lt. Comdr. L. P. Denny) / 55 rescued.
U 878	14.4.44	4.4.45	Na	KL J. Rodig	10.4.45 ✝ N. Atlantic S.W. of Ireland 47°35n/10°33w / D/Cs / DD HMS *Vanquisher* (Lt. Comdr. F. M. Osbourne), PE HMS *Tintagel Castle* (Lt. R. Atkinson) / 51 dead / ✝.
U 879	19.4.44	11.2.45	Kr	KL E. Manchen	30.4.45 ✝ N. Atlantic N.E. of Cape Hatteras: 36°34n/74°00w / D/Cs / PF USS *Natchez* (Lt. J. H. Stafford), DE's USS *Coffman* (Lt. Comdr. J. C. Crocker), USS *Bostwick* (Lt. Comdr. J. R. Davidson), USS *Thomas* (Lt. Comdr. D. M. Kellogg) / 52 dead / ✝.[180]
U 880	11.5.44	14.3.45	Be	KL G. Schötzau	16.4.45 ✝ N. Atlantic: 47°53n/30°26w / D/Cs / DE's USS *Frost* (Lt. Comdr. A. E. Ritchie), USS *Stanton* (Lt. Comdr. J. C. Kiley, Jr.) / 49 dead / ✝.[181]
U 881	27.5.44	7.4.45	Be	KL Dr. K.-H. Frischke	6.5.45 ✝ N. Atlantic S.E. of Newfoundland: 43°18n/47°44w / D/Cs / DE USS *Farquhar* (Lt. Comdr. D. E. Walter) / 53 dead / ✝.[182]
U 882	-------			(OL G. Drescher)	23.9.44 contract suspended, laid up incomplete; 30.3.45 ✝ Bremen, yard basin Deschimag-AG Weser: 53°08n/08°46e / bomb / air raid 8. USAAF / ↑ until 30.7.48, br.

1	2	3	4	5	6
U 889	4.8.44	5.4.45	Kr	KL F. Braeucker	13.5.45 Surrender Shelburne: 43°32n/65°12w, →Halifax, 28.5.45 →Canada, tests; August 1945 U.S. war prize, 10.(12.?).1.46 →United States, 20.11.47 ✝ N. Atlantic N.E. of Cape Cod: ≈42°37n/69°33w / torpedo SS USS *Flying Fish*.
U 890	-------			(OL F. Blaich)	29.7.44 ✝ Bremen, Deschimag-AG Weser, Industriehafen, Becken F: 53°08n/08°46e / bomb / air raid 8. USAAF / 23.9.44 contract canceled, ↑ until 7.8.46, br.
U 891	-------			(OL K. Mehne)	23.9.44 contract suspended, laid up incomplete; 30.3.45 ✝ Bremen, yard basin Deschimag-AG Weser: 53°08n/08°46e / bomb / air raid 8. USAAF / ↑ until 9.9.47, br.
U 892					30.9.43 suspension announced, 6.11.43 contract suspended, construction abandoned immediately after keel laying, taken up late 1943 on slip No. 9a Deschimag-AG Weser, 22.7.44 contract cancelled.
U 893– U 894					30.9.43 suspension announced, 6.11.43 contract suspended, 22.7.44 contract canceled.
U 1221	11.8.43			OL P. Ackermann	3.4.45 ✝ Kiel Fiord near buoy A 7: 54°20n/10°10,2e / bomb / air raid 8. USAAF / 7 dead / 11 rescued.
U 1222	1.9.43	15.4.44	Kr	KL H. Bielfeld	11.7.44 ✝ Biscay W. of La Rochelle: 46°31n/05°29w / D/Cs / Sun P (F/L I. F. B. Walters), 201 Sqn RAF / 56 dead / ✝.
U 1223	6.10.43			OL A. Kneip	14.4.45 decomm. Wesermünde, 5.5.45 (✝) W. of Wesermünde: 53°32n/08°35e / br.
U 1224	20.10.43			KL G. Preuß	donation of Germany to the Emperor of Japan, during work up training duplicate Japanese crew aboard, 15.2.44 Kiel transferred to Japan.
	28.2.44	1.4.44	Kr	KK S. Norita	comm. as *RO-501* for IJN, 13.5.44 ✝ mid-Atlantic N.W. of Cape Verde Is.: 18°08n/33°13w / D/Cs / DE USS *Francis M. Robinson* (Lt. Comdr. J. E. Johansen) during transfer to Japan with Japanese crew.
U 1225	10.11.43	19.6.44	Kr	OL E. Sauerberg	24.6.44 ✝ Arctic N.W. of Bergen: 63°00n/00°50w / D/Cs / Cat P (F/L D. E. Hornell), 162 Sqn RCAF / 56 dead / ✝.

1	2	3	4	5	6
U 1226	24.11.43	4.10.44	Kr	OL A.-W. Claussen	after 23.10.44 ✠ N. Atlantic / missing / 56 dead / ✠.[183]
U 1227	8.12.43			OL F. Altmeier	9.4.45 ✠ Kiel, Deutsche Werke inside dry-dock No. 1: 54°21n/10°09e / bomb / air raid 1, 3, and 8 Groups RAF Bomber Command, 10.4.45 decomm. / br.
U 1228	22.12.43	14.4.45	Kr	OL F.-W. Marienfeld	17.5.45 Surrender Portsmouth (N.H.) / August 1945 U.S. war prize, 5.2.46 ✠ N. Atlantic N.E. of Cape Cod: 42°30n/69°38w / torpedo SS USS *Sirago*.
U 1229	13.1.44	26.7.44	Dr	KK A. Zinke	20.8.44 ✠ N. Atlantic S.E. of Newfoundland: 42°20n/51°39w / D/Cs, rockets / Ave T-19 (Lt.[jg] A. X. Brokas), Ave T-16 (Lt.[jg] B. C. Sissler), Ave T-21 (Lt.[jg] M. J. Sherbring), Wil F-9 (Lt.[jg] J. Sulton, Jr.), Wil F-7 (Lt. J. B. Watson), VC-42 Sqn USN CVE USS *Bogue* (Capt. A. B. Vosseller) / 18 dead / 41 rescued.
U 1230	26.1.44			KL H. Hilbig	5.5.45 Surrender Heligoland, →Wilhelmshaven, 22.6.45 →Loch Ryan / 17.12.45 ✠ artillery DD HMS *Onslow*, DE HMS *Cubitt* 55°50n/10°05w / Op. Deadlight.
U 1231	9.2.44	27.4.45	Kr	OL H. Wicke	13.5.45 Surrender Loch Foyle; HMS/m *N 26*, August 1945 USSR war prize, 6.12.45 at Libau →USSR, 13.2.46 Soviet *N-26*. South Baltic Fleet. 9.6.49 *B-26*, 17.8.53 Reserve, 15.9.53 combat training hulk *KBP-33*, 27.12.56 training hulk *UTS-23*, § 13.1.68, Riga br.
U 1232	8.3.44			OL G. Roth	27.4.45 decomm. Wesermünde / May 45 captured by British forces, 4.3.46 ✠ 54°11,2n/07°24,7e foundered while under tow to scuttling place.
U 1233	22.3.44			OL H. Niemeyer	5.5.45 Surrender Fredericia, →Wilhelmshaven, 22.6.45 →Loch Ryan / 29.12.45 ✠ artillery DD HMS *Onslaught* 55°51n/08°54w / Op. Deadlight.
U 1234	19.4.44			KL H. Thurmann	14.5.44 ✠ 23h00 Gotenhafen Roads: 54°32,6n/18°37,3e / collision / German D/f *Anton* / 13 dead / 43 rescued / ↑ 15.5.44, →Gotenhafen, repaired Oderwerke Stettin.
				OL H. C. Wrede	5.5.45 (✠) Hörup Haff: 54°53n/09°52e / br.

1	2	3	4	5	6
U 1235	17.5.44	19.3.45	Be	KL F. Barsch	15.4.45 ✞ N. Atlantic: 47°54n/30°25w / D/Cs / DE's USS *Stanton* (Lt. Comdr. J. C. Kiley, Jr.), USS *Frost* (Lt. Comdr. A. E. Ritchie) / 57 dead / ✞.[184]
U 1236	-------			(KK R. Schendel)	construction abandoned 1944, 23.9.44 contract suspended; laid up incomplete, 3.5.45 (✞) Hamburg, Hansa basin, Oswald quay: 53°31,8n/10°00,1e / ↑ 7./8.1945. →Blankenese, br.
U 1237	-------				construction abandoned 1944, 23.9.44 contract suspended; laid up incomplete, 3.5.45 (✞) Hamburg Finkenwerder, Rüschkanal S.E. of U-boat pen Fink II: 53°32,5n/09°51,3e / 1945 br.
U 1238	-------				construction abandoned 1944, 23.9.44 contract suspended; laid up incomplete. 30.3.45 ✞ Hamburg Finkenwerder, Rüschkanal S.E. of U-boat pen Fink II: 53°32,5n/09°51,3e / bomb / air raid 8. USAAF / br.
U 1239					construction abandoned 1944, 23.9.44 contract suspended, 3.5.45 incomplete hull captured by British forces on slip No. 2 Deutsche Werft Hamburg, 31.12.45 blown up, br.
U 1240					construction abandoned 1944, 23.9.44 contract suspended, 3.5.45 incomplete hull captured by British forces on slip No. 2 Deutsche Werft Hamburg, 31.12.45 blown up, br.
U 1241					construction abandoned after keel laying owing to lack of manpower, broken up early 1944 on slip No. 2 Deutsche Werft Hamburg, 23.9.44 contract canceled.
U 1242					construction abandoned after keel laying owing to lack of manpower, broken up early 1944 on slip No. 2 Deutsche Werft Hamburg, 23.9.44 contract canceled.
U 1243					23.9.44 contract canceled.
U 1244					23.9.44 contract canceled.
U 1245– U 1250					30.9.43 suspension announced, 6.11.43 contract suspended, 22.7.44 contract canceled.
U 1251– U 1262					30.9.43 cancelation announced, 6.11.43 contract canceled.
U 1501– U 1506					30.9.43 suspension announced, 6.11.43 contract suspended, 22.7.44 contract canceled.

1	2	3	4	5	6
U 1507– U 1512					10.7.43 contract canceled, 6.11.43 cancelation confirmed.
U 1513– U 1515					30.9.43 suspension announced, 6.11.43 contract suspended, 22.7.44 contract canceled.
U 1516– U 1530					10.7.43 contract canceled, 6.11.43 cancelation confirmed.

Type IX D1

Oceangoing long-range high-speed combat U-boat type of conventional design developed in 1939–40, 1943–44 main propulsion unit removed and converted into transport U-boats
Surface/submerged displacement: 1610/1799 t
Overall length/beam/draught: 87.58 m/7.50 m/5.35 m
Standard main armament: 6 torpedo tubes (4 bow, 2 stern) with up to 25 torpedoes, tubes removed during conversion 1943-44

Building yard	Total no. ordered	Completed (comm.)	Under construction	Construction not started	Canceled after keel laying	Canceled prior to keel laying
Deschimag AG Weser Bremen	2	2	—	—	—	—
Total	2	2	—	—	—	—

1	2	3	4	5	6
U 180	16.5.42			FK W. Musenberg	30.9.43 decomm. Bordeaux, conversion to transport boat at Bordeaux, recomm. Bordeaux.
	2.4.44	22.8.44	Bo	OL R. Riesen	after 23.8.44 ✝ Biscay W. of Bordeaux / missing / 56 dead / ✝.[185]
U 195	5.9.42			KK H. Buchholz	17.10.43 decomm. Bordeaux, conversion to transport boat at Bordeaux, recomm. Bordeaux.
	?.5.44			OL F. Steinfeldt	6.5.45 taken over by Japan at Surabaya; 15.7.45 Japanese *I-506*; 8.45 Surrender Surabaya, 15.2.46 ✝ artillery LS HMS *LST 3036* 06°50s/114°42e.

Type IX D2

Oceangoing very long-range combat U-boat type of conventional design developed in 1939–40
Surface/submerged displacement: 1616/1804 t
Overall length/beam/draught: 87.58 m/7.50 m/5.35 m
Standard main armament: 6 torpedo tubes (4 bow, 2 stem) with up to 27 torpedoes

Building yard	Total no. ordered	Completed (comm.)	Under construction	Construction not started	Canceled after keel laying	Canceled prior to keel laying
Deschimag AG Weser Bremen	28	28	—	—	—	—
Total	28	28	—	—	—	—

1	2	3	4	5	6
U 177	14.3.42	2.1.44	Pa	KK H. Buchholz	6.2.44 ✠ S. Atlantic S.W. of Ascension: 10°35s/23°15w / D/Cs / Lib B-3 (Lt. [jg] C. I. Pinnell), VB-107 Sqn USN / 50 dead / 15 rescued.
U 178	14.2.42			KL W. Spahr	20.8.44 decomm. Bordeaux, unserviceable, laid up, 25.8.44 (✠) Bordeaux, U-boat pen: 44°52n/00°34w / 1947 br.
U 179	7.3.42	17.8.42	Kr	FK E. Sobe	8.10.42 ✠ S. Atlantic W. of Capetown: 33°28s/17°05e / D/Cs / DD HMS *Active* (Lt. Comdr. M. W. Tomkinson) / 61 dead / ✠.
U 181	9.5.42			KzS K. Freiwald	6.5.45 taken over by Japan at Singapore, 15.7.45 Japanese *I-501;* 7.8.45 Surrender Singapore, 16.2.46 (✠) D/Cs PF's HMS *Loch Glendhu*, HMS *Loch Lomond* 03°05,5n/100°41,5e.
U 182	30.6.42	11.12.42	Eg	KK N. Clausen	15.5.43 ✠ mid-Atlantic W. of Madeira: 31°40n/21°15w / D/Cs / Lib Q (1ˢᵗ Lt. E. A. Powers), 2nd A/S Sqn USAAF / 61 dead / ✠.[186]
U 196	11.9.42	30.11.44	Dj	OL H. W. Striegler	≈30.11.44 ✠ Indian Ocean ≈Sunda Strait / missing / 65 dead / ✠.[187]
U 197	10.10.42	6.4.43	Kr	KK R. Bartels	20.8.43 ✠ Indian Ocean S. of Madagascar: 28°40s/42°36e / D/Cs / Cat C (F/L O. Barnett), 259 Sqn RAF, Cat N (F/O C. E. Robin), 265 Sqn RAF / 66 dead / ✠.
U 198	3.11.42	20.4.44	Pa	OL B. Heusinger von Waldegg	12.8.44 ✠ Indian Ocean W. of Seychelles: 03°35s/52°49e / D/Cs / PF HMS *Findhorn* (Lt. Comdr. J. C. Dawson), PS HInMS *Godavari* (Comdr. A. B. Goord) / 66 dead / ✠.

1	2	3	4	5	6
U 199	28.11.42	16.5.43	Be	KL H.-W. Kraus	31.7.43 ♱ S. Atlantic E. of Rio de Janeiro: 23°54s/42°54w / D/Cs / Mar V (Lt.[jg] W. F. Smith), VP-74 Sqn USN, Cat No. 14 (Cadet A. M. Torres), Hud (Lt. S. C. Schnoor), 7th Air Base Corps, FAB / 49 dead / 12 rescued.
U 200	22.12.42	15.6.43	Kr	KL H. Schonder	24.6.43 ♱ N. Atlantic S.W. of Iceland: 58°15n/25°25w / D/Cs / Lib H (A/F/L A. W. Fraser), 120 Sqn RAF / 68 dead / ♱.[188]
U 847	23.1.43	29.7.43	Be	KL H. Kuppisch	27.8.43 ♱ mid-Atlantic: 28°19n/37°58w / homing torpedo / Ave (Lt. R. W. Long), Wil (Lt.[jg] F. M. Roundtree), Wil (Ens. J. H. Stewart), VC-1 Sqn USN CVE USS *Card* (Capt. M. R. Greer) / 62 dead / ♱.
U 848	20.2.43	21.9.43	Kr	KK W. Rollmann	5.11.43 ♱ S. Atlantic S.W. of Ascension: 10°10s/18°12w / D/Cs / Lib B-8 (Lt. W. E. Hill), Lib B-4 (Lt. S. K. Taylor, Jr.), Lib B-12 (Lt. C. A. Baldwin), Lib B-4 (Lt. W. R. Ford), VB-107 Sqn USN, Mit 41-12540 (Capt. P. Main), Mit 41-12629 (Maj. R. T. Akins), 1st Composite Sqn USAAF / 63 dead / ♱.
U 849	11.3.43	7.10.43	Fa	KL H.-O. Schultze	25.11.43 ♱ S. Atlantic E. of Ascencion: 06°30s/05°40w / D/Cs / Lib B-6 (Lt.[jg] M. V. Dawkins, Jr.), VB-107 Sqn USN / 63 dead / ♱.
U 850	17.4.43	20.11.43	Kr	FK K. Ewerth	20.12.43 ♱ mid-Atlantic S.W. of Azores: 32°54n/37°01w / D/Cs, homing torpedo / Ave T-12 (Lt.[jg] W. A. LaFleur), Ave T-19 (Lt.[jg] G. C. Goodwin), Ave T-18 (Lt.[jg] H. G. Bradshaw), Wil (Lt.[jg] I. G.. Cockroft), Wil (Lt. K. P. Hance). VC-19 Sqn USN CVE USS *Bogue* (Capt. J. B. Dunn) / 66 dead / ♱.
U 851	21.5.43	28.2.44	Kr	KK H. Weingaertner	after 27.3.44 ♱ mid-Atlantic / missing / 70 dead / ♱.[189]
U 852	15.6.43	20.1.44	Kr	KL H.-W. Eck	3.5.44 (♱) Indian Ocean S. of Cape Guardafui: 09°32n/50°45e / deliberately beached and blown up following D/Cs damage Wel E (F/O R. H. Mitchell), Wel T (W/C P. Green), Wel F (F/O E. W. Read), Wel D (W/O J. P. Ryall), Wel U (F/L J. Y. Wade), 621 Sqn RAF and Wel G (F/O J. R. Forrester), 8 Sqn RAF 2.5.44 / 7 dead / 59 rescued.
U 859	8.7.43	8.4.44	Kr	KL J. Jebsen	23.9.44 ♱ 06h32 Indian Ocean, Malacca Strait N.W. of Penang: 05°48,5n/100°02,7e / torpedo / SS HMS/m *Trenchant* (Lt. Comdr. A. R. Hezlet) / 47 dead / 19 rescued.

1	2	3	4	5	6
U 860	12.8.43	13.4.44	Kr	FK P. Büchel	15.6.44 ✠ S. Atlantic S. of St. Helena: 25°27s/05°30w / D/Cs, rockets / Ave T-12 (Ens. G. E. Edwards, Jr.), Ave T-33 (Lt. Comdr. H. M. Avery), Ave T-11 (Ens. M. J. Spear), Ave T-32 (Lt.[jg] W. F. Chamberlain), Ave T-1 (Lt.[jg] D. E. Weigle), Wil F-17 (Ens. T. J. Wadsworth), Wil F-23 (Ens. R. E. McMahon), VC-9 Sqn USN CVE USS *Solomons* (Capt. M. E. Crist) / 44 dead / 20 rescued.
U 861	2.9.43			KK J. Oesten	9.5.45 Surrender Trondheim, 29.5.45 sailed →Lisahally / 31.12.45 ✠ artillery DD ORP *Blyskawica* 55°25n/07°15w / Op. Deadlight.
U 862	7.10.43			KK H. Timm	6.5.45 taken over by Japan at Singapore, 15.7.45 Japanese *I-502;* 8.45 Surrender Singapore, 13.2.46 (✠) 03°05n/100°38,7e D/Cs PF's HMS *Loch Glendhu*, HMS *Loch Lomond*.
U 863	3.11.43	26.7.44	Dr	KL D. von der Esch	29.9.44 ✠ S. Atlantic S.E. of Recife: 10°45s/25°30w / D/Cs / Lib B-9 (Lt. J. T. Burton), Lib B-7 (Lt. E. A. Krug, Jr.), VB-107 Sqn USN / 69 dead / ✠.
U 864	9.12.43	7.2.45	Be	KK R.-R. Wolfram	9.2.45 ✠ North Sea N.W. of Bergen: 60°46n/04°35e / torpedo / SS HMS/m *Venturer* (Lt. J. S. Launders) / 75 dead / ✠.
U 871	15.1.44	31.8.44	Dr	KL E. Ganzer	26.9.44 ✠ N. Atlantic N.W. of Azores: 43°18n/36°28w / D/Cs / For P (F/L A. F. Wallace), 220 Sqn RAF / 69 dead / ✠.
U 872	10.2.44			KL P. O. Grau	29.7.44 ✠ Bremen, yard basin Deschimag-AG Weser: 53°06,9n/08°44,5e / bomb / air raid 8. USAAF / 1 dead / 10.8.44 decomm. / 1946 br.
U 873	1.3.44	31.3.45	Kr	KL F. Steinhoff	16.5.45 Surrender Portsmouth (N.H.) / August 1945 U.S. war prize, tests, 10.3.48 New York sold for scrap, 1948 br.
U 874	8.4.44			OL T. Petersen	9.5.45 Surrender Horten, 27.5.45 sailed →Lisahally / 31.12.45 ✠ artillery DD HMS *Offa* 55°47n/09°27w / Op. Deadlight.
U 875	21.4.44			KL G. Preuß	9.5.45 Surrender Bergen, 2.6.45 sailed →Lisahally / 31.12.45 ✠ artillery DD HMS *Offa* 55°41n/08°28w / Op. Deadlight.
U 876	24.5.44			KL R. Bahn	3.5.45 (✠) Eckernförde Bay: 54°29,5n/09°59,8e(?) / 1947 br.[190]

Type IX D/42

Oceangoing very long-range combat U-boat type of conventional design developed in 1942. First two units converted to transport U-boats during construction in 1944.

Surface/submerged displacement:		1616/1804 t				
Overall length/beam/draught:		87.58 m/7.50 m/5.35 m				
Standard main armament:		6 torpedo tubes (4 bow, 2 stern) with up to 27 torpedoes, after conversion to transport role in 1944 all bow torpedo tubes removed with 5 torpedoes remaining in the stern compartment				

Building yard	Total no. ordered	Completed (comm.)	Under construction	Construction not started	Canceled after keel laying	Canceled prior to keel laying
Deschimag AG Weser Bremen	24	1	1	—	—	22
Total	24	1	1	—	—	22

1	2	3	4	5	6
U 883	27.3.45			OL J. Uebel	5.5.45 Surrender Cuxhaven, →Wilhelmshaven; 21.6.45 sailed →Lisahally / 31.12.45 ✝ artillery DD HMS *Offa* 55°41n/08°40w / Op. Deadlight.
U 884	--------			(OL G. Lüders)	30.3.45 ✝ Bremen, Deschimag-AG Weser, Industriehafen: 53°06,9n/08°44,5e / bomb / air raid 8. USAAF / ↑ until 7.8.46, br.
U 885– U 888					30.9.43 suspension announced, 6.11.43 contract suspended, 22.7.44 contract canceled.
U 895– U 900					10.7.43 contract canceled, 6.11.43 cancelation confirmed.
U 1531– U 1542					10.7.43 contract canceled, 6.11.43 cancelation confirmed

Type X B

Oceangoing long-range mine-laying/supply U-boat type of conventional design developed in 1937

Surface/submerged displacement:	1763/2132 t
Overall length/beam/draught:	89.80 m/9.20 m/4.71 m
Standard main armament:	30 vertical mine tubes with 66 mines (SMA type), 2 stern torpedo tubes with up to 7 torpedoes, 1942–1944 in addition up to 8 reserve torpedoes in watertight containers alongside deck

Building yard	Total no. ordered	Completed (comm.)	Under Construction	Construction not started	Canceled after keel laying	Canceled prior to keel laying
Germaniawerft AG Kiel	8	8	—	—	—	—
Total	8	8	—	—	—	—

1	2	3	4	5	6
U 116	26.7.41	22.9.42	Lo	OL W. Grimme	after 6.10.42 ✠ N. Atlantic or Biscay / missing / 56 dead / ✠.[191]
U 117	25.10.41	22.7.43	Bo	KK H.-W. Neumann	7.8.43 ✠ N. Atlantic N.W. of Azores: 39°32n/38°21w / D/Cs, homing torpedo / Ave T-10 (Lt.[jg] A. H. Sallenger), Ave (Lt. C. R. Stapler), Ave (Lt.[jg] J. C. Forney) and Wil (Lt. N. D. Hodson), Wil (Lt.[jg] E. E. Jackson), VC-1 Sqn USN CVE USS *Card* (Capt. A. J. Isbell) / 62 dead / ✠.
U 118	6.12.41	25.5.43	Bo	KK W. Czygan	12.6.43 ✠ mid-Atlantic S.W. of Azores: 30°49n/33°49w / D/Cs / Ave T-12 (Lt.[jg] R. L. Steams), Ave (Lt.[jg] W. S. Fowler), Ave (Lt.[jg] H. E. Fryatt), Ave (Lt.[jg] W. F. Chamberlain), Wil (Lt.[jg] R. J. Johnson), Wil (Lt.[jg] R. J. Tennant), Wil (Lt.[jg] P. Perabo), VC-9 Sqn USN CVE USS *Bogue* (Capt. G. E. Short) / 43 dead / 16 rescued.
U 119	2.4.42	25.4.43	Bo	KL H.-T. von Kameke	24.6.43 ✠ N. Atlantic N.W. of Spain: 44°59n/12°24w / D/Cs, ramming / PS HMS *Starling* (Comdr. F. J. Walker) / 56 dead / ✠.
U 219	12.12.42			KK W. Burghagen	6.5.45 taken over by Japan at Jakarta, 15.7.45 Japanese *I-505*; ?.8.45 Surrender Jakarta / 3.2.46 (✠) artillery DD HNLMS *Kortenaer* 06°31s/104°54,8e.
U 220	27.3.43	8.9.43	Be	OL B. Barber	28.10.43 ✠ N. Atlantic: 48°53n/33°30w / D/Cs / Ave T-1 (Lt. F. M. Murray), Wil F-19 (Ens. H. L. Handshuh), VC-1 Sqn USN CVE USS *Block Island* (Capt. L. C. Ramsey) / 56 dead / ✠.[192]

1	2	3	4	5	6
U 233	22.9.43	29.5.44	Kr	KL H. Steen	5.7.44 ✝ 17h N. Atlantic S.E. of Halifax: 42°16n/59°49w / D/Cs, artillery, ramming / DE's USS *Baker* (Lt. Comdr. N. C. Hoffman), USS *Thomas* (Lt. Comdr. D. M. Kellogg) / 32 dead / 29 rescued.
U 234	2.3.44	16.4.45	Kr	KL J.-H. Fehler	19.5.45 Surrender Portsmouth (N.H.) / 8.45 U.S. war prize, 20.11.47 ✝ N. Atlantic N.E. of Cape Cod: ≈42°37n/69°33w / torpedo SS USS *Greenfish*.

Type XI

Oceangoing very long-range combat U-Cruiser type of conventional design developed in 1937–38

Surface/submerged displacement:	3140/3930 t
Overall length/beam/draught:	114.96 m/9.50 m/6.17 m
Standard main armament:	6 torpedo tubes (4 bow, 2 stern) with up to 12 torpedoes, four 5 inch guns in twin turrets

Building yard	Total no. ordered	Completed (comm.)	Under construction	Construction not started	Canceled after keel laying	Canceled prior to keel laying
Deschimag AG Weser Bremen	4	—	—	—	—	4
Total	4	—	—	—	—	4

1	2	3	4	5	6
U 112– U 115					Contract suspended in September 1939 before keel laying, contract canceled in May 1940.

Type XIV

Oceangoing supply U-boat type of conventional design developed in 1939–40

Surface/submerged displacement:	1688/1932 t
Overall length/beam/draught:	67.10 m/9.35 m/6.51 m
Standard main armament:	none except A/A artillery, carried for supply 618 t fuel oil, 13 t motor oil, miscellaneous provisions plus 4 spare torpedoes in upperdeck containers

Building yard	Total no. ordered	Completed (comm.)	Under construction	Construction not started	Canceled after keel laying	Canceled prior to keel laying
Deutsche Werke Kiel AG	13	10	—	—	3	—
Germaniawerft AG Kiel	11	—	—	—	4	7
Total	24	10	—	—	7	7

1	2	3	4	5	6
U 459	15.11.41	22.7.43	Bo	KK G. Wilamowitz-Moellendorff	24.7.43 ✠ N. Atlantic N.W. of Spain: 45°53n/10°38w / D/Cs / Wel Q (F/O W. T. H. Jennings), 172 Sqn RAF, Wel V (F/O J. Whyte), 547 Sqn RAF / 19 dead / 41 rescued.
U 460	24.12.41	30.8.43	Bo	KL E. Schnoor	4.10.43 ✠ N. Atlantic N. of Azores: 43°13n/28°58w / diving accident during attack Ave T-3 (Lt.[jg] R. L. Stearns), Ave T-9 (Lt.[jg] D. E. Weigle), Wil F-16 (Lt.[jg] E. S. Heim), Wil F-19 (Lt.[jg] D. O. Puckett), VC-9 Sqn USN CVE USS *Card* (Capt. A. J. Isbell) / 62 dead / 2 rescued.[193]
U 461	30.1.42	27.7.43	Bo	KK W.-H. Stiebler	30.7.43 ✠ 12h06 N. Atlantic N.W. of Spain: 45°33n/10°47w / D/Cs / Sun U (F/L D. Marrows), 461 Sqn RAAF / 53 dead / 15 rescued.
U 462	5.3.42	27.7.43	Bo	OL B. Vowe	30.7.43 ✠ 12h14 N. Atlantic N.W. of Spain: 45°33n/10°48w / D/Cs, artillery / Hal S (F/O A. van Rossum), 502 Sqn RAF and PS's HMS *Kite* (Lt. Comdr. W. E. R. Segrave), HMS *Wren* (Lt. Comdr. R. M. Aubrey), HMS *Woodcock* (Lt. Comdr. C. Gwinner), HMS *Woodpecker* (Lt. Comdr. R. E. S. Hugonin), HMS *Wild Goose* (Comdr. F. J. Walker) / 1 dead / 64 rescued.

1	2	3	4	5	6
U 463	2.4.42	12.5.43	Bo	KK L. Wolfbauer	16.5.43 ✠ N. Atlantic N.W. of Spain: 45°57n/11°40w / D/Cs / Hal R (F/O A. J. W. Birch), 58 Sqn RAF / 57 dead / ✠.[194]
U 464	30.4.42	14.8.42	Be	KL O. Harms	20.8.42 (✠) 07h10 N. Atlantic S.E. of Iceland: 61°25n/14°40w / following D/Cs damage Cat 1 (Lt.[jg] R. B. Hopgood), VP-73 Sqn USN / 2 dead / 52 rescued.
U 487	21.12.42	15.6.43	Bo	OL H. Metz	13.7.43 ✠ mid-Atlantic: 27°15n/34°18w / D/Cs / Ave (Lt. R. P. Williams), Ave (Lt.[jg] J. F. Schoby), Wil (Lt.[jg] E. H. Steiger), Wil (Lt. Comdr. C. W. Brewer), VC-13 Sqn USN CVE USS *Core* (Capt. M. R. Greer) / 31 dead / 33 rescued.
U 488	1.2.43	22.2.44	Bo	OL B. Studt	26.4.44 ✠ mid-Atlantic: 17°54n/38°05w / D/Cs / DE's USS *Frost* (Lt. Comdr. J. H. McWhorter), USS *Huse* (Lt. Comdr. R. H. Wanless), USS *Barber* (Lt. Comdr. E. T. B. Sullivan), USS *Snowden* (Lt. Comdr. N. W. Swanson) / 64 dead / ✠.
U 489	8.3.43	25.7.43	Kr	OL A. Schmandt	4.8.43 (✠) N. Atlantic S.E. of Iceland: 61°11n/14°38w / following D/Cs damage Sun G (F/O A. A. Bishop), 423 Sqn RCAF / 1 dead / 53 rescued.
U 490	27.3.43	6.5.44	Kr	OL W. Gerlach	12.6.44 ✠ N. Atlantic N.W. of Azores: 42°47n/40°08w / D/Cs, artillery / DE's USS *Frost* (Lt. Comdr. J. H. McWhorter), USS *Inch* (Lt. Comdr. D. A. Tufts), USS *Huse* (Lt. J. H. Batcheller, Jr.) / 60 rescued.
U 491				(OL G. Kellerstrass)	(keel laid 31.7.43) construction abandoned June 1944, ≈75% complete, 23.9.44 contract suspended, incomplete hull captured by British forces May 45 on slip No. 3 Deutsche Werke Kiel, br.
U 492					(keel laid 28.8.43) construction abandoned June 1944, ≈75% complete, 23.9.44 contract suspended, incomplete hull captured by British forces May 45 on slip No. 3 Deutsche Werke Kiel, br.
U 493					(keel laid 25.9.43) construction abandoned June 1944, ≈75% complete, 23.9.44 contract suspended, incomplete hull captured by British forces May 45 on slip No. 3 Deutsche Werke Kiel, br.

1	2	3	4	5	6
U 494					(keel laid 1.11.43) 3.6.44 contract suspended. 23.9.44 contract canceled, incomplete hull broken up October 1944 on slip No. 8 Germaniawerft Kiel.
U 495					(keel laid 12.11.43) 3.6.44 contract suspended, 22.7.44 contract canceled, incomplete hull broken up October 1944 on slip No. 8 Germaniawerft Kiel.
U 496					(keel laid 8.2.44) 3.6.44 contract suspended, 22.7.44 contract canceled, incomplete hull broken up October 1944 on slip No. 7 Germaniawerft Kiel.
U 497					(keel laid ?.2.44) 3.6.44 contract suspended, 22.7.44 contract canceled, incomplete hull broken up during May 1944 on slip No. 7 Germaniawerft Kiel.
U 498– U 500					3.6.44 contract suspended before keel laying, 22.7.44 contract canceled.
U 2201– U 2204					3.6.44 contract suspended before keel laying, 22.7.44 contract canceled.

Type V 80

Small experimental U-boat type of advanced design developed in 1938–39 for Walter turbine propulsion system

Surface/submerged displacement: 73/76 t
Overall length/beam/draught: 22.05 m/2.10 m/3.20 m
Standard main armament: none

Building yard	Total no. ordered	Completed (comm.)	Under construction	Construction not started	Canceled after keel laying	Canceled prior to keel laying
Germaniawerft AG Kiel	1	1	—	—	—	—
Total	1	1	—	—	—	—

1	2	3	4	5	6
V 80	30.9.40				experimental boat, decomm. late 1942 at Hela, laid up Hela. 29.3.45 (✝) off Hela.

Type V 300

Experimental U-boat type of advanced design developed in 1940–41 for Walter turbine propulsion system

Surface/submerged displacement: 610/655 t
Overall length/beam/draught: 52.08 m/4.0.3 m/5.49 m
Standard main armament: 2 bow torpedo tubes with up to 6 torpedoes

Building yard	Total no. ordered	Completed (comm.)	Under construction	Construction not started	Canceled after keel laying	Canceled prior to keel laying
Germaniawerft AG Kiel	1	—	—	—	—	1
Total	1	—	—	—	—	1

1	2	3	4	5	6
U 791					7.8.42 contract canceled prior to keel laying.

Type Wa 201, Wk 202

Small experimental U-boat type of advanced design developed in 1942 for Walter turbine propulsion system, Wa 201 designed at Blohm & Voss AG, Wk 202 designed at Germaniawerft AG.

Surface/submerged displacement: Wa 201: 277/309 t, Wk 202: 236/259 t

Overall length/beam/draught: Wa 201: 39.05 m/4.50 m/4.30 m; Wk 202: 34.64 m/4.50 m /4.55 m

Standard main armament: 2 bow torpedo tubes with 4 torpedoes

Building yard	Total no. ordered	Completed (comm.)	Under construction	Construction not started	Canceled after keel laying	Canceled prior to keel laying
Blohm & Voss AG Hamburg	2	2	—	—	—	—
Germaniawerft AG Kiel	2	2	—	—	—	—
Total	4	4	—	—	—	—

1	2	3	4	5	6
U 792	16.11.43			OL H.-D. Duis	Wa 201 experimental boat for Walter propulsion unit; 4.5.45 (✝) 01h30 Audorfer See, Kaiser Wilhelm-Canal km 67: 54°19,5n/09°43e / ↑ 26.5.45, →Kiel, quay Howaldtswerke, br.
U 793	24.4.44			OL F. Schmidt	Wa 201 experimental boat for Walter propulsion unit; 4.5.45 (✝) 01h30 Audorfer See, Kaiser Wilhelm-Canal km 67: 54°19,5n/09°43e / ↑ 15.6.45, →Kiel, quay Howaldtswerke, br.
U 794	14.11.43			OL P. Becker	Wk 202 experimental boat for Walter propulsion unit; 5.5.45 (✝) Gelting Bay: 54°48n/09°49e / br.
U 795	22.4.44			OL H. Selle	Wk 202 experimental boat for Walter propulsion unit; 22.2.45 decomm. Kiel, laid up on quay at Germaniawerft N. of slip No. 8 / 3.5.45 blown up / propulsion unit cannibalized from 14.8.45, hull br.

1. The Type VII B boat U 53 building on slip #2 at the Germaniawerft AG Kiel on 20 September 1938. The pressure hull is already complete, plating of the outer saddle tanks has just started. Forward of the conning tower is the massive deck gun mount. In the background are U 48 (left) and U 52 in a more advanced state of completion.

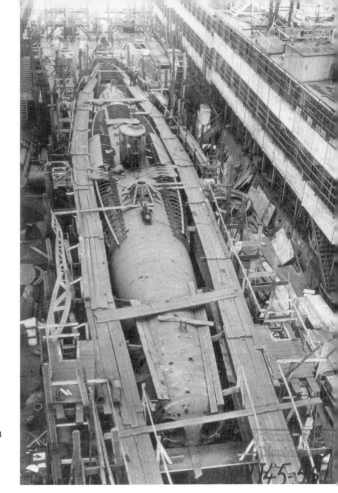

2. U 53 seven months later ready for launching on 6 May 1939 from the covered slipway #2, showing the clean lines of the German Type VII design, which became the workhorse of the German U-boat arm during the war.

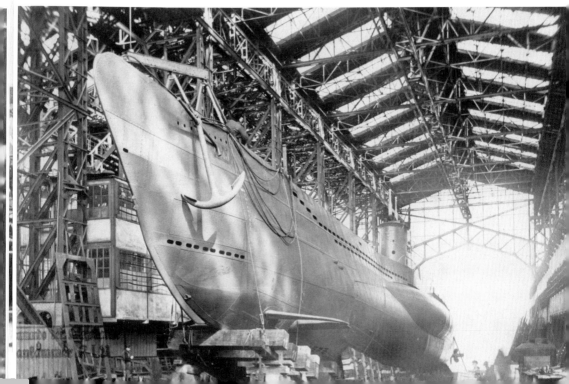

27. Prefabricated sections #1 and #4 of Type XXIII boats in a devastated assembly building at Deutsche Werft AG Hamburg following the USAAF raid on 30 March 1945. Intended for final assembly at Germaniawerft AG Kiel as U 4719–U 4723, none of these boats ever materialized.

28. Two U-boat hulks lying stranded on the banks of the river Oder just north of Stettin in summer 1945. Next to the camera is U 902 with U 108 behind. Both boats were heavily damaged by bombs in an air raid on Stettin on 11 April 1944. At the end of March 1945, it was intended to use both hulks as block ships on the Oder, but the confused military situation eventually prohibited the execution of the plan. Note that U 108 still carries the Ice bear emblem at the conning tower front.

29. Surrendered U-boats arriving at Wilhelmshaven on transfer from Cuxhaven on 13 May 1945, making fast inside the Tirpitz lock. From left to right U 291, U 1198 and U 779 with U 883 on the outer left just coming alongside, behind are U 1194 and U 1103 (covered by U 779).

30. Three German U-boats after surrender in May 1945 alongside at Lisahally, Northern Ireland. The streamlined hulls of the outer Type XXI boats U 2506 and U 2513 differ markedly from the technologically out-dated Type IX C/40 design of U 802. All three boats had been temporarily handed over to the US Navy when the photo was taken.

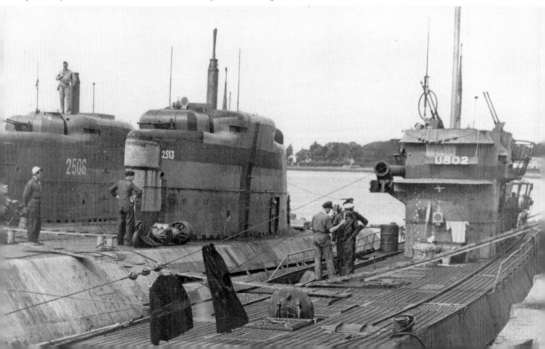

31. Early on 5 May 1945 twenty-three German U-boats were scuttled at Wilhelmshaven inside the western box of the still incomplete Raeder lock. Some of the boats had been decommissioned and laid up before. Here the partly submerged wrecks of the Type VII C boats U 382 (left) and U 339 can be seen alongside the outer concrete wall of the lock.

32. The end of U 96, which had sunk more than 200,000 grt of Allied shipping between 1940 and 1942 before being used as a school boat in the Baltic. Sunk in a US air attack on Wilhelmshaven on 30 March 1945 after being laid up, here the forward part of the boat is being salvaged in 1947 from the Hipper basin at Wilhelmshaven. Postwar, U 96 became famous from the novel and the movie 'Das Boot'.

Type XVII B

Coastal U-boat type of advanced design with Walter turbine propulsion system developed in 1942–43
Surface/submerged displacement: 306/337 t
Overall length/beam/draught: 41.45 m/4.50 m/4.30 m
Standard main armament: 2 bow torpedo tubes with up to 4 torpedoes

Building yard	Total no. ordered	Completed (comm.)	Under construction	Construction not started	Canceled after keel laying	Canceled prior to keel laying
Blohm & Voss AG Hamburg	12	3	2	—	1	6
Total	12	3	2	—	1	6

1	2	3	4	5	6
U 1405	21.12.44			OL W. Rex	5.5.45 (✠) Eckernförde Bay: 54°30,9n/10°02e / br.
U 1406	8.2.45			OL W. Klug	5.5.45 Surrender Cuxhaven, 7.5.45 (✠) Cuxhaven, Fischereihafen / ↑, August 1945 U.S. war prize, 14.9.45 as deck load on US transport ship *Shoemaker* →United States: tests, 18.5.48 New York sold for scrap, 1948 br.
U 1407	29.3.45			OL H. Heitz	5.5.45 Surrender Cuxhaven, 7.5.45 (✠) Cuxhaven, Fischereihafen / ↑, British war prize, HMS/m *N 25*, 1946/49 HMS/m *Meteorite S 94;* 7.9.49 →Vickers Yard, Barrow, br.
U 1408				(OL H. Selle)	3.3.45 construction abandoned while 90% complete awaiting launching on building place at Blohm & Voss Hamburg N. of dry-dock Elbe 17, 8.4.45 bomb damage air raid 4, 6 (RCAF) and 8 Groups RAF Bomber Command, 3.5.45 captured by British forces, br.
U 1409				(OL G. Schauenburg)	3.3.45 construction abandoned while 80% complete awaiting launching on building place at Blohm & Voss Hamburg N. of dry-dock Elbe 17, 8.4.45 bomb damage air raid 4, 6 (RCAF) and 8 Groups RAF Bomber Command, 3.5.45 captured by British forces, br.
U 1410					(keel laid 31.12.43) 13.3.44 contract suspended, 22.7.44 contract canceled, material partly used for U 798, pressure hull parts captured by British forces May 45 at Blohm & Voss Hamburg W. of dry dock Elbe 17.

1	2	3	4	5	6
U 1411– U 1416					30.9.43 suspension announced, 6.11.43 contract suspended, 22.7.44 contract canceled.

In addition, the building yards Blohm & Voss AG at Hamburg and Nordseewerke Emden received a building order for, respectively, 48 and 12 Type XVII B boats by telex on 6.7.43. These orders were subsequently canceled on 30.9.43 before the arrival of written confirmation and the assignment of official U-numbers.

Type XVII G

Coastal U-boat type of advanced design with Walter turbine propulsion system developed in 1942–43
Surface/submerged displacement: 314/345 t
Overall length/beam/draught: 39.51 m/4.50 m/4.72 m
Standard main armament: 2 bow torpedo tubes with up to 4 torpedoes

Building yard	Total no. ordered	Completed (comm.)	Under construction	Construction not started	Canceled after keel laying	Canceled prior to keel laying
Germaniawerft AG Kiel	12	—	—	—	—	12
Total	12	—	—	—	—	12

1	2	3	4	5	6
U 1081– U 1092					30.9.43 suspension announced, 6.11.43 contract suspended, 22.7.44 contract canceled.

In addition, the building yard Germaniawerft AG at Kiel received a building order for 48 Type XVII G boats by telex on 6.7.43. This order was subsequently canceled on 30.9.43 before the arrival of written confirmation and the assignment of official U–numbers.

Type XVII K

Small experimental U-boat type of advanced design developed in 1944 for closed-cycle propulsion system

Surface/submerged displacement: 308/340 t
Overall length/beam/draught: 40.71 m/4.50 m/≈4.90 m
Standard main armament: none

Building yard	Total no. ordered	Completed (comm.)	Under construction	Construction not started	Canceled after keel laying	Canceled prior to keel laying
Germaniawerft AG Kiel	1	—	1	—	—	—
Total	1	—	1	—	—	—

1	2	3	4	5	6
U 798	-------			(OL H. Apel)	experimental boat for closed-cycle propulsion unit; 3.5.45 blown up before installation of propulsion unit on fitting out quay Germaniawerft Kiel, br.

Type XVIII

Oceangoing U-boat type of advanced design with Walter turbine propulsion system developed in 1942–43

Surface/submerged displacement:	1485/1652 t
Overall length/beam/draught:	71.50 m/8.00 m/6.36 m
Standard main armament:	6 bow torpedo tubes with up to 23 torpedoes

Building yard	Total no. ordered	Completed (comm.)	Under construction	Construction not started	Canceled after keel laying	Canceled prior to keel laying
Germaniawerft AG Kiel	2	—	—	—	1	1
Total	2	—	—	—	1	1

1	2	3	4	5	6
U 796					(keel laid 27.12.43) 27.3.44 contract canceled, incomplete pressure hull broken up 1944 on slip No. 7 Germaniawerft Kiel.
U 797					27.3.44 contract canceled prior to keel laying.

Type XX

Oceangoing cargo transport U-boat type of conventional design developed in 1943
Surface/submerged displacement: 2708/2962 t
Overall length/beam/draught: 77.10 m/9.15 m/6.60 m
Standard main armament: none. 800 t cargo capacity including 50 t internal dry stowage capacity

Building yard	Total no. ordered	Completed (comm.)	Under construction	Construction not started	Canceled after keel laying	Canceled prior to keel laying
Germaniawerft AG Kiel	30	—	3	—	—	27
Total	30	—	3	—	—	27

1	2	3	4	5	6
U 1601– U 1615					construction abandoned 27.5.44 before keel laying, 3.6.44 contract suspended, 22.7.44 contract canceled.
U 1701					(keel laid 21.2.44) construction abandoned 27.5.44, 3.6.44 contract suspended, 15.8.44 completion planned as H_2O_2-transporter; construction abandoned January 1945, incomplete hull captured by British forces May 45 on slip No. 3 of Germaniawerft Kiel, br 1946.
U 1702					(keel laid 10.3.44) construction abandoned 27.5.44, 3.6.44 contract suspended, 15.8.44 completion planned as H_2O_2-transporter; construction abandoned January 1945, incomplete hull captured by British forces May 45 on slip No. 5 of Gennaniawerft Kiel, br 1946.
U 1703					(Keel laid 4.44) construction abandoned 27.5.44, 3.6.44 contract suspended, 15.8.44 completion planned as H_2O_2-transporter; construction abandoned January 1945, incomplete pressure hull captured by British forces May 45 on slip No. 6 of Gernianiawerft Kiel, br 1946.
U 1704– U 1715					construction abandoned 27.5.44 before keel laying, 3.6.44 contract suspended, 22.7.44 contract canceled.

Type XXI

Oceangoing U-boat type of advanced design with enlarged accumulator battery capacity developed in 1943

Surface/submerged displacement: 1621/1819 t
Overall length/beam/draught: 76.70 m/8.00 m/6.32 m
Standard main armament: 6 bow torpedo tubes with up to 23 torpedoes

Building yard	Total no. ordered	Completed (comm.)	Under construction	Construction not started	Canceled after keel laying	Canceled or abandoned
Deschimag AG Weser Bremen	88	41	19	25	3	—
Blohm & Voss AG Hamburg	262	47	14	18	3	180
F. Schichau GmbH Danzig	142	30	12	32	—	68
Bremer Vulkan Vegesacker Werft	88	—	—	—	—	88
Total	580	118	45	75	6	336

1	2	3	4	5	6
U 2501	27.6.44			OL (Ing) H. Noack i.V.	20.11.44 → Hamburg, →training boat 8.KLA Hamburg, 3.5.45 (✝) 07h00 Hamburg, entrance to west box of U-boat pen Elbe II: 53°32n/09°57e / br.
U 2502	19.7.44			KL H. Franke	9.5.45 Surrender Horten, 3.6.45 sailed →Lisahally / 3.1.46 ✝ artillery DD ORP *Piorun* 56°06n/09°00w / Op. Deadlight.
U 2503	1.8.44	3.5.45	Ki	KL K.-J. Wächter	4.5.45 (✝) 05h12 Baltic, Great Belt S.W. Ömö: 55°09n/11°07e / following rocket damage Bft R, C, E, G, E1, 236 Sqn RAF, Mos A, U, K, C, T, Z, 254 Sqn RAF 3.5.45 / 13 dead / ? rescued.
U 2504	12.8.44			OL (Ing) H. Hinrichs i.V.	19.11.44 → Hamburg, →training boat 8.KLA Hamburg, 3.5.45 (✝) Hamburg, Vulkan basin alongside Blaufries jetty / br.
U 2505	7.11.44			OL J. Düppe	3.5.45 (✝) 07h Hamburg, west box U-boat pen Elbe II: 53°32n/09°57e / partly br.
U 2506	31.8.44			KL H. von Schroeter	9.5.45 Surrender Bergen, 17.6.45 sailed →Lisahally / 5.1.46 ✝ artillery DD HMS *Onslaught* 55°37n/07°30w / Op. Deadlight.
U 2507	8.9.44			KL P. Siegmann	5.5.45 (✝) 05h55 Gelting Bay, near Kalkgrund LF / br.

1	2	3	4	5	6
U 2508	26.9.44			OL U. Christiansen	3.5.45 (✞) Kiel / br.
U 2509	21.9.44			KK R. Schendel	8.4.45 ✞ Hamburg, Blohm & Voss yard, basin E off 150 t crane / bomb / air raid 4, 6 (RCAF) and 8 Groups RAF Bomber Command / none dead / ↑ 7./8.45, →Blankenese, br.
U 2510	27.9.44			OL W. Herrmann	2.5.45 (✞) Travemünde: 53°59n/10°56e / br.
U 2511	29.9.44			KK A. Schnee	9.5.45 Surrender Bergen, 17.6.45 sailed →Lisahally / 7.1.46 ✞ artillery DD HMS *Solebay* 55°33,1n/07°38,1w / Op. Deadlight.
U 2512	10.10.44			KL H. Nordheimer	8.5.45 (✞) Eckernförde Bay, off Hemmelmark: 54°28,5n/09°54,1e (?) / br.
U 2513	12.10.44			FK E. Topp	9.5.45 Surrender Horten, 3.6.45 sailed →Lisahally / U.S. war prize, 6.8.45 →United States, .7.46 comm. USS *U 2513*, tests; 8.7.49 decomm., 7.10.51 ✞ Atlantic W. of Key West: 24°53n/83°15w / DD USS *Robert A. Owens* / A/S weapon test.
U 2514	17.10.44			KL R.-B. Wahlen	8.4.45 ✞ Hamburg, Blohm & Voss. Norderelbe quay between dry-dock Elbe 17 and slip No. 3 / bomb / air raid 4, 6 (RCAF) and 8 Groups RAF Bomber Command / none dead / ↑ 7./8.45, →Blankenese, br.
U 2515	19.10.44			OL G. Linder	17.1.45 ✞ Hamburg, Blohm & Voss Kuhwarder basin inside dry-dock No. 3 / bomb / air raid 8. USAAF / none dead / br.
U 2516	24.10.44			OL E. Kallipke	9.4.45 ✞ Kiel, Deutsche Werke inside dry-dock I / bomb / air raid 1, 3, and 8 Groups RAF Bomber Command / none dead / br.
U 2517	31.10.44			OL H. Hansen	5.5.45 (✞) Gelting Bay: 54°48n/09°49e / br.
U 2518	4.11.44			KL E. Weidner	9.5.45 Surrender Horten, 3.6.45 sailed →Lisahally, British war prize, 13.2.46 →Cherbourg, 15.2.51 →France, 9.4.51 French *Roland Morillot* (S 613), 15.4.67 Reserve, decomm. 12.10.67, Q 426, 21.5.69 sold to SPA Lotti, La Spezia, Italy, br after 6.8.69.
U 2519	15.11.44			KK P. E. Cremer	3.5.45 (✞) Kiel, Tirpitz basin No. 22 berth / br.

1	2	3	4	5	6
U 2520	25.12.44			KK R. Schendel	3.5.45 (✠) Kiel, Tirpitz basin Gneisenau jetty / br.
U 2521	21.11.44	4.5.45	Fl	OL J. Methner	4.5.45 ✠ Baltic, Flensburg Fiord: 54°49,1 n/09°50,1e (?) / rockets / air strike Typhoons, 184 Sqn RAF and 245 Sqn RAF / 44 dead / 5 rescued.[195]
U 2522	22.11.44			KL H.-T. Queck	5.5.45 (✠) Gelting Bay: 54°48n/09°49e / br.
U 2523	26.12.44			KL H.-H. Ketels	17.1.45 ✠ Hamburg, Blohm & Voss fitting out quay Steinwarder Ufer berth IV / bomb / air raid 8. USAAF / br.
U 2524	16.1.45			KL E. von Witzendorff	3.5.45 (✠) Baltic E. of Fehmarn: 54°26,3n/11°33,9e / 1 dead.
U 2525	12.12.44			KL P.-F. Otto	5.5.45 (✠) Gelting Bay: 54°48n/09°49e / br.
U 2526	15.12.44			OL O. Hohmann	2.5.45 (✠) Travemünde: 53°59n/10°56e / br.
U 2527	23.12.44			OL H. Götze	2.5.45 (✠) Travemünde: 53°59n/10°56e / br.
U 2528	9.12.44			KL O. Curio	2.5.45 (✠) Travemünde: 53°59n/10°56e / br.
U 2529	22.2.45			OL E Kallipke	9.5.45 Surrender Kristiansand, 3.6.45 sailed →Loch Ryan / HMS/m N 27, USSR war prize, 6.12.45 at Libau →USSR, 13.2.46 Soviet N-27, South Baltic Fleet, 9.6.49 B-27, 10.6.55 Reserve, 19.9.55 block ship BSh-28, 9.1.57 training hulk UTS-3, § 1.9.72, br.
U 2530	30.12.44			KL M. Bokelberg	31.12.44 ✠ Hamburg, Blohm & Voss fitting out berth IV / bomb / air raid 8. USAAF / none dead / ↑ ?.1.45, docked, 17.1.45 ✠ Kuhwarder basin inside dry-dock No. 5 / bomb / air raid 8. USAAF / none dead / br.
U 2531	10.1.45			KL H. Niss	2.5.45 (✠) Travemünde: 53°59n/10°56e / br.
U 2532	--------			(OL O. Hübschen)	31.12.44 ✠ Hamburg, Blohm & Voss fitting out quay Steinwarder Ufer berth V / bomb / air raid 8. USAAF / during salvage attempt 17.1.45 ✠ together with salvage ships Hiev and Griep / bomb / air raid 8. USAAF / br.
U 2533	18.1.45			OL H. Günther	2.5.45 (✠) Travemünde: 53°59n/10°56e / br.
U 2534	17.1.45			KL U. Drews	3.5.45 (✠) Baltic E. of Fehmarn: 54°26,8n/11°34e(?) / br.[196]

1	2	3	4	5	6
U 2535	28.1.45			KL O. Bitter	2.5.45 (✠) Travemünde: 53°59n/10°56e / br.
U 2536	6.2.45			OL U. Vöge	2.5.45 (✠) Travemünde: 53°59n/10°56e / br.
U 2537	-------			(OL M. Dobbert)	31.12.44 ✠ Hamburg, Blohm & Voss fitting out quay Steinwarder Ufer berth I / bomb / air raid 8. USAAF / br.
U 2538	16.2.45			OL H. Klapdor	8.5.45 (✠) 04h45 Baltic, off S.W. coast of Aerö near Marstal: 54°53,5n/10°15,7e / 1948 br.
U 2539	21.2.45			OL J. Johann i.V.	3.5.45 (✠) Kiel / br.
U 2540	24.2.45			OL R. Schultze	4.5.45 (✠) near Flensburg Light vessel / ↑ 1957; 1.9.60 German Bundesmarine: experimental boat *Wilhelm Bauer*, 1984 museum ship Deutsches Schiffahrtsmuseum at Bremerhaven.
U 2541	1.3.45			KL R.-B. Wahlen	5.5.45 (✠) Gelting Bay: 54°48n/09°49e / br.
U 2542	5.3.45			OL O. Hübschen	3.4.45 ✠ Kiel, Tirpitz basin / bomb / air raid 8. USAAF / none dead / br.
U 2543	7.3.45			OL G. Stolzenburg	3.5.45 (✠) Kiel / br.
U 2544	10.3.45			OL R. Meinlschmidt	5.5.45 (✠) Kattegat S.E. of Aarhus: 56°06,5n/10°27,9e / ↑ 1952, br.
U 2545	8.4.45			OL H.-B. Frhr. Von Müffling	3.5.45 (✠) Kiel / br.
U 2546	21.3.45			OL M. Dobbert	3.5.45 (✠) Kiel / br.
U 2547	--------			(OL F. Richter)	11.3.45 severe bomb damage during air raid 8. USAAF while fitting out, construction abandoned, laid up, 3.5.45 (✠) Hamburg, west side of Vorhafen alongside Tollerort jetty: 53°32,4n/09°57,1e / br.
U 2548	9.4.45			OL K.-E. Utischill	3.5.45 (✠) Kiel harbour S.W. of buoy B.2: 54°21,1n/10°09,6e / br.
U 2549				(OL K. Sureth)	3.5.45 captured almost completed by British forces on slip No. 6 at Blohm & Voss Hamburg, launching blocked by damaged U 2550 / br.
U 2550				(OL G. Wolff)	construction abandoned after severe bomb damage air raid 8. USAAF and RAF Bomber Command 20.3.45 and 8.4.45, 3.5.45 captured incomplete by British forces on slip No. 6 at Blohm & Voss Hamburg / br.

1	2	3	4	5	6
U 2551	?.4.45			KL G. Schaar	5.5.45 (✝) Flensburg-Solitude: 54°49,7n/09°28,7e / grounded / 23.7.45 blown up by Royal Navy / br.
U 2552	20.4.45			KL J. Rudolph	3.5.45 (✝) Kiel harbour S.W. of buoy B.2: 54°21,1n/10°09,6e / br.
U 2553				(OL H.-D. Wilke)	3.5.45 captured incomplete by British forces on slip No. 8 at Blohm & Voss Hamburg / 1945–46 br.
U 2554				(OL G. Linder)	3.5.45 captured incomplete by British forces on slip No. 8 at Blohm & Voss Hamburg / 1945–46 br.
U 2555				(KL J. Vanselow)	3.5.45 captured incomplete by British forces on slip No. 10 at Blohm & Voss Hamburg / 1945–46 br.
U 2556				(KL E. Wolf)	3.5.45 captured incomplete by British forces on slip No. 10 at Blohm & Voss Hamburg / 1945–46 br.
U 2557				(OL H.-H. Nibbe)	3.5.45 captured incomplete by British forces on slip No. 9 at Blohm & Voss Hamburg / 1945–46 br.
U 2558				(OL F. Brunke)	3.5.45 captured incomplete by British forces on slip No. 10 at Blohm & Voss Hamburg / 1945–46 br.
U 2559				(KL M. Bokelberg)	3.5.45 captured incomplete by British forces on slip No. 9 at Blohm & Voss Hamburg / 1945–46 br.
U 2560				(KL F. Henning)	3.5.45 captured incomplete by British forces on slip No. 9 at Blohm & Voss Hamburg / 1945–46 br.
U 2561				(KK E. G. Heinicke)	3.5.45 captured incomplete by British forces on slip No. 9 at Blohm & Voss Hamburg / 1945–46 br.
U 2562				(OL H.-A. Isermeyer)	3.5.45 captured incomplete by British forces on slip No. 8 at Blohm & Voss Hamburg / 1945–46 br.
U 2563					3.5.45 captured incomplete by British forces on slip No. 8 at Blohm & Voss Hamburg / 1945-46 br.
U 2564					3.5.45 captured incomplete by British forces on slip No. 9 at Blohm & Voss Hamburg / 1945-46 br.
U 2565– U 2567					completion planned during emergency building program of 29.1.45, but no keel laid. Prefabricated sections partly completed.

1	2	3	4	5	6
U 2568– U 2575					completion planned during emergency building program of 29.1.45, but 12.3.45 contract suspended. No keel laid, prefabricated sections partly completed.
U 2576– U 2608					no keel laid. Prefabricated sections partly completed, 29.1.45 contract suspended.
U 2609– U 2720					27.9.44 contract canceled, construction shifted to Vegesacker Werft Bremen. New U-numbers assigned (See U 3177–U 3288).
U 2721– U 2762					27.9.44 contract canceled, construction shifted to Schichau-Werft Danzig. New U-numbers assigned (See U 3643–U 3684).
U 3001	20.7.44			KL W. Peters	26.11.44 →Bremen, – training boat 6.KLA Bremen, April 1945 →Wesermünde, 5.5.45 (✠) N.W. of Wesermünde / br.
U 3002	6.8.44			FK H. Kaiser	2.5.45 (✠) Travemünde: 53°59n/10°56e / br.
U 3003	22.8.44			OL L. Kregelin	4.4.45 ✠ Kiel, Howaldtswerke / bomb / air raid 8. USAAF / br.
U 3004	30.8.44			KL O. Peschel	3.5.45 (✠) Hamburg, inside west box U-boat pen Elbe II: 53°32n/09°57e / partly br.
U 3005	20.9.44			KL J. Hinrichs	5.5.45 (✠) W. of Wesermünde / br.
U 3006	5.10.44			OL E. Fischer	5.5.45 (✠) 07h Wilhelmshaven, western entrance to Raeder lock / br.
U 3007	22.10.44			KL H. Manseck	24.2.45 ✠ Bremen, yard basin Deschimag-AG Weser: 53°08n/08°46e / bomb / air raid 8. USAAF / 1 dead / ↑ until 20.6.47, br.
U 3008	19.10.44			KL H. Manseck	21.5.45 Surrender Kiel, → Wilhelmshaven, 21.6.45 sailed →Lisahally, U.S. war prize, 6.8.45 →United States, comm. 24.7.46 USS *U 3008*, tests; decomm. 18.6.48, →Puerto Rico, explosive tests, 15.9.55 sold for scrap Loudes Iron & Metal Co., Puerto Rico, br 1956
U 3009	10.11.44			KL K. Schimpf	5.5.45 (✠) W. of Wesermünde / br.
U 3010	11.11.44			FK E. Topp	2.5.45 (✠) Lübeck, Flenderwerke (?): 53°54n/10°47e / br.
U 3011	21.12.44			OL O. Fränzel	2.5.45 (✠) Travemünde: 53°59n/10°56e / br.

1	2	3	4	5	6
U 3012	4.12.44			KL F. Meier i.V.	3.5.45 ✠ Baltic E. of Fehmarn: 54°27n/11°32,5e(?) / rockets / 9. USAAF XXIX TAC ? / all rescued.
U 3013	22.11.44			KL V. Simmermacher	2.5.45 (✠) Travemünde: 53°59n/10°56e / br.
U 3014	17.12.44			KL K.-H. Marbach	3.5.45 (✠) Neustadt / br.
U 3015	17.12.44			KL P. O. Grau	5.5.45 (✠) Gelting Bay: 54°48n/09°49e / br.
U 3016	5.1.45			OL B. Meentzen	2.5.45 (✠) Travemünde: 53°59n/10°56e / br.
U 3017	5.1.45			OL R. Lindschau	9.5.45 Surrender Horten, 3.6.45 sailed →Lisahally, British war prize, HMS/m *N 41*, tests / 25.10.49 →Messr. John Cashmore Ltd., Newport/Mon, br.
U 3018	7.1.45			OL S. Breinlinger	2.5.45 (✠) Travemünde: 53°59n/10°56e / br.
U 3019	23.12.44			OL E.-A. Racky	2.5.45 (✠) Travemünde: 53°59n/10°56e / br.
U 3020	23.12.44			OL H. Mäueler	2.5.45 (✠) Travemünde: 53°59n/10°56e / br.
U 3021	12.1.45			OL K. van Meeteren	2.5.45 (✠) Travemünde: 53°59n/10°56e / br.
U 3022	25.1.45			KL P. Weber	3.5.45 (✠) Kiel-Wik / br.
U 3023	22.1.45			OL E. Harms	2.5.45 (✠) Travemünde: 53°59n/10°56e / br.
U 3024	13.1.45			OL F. Blaich	3.5.45 (✠) Neustadt / br.
U 3025	20.1.45			KL H. Vogel	2.5.45 (✠) Travemünde: 53°59n/10°56e / br.
U 3026	22.1.45			OL G. Drescher	2.5.45 (✠) Travemünde: 53°59n/10°56e / br.
U 3027	25.1.45			KL K. Mehne	2.5.45 (✠) Travemünde: 53°59n/10°56e / br.
U 3028	27.1.45			KL E. Christophersen	3.5.45 (✠) Kiel / br.
U 3029	5.2.45			KL H. Lamby	3.5.45 (✠) Kiel Fiord / br.
U 3030	14.2.45			OL B. Luttmann	8.5.45 (✠) Eckernförde Bay: 54°30,8n/10°06,2e (?) / br.
U 3031	28.2.45			OL H. Sach	3.5.45 (✠) Kiel/br.
U 3032	12.2.45			OL H. Slevogt	3.5.45 ✠ Baltic E. of Fehmarn: 54°26,5n/11°32,2e / rockets / Typhoons. 184 Sqn RAF / 36 dead / 24 rescued.
U 3033	27.2.45			OL P. Callsen	5.5.45 (✠) Flensburg Fiord, Wassersleben Bay / br.

1	2	3	4	5	6
U 3034	31.3.45			OL H. Willner	5.5.45 (✠) Flensburg Fiord, Wassersleben Bay / br.
U 3035	1.3.45			OL E.-A. Gerke	9.5.45 Surrender Egersund. →Stavanger, 31.5.45 sailed →Lisahally / HMS/m *N 28*, USSR war prize, 16.12.45 at Libau →USSR, 13.2.46 Soviet *N-28*, South Baltic Fleet, 9.6.49 *B-28*, 29.12.55 Reserve, 18.1.56 floating torpedo fire station *PZS-34*, § 25.3.58, br.
U 3036	-------			(KL J. Knecht)	30.3.45 ✠ Bremen, Deschimag-AG Weser yard basin, Querbollwerk / bomb / air raid 8. USAAF / br.
U 3037	3.3.45			KL G.-A. Janssen	2.5.45 (✠) Travemünde: 53°59n/10°56e / br.
U 3038	4.3.45			OL M. Brünig	3.5.45 (✠) Kiel / br.
U 3039	8.3.45			KL G. Ruperti	3.5.45 (✠) Kiel / br.
U 3040	8.3.45			OL H. Robbert	3.5.45 (✠) Kiel / br.
U 3041	10.3.45			KL H. Hornkohl	9.5.45 Surrender Horten, 3.6.45 sailed →Lisahally / HMS/m *N29*, USSR war prize, 12.12.45 at Libau →USSR, 13.2.46 Soviet *N-29*, South Baltic Fleet, 9.6.49 *B-29*, 29.12.55 Reserve, 18.1.56 floating torpedo fire station *PZS-II*, § 25.3.58, br.
U 3042				(KL K. Petersen)	27.4.45 captured incomplete by British forces on slip No. 5 at Deschimag-AG Weser following bomb damage air raid RAF Bomber Command 22.2.45 / br.
U 3043				(KL G. Kellerstrass)	27.4.45 captured incomplete by British forces on slip No. 5 at Deschimag-AG Weser, launching blocked by damaged U 3042 / br.
U 3044	27.3.45			KL D. von Lehsten	5.5.45 (✠) Gelting Bay: 54°48n/09°49e / br.
U 3045	-------			(KL W. Peters)	30.3.45 ✠ Bremen, yard basin Deschimag-AG Weser: 53°08n/08°46e / bomb / air raid 8. USAAF / ↑ until 21.5.48, br.
U 3046	-------			(OL J. van Stipriaan)	30.3.45 ✠ Bremen, yard basin Deschimag-AG Weser: 53°08n/08°46e / bomb / air raid 8. USAAF / ↑ until 19.3.48, br.
U 3047	-------			(OL W. Seiler)	5.5.45 (✠) W. of Wesermünde / br.

1	2	3	4	5	6
U 3048				(KL H. Laubert)	27.4.45 captured incomplete by British forces on slip No. 5 at Deschimag-AG Weser following bomb damage air raid RAF Bomber Command 22.2.45 / br.
U 3049				(OL H.-F. Geisler)	27.4.45 captured incomplete by British forces on slip No. 5 at Deschimag-AG Weser, launching blocked by damaged U 3048 / br.
U 3050				(OL E. Reimann)	5.5.45 (✞) W. of Wesermünde / br.
U 3051				(OL H. Müller-Koelbl)	5.5.45 (✞) W. of Wesermünde / br.
U 3052				(KL D. Beck)	27.4.45 captured incomplete by British forces on slip No. 5 of Deschimag-AG Weser following severe bomb damage air raid RAF Bomber Command 22.2.45 / br.
U 3053				(KL C. Billich)	27.4.45 captured incomplete by British forces on slip No. 5 of Deschimag-AG Weser, br.
U 3054				(OL C. Neuland)	27.4.45 captured incomplete by British forces on slip No. 1 of Deschimag-AG Weser, br.
U 3055				(OL H. Fritz)	27.4.45 captured incomplete by British forces on slip No. 1 of Deschimag-AG Weser. br.
U 3056				(OL G. Fröhlich)	27.4.45 captured incomplete by British forces on slip No. 5 of Deschimag-AG Weser, br.
U 3057				(OL H. Neumann)	27.4.45 captured incomplete by British forces on slip No. 5 of Deschimag-AG Weser, br.
U 3058				(KL R. Wurmbach)	27.4.45 captured incomplete by British forces on slip No. 3 of Deschitnag-AG Weser, br.
U 3059				(KL J. Knecht)	27.4.45 captured incomplete by British forces on slip No. 3 of Deschimag-AG Weser, br.
U 3060				(KL F. Bart)	27.4.45 captured incomplete by British forces on slip No. 4 of Deschimag-AG Weser, br.
U 3061				(KL F. Schlömer)	27.4.45 captured incomplete by British forces on slip No. 4 of Deschimag-AG Weser, br.
U 3062				(OL K.-H. Schröter)	27.4.45 captured incomplete by British forces on slip No. 4 of Deschimag-AG Weser, br.

1	2	3	4	5	6
U 3063					27.4.45 captured incomplete by British forces on slip No. 4 of Deschimag-AG Weser, br.
U 3064– U 3065					completion planned during emergency building program of 29.1.45, but no keel laid: prefabricated sections partly completed.
U 3066- U 3073					no keel laid, contract suspended 29.1.45. but 24.3.45 construction resumed. Prefabricated sections partly completed.
U 3074– U 3082					no keel laid, 29.1.45 contract suspended.
U 3083– U 3088					Scheduled for assembly in U-boat building pen Valentin, construction not started, 29.1.45 construction suspended.
U 3089– U 3176					Scheduled for assembly in U-boat building pen Valentin, construction not started, 29.1.45 construction suspended.
U 3177– U 3288					Scheduled for assembly in U-boat building pen Valentin, construction not started, 29.1.45 contract suspended.
U 3501	29.7.44			KL J. Schmidt-Weichert	4.10.44 →Danzig, →7.KLA Danzig instruction boat, 1945 →Wesermünde, generating plant, 5.5.45 (✠) W. bank of Weser river W. of Wesermünde / br.
U 3502	19.8.44			OL H. Schultz	3.5.45 (✠) Hamburg, Vorhafen basin alongside Tollerort jetty: 53°32,4n/09°57,1e while used as floating generating plant following bomb damage air raid 4, 6 (RCAF) and 8 Groups RAF Bomber Command 8.4.45 / br.
U 3503	9.9.44	3.5.45	Ki	OL H. Deiring	8.5.45 (✠) Baltic W. of Göteborg: 57°39n/11°44e / ↑ 24.8.46, →Göteborg, 1946/47 br Nya Varvet Navy Yard, Göteborg.[197]
U 3504	23.9.44			KI. K. H. Siebold	5.5.45 (✠) Wilhelmshaven. western entrance to Raeder lock / br
U 3505	7.10.44			OL H. Willner	3.4.45 ✠ 17h30 Kiel, Tirpitz basin No. 18 berth / bomb / air raid 8. USAAF / 1 dead / br.
U 3506	14.10.44			KL G. Thäter	3.5.45 (✠) 07h Hamburg, inside west box U-boat pen Elbe II: 53°32n/09°57e / partly br.
U 3507	19.10.44			OL H.-J. Schley	2.5.45 (✠) Travemünde: 53°59n/10°56e / br.

1	2	3	4	5	6
U 3508	2.11.44			KL D. von Lehsten	30.3.45 ✠ Wilhelmshaven, Bauhafen basin / bomb / air raid 8. USAAF / none dead / br.
U 3509	29.1.45			OL W. Neitzsch i.V.	5.5.45 (✠) W. of Wesermünde / br.
U 3510	11.11.44			OL E.-W. Schwirley	5.5.45 (✠) Gelting Bay: 54°48n/09°49e / br.
U 3511	18.11.44			KL H. Schrenk	2.5.45 (✠) Travemünde: 53°59n/10°56e / br.
U 3512	27.11.44			KL H. Hornkohl	8.4.45 ✠ Hamburg, Howaldtswerke inside floating dry-dock No. 5 off building slips / bomb / 4, 6 (RCAF) and 8 Groups RAF Bomber Command / none dead / br.
U 3513	2.12.44			OL O.-H. Nachtigall	2.5.45 (✠) Travemünde: 53°59n/10°56e / br.
U 3514	9.12.44			OL G. Fritze	9.5.45 Surrender Bergen, 6.6.45 sailed →Lisahally / 12.2.46 ✠ artillery PF HMS *Loch Arkaig* 56°00n/10°05w / Op. Deadlight, last boat sunk during this operation.
U 3515	14.12.44			OL F. Kuscher	9.5.45 Surrender Horten, 3.6.45 sailed →Lisahally / HMS/m *N 30*, USSR war prize, 2.2.46 at Libau →USSR, 13.2.46 Soviet *N-30*, South Baltic Fleet, 9.6.49 *B-30*, 29.12.55 Reserve, 18.1.56 floating torpedo fire station *PZS-35*, 2.7.58 test hulk *B-100*, § 25.9.59, 30.11.59 sold for scrap.
U 3516	18.12.44			OL H. Grote	2.5.45 (✠) Travemünde: 53°59n/10°56e / br.
U 3517	22.12.44			KL H. Münster	2.5.45 (✠) Travemünde: 53°59n/10°56e / br.
U 3518	29.12.44			KL H. Brünning	3.5.45 (✠) Kiel / br.
U 3519	15.12.44			KL R. von Harpe	2.3.45 ✠ 12h45 Baltic N. of Warnemünde: 54°15,4n/12°04,4e / British air-laid mine, field "Sweet Pea I" / 75 dead / 3 rescued / 1949 blown up, ↑, br.
U 3520	23.12.44			KL S. Ballert	31.1.45 ✠ 03h35 Baltic, Flensburg Fiord N.E. of Surendorf: 54°30,9n/10°06,1e / British air-laid mine, field "Forgetmenot" / 85 dead / ✠ / ↑ , br.
U 3521	14.1.45			OL G. Keller	2.5.45 (✠) Travemünde: 53°59n/10°56e / br.
U 3522	21.1.45			OL D. Lenzmann	2.5.45 (✠) Travemünde: 53°59n/10°56e / br.

1	2	3	4	5	6
U 3523	23.1.45	2.5.45	Tr	OL W. Müller	6.5.45 ✞ 18h39 North Sea, Skagerrak: 57°52n/10°49e / D/Cs / Lib G (F/L T. H. E. Goldie), 86 Sqn RAF / 58 dead / ✞.[198]
U 3524	26.1.45	4.5.45	Fl	KK H.-L. Witt	5.5.45 (✞) Gelting Bay: 54°48n/09°49e / br.
U 3525	31.1.45			KL F. Kranich	3.5.45 (✞) Kiel / br.
U 3526	22.3.45			OL K. Hilbig	5.5.45 (✞) Gelting Bay: 54°48n/09°49e / br.
U 3527	10.3.45			KL W. Kronenbitter	5.5.45 (✞) W. bank river Weser W. of Wesermünde / br.
U 3528	18.3.45			KL H. Zwarg	5.5.45 (✞) W. bank river Weser W. of Wesermünde / br.
U 3529	22.3.45			OL K. H. Schmidt	5.5.45 (✞) Gelting Bay: 54°48n/09°49e / br.
U 3530	22.3.45			KL W. Brauel	3.5.45 (✞) Kiel / br.
U 3531	-------			(OL G. Bergner)	March 1945 towed to Kiel prior to completion to avoid capture by USSR forces / 24.3.45 contract suspended / 3.5.45 (✞) Kiel, Tirpitz basin No. 37 berth, br.
U 3532	-------			(OL H. Niemeyer)	March 1945 towed to Brunsbüttel prior to completion to avoid capture by USSR forces / 24.3.45 contract suspended / May 1945 captured by British forces at Brunsbüttel, br.
U 3533	-------			(OL K. Jaenicke)	March 1945 towed to Kiel prior to completion to avoid capture by USSR forces / 24.3.45 contract suspended / 3.5.45 (✞) Kiel, south side of Tirpitz jetty, br.
U 3534	-------			(KL H. Wolff)	March 1945 towed to Kiel prior to completion to avoid capture by USSR forces / 24.3.45 contract suspended / 3.5.45 (✞) Kiel, south side of Tirpitz jetty, br.
U 3535				(OL W. Zenker)	95% completed Schichau-Werft Danzig, slip No. 4, 24.3.45 contract suspended, 30.3.45 captured by USSR forces, 12.4.45 Soviet *TS*-5, 15.7.45 launched, →Libau, 8.3.47 *R-1*, 7./8.8.47 ✞ Baltic 20 sm N.W. of Cape Ristna: ≈59°15n/21°30e, § 20.9.47.

1	2	3	4	5	6
U 3536				(OL H. Gode)	95% completed Schichau-Werft Danzig, slip No. 4, 24.3.45 contract suspended, 30.3.45 captured by USSR forces, 12.4.45 Soviet *TS-6*. 15.7.45 launched, →Libau, 8.3.47 *R-2*, 7./8.8.47 ✞ Baltic 20 sm N.W. of Cape Ristna: ≈59°15n/21°30e, § 20.9.47.
U 3537				(OL H. Korndörfer)	24.3.45 contract suspended, 30.3.45 captured incomplete at Schichau-Werft Danzig, slip No. 3, by USSR forces, 12.4.45 Soviet *TS-7*, 15.7.45 launched, →Libau, 8.3.47 *R-3*,7./8.8.47 ✞ Baltic 20 sm N.W. of Cape Ristna: ≈59°15n/21°30e, § 20.9.47.
U 3538					24.3.45 contract suspended, 30.3.45 captured incomplete at Schichau-Werft Danzig, slip No. 3, by USSR forces, 12.4.45 Soviet *TS-8*, 15.7.45 launched, →Libau, 8.3.47 *R-4*, 7./8.8.47 ✞ Baltic 20 sm N.W. of Cape Ristna: ≈59°15n/21°30e, § 20.9.47.
U 3539					24.3.45 contract suspended, 30.3.45 captured incomplete at Schichau-Werft Danzig, slip No. 2, by USSR forces, 12.4.45 Soviet *TS-9*, summer 1945 launched, →Libau, 8.3.47 *R-5*, 7./8.8.47 ✞ Baltic 20 sm N.W. of Cape Ristna: ≈59°15n/21°30e, § 20.9.47.
U 3540					24.3.45 contract suspended. 30.3.45 captured incomplete at Schichau-Werft Danzig, slip No. 2, by USSR forces, 12.4.45 Soviet *TS-10*, summer 1945 launched, →Libau, 8.3.47 *R-6*, § 28.2.48, br.
U 3541					29.1.45 contract suspended, 30.3.45 captured incomplete at Schichau-Werft Danzig, slip No. 6, by USSR forces, 12.4.45 Soviet *TS-11*, summer 1945 launched, →Libau, 8.3.47 *R-7*, § 28.2.48, br.
U 3542					29.1.45 contract suspended, 30.3.45 captured incomplete at Schichau-Werft Danzig, slip No. 3, by USSR forces, 12.4.45 Soviet *TS-12*, summer 1945 launched, →Libau, 8.3.47 *R-8*, § 28.2.48, br.

1	2	3	4	5	6
U 3543– U 3547					no keel laid, prefabricated sections partly completed, 29.1.45 contract suspended, 30.3.45 captured by USSR forces, 12.4.45 Soviet *TS-13*, *TS-15*, *TS-17* to *TS-19*, § 9.4.47, br.
U 3548– U 3554					no keel laid, prefabricated sections partly completed, 29.1.45 contract suspended, 30.3.45 captured by USSR forces, 12.2.46 Soviet *TS-32* to *TS-38*, § 9.4.47, br.
U 3555– U 3571					construction of prefabricated sections not started, 29.1.45 contract suspended.
U 3572– U 3642					construction of prefabricated sections not started, 29.1.45 contract suspended.
U 3643– U 3684					construction of prefabricated sections not started, 29.1.45 contract suspended.

In addition the following building yards received building orders for Type XXI boats by telex on 6.7.43:

Deutsche Werft AG Hamburg	24 boats
Danziger Werft AG	12 boats
F. Schichau GmbH Danzig	18 boats
Deschimag AG Weser Bremen	24 boats
Lübecker Flender-Werke AG	12 boats
Kriegsmarinewerft Wilhelmshaven	12 boats.

These orders were subsequently canceled on 30.9.43 before the arrival of written confirmation and the assignment of official U-numbers.

Type XXII

Coastal U-boat type of advanced design with Walter propulsion system developed in 1943
Surface/submerged displacement: 155/ ≈170 t
Overall length/beam/draught: 27.10 m/3.00 m/4.20 m
Standard main armament: 3 torpedo tubes (2 bow, 1 stern) with 3 torpedoes

Building yard	Total no. ordered	Completed (comm.)	Under construction	Construction not started	Canceled after keel laying	Canceled prior to keel laying
Howaldtswerke Kiel AG	2	—	—	—	—	2
Total	2	—	—	—	—	2

1	2	3	4	5	6
U 1153– U 1154					30.9.43 cancelation announced, 6.11.43 contract canceled.

In addition the building yards Howaldtswerke Kiel AG and Howaldtswerke Hamburg AG received building orders for 36 Type XXII boats each by telex on 6.7.43. These orders were subsequently canceled on 30.9.43 before the arrival of written confirmation and the assignment of official U-numbers.

Type XXIII

Coastal U-boat type of advanced design with enlarged accumulator battery capacity developed in 1943

Surface/submerged displacement: 234/258 t
Overall length/beam/draught: 34.68 m/3.02 m/3.66 m
Standard main armament: 2 bow torpedo tubes with 2 torpedoes

Building yard	Total no. ordered	Completed (comm.)	Under construction	Construction not started	Contract shifted	Canceled or abandoned
Deutsche Werft AG Hamburg	120 (+30)	49	2	—	131	18
Germaniawerft AG Kiel	50 (+141)	12 (11)	6	12	—	161
Ansaldo Genoa	30	—	—	—	30	—
Cantiere Riuniti Dell Adriatico Monfalcone	15	—	—	—	15	—
Deutsche Werft AG Toulon	30	—	—	—	30	—
Deutsche Werft AG Nikolaev	15	—	—	—	15	—
Schiffswerft Linz AG	0 (+15)	—	—	—	15	—
Total	260	61 (60)	8	12	—	179

1	2	3	4	5	6
U 2321	12.6.44			OL H.-H. Barschkies	9.5.45 Surrender Kristiansand, 29.5.45 sailed →Loch Ryan / 27.11.45 ✝ artillery DD's HMS *Onslow*, ORP *Blyskawica* 56°10n/10°05w / Op. Deadlight.
U 2322	1.7.44			OL F. Heckel	9.5.45 Surrender Stavanger, 27.5.45 sailed →Loch Ryan / 27.11.45 ✝ artillery DD's HMS *Onslow*, ORP *Blyskawica* 56°10n/10°05w / Op. Deadlight.
U 2323	18.7.44			LT W. Angermann	26.7.44 ✝ 16h35 Baltic, Kiel Fiord W. of Möltenort: 54°22,8n/10°11,2e / British air-laid mine, field "Forgetmenot" / 2 dead / 12 rescued / ↑ ?.8.44, from March 1945 repaired Germaniawerft Kiel / May 45 captured by British forces on slip No. 7 Germaniawerft Kiel, 1946 br.
U 2324	25.7.44	2.4.45	St	KL K. von Rappard	9.5.45 Surrender Stavanger, 27.5.45 sailed →Loch Ryan / 27.11.45 ✝ artillery DD's HMS *Onslow*, ORP *Blyskawica* 56°10n/10°05w / Op. Deadlight.

1	2	3	4	5	6
U 2325	3.8.44			OL K. Eckel	9.5.45 Surrender Kristiansand, 29.5.45 sailed →Loch Ryan / 28.11.45 ✝ artillery DD's HMS *Onslaught*, ORP *Piorun* 56°10n/10°05w / Op. Deadlight.
U 2326	11.8.44	4.5.45	St	OL K. Jobst	14.5.45 Surrender Dundee, →Lisahally, British war prize, HMS/m *N 35*, tests; 13.2.46 →Cherbourg →France, 6.12.46 ✝ off Toulon: 43°07n/05°55e / diving accident / 17 dead / ↑, br.
U 2327	19.8.44			OL H. Schulz	3.5.45 (✝) 03h Hamburg-Finkenwerder, U-boat pen Fink II inside box No. 3: 53°33n/09°58e / br.
U 2328	25.8.44			OL P. Lawrence	9.5.45 Surrender Bergen, 2.6.45 sailed →Loch Ryan / 27.11.45 ✝ foundered while under tow 56°12n/09°48w / Op. Deadlight.
U 2329	1.9.44			OL H. Schlott	9.5.45 Surrender Stavanger, 27.5.45 sailed →Loch Ryan / 28.11.45 ✝ artillery DD's HMS *Onslaught*, ORP *Piorun* 56°10n/10°05w / Op. Deadlight.
U 2330	7.9.44			OL H. Beckmann	3.5.45 (✝) Kiel: 54°19n/10°10e / br.
U 2331	12.9.44			OL H.-W. Pahl	10.10.44 ✝ Baltic off Hela: 54°35n/18°47e / marine accident / 15 dead / 4 rescued / ↑, →Gotenhafen, ?.10.44 decomm., 7.1.45 ready for transfer →Kiel, under repair Germaniawerft; 3.5.45 (✝) Kiel. Germaniawerft inside floating dock / br.
U 2332	13.11.44			OL H.-J. Junker	3.5.45 (✝) 03h Hamburg-Finkenwerder, U-boat pen Fink II inside box No. 3: 53°33n/09°51e / br.
U 2333	18.12.44			OL H. Baumann	5.5.45 (✝) Gelting Bay: 54°48n/09°49e / br.
U 2334	21.9.44			OL W. Angermann	9.5.45 Surrender Kristiansand, 29.5.45 sailed →Loch Ryan / 28.11.45 ✝ artillery DD's HMS *Onslaught*, ORP *Piorun* 56°10n/10°05w / Op. Deadlight.
U 2335	27.9.44			OL K.-D. Benthin	9.5.45 Surrender Kristiansand, 29.5.45 sailed →Loch Ryan / 28.11.45 ✝ artillery DD's HMS *Onslaught*, ORP *Piorun* 56°10n/10°05w / Op. Deadlight.
U 2336	30.9.44	1.5.45	Kr	KL E. Klusmeier	15.5.45 Surrender Kiel, →Wilhelmshaven, 21.6.45 sailed →Lisahally / 3.1.46 ✝ artillery DD HMS *Offa* 56°06n/09°00w / Op. Deadlight.

1	2	3	4	5	6
U 2337	4.10.44			OL G. Behnisch	9.5.45 Surrender Kristiansand, 29.5.45 sailed →Loch Ryan / 28.11.45 ✞ artillery DD's HMS *Onslaught*, ORP Mos M 56°10n/10°05w / Op. Deadlight.
U 2338	9.10.44	4.5.45	Ge	OL D.-K. Kaiser	4.5.45 ✞ 15h40 Baltic N.E. of Fredericia: 55°34,2n/09°49,3e / rockets / Bft R, A, C, E, F, W, K, 236 Sqn RAF, Mos M, Q, A, Z, T, J, K, 254 Sqn RAF / 12 dead / 1 rescued / ↑ 1952, br.
U 2339	16.11.44			OL G. Woermann	5.5.45 (✞) Gelting Bay: 54°48n/09°49e / br.
U 2340	16.10.44			OL E. Klusmeier	30.3.45 ✞ Hamburg-Finkenwerder. Rüschkanal, inside pontoon dock S.E. of U-boat pen Fink II: 53°33n/09°51e / bomb / air raid 8. USAAF / none dead / ↑ ?.8.45, →Blankenese, br.
U 2341	21.10.44			OL H. Böhm	5.5.45 Surrender Cuxhaven, →Wilhelmshaven, 21.6.45 sailed →Lisahally / 31.12.45 ✞ artillery DD's HMS *Onslaught*, ORP *Blyskawica* 55°44n/08°19w / Op. Deadlight.
U 2342	1.11.44			OL B. Schad von Mittelbiberach	26.12.44 ✞ 22h40 Baltic N. of Swinemünde: 54°01,8n/14°15,2e / British air-laid mine, field "Geranium" / 7 dead / 4 rescued / 30.10.-3.11.54 blown up, ↑, →Karlshagen, br.
U 2343	6.11.44			KL H.-L. Gaude	5.5.45 (✞) Gelting Bay: 54°48n/09°49e / br.
U 2344	10.11.44			OL H. Ellerlage	18.2.45 ✞ 15h14 Baltic N. of Heiligendamm: 54°17,3n/11°46,3e / collision U 2336 / 11 dead / 10 rescued / ↑ 22.1.55, →Rostock, Neptun-Werft. preserved, but not repaired; 1958 br Rostock.
U 2345	15.11.44			OL K. Steffen	9.5.45 Surrender Stavanger, 27.5.45 sailed →Loch Ryan / 27.11.45 ✞ demolition charge 56°10n/10°05w / Op. Deadlight.
U 2346	20.11.44			OL H. von der Höh	5.5.45 (✞) Gelting Bay: 54°48n/09°49e / br.
U 2347	2.12.44			OL W. Ulbing	5.5.45 (✞) Gelting Bay: 54°48n/09°49e / br.
U 2348	4.12.44			OL G. Goschzik	9.5.45 Surrender Stavanger, 27.5.45 sailed →Loch Ryan, August 1945 British war prize, HMS/m *N 21*, 30.12.45 →Lisahally, laid up / April 1949 →Leigh & Co., Belfast, br.

1	2	3	4	5	6
U 2349	11.12.44			OL H.-G. Müller	5.5.45 (✝) Gelting Bay: 54°48n/09°49e / br.
U 2350	23.12.44			OL W. Schauer	9.5.45 Surrender Kristiansand, 29.5.45 sailed →Loch Ryan / 28.11.45 ✝ artillery DD's HMS *Onslaught*. ORP *Piorun* 56°10n/10°05w / Op. Deadlight.
U 2351	30.12.44			OL W. Brückner	9.5.45 Surrender Flensburg, →Kiel. →Wilhelmshaven, 21.6.45 sailed →Lisahally / 3.1.46 ✝ artillery DD HMS *Offa* 55°50n/08°20w / Op. Deadlight.
U 2352	11.1.45			OL S. Budzyn	5.5.45 (✝) Hörup Haff: 54°53n/09°52e / br.
U 2353	9.1.45			OL J. Hillmann	9.5.45 Surrender Kristiansand, 29.5.45 sailed →Loch Ryan, *N 31;* USSR war prize, 1.11.45 →Lisahally, 23.11.45 sailed →Libau / 4.12.45 →USSR, Soviet *M-31*, 1963 br.
U 2354	11.1.45			OL D. Wex	9.5.45 Surrender Kristiansand, 29.5.45 sailed →Loch Ryan / 22.12.45 ✝ artillery DD HMS *Onslow* 56°00n/10°05w / Op. Deadlight.
U 2355	12.1.45			OL H.-H. Franke	3.5.45 (✝) Baltic, Kiel Fiord N.W. of Laboe: 54°24,4n/10°12e / br.
U 2356	12.1.45			OL F. Hartel	5.5.45 Surrender Cuxhaven, →Wilhelmshaven, 21.6.45 sailed →Lisahally / 6.1.46 ✝ artillery DD HMS *Onslaught* 55°50n/08°20w / Op. Deadlight.
U 2357	13.1.45			OL E. Heinrich	5.5.45 (✝) Gelting Bay: 54°48n/09°49e / br.
U 2358	16.1.45			OL G. Breun	5.5.45 (✝) Gelting Bay: 54°48n/09°49e / br.
U 2359	16.1.45	29.4.45	Ki	OL G. Bischoff	2.5.45 ✝ Baltic S.W. of Göteborg: 57°29n/11°24e / rockets / Mos A, B, J, 235 Sqn RAF, Mos K, F, 143 Sqn RAF, Mos L, Z, V, M, N, S, 248 Sqn RAF / 12 dead / ✝.
U 2360	23.1.45			OL K. Schrobach	5.5.45 (✝) Gelting Bay: 54°48n/09°49e / br.
U 2361	3.2.45			OL H. von Hennig	9.5.45 Surrender Kristiansand, 29.5.45 sailed →Loch Ryan / 27.11.45 ✝ artillery DD's HMS *Onslow*, ORP *Blyskawica* 56°10n/10°05w / Op. Deadlight.
U 2362	5.2.45			OL M. Czekowski	5.5.45 (✝) Gelting Bay: 54°48n/09°49e / br.

1	2	3	4	5	6
U 2363	5.2.45			OL K. Frahm	9.5.45 Surrender Kristiansand, 29.5.45 sailed →Loch Ryan / 28.11.45 ✠ artillery DD's HMS *Onslaught*, ORP *Piorun* 56°10n/10°05w / Op. Deadlight.
U 2364	14.2.45			KL G. Remus	5.5.45 (✠) Gelting Bay: 54°48n/09°49e / br.
U 2365	2.3.45	4.5.45	Ge	OL U. Christiansen	8.5.45 (✠) Baltic N.W. of Anholt I.: 56°51n/11°49e / ↑ ?.6.56. German Bundesmarine, comm. 15.8.57: *Hai*, 14.9.66 ✠ 18h45 North Sea: 55°15n/04°22e / marine accident / 19 dead / 1 rescued / ↑ 24.9.66, br Rheinstahl Nordseewerke Emden 1968.[199]
U 2366	10.3.45			OL K. Jäckel	5.5.45 (✠) Gelting Bay: 54°48n/09°49e / br.
U 2367	17.3.45			OL H. Schröder	9.5.45 (✠) Baltic S.E. of Schleimünde: 54°35,9n/10°11,9e (?) / ↑ ?.8.56, German Bundesmarine, comm. 1.10.57: *Hecht*, 30.9.68 decomm. Kiel / 1969 br Kiel.
U 2368	11.4.45			OL F. Ufermann	5.5.45 (✠) Gelting Bay: 54°48n/09°49e / br.
U 2369	18.4.45			OL H.-W. Pahl	5.5.45 (✠) Gelting Bay: 54°48n/09°49e / br.
U 2370	-------			(OL D. Bornkessel)	3.5.45 (✠) 03h Hamburg-Finkenwerder, U-boat pen Fink II inside box No. 3: 53°33n/09°51e / br.
U 2371				(OL J. Kühne)	3.5.45 (✠) 03h Hamburg-Finkenwerder, U-boat pen Fink II inside box No. 3: 53°33n/09°51e / br.
U 2372– U 2377					prefabricated sections completed at Deutsche Werft, Hamburg (yard No. 526-531); February 1945 delivered →Germaniawerft AG, Kiel for assembly of U 4713–U 4718.
U 2378– U 2389					prefabricated sections partly completed at Deutsche Werft, Hamburg (yard No. 532-543), final assembly intended as U 4719–U 4730 at Germaniawerft AG Kiel.
U 2390– U 2400					1.12.44 ? contract cancelled, shifted to Germaniawerft AG Kiel
U 2401– U 2404					July 1944 construction abandoned at Ansaldo, Genoa, 24.8.44 contract suspended, later shifted under new U-number to Germaniawerft AG Kiel. Incomplete hulls final fate?

1	2	3	4	5	6
U 2405– U 2430					construction not started, 24.8.44 contract suspended, later shifted under new U-number to Germaniawerft AG Kiel.
U 2431– U 2432					July 1944 construction abandoned at Cantiere Riuniti dell Adriatico, Monfalcone, 24.8.44 contract suspended, later shifted under new U-number to Germaniawerft AG Kiel. Incomplete hulls 1.5.45 blown up on slip, br.
U 2433– U 2445					construction not started, 24.8.44 contract suspended, later shifted under new U-number to Germaniawerft AG Kiel.
U 2446– U 2460					contract originally placed with Deutsche Werft Nikolaev, 1.5.44 shifted to Schiffswerft Linz AG, construction not started, August 1944 contract suspended, later shifted under new U-number to Germaniawerft AG Kiel.
U 4001– U 4070					construction not started. 29.9.44 contract canceled.
U 4701	10.1.45			OL A. Wiechmann	5.5.45 (✞) Hörup Haff: 54°53n/09°52e / br.
U 4702	12.1.45			OL E. Seeliger	5.5.45 (✞) Gelting Bay: 54°48n/09°49e / br.
U 4703	21.1.45			OL H. U. Scholz	5.5.45 (✞) Gelting Bay: 54°48n/09°49e / br.
U 4704	14.3.45			OL G. Franceschi	5.5.45 (✞) Hörup Haff: 54°53n/09°52e / br.
U 4705	2.2.45			OL M. Landt-Hayen	3.5.45 (✞) Kiel: 54°20n/10°09e / br.
U 4706	7.2.45			OL M. Schneider	Kristiansand, unserviceable; May 45 captured by British forces, October 1948 transferred →Norway: KNM *Knerten;* decomm. following fire damage, 14.4.50 sold Royal Norwegian Yacht Club, floating store ship, br 1954.
U 4707	20.2.45			OL J. Leder	5.5.45 (✞) Gelting Bay: 54°48n/09°49e / br.
U 4708	-------			(OL D. Schultz)	9.4.45 ✞ Kiel, U-boat pen Kilian South box / bomb / air raid 1, 3, and 8 Groups RAF Bomber Command / 5 dead / wreck still present.
U 4709	3.3.45			OL P. Berkemann	3.5.45 (✞) Kiel, Germaniawerft inside floating dock / br.
U 4710	1.5.45			OL L.-F. von Friedeburg	5.5.45 (✞) Gelting Bay: 54°48n/09°49e / br.

1	2	3	4	5	6
U 4711	21.3.45			OL S. Endler	3.5.45 (✠) Kiel, Germaniawerft inside floating dock / br.
U 4712	3.4.45			KL K. Fleige	3.5.45 (✠) Kiel, Germaniawerft inside floating dock / br.
U 4713	-------			(LT W. Käding)	completed, but not formally accepted; 3.5.45 (✠) Kiel, Germaniawerft inside floating dock / br.
U 4714	-------			(OL H. von Ahlefeld)	completed, but not formally accepted; 3.5.45 (✠) Kiel, Germaniawerft inside floating dock / br.
U 4715				(OL L. Wäninger)	completed except battery cells on slip No. 8 at Germaniawerft Kiel, 1946 br.
U 4716				(OL C. Ostrowitzky)	captured by British forces 95% complete on slip No. 8 at Germaniawerft Kiel, 1946 br.
U 4717				(OL G. Popp)	captured by British forces 95% complete on slip No. 8 at Germaniawerft Kiel, 1946 br.
U 4718				(OL H. Warnecke)	captured by British forces 95% complete on slip No. 8 at Germaniawerft Kiel, 1946 br.
U 4719– U 4723					completion planned until the end of May 1945 according to emergency program of 29.1.45, construction of prefabricated sections partly started at Deutsche Werft AG Hamburg.
U 4724– U 4730					construction of prefabricated sections partly started at Deutsche Werft AG Hamburg, 29.1.45 contract suspended.
U 4731– U 4750					construction of prefabricated sections not started, 29.1.45 contract suspended.
U 4751– U 4891					construction of prefabricated sections not started, 29.1.45 contract suspended.

Type XXVI W

Seagoing U-boat type of advanced design with Walter propulsion system developed in 1944
Surface/submerged displacement: 842/926 t
Overall length/beam/draught: 56.20 m/5.44 m/5.90 m
Standard main armament: 10 torpedo tubes (4 bow, 6 side) with 10 torpedoes

Building yard	Total no. ordered	Completed (comm.)	Under construction	Construction not started	Canceled after keel laying	Canceled prior to keel laying
Blohm & Voss AG Hamburg	100	—	2	2	—	96
Total	100	—	2	2	—	96

1	2	3	4	5	6
U 4501– U 4502					no keel laid, only pressure hull sections partly completed in building shops at Blohm & Voss Hamburg.
U 4503– U 4504					construction of prefabricated sections not started.
U 4505– U 4600					construction not started, 28.3.45 contract canceled.

Foreign submarines captured by German forces and designated for service in the Kriegsmarine

UA (ex Turkish *Batiray*)

Seagoing U-boat type of conventional design developed in 1936
Surface/submerged displacement: 1128/1284 t
Overall length/beam/draught: 86.65 m/6.80 m/4.07 m
Standard main armament: 6 torpedo tubes (4 bow, 2 stern) with 12 torpedoes

1	2	3	4	5	6
UA	21.9.39			OL U.-P. Graf von und zu Arco-Zinneberg	September 1939 taken over while fitting out at Germaniawerft Kiel; comm. Kiel; 15.3.45 decomm. Kiel, laid up, 3.5.45 (✝) Kiel, br.

UB (ex HMS/m *Seal*)

Seagoing minelaying U-boat type of conventional design developed in 1930
Surface/submerged displacement: 1770/2113 t
Overall length/beam/draught: 89.31 m/7.74 m/5.18 m
Standard main armament: 6 bow torpedo tubes with 12 torpedoes and 50 moored mines on rails in upperdeck casing

1	2	3	4	5	6
UB	30.11.40			FK B. Mahn	5.5.40 captured by German aircraft of 1. BoFlGr. 196 (OL. K. Schmidt) Kattegat E. of Laesö following mine damage and engine failure 4.5.40; towed →Frederikshavn by SC *UJ 128*, 11.5.40 →Kiel. 23.7.40 renamed *UB*. comm. Kiel; 31.7.41 decomm. Kiel, cannibalized, 1942 converted to explosives test vessel, hulk 3.5.45 (✝) Kiel-Friedrichsort Road N.E. of Stickenhörn quay, br.

UC 1 (ex Norwegian *B 5*)
UC 2 (ex Norwegian *B 6*)

Coastal U-boat type of conventional design developed in 1915–23
Surface/submerged displacement: 427/554 t
Overall length/beam/draught: 51.00 m/5.34 m/3.50 m
Standard main armament: 4 torpedo tubes (2 bow, 2 stern) with 6 torpedoes

1	2	3	4	5	6
UC 1	20.11.40			KL G. Lange	9.4.40 captured at Kristiansand; 26.10.40 renamed *UC 1*, 4.1.42 decomm. Kiel following fire damage 20.12.41 Deutsche Werke Kiel, br.
UC 2	17.11.41			OL H. Waldkirch	19.5.40 captured at Flörö; 21.5.40 →Bergen, 26.10.40 renamed *UC 2*, 22.11.43 decomm. Bergen, 1944 cannibalized, hulk 4.10.44 ✝ Bergen, Laksevaag Yard: 60°23n/05°18e / bomb / air raid 6 (RCAF) and 8 Groups RAF Bomber Command, ↑, 1945 br.

UD 1 (ex Dutch *O 8*)

(ex HMS/m *H 6*, interned on 18.1.16 after stranding on Ameland Island. Sold to the Netherlands
Coastal U-boat type of conventional design developed in 1913

Surface/submerged displacement:	359/429 t
Overall length/beam/draught:	46.20 m/4.86 m/3.87 m
Standard main armament:	4 bow torpedo tubes with 8 torpedoes

1	2	3	4	5	6
UD 1	21.11.40			OL F. Weidner	14.5.40 captured at Den Helder; 8.7.40 →Kiel, 23.7.40 renamed *UD 1*, comm. Kiel 22.11.43 15h00 decomm. Kiel, Kriegsmarine dockyard, laid up, hulk 3.5.45 (✝) Kiel, br.

UD 2 (ex Dutch *O 12*)

Seagoing U-boat type of conventional design developed in 1937

Surface/submerged displacement:	555/715 t
Overall length/beam/draught:	60.50 m/5.38 m/3.55 m
Standard main armament:	5 torpedo tubes (4 bow, 2 stem) with 10 torpedoes

1	2	3	4	5	6
UD 2	30.1.43			OL G. Scholz	14.5.40 captured at Rijkswerf, Den Helder following (✝) 14.5.40, ↑ 1940, repaired at Wilton-Fijenoord, Rotterdam, comm. Rotterdam; 6.7.44 decomm. Kiel, 1945 laid up Kiel on quay opposite to railroad station, 4.5.45 captured by British forces, br.

UD 3 (ex Dutch *O 25*)
UD 4 (ex Dutch *O 26*)
UD 5 (ex Dutch *O 27*)

Seagoing U-boat type of conventional design developed in 1937

Surface/submerged displacement:	949/1054 t
Overall length/beam/draught:	77.53 m/6.55 m/3.90 m
Standard main armament:	8 torpedo tubes (4 bow, 2 stern, 2 in upperdeck) with 14 torpedoes

1	2	3	4	5	6
UD 3	8.6.41			OL J. Seeger	14.5.40 captured at building yard Schiedam following (✝) 14.5.40 in Nieuwe Waterweg, ↑ 7.6.40, 23.7.40 renamed *UD 3*, repaired and completed at Wilton-Fijenoord. Schiedam, comm. Rotterdam; 13.10.44 decomm. Kiel following battery fire, laid up, 4.5.45 captured by British forces Kiel, Kriegsmarine dockyard, br.
UD 4	28.1.41			KL F. Bart	14.5.40 captured on slip at building yard Rotterdamsche Droogdok, 1.6.40 completion ordered, 23.7.40 renamed *UD 4*, comm. Rotterdam; 3.45 decomm. Kiel, Kriegsmarine dockyard, laid up, 4.5.45 captured by British forces Kiel, Kriegsmarine dockyard, br.
UD 5	1.11.41			KL H. U. Scheltz	14.5.40 captured on slip at building yard Rotterdamsche Droogdok, 1.6.40 completion ordered, 23.7.40 renamed *UD 5*, comm. Rotterdam; 9.5.45 Surrender Bergen, 30.5.45 sailed →Lisahally, 13.7.45 at Lisahally Dutch *O 27*, 10.5.47 *S 807*, decomm. 14.11.59, 23.12.60 sold to scrap to Jos Desmet, Antwerp, 1961 br.

UF 1 (ex French *L'Africaine*)
UF 2 (ex French *La Favorite*)
UF 3 (ex French *L'Astree*)

Seagoing U-boat type of conventional design developed in 1934
Surface/submerged displacement: 818/928 t
Overall length/beam/draught: 68.15 m/5.33 m/4.57 m
Standard main armament: 9 torpedo tubes (4 bow, 2 stern, 3 in upperdeck) with ? torpedoes

1	2	3	4	5	6
UF 1					13.6.40 captured incomplete on slip at building yard Atelier et Chant. Worms & Cie, Le Trait, 31.10.40 completion ordered, 5.5.41 renamed *UF 1*, construction abandoned November 1943, 23.8.44 incomplete hull blown up on slip, recaptured by Allied Forces August 1944, returned to France.

1	2	3	4	5	6
UF 2	5.11.42			OL H. Gehrken	3.6.40 captured incomplete on slip at building yard Atelier et Chant. Worms & Cie, Le Trait, 31.10.40 completion ordered, 5.5.41 renamed *UF 2*, comm. Le Trait; 5.7.44 decomm. Gotenhafen, 1945 (✠) Gotenhafen ?
UF 3					19.6.40 captured incomplete on slip at building yard Anciens Chantier Dubigeon, Nantes; 31.10.40 completion ordered, 5.5.41 renamed *UF 3*, 3.12.41 construction abandoned, 9.8.44 incomplete hull blown up on slip, recaptured by Allied Forces August 1944, returned to France.

Ex French *Roland Morillot*-class submarine

Oceangoing U-boat type of conventional design developed in 1937
Surface/submerged displacement: 1817/2416 t
Overall length/beam/draught: 102.50 m/8.30 m/4.60 m
Standard main armament: 10 torpedo tubes (4 bow, 2 stern, 4 in upperdeck) with 14–18 torpedoes

1	2	3	4	5	6
ex La Martinique					19.6.40 captured incomplete on slip at building yard Arsenal Cherbourg, 31.10.40 completion ordered, 30.5.41 construction abandoned owing to lack of material, probably br.

UIT 1 (ex Italian *R 10*)
UIT 2 (ex Italian *R 11*)
UIT 3 (ex Italian *R 12*)
UIT 4 (ex Italian *R 7*)
UIT 5 (ex Italian *R 8*)
UIT 6 (ex Italian *R 9*)

Seagoing transport U-boat type of conventional design developed in 1941–42
Surface/submerged displacement: 1300/2220 t
Overall length/beam/draught: 86.50 m/7.86 m/5.34 m
Standard main armament: none except AA-guns

1	2	3	4	5	6
UIT 1	-------			(OL H. Böhm)	9.9.43 captured incomplete on slip of building yard Odero-Terni-Orlando, Muggiano-La Spezia, construction continued, launched 12.7.44, 19.7.44 →Genoa for completion, delivery delayed by lack of material; 4.9.44 ✠ Genoa: 44°24n/08°54e / bomb / air raid 15. USAAF / 1946 br.
UIT 2	-------				9.9.43 captured incomplete on slip of building yard Odero-Terni-Orlando, Muggiano-La Spezia, construction continued, launched 6.7.1944, delivery delayed by lack of material, 5.9.44 contruction suspended; 24.4.45 (✠) La Spezia, ↑ 1946, § 1947, →floating oil tank *GR 522*.
UIT 3					9.9.43 captured incomplete on slip of building yard Odero-Terni-Orlando. Muggiano-La Spezia, construction continued, delivery delayed by lack of material, 5.9.44 construction suspended; launched 29.9.44?, 24.4.45 (✠) La Spezia, East jetty, ↑ 1946, § 27.3.47, →floating oil tank *GR 523*.
UIT 4	-------				9.9.43 captured 75% complete on slip of building yard Cantiere Riuniti dell Adriatico, Monfalcone, construction resumed, launched 31.10.43, delivery delayed by lack of material; 25.5.44 ✠ Monfalcone: 45°48n/13°32e / bomb / air raid 15. USAAF / ↑ 31.5.46, § 27.3.47, 1948 br.
UIT 5	-------				9.9.43 captured 72% complete on slip of building yard Cantiere Riuniti dell Adriatico, Monfalcone, construction resumed, launched 28.12.43, delivery delayed by lack of material; 20.4.44 ✠ Monfalcone: 45°48n/13°32e / bomb / air raid 15. USAAF / ↑ 3.6.46, § 27.3.47, 1948 br.
UIT 6	-------				9.9.43 captured 67% complete on slip of building yard Cantiere Riuniti dell Adriatico, Monfalcone, construction resumed, launched 27.2.44, delivery delayed by lack of material; 5.9.44 construction abandoned; 16.3.45 ✠ Monfalcone: 45°48n/13°32e / bomb / Lib, air raid 37 Sqn and 70 Sqn RAF / ↑ ?.6.46, § 27.3.47, 1948 br.

UIT 7 (ex Italian *CM 1*)
UIT 8 (ex Italian *CM 2*)

Coastal U-boat type of conventional design developed in 1943
Surface/submerged displacement:	92/114 t
Overall length/beam/draught:	32.95 m/2.89 m/2.77 m
Standard main armament:	2 torpedo tubes with 2 torpedoes

1	2	3	4	5	6
UIT 7	4.1.45 (?)				9.9.43 captured incomplete at building yard Cantiere Riuniti dell Adriatico, Monfalcone, construction resumed, delivery delayed by lack of material, 1944 →transferred to Navy of Italian Social Republic; April 45 captured at Monfalcone by Italian guerrilla forces, →Italy, § 1.2.48, br.
UIT 8	-------				9.9.43 captured incomplete on slip of building yard Cantiere Riuniti dell Adriatico, Monfalcone, construction resumed, launched February 1944, delivery delayed by lack of material and bomb damage air raid 15. USAAF on 25.5.44, 1.5.45 (✝) Monfalcone: 45°48n/13°32e / ↑ 7.10.50, br, partly preserved at the Museo Navale, Trieste.

UIT 21 (ex Italian *Giuseppe Finzi*)

Seagoing U-boat type of conventional design developed in 1933–34
Surface/submerged displacement:	1550/2060 t
Overall length/beam/draught:	84.30 m/7.71 m/5.21 m
Standard main armament:	8 torpedo tubes (4 bow, 4 stern) with 16 torpedoes, all removed in 1943 during conversion to transport boat

1	2	3	4	5	6
UIT 21	14.10.43			OL F. Steinfeldt	9.9.43 captured at Bordeaux after Italian Surrender, comm. Bordeaux; 15.4.44 decomm. Bordeaux owing to material breakdown, laid up Bordeaux U-boat pen, 25.8.44 (✝) Bordeaux inside U-boat pen, br.

UIT 22 (ex Italian *Alpino Bagnolini*) UIT 23 (ex Italian *Reginaldo Giuliani*)

Seagoing U-boat type of conventional design developed in 1937–38
Surface/submerged displacement:	1166/1484 t
Overall length/beam/draught:	76.10 rn/7.12 m/4.55 m
Standard main armament:	8 torpedo tubes (4 bow, 4 stern) with 12 torpedoes, all removed in 1943 during conversion to transport boat

1	2	3	4	5	6
UIT 22	14.10.43	26.1.44	Bo	OL K. Wunderlich	9.9.43 captured at Bordeaux after Italian Surrender, comm. Bordeaux; 11.3.44 h ✝ S. of Capetown: 41°28s/17°40e / D/Cs / Cat D (F/L F. J. Roddick), Cat P (F/L E. S. S. Nash), Cat A (F/L A. H. Surridge), 262 Sqn RAF/ 55 dead / ✝.
UIT 23	6.12.43	14.2.44	Sh	OL H. W. Striegler i.V.	10.9.43 captured by IJN at Singapore after Italian Surrender, 22.10.43 handed over to the Kriegsmarine, comm. Singapore; 15.2.44 ✝ 08h22 Malacca Strait: 04°27n/100°11e / torpedo / SS HMS/m *Tally Ho* (Lt. Comdr. L. W. A. Bennington) / 31 dead / 14 rescued.

UIT 24 (ex Italian *Commandante Cappellini*)

Seagoing U-boat type of conventional design developed in 1937–38
Surface/submerged displacement: 1060/1313 t
Overall length/beam/draught: 73.10 m/8.15 m/5.12 m
Standard main armament: 8 torpedo tubes (4 bow, 4 stern) with 16 torpedoes, all removed in 1943 during conversion to transport boat

1	2	3	4	5	6
UIT 24	6.12.43			OL H. Pahls	10.9.43 captured by IJN at Singapore after Italian Surrender, 22.10.43 handed over to the Kriegsmarine, comm. Singapore; 6.5.45 captured at Kobe by IJN after German Surrender, 15.7.45 Japanese SS *I-503*, September 1945 captured by U.S. forces at Mitsubishi Yard Kobe, 15.4.46 (✝) Kii Suido by U.S. T.F. 96.5.

UIT 25 (ex Italian *Luigi Torelli*)

Seagoing U-boat type of conventional design developed in 1937–38
Surface/submerged displacement: 1191/1489 t
Overall length/beam/draught: 76.04 m/7.91 m/4.72 m
Standard main armament: 8 torpedo tubes (4 bow, 4 stern) with 16 torpedoes, all removed in 1943 during conversion to transport boat

1	2	3	4	5	6
UIT 25	6.12.43			OL A. Meier	10.9.43 captured by IJN at Singapore after Italian Surrender, 22.10.43 handed over to the Kriegsmarine, comm. Singapore; 6.5.45 captured at Kobe by IJN after German Surrender, 15.7.45 Japanese SS *I-504*, September 1945 captured by U.S. forces at Kawasaki Yard Kobe, 15.4.46 (✝) Kii Suido by U.S. T.F. 96.5.

Ex Italian *Tritone*-class submarines

Oceangoing U-boat type of conventional design developed in 1941[200]

Surface/submerged displacement:	1128/1284 t
Overall length/beam/draught:	86.65 m/6.80 m/4.12 m
Standard main armament:	6 torpedo tubes (4 bow, 2 stern) with 12 torpedoes

1	2	3	4	5	6
ex *Sparide*					9.9.43 (⚓) La Spezia at Italian Surrender, captured, ↑ 1944, 18.3.44 completion ordered as midget submarine carrier; 7.8.44 →Genoa, 4.9.44 ⚓ Genoa: 44°24n/08°54e / bomb / air raid 15. USAAF / ↑ ≈1946, § 27.3.47, br.
ex *Murena*					9.9.43 (⚓) La Spezia at Italian Surrender, captured, ↑ 1943, 18.3.44 completion ordered as midget submarine carrier; 28.7.44 →Genoa, 4.9.44 ⚓ Genoa: 44°24n/08°54e / bomb / air raid 15. USAAF / ↑ 1946, § 27.3.47, br.
ex *Grongo*					9.9.43 (⚓) incomplete La Spezia at Italian Surrender, captured, ↑ 1944, 18.3.44 completion ordered as midget submarine carrier; 31.7.44 →Genoa, 4.9.44 ⚓ Genoa: 44°24n/08°54e / bomb / air raid 15. USAAF / ↑ ≈1946, § 27.3.47, br.
ex *Nautilo*					11.9.43 captured intact Venice at Italian Surrender, 23.11.43 completion ordered at Pola as transport for Aegean Sea theatre, →Pola, 9.1.44 ⚓ 12h00 Pola: 44°52n/13°51e / bomb / air raid 15. USAAF / none dead / ↑ 1944, laid up Pola; May 1945 captured by Yugoslavian guerrilla forces, 1949 repaired. →Yugoslavian *Sava*, 1971 decomm., br.

Ex Italian *Adua*-class submarine

Seagoing U-boat type of conventional design developed in 1936

Surface/submerged displacement:	698/866 t
Overall length/beam/draught:	60.18 m/6.45 m/4.70 m
Standard main armament:	6 torpedo tubes (4 bow, 2 stern) with 12 torpedoes, 3 transport containers for midget submarines on upperdeck

1	2	3	4	5	6
ex *Beilul*					9.9.43 captured intact at Cantiere Riuniti dell Adriatico, Monfalcone at Italian Surrender, 23.11.43 completion ordered as transport for Aegean Sea theatre; 20.4.44 ⚓ Monfalcone: 45°48n/13°32e / bomb / air raid 15. USAAF / ↑ 1946, § 27.3.47, br.

APPENDIX I

CHRONOLOGICAL LIST OF GERMAN U-BOAT LOSSES DURING WORLD WAR II

Symbols and abbreviations for causes of loss used in the list:

S	Ships	BR	Area bombing raid
AL	Shore-based aircraft	C	Collision
AS	Ship-based aircraft	OC	Miscellaneous causes
S/AL	Ships and shore-based aircraft	M	Unknown causes – Missing
S/AS	Ships and ship-borne aircraft	D	Decommissioned
SS	Submarine	SC	Scuttled
MS	Sea mine	≈	Probably
MA	Air-laid mine	↑	Raised and recommissioned

Date	U-No.	Cause	Date	U-No.	Cause	Date	U-No.	Cause
14.09.39	U 39	S	25.02.40	U 63	S	30.10.40	U 32	S
20.09.39	U 27	S	11.03.40	U 31 ↑	AL	02.11.40	U 31	S
after 23.09.39	U 12	M	≈13.03.40	U 44	M	≈28.11.40	U 104	M
13.10.39	U 40	MS	after 20.03.40	U 22	M	07.03.41	U 70	S
13.10.39	U 42	S	06.04.40	U 1	MS	≈07.0.3.41	U 47	M
14.10.39	U 45	S	≈06.04.40	U 50	M	17.03.41	U 99	S
25.10.39	U 16	MS	13.04.40	U 64	AS	17.03.41	U 100	S
29.11.39	U 35	S	15.04.40	U 49	S	23.03.41	U 551	S
04.12.39	U 36	SS	31.05.40	U 13	S	05.04.41	U 76	S
30.01.40	U 55	S/AL	after 21.06.40	U 122	M	28.04.41	U 65	S
30.01.40	U 15	C	01.07.40	U 102	S	09.05.41	U 110	S
05.02.40	U 41	S	01.07.40	U 26	S/AL	02.06.41	U 147	S
12.02.40	U 33	S	≈02.08.40	U 25	M	18.06.41	U 138	S
≈13.02.40	U 54	MS	20.08.40	U 51	SS	27.06.41	U 556	S
24.02.40	U 53	S	03.09.40	U 57 ↑	C	29.06.41	U 651	S

Date	U-No.	Cause	Date	U-No.	Cause	Date	U-No.	Cause
31.07.41	U B	D	14.04.42	U 85	S	27.09.42	U 165	AL
03.08.41	U 401	S	02.05.42	U 74	S	02.10.42	U 512	AL
10.08.41	U 144	SS	09.05.42	U 352	S	05.10.42	U 619	AL
25.08.41	U 452	S/AL	28.05.42	U 568	S/AL	05.10.42	U 582	AL
27.08.41	U 570	AL	02.06.42	U 652	S/AL	after 06.10.42	U 116	M
10.09.41	U 501	S	13.06.42	U 157	S	08.10.42	U 179	S
11.09.41	U 207	S	30.06.42	U 158	AL	09.10.42	U 171	MA
04.10.41	U 111	S	03.07.42	U 215	S	12.10.42	U 597	AL
12.10.41	U 579	D	06.07.42	U 153	AL	15.10.42	U 661	S
19.10.41	U 204	S	06.07.42	U 502	AL	16.10.42	U 353	S
11.11.41	U 580	C	07.07.42	U 701	AL	20.10.42	U 216	AL
15.11.41	U 583	C	11.07.42	U 136	S	22.10.42	U 412	AL
16.11.41	U 433	S	15.07.42	U 576	S/AL	24.10.42	U 599	AL
28.11.41	U 95	SS	17.07.42	U 751	AL	27.10.42	U 627	AL
≈29.11.41	U 206	M	24.07.42	U 90	S	30.10.42	U 520	AL
07.12.41	U 208	S	30.07.42	U 166	S	30.10.42	U 559	S/AL
15.12.41	U 127	S	31.07.42	U 213	S	30.10.42	U 658	AL
16.12.41	U 557	C	31.07.42	U 588	S	≈04.11.42	U 132	M
17.12.41	U 131	S/AS	31.07.42	U 754	AL	05.11.42	U 408	AL
18.12.41	U 434	S	02.08.42	U 573	D	12.11.42	U 272	C
19.12.41	U 574	S	03.08.42	U 335	SS	12.11.42	U 660	S
21.12.41	U 451	AL	04.08.42	U 372	S/AL	13.11.42	U 411	AL
21.12.41	U 567	S	06.08.42	U 612 ↑	C	14.11.42	U 605	AL
23.12.41	U 79	S	06.08.42	U 210	S	14.11.42	U 595	AL
28.12.41	U 75	S	after 06.08.42	U 578	M	15.11.42	U 259	AL
04.01.42	U C1	D	08.08.42	U 379	S	15.11.42	U 98	S
12.01.42	U 374	SS	20.08.42	U 464	AL	16.11.42	U 173	S
15.01.42	U 577	AL	22.08.42	U 654	AL	17.11.42	U 331	AL
15.01.42	U 93	S	28.08.42	U 94	S/AL	≈20.11.42	U 184	M
02.02.42	U 581	S	01.09.42	U 756	S	21.11.42	U 517	AS
06.02.42	U 82	S	02.09.42	U 222	C	30.11.42	U 256	D
01.03.42	U 656	AL	03.09.42	U 705	AL	08.12.42	U 254	C
14.03.42	U 133	MS	03.09.42	U 162	S	08.12.42	U 611	AL
15.03.42	U 503	AL	12.09.42	U 88	S	after 14.12.42	U 626	M
24.03.42	U 655	S	14.09.42	U 589	S/AS	26.12.42	U 357	S
27.03.42	U 587	S	15.09.42	U 261	AL	27.12.42	U 356	S
≈30.03.42	U 585	M	16.09.42	U 457	S	after 03.01.43	U 337	M
≈31.03.42	U 702	MS	21.09.42	U 446 ↑	MA	06.01.43	U 164	AL
14.04.42	U 252	S	≈25.09.42	U 253	M	13.01.43	U 224	S

Date	U-No.	Cause	Date	U-No.	Cause	Date	U-No.	Cause
13.01.43	U 507	AL	06.04.43	U 167	AL	15.05.43	U 266	AL
after 20.01.43	U 553	M	06.04.43	U 632	AL	15.05.43	U 176	S/AL
21.01.43	U 301	SS	after 06.04.43	U 376	M	15.05.43	U 182	AL
after 30.01.43	U 519	M	07.04.43	U 644	SS	16.05.43	U 463	AL
03.02.43	U 265	AL	08.04.43	U 416	D	17.05.43	U 128	S/AL
04.02.43	U 187	S	08.04.43	U 733 ↑	C	17.05.43	U 657	S
06.02.43	U 609	S	14.04.43	U 526	MA	17.05.43	U 646	AL
07.02.43	U 624	AL	17.04.43	U 175	S	19.05.43	U 954	S
12.02.43	U 442	AL	after 19.04.43	U 602	M	19.05.43	U 273	AL
13.02.43	U 620	AL	23.04.43	U 189	AL	20.05.43	U 258	AL
15.02.43	U 529	AL	23.04.43	U 191	S	21.05.43	U 303	SS
17.02.43	U 201	S	24.04.43	U 710	AL	22.05.43	U 569	AS
17.02.43	U 69	S	25.04.43	U 203	S/AS	23.05.43	U 752	AS
17.02.43	U 205	S/AL	27.04.43	U 174	AL	25.05.43	U 414	S
19.02.43	U 562	S/AL	29.04.43	U 332	AL	25.05.43	U 467	AL
19.02.43	U 268	AL	30.04.43	U 227	AL	26.05.43	U 436	S
21.02.43	U 623	AL	02.05.43	U 465	AL	28.05.43	U 304	AL
22.02.43	U 225	S	04.05.43	U 659	C	28.05.43	U 755	AL
22.02.43	U 606	S	04.05.43	U 439	C	30.05.43	U 418	AL
23.02.43	U 443	S	04.05.43	U 109	AL	31.05.43	U 563	AL
23.02.43	U 522	S	05.05.43	U 638	S	31.05.43	U 440	AL
24.02.43	U 649	C	06.05.43	U 630	S	02.06.43	U 202	S
04.03.43	U 87	S	06.05.43	U 192	S	02.06.43	U 105	AL
04.03.43	U 83	AL	06.05.43	U 125	S	02.06.43	U 521	S
08.03.43	U 156	AL	06.05.43	U 531	S	04.06.43	U 308	SS
08.03.43	U 633	S	06.05.43	U 438	S	05.06.43	U 217	AS
11.03.43	U 432	S	07.05.43	U 447	AL	05.06.43	U 594	AL
11.03.43	U 444	S	≈07.05.43	U 209	M	11.06.43	U 417	AL
12.03.43	U 130	S	08.05.43	U 663	M	12.06.43	U 118	AS
13.03.43	U 163	S	after 09.05.43	U 381	M	14.06.43	U 334	S
19.03.43	U 5	OC	11.05.43	U 528	S/AL	14.06.43	U 564	AL
19.03.43	U 384	AL	12.05.43	U 186	S	16.06.43	U 97	AL
≈21.03.43	U 665	M	12.05.43	U 89	S/AS	20.06.43	U 388	AL
22.03.43	U 524	AL	12.05.43	U 456	OC	24.06.43	U 119	S
25.03.43	U 469	AL	13.05.43	U 753	S/AL	24.06.43	U 194	AL
27.03.43	U 169	AL	14.05.43	U 235 ↑	BR	24.06.43	U 200	AL
29.03.43	U 77	AL	14.05.43	U 236 ↑	BR	24.06.43	U 449	S
02.04.43	U 124	S	14.05.43	U 237 ↑	BR	03.07.43	U 126	AL
05.04.43	U 635	AL	14.05.43	U 640	AL	03.07.43	U 628	AL

Date	U-No.	Cause	Date	U-No.	Cause	Date	U-No.	Cause
05.07.43	U 535	AL	02.08.43	U 106	AL	08.10.43	U 419	AL
07.07.43	U 951	AL	03.08.43	U 572	AL	13.10.43	U 402	AS
08.07.43	U 514	AL	04.08.43	U 489	AL	16.10.43	U 470	AL
09.07.43	U 232	AL	05.08.43	U 34 ↑	C	16.10.43	U 533	AL
09.07.43	U 435	AL	07.08.43	U 84	AL	16.10.43	U 844	AL
09.07.43	U 590	AL	07.08.43	U 117	AS	16.10.43	U 964	AL
12.07.43	U 409	S	07.08.43	U 615	AL	17.10.43	U 841	S
12.07.43	U 506	AL	09.08.43	U 664	AS	17.10.43	U 540	AL
12.07.43	U 561	S	11.08.43	U 604	SC	17.10.43	U 631	S
13.07.43	U 607	AL	11.08.43	U 468	AL	20.10.43	U 378	AS
13.07.43	U 487	AS	11.08.43	U 525	AS	after 20.10.43	U 420	M
14.07.43	U 160	AS	18.08.43	U 403	AL	21.10.43	U 431	AL
15.07.43	U 135	S/AL	20.08.43	U 197	AL	22.10.43	U 52	D
15.07.43	U 509	AS	20.08.43	U 670	C	22.10.43	U 101	D
15.07.43	U 759	AL.	22.08.43	U 458	S	23.10.43	U 274	S/AL
16.07.43	U 67	AS	24.08.43	U 185	AS	24.10.43	U 566	AL
19.07.43	U 513	AL	25.08.43	U 523	S	28.10.43	U 220	AS
20.07.43	U 558	AL	27.08.43	U 134	S	29.10.43	U 282	S
21.07.43	U 662	AL	27.08.43	U 847	AS	31.10.43	U 306	S
23.07.43	U 527	AS	28.08.43	U 639	SS	31.10.43	U 584	AS
23.07.43	U 613	S	30.08.43	U 634	S	31.10.43	U 732	S
23.07.43	U 598	AL	≈30.08.43	U 669	M	00.11.43	U 46	D
24.07.43	U 459	AL	08.09.43	U 983	C	00.11.43	U 48	D
24.07.43	U 622	BR	08.09.43	U 760	OC	01.11.43	U 405	S
after 25.07.43	U 375	M	12.09.43	U 617	AL	02.11.43	U 340	SC
26.07.43	U 359	AL	16.09.43	U 511	D	05.11.43	U 848	AL
28.07.43	U 159	AL	19.09.43	U 341	AL	06.11.43	U 226	S
28.07.43	U 404	AL	≈20.09.43	U 338	M	06.11.43	U 842	S
after 28.07.43	U 647	M	20.09.43	U 346	OC	09.11.43	U 707	AL
29.07.43	U 614	AL	22.09.43	U 229	S	10.11.43	U 966	AL
30.07.43	U 591	AL	27.09.43	U 161	AL	12.11.43	U 508	AL
30.07.43	U 504	S	27.09.43	U 221	AL	16.11.43	U 280	AL
30.07.43	U 43	AS	04.10.43	U 279	AL	18.11.43	U 718	C
30.07.43	U 461	AL	04.10.43	U 422	AS	19.11.43	U 211	AL
30.07.43	U 462	S/AL	04.10.43	U 460	OC	20.11.43	U 536	S
31.07.43	U 199	AL	04.10.43	U 389	AL	20.11.43	U 768	C
≈01.08.43	U 383	AL	05.10.43	U 336	AL	21.11.43	U 538	S
01.08.43	U 454	AL	08.10.43	U 643	AL	22.11.43	U C2	D
02.08.43	U 706	AL	08.10.43	U 610	AL	22.11.43	U D1	D

Date	U-No.	Cause	Date	U-No.	Cause	Date	U-No.	Cause
after 22.11.43	U 648	M	15.02.44	U 1224	D	05.04.44	U 288	AS
25.11.43	U 849	AL	18.02.44	U 7	OC	05.04.44	U 455	MS
25.11.43	U 600	S	18.02.44	U 406	S	06.04.44	U 302	S
26.11.43	U 542	AL	after 18.02.44	U 603	M	07.04.44	U 856	S
29.11.43	U 86	S	19.02.44	U 264	S	08.04.44	U 2	C
after 12.12.43	U 645	M	19.02.44	U 386	S	08.04.44	U 962	S
13.12.43	U 172	S/AS	after 19.02.44	U 709	M	09.04.44	U 515	S/AS
13.12.43	U 391	AL	24.02.44	U 257	S	10.04.44	U 68	AS
13.12.43	U 593	S	24.02.44	U 761	S/AL	after 10.04.44	U 986	M
after 15.12.43	U 972	M	after 24.02.44	U 713	M	11.04.44	U 108	BR
16.12.43	U 73	S	25.02.44	U 601	AL	14.04.44	U 448	S
20.12.43	U 850	AS	26.02.44	U 91	S	15.04.44	U IT21	D
21.12.43	U 284	SC	00.03.44	U 103	D	16.04.44	U 550	S
23.12.43	U 345	D	01.03.44	U 358	S	17.04.44	U 342	AL
08.01.44	U 426	AL	04.03.44	U 472	S/AS	17.04.44	U 29	D
08.01.44	U 757	S	05.03.44	U 366	AS	19.04.44	U 974	SS
09.01.44	U 81	BR	06.03.44	U 744	S	22.04.44	U 311	S
13.01.44	U 231	AL	06.03.44	U 973	AS	after 23.04.44	U 193	M
≈16.01.44	U 305	M	10.03.44	U 343	S	26.04.44	U 488	S
16.01.44	U 544	AS	10.03.44	U 450	S	27.04.44	U 803 ↑	MA
17.01.44	U 377	S	10.03.44	U 625	AL	29.04.44	U 421	BR
19.01.44	U 641	S	10.03.44	U 845	S	01.05,44	U 277	AS
20.01.44	U 263	M	11.03.44	U IT22	AL	02.05.44	U 674	AS
28.01.44	U 571	AL	11.03.44	U 380	BR	02.05.44	U 959	AS
28.01.44	U 271	AL	11.03.44	U 410	BR	03.05.44	U 852	AL
30.01.44	U 314	S	13.03.44	U 575	S/AL	04.05.44	U 371	S
30.01.44	U 364	AL	15.03.44	U 653	S/AS	04.05.44	U 846	AL
31.01.44	U 592	S	16.03.44	U 392	S/AL	06.05.44	U 473	S
04.02.44	U 854 ↑	MA	17.03.44	U 28	OC	06.05.44	U 66	S/AS
06.02.44	U 177	AL	17.03.44	U 801	S/AS	06.05.44	U 765	S/AS
08.02.44	U 762	S	17.03.44	U 1013 ↑	C	14.05.44	U 1234 ↑	C
09.02.44	U 238	S	19.03.44	U 1059	AS	after 14.05.44	U 240	M
09.02.44	U 734	S	24.03.44	U 1102 ↑	OC	15.05.44	U 731	S/AL
10.02.44	U 666	AS	25.03.44	U 976	AL	17.05.44	U 616	S/AL
11.02.44	U 283	AL	29.03.44	U 961	S	18.05.44	U 241	AL
11.02.44	U 424	S	after 27.03.44	U 851	M	19.05.44	U 960	S/AL
11.02.44	U 545	AL	30.03.44	U 223	S	19.05.44	U 1015	C
14.02.44	U 738 ↑	C	≈01.04.44	U 355	M	21.05.44	U 453	S
15.02.44	U IT23	SS	02.04.44	U 360	S	24.05.44	U 675	AL

Date	U-No.	Cause	Date	U-No.	Cause	Date	U-No.	Cause
25.05.44	U 476	AL	05.07.44	U 642	BR	19.08.44	U 967	SC
25.05.44	U 990	AL	05.07.44	U 952	BR	20.08.44	U 9	BR
27.05.44	U 292	AL	06.07.44	U 678	S	20.08.44	U 178	D
29.05.44	U 549	S	08.07.44	U 243	AL	20.08.44	U 188	D
31.05.44	U 289	S	11.07.44	U 1222	AL	20.08.44	U 413	S
03.06.44	U 477	AL	14.07.44	U 415	MA	20.08.44	U 1229	AS
04.06.44	U 505	S	15.07.44	U 319	AL	21.08.44	U 230	SC
07.06.44	U 629	AL	17.07.44	U 361	AL	after 21.08.44	U 743	M
07.06.44	U 955	AL	17.07.44	U 347	AL	22.08.44	U 344	AS
08.06.44	U 373	AL	18.07.44	U 672	SC	≈23.08.44	U 180	M
08.06.44	U 740	AL	18.07.44	U 742	AL	24.08.44	U 354	S
08.06.44	U 970	AL	21.07.44	U 212	S	24.08.44	U 445	S
10.06.44	U 821	AL	24.07.44	U 239	BR	24.08.44	U 766	D
11.06.44	U 980	AL	24.07.44	U 1164	BR	after 24.08.44	U 925	M
12.06.44	U 490	S	26.07.44	U 214	S	25.08.44	U 18	SC
13.06.44	U 715	AL	26.07.44	U 2323 ↑	MA	25.08.44	U 24	SC
15.06.44	U 860	AS	29.07.44	U 872	BR	26.08.44	U 667	MA
15.06.44	U 987	SS	30.07.44	U 250	S	28.08.44	U 1166	D
17.06.44	U 423	AL	31.07.44	U 333	S	01.09.44	U 247	S
18.06.44	U 767	S	00.08.44	U 123	D	02.09.44	U 394	S/AS
22.06.44	U 988	AL	01.08.44	U 3	D	05.09.44	U 362	S
24.06.44	U 971	S/AL	01.08.44	U 4	D	after 08.09.44	U 865	M
24.06.44	U 1225	AL	after 02.08.44	U 984	M	09.09.44	U 484	S
25.06.44	U 269	S	04.08.44	U 671	S	10.09.44	U 20	SC
26.06.44	U 317	AL	06.08.44	U 736	S	10.09.44	U 23	SC
26.06.44	U 719	S	06.08.44	U 471	BR	11.09.44	U 19	SC
27.06.44	U 998	D	06.08.44	U 969	BR	after 11.09.44	U 855	M
30.06.44	U 441	S/AL	07.08.44	U 6	D	15.09.44	U 1054	D
30.06.44	U 478	AL	10.08.44	U 608	S/AL	after 16.09.44	U 703	M
00.07.44	U 10	D	11.08.44	U 385	S/AL	19.09.44	U 407	S
00.07.44	U 21	D	12.08.44	U 981	AL	19.09.44	U 867	SC
02.07.44	U 543	AS	12.08.44	U 198	S	23.09.44	U 859	SS
03.07.44	U 154	S	13.08.44	U 270	AL	24.09.44	U 596	BR
03.07.44	U 1191	S	15.08.44	U 618	S/AL	after 24.09.44	U 921	M
04.07.44	U D2	D	15.08.44	U 741	S	26.09.44	U 871	AL
05.07.44	U F2	D	18.08.44	U 107	AL	29.09.44	U 863	AL
05.07.44	U 233	S	18.08.44	U 621	S	29.09.44	U 1000	D
05.07.44	U 390	S	18.08.44	U 129	D	29.09.44	U 276	D
05.07.44	U 586	BR	19.08.44	U 466	SC	30.09.44	U 565	SC

Date	U-No.	Cause	Date	U-No.	Cause	Date	U-No.	Cause
30.09.44	U 1062	S	00.01.45	U 30	D	27.02.45	U 1279	S
04.10.44	U 228	BR	05.01.45	U 11	D	28.02.45	U 60	D
04.10.44	U 437	BR	after 9.01.45	U 1020	MS	00.03.45	U 555	D
04.10.44	U 993	BR	16.01.45	U 248	S	02.03.45	U 3519	MA
06.10.44	U 168	SS	17.01.45	U 2523	BR	03.03.45	U 14	D
10.10.44	U 2331 ↑	OC	17.01.45	U 2515	BR	07.03.45	U 1302	S
12.10.44	U 92	D	21.01.45	U 1199	S	after 07.03.45	U 857	M
13.10.44	U D3	D	26.01.45	U 1051	S	10.03.45	U 275	MS
15.10.44	U 777	BR	27.01.45	U 1172	S	11.03.45	U 681	AL
16.10.44	U 1006	S	29.01.45	U 763	SC	11.03.45	U 682	BR
21.10.44	U 957	D	after 29.01.45	U 480	MS	12.03.45	U 260	MS
23.10.44	U 256	D	31.01.45	U 745	MS	≈12.03.45	U 296	M
after 23.10.44	U 1226	M	31.01.45	U 3520	MA	14.03.45	U D4	D
24.10.44	U 673	C	00.02.45	U 17	D	14.03.45	U 714	S
27.10.44	U 1060	AS	00.02.45	U 552	D	≈14.03.45	U 1021	MS
10.11.44	U 537	SS	03.02.45	U 327	S	15.03.45	U A	D
11.11.44	U 771	SS	04.02.45	U 1014	S	15.03.45	U 367	MS
after 12.11.44	U 1200	M	09.02.45	U 864	SS	16.03.45	U 758	D
15.11.44	U 985	D	09.02.45	U 923	MA	after 16.03.45	U 1106	M
25.11.44	U 482	S/AL	11.02.45	U 869	S	17.03.45	U 246	S
after 27.11.44	U 479	MS	after 12.02.45	U 676	MS	18.03.45	U 866	S
28.11.44	U 80	OC	14.02.45	U 989	S	20.03.45	U 382	D
≈30.11.44	U 196	M	15.02.45	U 96	D	20.03.45	U 62	D
after 06.12.44	U 297	M	15.02.45	U 1053	OC	after 22.03.45	U 1169	M
09.12.44	U 387	S	16.02.45	U 309	S	23.03.45	U 1003	SC
12.12.44	U 416	C	17.02.45	U 425	S	24.03.45	U 704	D
13.12.44	U 365	AS	17.02.45	U 1273	MA	26.03.45	U 399	S
after 14.12.44	U 400	MS	17.02.45	U 1278	S	27.03.45	U 61	D
17.12.44	U 772	S	18.02.45	U 2344	C	27.03.45	U 722	S
18.12.44	U 1209	OC	20.02.45	U 1276	S	27.03.45	U 905	S
19.12.44	U 737	C	after 20.02.45	U 683	M	30.03.45	U 72	BR
26.12.44	U 2342	MA	22.02.45	U 300	S	30.03.45	U 348	BR
after 26.12.44	U 679	MS	22.02.45	U 795	D	30.03.45	U 350	BR
27.12.44	U 877	S	23.02.45	U 339	D	30.03.45	U 429	BR
28.12.44	U 735	BR	24.02.45	U 927	AL	30.03.45	U 430	BR
29.12.44	U 322	S	24.02.45	U 1208	S	30.03.45	U 870	BR
31.12.44	U 547	D	24.02.45	U 3007	BR	30.03.45	U 965	S
31.12.44	U 2530	BR	27.02.45	U 71	D	30.03.45	U 1131	BR
after 01.01.45	U 650	S	27.02.45	U 1018	S	30.03.45	U 1167	BR

Date	U-No.	Cause	Date	U-No.	Cause	Date	U-No.	Cause
30.03.45	U 2340	BR	16.04.45	U 78	OC	02.05.45	U 3013	SC
30.03.45	U 3508	BR	16.04.45	U 880	S	02.05.45	U 3016	SC
31.03.45	U 8	D	16.04.45	U 1274	S	02.05.45	U 3018	SC
00.04.45	U 56	D	after 17.04.45	U 398	M	02.05.45	U 3019	SC
00.04.45	U 57	D	19.04.45	U 251	AL	02.05.45	U 3020	SC
00.04.45	U 58	D	19.04.45	U 548	S	02.05.45	U 3021	SC
00.04.45	U 59	D	21.04.45	U 636	S	02.05.45	U 3023	SC
02.04.45	U 321	AL	22.04.45	U 518	S	02.05.45	U 3025	SC
02.04.45	U 262	D	23.04.45	U 183	SS	02.05.45	U 3026	SC
03.04.45	U 1221	BR	after 23.04.45	U 1055	M	02.05.45	U 3027	SC
03.04.45	U 2542	BR	24.04.45	U 546	S	02.05.45	U 3037	SC
03.04.45	U 3505	BR	25.04.45	U 326	AL	02.05.45	U 3507	SC
04.04.45	U 749	BR	25.04.45	U 1197	D	02.05.45	U 3511	SC
04.04.45	U 237	BR	27.04.45	U 1232	D	02.05.45	U 3513	SC
04.04.45	U 3003	BR	29.04.45	U 1017	AL	02.05.45	U 3516	SC
05.04.45	U 242	MS	29.04.45	U 307	S	02.05.45	U 3517	SC
06.04.45	U 1195	S	29.04.45	U 286	S	02.05.45	U 3521	SC
08.04.45	U 1001	S	30.04.45	U 879	S	02.05.45	U 3522	SC
08.04.45	U 2509	BR	30.04.45	U 1107	AL	03.05.45	U 475	SC
08.04.45	U 2514	BR	after 30.04.45	U 325	MS	03.05.45	U 560	SC
08.04.45	U 3512	BR	01.05.45	U 612	SC	03.05.45	U 747	SC
08.04.45	U 774	S	01.05.45	U 929	SC	03.05.45	U 876	SC
09.04.45	U 677	BR	01.05.45	U 1308	SC	03.05.45	U 922	SC
09.04.45	U 804	AL	02.05.45	U 316	SC	03.05.45	U 924	SC
09.04.45	U 843	AL	02.05.45	U 1007	AL.	03.05.45	U 958	SC
09.04.45	U 982	BR	02.05.45	U 1170	SC	03.05.45	U 1192	SC
09.04.45	U 1065	AL	02.05.45	U 1196	SC	03.05.45	U 1201	SC
09.04.45	U 1227	BR	02.05.45	U 2359	AL	03.05.45	U 1205	SC
09.04.45	U 2516	BR	02.05.45	U 2510	SC	03.05.45	U 1210	AL
10.04.45	U 878	S	02.05.45	U 2526	SC	03.05.45	U 1275	SC
after 11.04.45	U 396	M	02.05.45	U 2527	SC	03.05.45	U 2327	SC
12.04.45	U 486	SS	02.05.45	U 2528	SC	03.05.45	U 2330	SC
12.04.45	U 1024	S	02.05.45	U 2531	SC	03.05.45	U 2332	SC
14.04.45	U 1206	OC	02.05.45	U 2533	SC	03.05.45	U 2355	SC
14.04.45	U 235	OC	02.05.45	U 2535	SC	03.05.45	U 2501	SC
14.04.45	U 1223	D	02.05.45	U 2536	SC	03.05.45	U 2504	SC
15.04.45	U 285	S	02.05.45	U 3002	SC	03.05.45	U 2505	SC
15.04.45	U 1063	S	02.05.45	U 3010	SC	03.05.45	U 2508	SC
15.04.45	U 1235	S	02.05.45	U 3011	SC	03.05.45	U 2519	SC

Date	U-No.	Cause	Date	U-No.	Cause	Date	U-No.	Cause
03.05.45	U 2520	SC	05.05.45	U 37	SC	05.05.45	U 999	SC
03.05.45	U 2524	SC	05.05.45	U 38	SC	05.05.45	U 1016	SC
03.05.45	U 2534	SC	05.05.45	U 120	SC	05.05.45	U 1025	SC
03.05.45	U 2539	SC	05.05.45	U 121	SC	05.05.45	U 1056	SC
03.05.45	U 2543	SC	05.05.45	U 137	SC	05.05.45	U 1101	SC
03.05.45	U 2545	SC	05.05.45	U 139	SC	05.05.45	U 1132	SC
03.05.45	U 2546	SC	05.05.45	U 140	SC	05.05.45	U 1161	SC
03.05.45	U 2548	SC	05.05.45	U 141	SC	05.05.45	U 1162	SC
03.05.45	U 2552	SC	05.05.45	U 142	SC	05.05.45	U 1193	SC
03.05.45	U 3004	SC	05.05.45	U 146	SC	05.05.45	U 1204	SC
03.05.45	U 3012	AL	05.05.45	U 148	SC	05.05.45	U 1207	SC
03.05.45	U 3014	SC	05.05.45	U 151	SC	05.05.45	U 1234	SC
03.05.45	U 3022	SC	05.05.45	U 152	SC	05.05.45	U 1303	SC
03.05.45	U 3024	SC	05.05.45	U 236	SC	05.05.45	U 1304	SC
03.05.45	U 3028	SC	05.05.45	U 267	SC	05.05.45	U 1306	SC
03.05.45	U 3029	SC	05.05.45	U 290	SC	05.05.45	U 1405	SC
03.05.45	U 3031	SC	05.05.45	U 323	SC	05.05.45	U 2333	SC
03.05.45	U 3032	AL	05.05.45	U 349	SC	05.05.45	U 2339	SC
03.05.45	U 3038	SC	05.05.45	U 351	SC	05.05.45	U 2343	SC
03.05.45	U 3039	SC	05.05.45	U 370	SC	05.05.45	U 2346	SC
03.05.45	U 3040	SC	05.05.45	U 393	SC	05.05.45	U 2347	SC
03.05.45	U 3502	SC	05.05.45	U 397	SC	05.05.45	U 2349	SC
03.05.45	U 3506	SC	05.05.45	U 428	SC	05.05.45	U 2352	SC
03.05.45	U 3518	SC	05.05.45	U 534	AL	05.05.45	U 2357	SC
03.05.45	U 3525	SC	05.05.45	U 554	SC	05.05.45	U 2358	SC
03.05.45	U 3530	SC	05.05.45	U 579	AL	05.05.45	U 2360	SC
03.05.45	U 4705	SC	05.05.45	U 708	SC	05.05.45	U 2362	SC
03.05.45	U 4709	SC	05.05.45	U 717	SC	05.05.45	U 2364	SC
03.05.45	U 4711	SC	05.05.45	U 721	SC	05.05.45	U 2366	SC
03.05.45	U 4712	SC	05.05.45	U 733	SC	05.05.45	U 2368	SC
04.05.45	U 711	AS	05.05.45	U 746	SC	05.05.45	U 2369	SC
04.05.45	U 792	SC	05.05.45	U 748	SC	05.05.45	U 2507	SC
04.05.45	U 793	SC	05.05.45	U 750	SC	05.05.45	U 2517	SC
04.05.45	U 904	SC	05.05.45	U 794	SC	05.05.45	U 2522	SC
04.05.45	U 1168	SC	05.05.45	U 822	SC	05.05.45	U 2525	SC
04.05.45	U 2338	AL	05.05.45	U 827	SC	05.05.45	U 2541	SC
04.05.45	U 2503	AL	05.05.45	U 828	SC	05.05.45	U 2544	SC
04.05.45	U 2521	AL	05.05.45	U 903	SC	05.05.45	U 2551	SC
04.05.45	U 2540	SC	05.05.45	U 926	D	05.05.45	U 3001	SC

Date	U-No.	Cause	Date	U-No.	Cause	Date	U-No.	Cause
05.05.45	U 3005	SC	05.05.45	U 3527	SC	07.05.45	U 1406	SC
05.05.45	U 3006	SC	05.05.45	U 3528	SC	07.05.45	U 1407	SC
05.05.45	U 3009	SC	05.05.45	U 3529	SC	08.05.45	U 320	AL
05.05.45	U 3015	SC	05.05.45	U 4701	SC	08.05.45	U 2365	SC
05.05.45	U 3033	SC	05.05.45	U 4702	SC	08.05.45	U 2512	SC
05.05.45	U 3034	SC	05.05.45	U 4703	SC	08.05.45	U 2538	SC
05.05.45	U 3044	SC	05.05.45	U 4704	SC	08.05.45	U 3030	SC
05.05.45	U 3501	SC	05.05.45	U 4707	SC	08.05.45	U 3503	SC
05.05.45	U 3504	SC	05.05.45	U 4710	SC	09.05.45	U 2367	SC
05.05.45	U 3509	SC	06.05.45	U 853	S	16.05.45	U 287	SC
05.05.45	U 3510	SC	06.05.45	U 881	S	20.05.45	U 963	SC
05.05.45	U 3524	SC	06.05.45	U 1008	SC	24.05.45	U 979	SC
05.05.45	U 3526	SC	06.05.45	U 3523	AL	03.06.45	U 1277	SC

APPENDIX 2

TABULAR MONTHLY OVERVIEW ON THE CAUSES OF U-BOAT LOSSES

Year →	1939				1940												1941												1942					
Month →	S	O	N	D	J	F	M	A	M	J	J	A	S	O	N	D	J	F	M	A	M	J	J	A	S	O	N	D	J	F	M	A	M	J
FRONTLINE BOATS																																		
Ship S	2	2				4		1	1	1	1					1	4	2	1	4		4		1	2	2	1	7	1	2	2	2	2	1
Shore-based Aircraft AL							1									1								1			1	1	1	2	2			1
Ship-based Aircraft AS								1																						2				
Ship/Shore-based Aircraft S/AL				1	1						1													1								1	1	1
Ship/Ship-based Aircraft S/AS																																		
Submarine SS				1								1													1	1	1							
Sea Mine MS	2				1	1	1										1							1			1		1	2				
Aerial Mine MA																																		
Area Bombing Raid BR																																		
Collision C					1								1														1							
Other Causes OC																																		
Missing M	1					2	1		1		1			1			1							1		1				1				
Decommissioned D																																		
Scuttled SC																																		
Total	3	4	1	1	2	5	3	4	1	1	2	2	1	1	1	2	5	2	1	4		4		4	2	2	3	10	3	2	7	2	3	3
HOME BOATS																																		
Shore-based Aircraft AL																							1											
Sea Mine MS																																		
Aerial Mine MA																																		
Area Bombing Raid BR																																		
Collision C																											2							
Other Causes OC																							1		1									
Decommissioned D																										1			1					
Scuttled SC																																		
Total																					1		1			1	2		1					
Grand Total	3	4	1	1	2	5	3	4	1	1	2	2	1	1	1	2	5	2	1	4	1	4	1	4	2	3	5	10	4	2	7	2	3	3

	1942						1943												1944												1945					Grand Total
Month	J	A	S	O	N	D	J	F	M	A	M	J	J	A	S	O	N	D	J	F	M	A	M	J	J	A	S	O	N	D	J	F	M	A	M	Total
FRONTLINE BOATS																																				
Ship S	6	2	4	3	3	2	5	7	8	6	11	5	4	4	1	5	7	2	5	9	7	8	5	5	9	8	5	1	1	4	5	12	8	17	2	235
Shore-based Aircraft AL	5	2	3	10	6	1	2	7	7	8	16	8	23	11	4	13	8	1	1	4	3	1	7	14	6	3	2	5			1	1	8	8	7	204
Ship-based Aircraft AS				1						2	2	6	5	5	5		1	1	1			2	3	1	1	2	3	1	1	1					1	40
Ship/Shore-based Aircraft S/AL	1	2					2		1	4		2		1	1				1	2	1	3	2	2		3	1	1		1						30
Ship/Ship-based Aircraft S/AS		1						1	1							1			1	3	1	1														12
Submarine SS	1					1	1			1	1	1		1		1	1	2		1	3	1		1				1	2			1	3	2		21
Sea Mine MS								1							1		1					1						1	1		3	1	3	2		19
Aenal Mine MA			1							1										1						1						1				5
Area Bombing Raid BR															1					2	1				3	3	1	3		1			3	2		21
Collision C				1						2																		1	1	1						8
Other Causes OC										1					1	1											1		1			1		2		7
Missing M	1	1		2	1		3		1	2	3		2	2	1	1	1	2		3	1	3				4	4	2	1		1	1	4	3		63
Decommissioned D	1		1												1	1	3	1		1	2	1			1	5	1	3	1			2	2	3	1	22
Scuttled SC														1	1			1							1	5	5	5				1	1		15	30
Total	12	9	16	13	5	7	17	14	16	41	16	38	23	8	26	17	8	14	19	21	19	21	24	21	34	20	11	7	12	8	18	22	39	26		717
HOME BOATS																																				
Shore-based Aircraft AL																											1	1	1		1	1	1	5	5	5
Sea Mine MS			1																												1		1			1
Arial Mine MA													1								1	1							1		1	1	1			8
Area Bombing Raid BR										3										1	1	1		3			1		1	2	2	1	8	11		31
Collision C		1	1	1			1			1					2	1	2		1	1	1	2	2					1	1			1				19
Other Causes OC							1							1	1		1		2	1	2						1	1	1				1			8
Decommissioned D											1							2	4	1	1	1	1		4	4	2	1	1		2	7	8	5		47
Scuttled SC														2	2	2	6	1												1	6	10	18	17	183	184
Total	12	10	11	16	14	5	7	18	15	18	44	16	38	23	10	28	23	9	14	23	25	23	24	29	38	22	14	8	15	14	28	40	56	40	188	303
Grand Total	12	10	11	16	14	5	7	18	15	18	44	16	38	25	10	28	23	9	14	23	25	23	24	29	38	22	14	8	15	14	28	40	56	56	214	1020

APPENDIX 3

DISTRIBUTION OF GERMAN FRONT-LINE U-BOATS ON 8 MAY 1945

In operational area:

British Coastal Waters:

Firth of Forth	U 2326, U 2336
North Minch–N. of Scotland	U 764
Minch Canal	U 901
Approaches to North Channel	U 956, U 1105
Irish Sea	U 825
SW of Ireland	U 1010
Western exit of English Channel	U 244, U 776
English Channel	U 249, U 1023
American East Coast	U 530

Homebound from:

Arctic	U 278, U 313, U 318, U 992
British coastal waters:	
Thames–Scheldt area	U 245
Firth of Forth	U 2324
North Minch	U 739
Approaches to North Channel	U 293, U 1305
Mining operation in the Clyde	U 218
SW of Ireland	U 826
Icelandic coast off Reykjavik	U 979
North Atlantic–Weather reporting boat	U 1009
Canadian East coast	U 190
Transport mission Far East–Europe	U 532
Transfer passage St. Nazaire, France–Norway	U 255

Outbound to:

British coastal waters:	
Approaches to North Channel	U 1109
Western exit of English Channel	U 977, U 1272, U 1277
Mining operation off Portland	U 963
West of Gibraltar	U 541
Gibraltar–Western Mediterranean	U 485

Canadian East Coast	U 889
American East Coast	U 805, U 858, U 1228, U 1231
Caribbean	U 873
Transport mission Kiel, Germany-Far East	U 234
Supply mission Kiel, Germany-St. Nazaire, France	U 516
Transfer passage Germany-Norway	U 1110, U 1194, U 1198, U 2365, U 3008, U 3503
Operational area not yet assigned	U 287, U 320, U 802, U 1005, U 1058

In Port:

Norway:

Horten	U 170, U 874, U 975, U 1108, U 2502, U 2513, U 2518, U 3017, U 3041, U 3515
Kristiansand-South	U 281, U 299, U 369, U 712, U 1163, U 2321, U 2325, U 2334, U 2335, U 2337, U 2350, U 2353, U 2354, U 2361, U 2363, U 2529, U 4706
Egersund	U 3035
Stavanger	U 637, U 1171, U 2322, U 2329, U 2345, U 2348
Bergen	U 298, U 324. U 328, U 539, U 778, U 868, U 875, U 907, U 928, U 930, U 991, U 1002, U 1004, U 1022, U 1052, U 1057, U 1061, U 1104, U 1202, U 1271, U 1301, U 1307, U 2328, U 2506, U 2511, U 3514, UD 5
Trondheim	U 310. U 315, U 483, U 775, U 861, U 953, U 994, U 995, U 1019, U 1064
Trondheim-Lo-Fiord	U 773, U 978, U 1203
Narvik	U 294, U 295, U 312, U 363, U 427, U 481, U 668, U 716, U 968, U 997, U 1165

France:

St. Nazaire	U 510

Far East:

Jakarta	U 219
Singapore	U 181, U 862
Surabaya	U 195
Kobe	UIT 24, UIT 25

Germany:

Cuxhaven	U 291, U 1103
Heligoland	U 368, U 720, U 1230
Flensburg	U 2351

Denmark:

Aarhus	U 806
Fredericia-Baring Bay	U 155, U 680, U 1233

APPENDIX 4

GERMAN U-BOATS SURRENDERING OR CAPTURED BY ALLIED FORCES AT THE END OF WORLD WAR II

Surrendered at sea and brought in to

British ports:	U 244, U 249, U 255, U 278, U 293, U 294, U 295, U 312, U 313, U 318, U 363, U 427, U 481, U 485, U 516, U 532, U 541, U 668, U 716, U 764, U 776, U 802, U 825, U 826, U 956, U 968, U 992, U 997, U 1009, U 1010, U 1023, U 1058, U 1105. U 1109, U 1165, U 1231, U 1305, U 2326
American ports:	U 234, U 805, U 858, U 873, U 1228
Canadian ports:	U 190, U 889
Occupied German ports:	U 739, U 1102, U 1110, U 1194, U 1198, U 2336, U 3008

Captured afloat in occupied ports

Norway:

Horten	U 170, U 874. U 975, U 1108, U 2502, U 2513, U 2518, U 3017, U 3041, U 3515
Kristiansand-South	U 281, U 299, U 369, U 712, U 985*, U 1163, U 2321, U 2325, U 2334, U 2335, U 2337, U 2350, U 2353, U 2354, U 2361, U 2363, U 2529, U 3035, U 4706
Stavanger	U 637, U 673*, U 901, U 1171, U 2322, U 2324, U 2329, U 2345, U 2348
Bergen	U 218, U 228*, U 245, U 256*, U 298, U 324, U 328, U 437*, U 539, U 778, U 868, U 875, U 907, U 926*, U 928, U 930, U 991, U 993*, U 1002, U 1004, U 1005, U 1022, U 1052, U 1057, U 1061, U 1104, U 1202, U 1271, U 1272, U 1301, U 1307, U 2328, U 2506, U 2511, U 3514, UD 5
Trondheim	U 310, U 315, U 483, U 775, U 861, U 953, U 994, U 995, U 1019, U 1064
Trondheim-Lo-Fiord	U 773, U 978, U 1203

France:

St. Nazaire	U 510
Lorient	U 123*, U 129*
La Pallice	U 766*

Far East:

Jakarta	U 219
Singapore	U 181, U 862
Surabaya	U 195
Kobe	UIT 24, UIT 25

Germany:

Cuxhaven	U 291, U 779, U 883, U 1103, U 1406, U 1407, U 2341, U 2356
Heligoland	U 143, U 145, U 149, U 150, U 368, U 720, U 1230
Wesermünde	U 1197*, U 1232*
Flensburg	U 2351

Denmark:

Aarhus	U 806
Fredericia-Baring Bay	U 155, U 680, U 1233

Captured incomplete in building yards

Bremer Vulkan Vegesacker Werft	U 1280*, U 1281*, U 1282*
Deschimag AG Weser Bremen	U 3042*, U 3043*, U 3048*, U 3049*, U 3052*, U 3053*, U 3054*, U 3055*, U 3056*, U 3057*, U 3058*, U 3059*, U 3060*, U 3061*, U 3062*, U 3063*
Howaldtswerke AG Hamburg	U 686*, U 687*, U 688*
H.C. Stülckens Werft Hamburg	U 908*
Deutsche Werft AG Hamburg	U 1239*, U 1240*
Blohm & Voss AG Hamburg	U 1408*, U 1409*, U 2549*, U 2550*, U 2553*, U 2554*, U 2555*, U 2556*, U 2557*, U 2558*, U 2559*, U 2560*, U 2561*, U 2562*, U 2563*, U 2564*
Howaldtswerke AG Kiel	U 1133*, U 1134*, U 1135*
Deutsche Werke Kiel AG	U 491*, U 492*, U 493*
Germaniawerft AG Kiel	U 798*, U 1701*, U 1702*, U 1703*, U 2323*, U 4715*, U 4716*, U 4717*, U 4718*
Flender-Werft Lübeck	U 329*

Captured by the Russian Army at Danzig on 30 March 1945 or elsewhere thereafter

Danziger Werft AG	U 1174*, U 1176*, U 1177*
F. Schichau GmbH Danzig	U 3535*, U 3536*, U 3537*, U 3538*, U 3539*, U 3540*, U 3541*, U 3542*
Various locations	U 2*, U 4*, U 6*, U 10*, U 21*, U 803*, U 902*

(* U-boat in state of decommission, not yet commissioned, or incomplete)

CHARTS

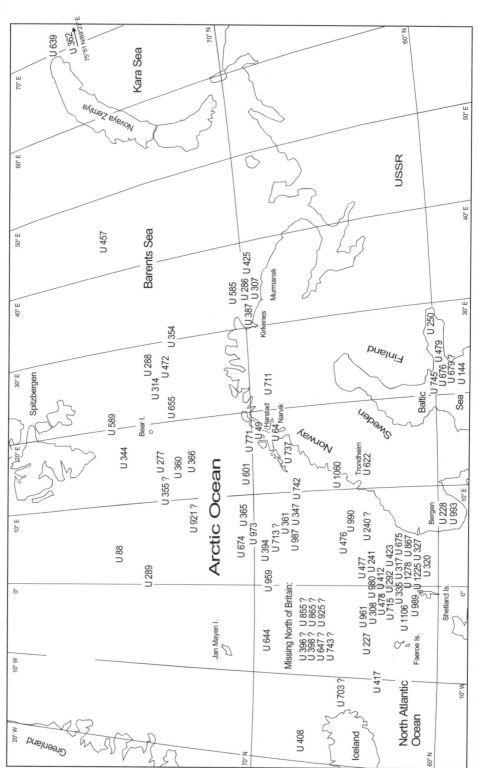

1. Arctic Ocean and Baltic Sea

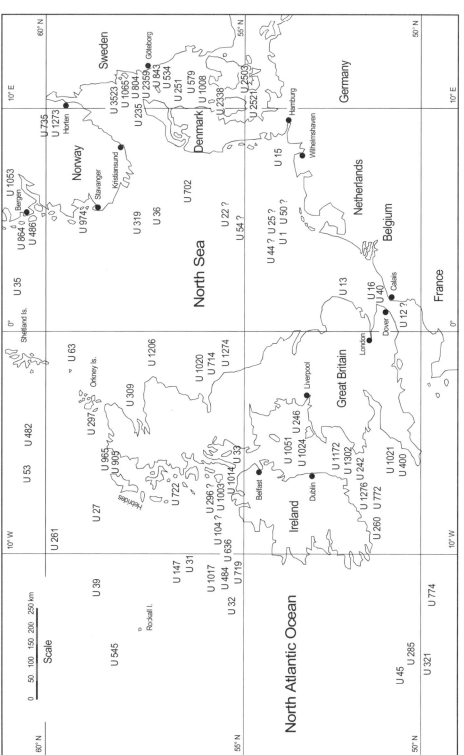

2. North Sea and British Coastal Waters

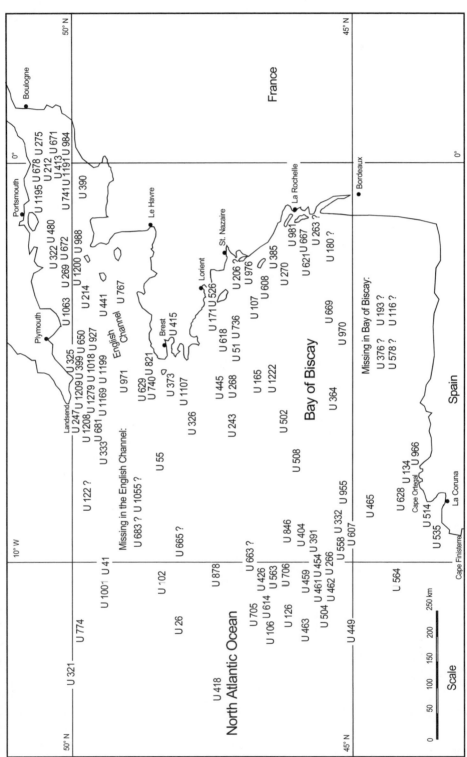

3. Bay of Biscay

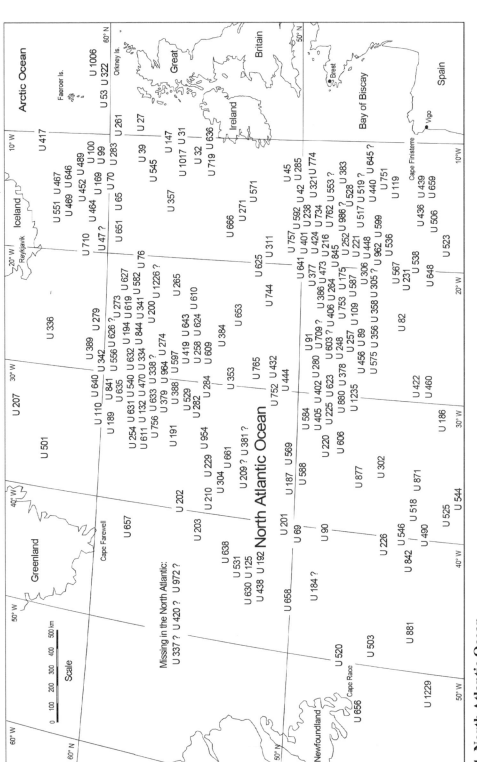

4. North Atlantic Ocean

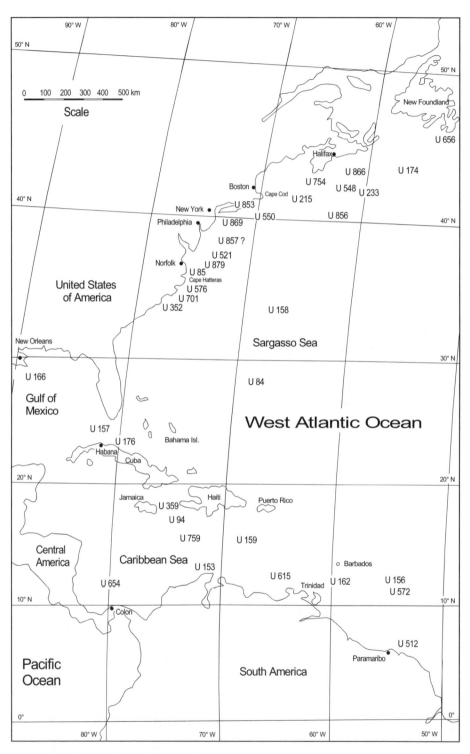

5. West Atlantic Ocean and Caribbean Sea

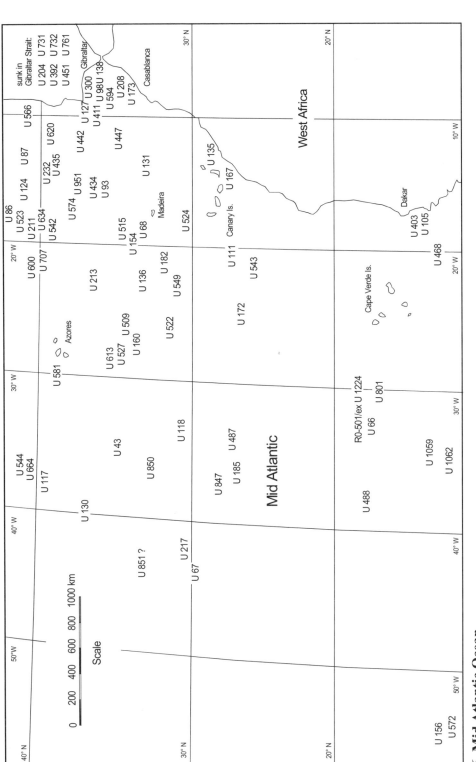

6. Mid Atlantic Ocean

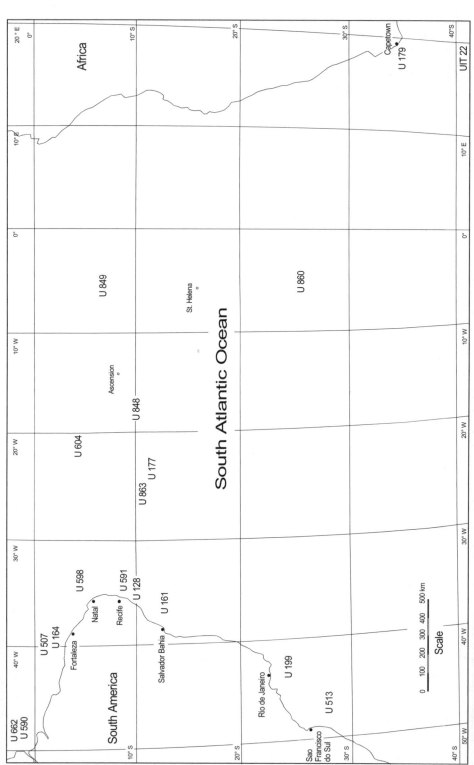

South Atlantic Ocean

Africa

South America

South Atlantic Ocean

St. Helena

Ascension

U 662
U 590

U 507
U 164

Fortaleza

Natal

U 598

Recife

U 591

U 128

U 161

Salvador Bahia

Rio de Janeiro

U 199

U 513

Sao Francisco do Sul

U 604

U 863 U 177

U 848

U 849

U 860

Capetown
U 179

Scale

0   100 200 300 400 500 km

7. South Atlantic Ocean

UIT 22

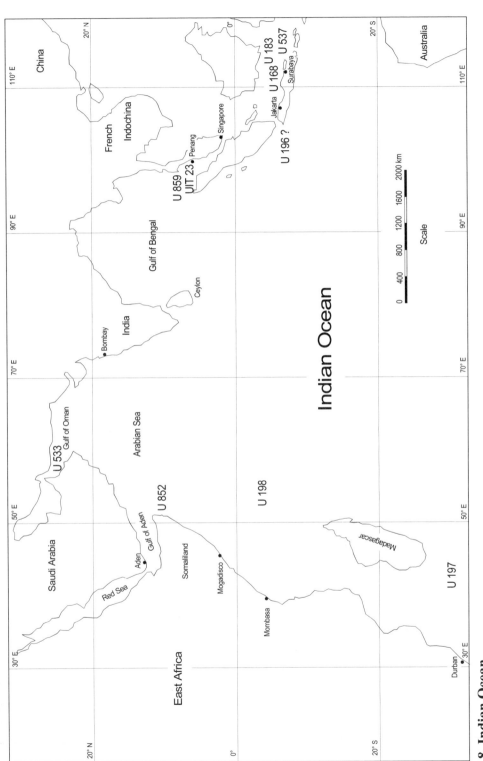

8. Indian Ocean

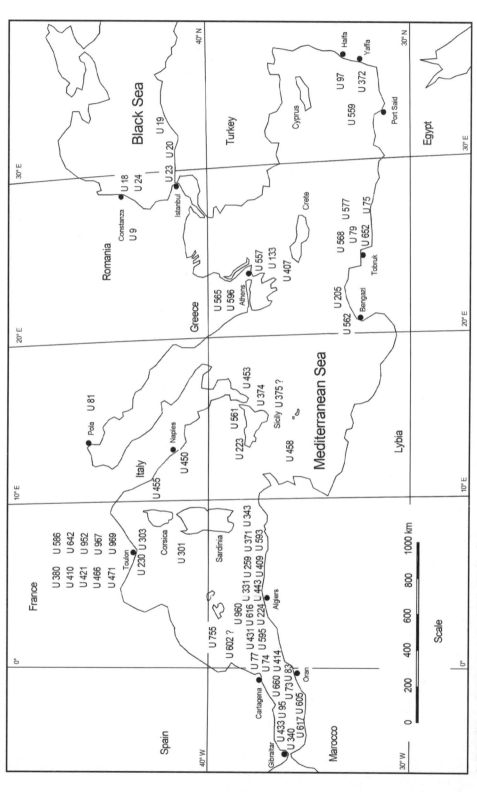

9. **Mediterranean Sea and Black Sea**

NOTES

Chapter 2

1. Originally the U-numbers U 66-U 68 were assigned to a contract for three Type IX B boats placed on 15 December 1937. In September 1939 the U-numbers were transferred to a contract for three Type IX C boats placed on 7 August 1939 as a ruse de guerre.

2. Originally the contract for U 69-U 70 was placed as Type VII B boats designated as U 99-U 100, changed into Type VII C on 22 December 1938. In September 1939 the U-Numbers were changed into U 69-U 70 as a ruse de guerre.

3. Originally the contract for U 71-U 72 was placed with the U-Numbers designated as U 101-U 102. In September 1939 the U-Numbers were changed into U 71-U 72 as a ruse de guerre.

4. Originally the boat was ordered by the Chinese government but the contract was eventually taken over by the Kriegsmarine.

5. Originally the contract for U 93-U 98 was placed as Type VII B boats, changed into Type VII C on 22 December 1938.

6. Originally the contract for U 99-U 102 was placed with the U-numbers designated as U 69-U 72. In September 1939 the U-numbers were changed into U 99-U 102 as a ruse de guerre.

7. Originally the U-numbers 120–121 were assigned to Type X B boats placed on 7 August 1939 with Germania Werft AG Kiel under yard numbers 625–626. The contracts were canceled in 1939 with the U-numbers reassigned to two Type II B boats under construction at the Lübecker Flender-Werke AG. These boats were originally ordered by the Chinese government but were taken over by the Kriegsmarine after the beginning of the war.

8. Originally the U-numbers U 122-U 124 were assigned to a contract for three Type IX C boats placed on 7 August 1939. In September 1939 the U-numbers were transferred to a contract for three Type IX C boats placed on 15 December 1937 as a ruse de guerre.

9. Originally the contract for U 177-U 180 was placed on 23 December 1939 as Type IX C boats.

10. Originally the contract for U 494–U 498 was placed on 22 September 1942 with Deutsche Werke Kiel AG under yard numbers 325–329.

11. Originally the contract for U 499–U 500 was placed on 17 April 1943 with Deutsche Werke Kiel AG under yard numbers 332–333.

12. The addition "St" indicates that the pressure hull was to be constructed from normal ship building steel of Type St 52.

13. The addition "CM" indicates that the pressure hull was to be constructed from special armored steel of Type CM 351 produced by the F. Krupp AG Essen.

14. Originally the contract for U 796–U 797 was placed on 4 January 1943 with Deutsche Werke Kiel AG under yard numbers 330–331.

15. Originally the contract for U 825–U 826 was placed on 10 April 1941 with Stettiner Oderwerke AG under yard numbers 843–844.

16. Originally the contract for U 827–U 828 was placed on 10 April 1941 with Stettiner Oderwerke AG under yard numbers 845–846.

17. Originally the contract for U 829–U 832 was placed on 25 August 1941 with Stettiner Oderwerke AG under yard numbers 847–850.

18. Originally the contract for U 903–U 904 was placed on 10 April 1941 with Vulcan Stettiner Maschinenbau AG under yard numbers 16–17. On 6 August 1942 it was temporarily shifted to Stülckenswerft Hamburg.

19. Originally the contract for U 905–U 908 was placed on 5 June 1941 with Vulcan Stettiner Maschinenbau AG under yard numbers 18–21.

20. Wartime records are inconclusive whether U 1103–U 1106 were built as Type VII C or Type VII C/41 boats.

21. Wartime records are inconclusive whether U 1199–U 1204 were built as Type VII C or Type VII C/41 boats.

22. Originally the U-numbers U 1286–U 1291 were contracted as Type VII C/41 boats. On 25 June 1943 the contract was altered to Type VII C/42 St boats, retaining the previously allocated U-numbers.

23. Originally the contract for U 1501–U 1506 was placed on 2 January 1943 with Deschimag AG Weser Bremen under yard numbers 1115–1120.

24. Originally the contract for U 1601–U 1615 was placed on 3 March 1943 with Deutsche Werft AG Hamburg under yard numbers 452–466.

25. Originally the contract for U 1701–U 1715 was placed on 3 March 1943 with Bremer Vulkan Vegesacker Werft under yard numbers 93–107.

26. Originally the contract for U 2201–U 2204 was placed on 17 April 1943 with Deutsche Werke Kiel AG under yard numbers 334–337.

27. Originally the contract for U 2332–U 2333 was placed on 20 September 1943 with Deutsche Werft AG Hamburg under yard numbers 486–487. It was modified in July 1944, so that the Deutsche Werft AG completed only the prefabricated sections which were then delivered to Germania Werft AG Kiel for final assembly.

28. Originally the contract for U 2371–U 2400 was placed on 20 September 1943 with Deutsche Werft AG Toulon (yard numbers ?).

29. Originally the contract for U 2446–U 2460 was placed on 20 September 1943 with Deutsche Werft AG Nikolaev (yard numbers ?).

30. Originally the construction of these 112 boats was allocated to Blohm & Voss Hamburg under the U-numbers U 2609–U 2720, contracted on 6 November 1943 and 6 May 1944.

31. Originally the construction of these 42 boats was allocated to Blohm & Voss Hamburg under the U-numbers U 2721–U 2762, contracted on 6 May 1944.

32. This contract was later shifted to Germaniawerft AG Kiel (see note 26).

33. Originally the contract for U 4501–U 4600 was placed on 26 May 1944 with F. Schichau GmbH Danzig under yard numbers 1801–1900.

34. Previously the 141 boats of this contract were allocated to Deutsche Werft AG Hamburg (U 2390–U 2400, U 4001–U 4070), Ansaldo Genoa (U 2401–U 2430), Cantiere Riuniti Dell Adriatico Monfalcone (U 2431–U 2445) and Schiffswerft Linz AG (U 2446–U 2460).

Chapter 3

1. U 25 was ordered to operate against Allied shipping in the Bay of Biscay. When it failed to report its position after sailing from Wilhelmshaven, the boat was posted as missing effective 2 August 1940. In the absence of Allied attacks to account for its loss, it is probable that U 25 was lost to mining in the British mine barrage Field No. 7 while outbound in the North Sea. Field No. 7 was laid on its exit route on 3 March 1940 by the destroyers HMS *Express*, HMS *Esk*, HMS *Icarus*, and HMS *Impulsive*.

2. Original postwar assessment changed by the Foreign Documents Section of the Naval Historical Branch of U.K. Ministry of Defence (hereafter cited as FDS/NHB) in December 1993. The attack by the submarine HMS *Porpoise* on 16 April 1940 in position 58°18n/05°47e, formerly credited with the destruction of U 1, was actually directed against U 3 inflicting no damage. U 1 was ordered to operate in a waiting position to the west of Obrestad, Norway. When the boat failed repeatedly to report its position, it was posted as missing effective 21 April 1940. U 1 was lost to mining in the British mine barrage Field No. 7 while outbound in the North Sea. Field No. 7 was laid on its exit route on 3 March 1940 by the destroyers HMS *Express*, HMS *Esk*, HMS *Icarus*, and HMS *Impulsive*.In June 2007 a Dutch diving company salvaged the anti-aircraft gun of U 1 from the waters North of Terschelling.

3. U 12 was ordered to operate in the English Channel against the cross-channel troop transports between Britain and France. It made no report after sailing from Wilhelmshaven. The boat was posted as missing effective 20 October 1939. In the absence of an Allied attack to account for its loss, there is a possibility that U 12 was lost to mining in the Dover-Calais mine barrage during the outbound or return trip through the Straits of Dover. The body of its commanding officer, Kaptlt. von der Ropp, was washed ashore on the French coast near Dunkirk on 29 October 1939.

4. U 16 reported last early on 25 October 1939 about heavy damage and the intention to scuttle. When the boat failed to report thereafter, it was posted as missing. On 25 October 1939, the wreck of U 16 was discovered by British forces on the Goodwin Sands. A British salvage attempt failed. Nineteen dead crew members were recovered by the Royal Navy or washed ashore on the French and Dutch coast. It is possible that the damage reported by U 16 was the result of striking a mine in the Dover barrage.

5. U 22 was originally ordered to operate against enemy shipping east of the Orkney Islands. On 22 March 1940, the boat was ordered to patrol temporarily off Ryvingen, Norway, to guard German merchant vessels. It made no report after sailing from Wilhelmshaven. U 22 was posted as missing effective 27 March 1940. There is presently no plausible explanation for its loss.

6. Original postwar assessment changed by FDS/NHB in June 1991. The attack by the destroyer HMS *Wolverine* on 8 March 1941 in position 60°47n/19°13w, formerly credited with the destruction of U 47, was actually directed against U A inflicting severe damage. U 47 was operating against convoy OB.293 when it reported for the last time early on 7 March 1941. After it failed repeatedly to report its position, the boat was posted as missing effective 7 March 1941. There is presently no convincing explanation for its loss. However, unlike to previous attribution by the FDS/NHB, the British whaling ship *Terje Viken* was not attacked by U 47 early on 7 March 1941, but torpedoed by its sister boat U 70.

7. Postwar assessment of 1947 changed by the FDS/NHB in December 1993. The attack by the destroyer HMS *Hero* on 10 April 1940 in position 62°54n/01°56w, formerly credited with the destruction of U 50, was very probably directed against a nonsub target. U 50 was originally ordered to operate in a waiting position northeast of the Shetlands. It made no report after sailing from Wilhelmshaven. The boat was posted as missing effective 13 April 1940. In the absence of an Allied attack to account for its loss, it is probable that U 50 was lost to mining in the British mine barrage Field No. 7 while outbound in the North Sea. Field No. 7 was laid on its exit route on 3 March 1940 by the destroyers HMS *Express*, HMS *Esk*, HMS *Icarus*, and HMS *Impulsive.*

8. The wreck of U 54 was located in 1989 in the given position. Original postwar assessment changed by FDS/NHB in June 1983. U 54 was ordered to operate against enemy shipping off Cape Finisterre, Spain. Outbound routed through the North Sea, it made no report after sailing from Heligoland. The boat was therefore posted as missing effective 14 February 1940. Parts of two of its torpedoes were recovered on 14 March 1940 by the German patrol boat *V 1101* in the approximate position 54°57n/06°45e and on 16 April 1940 by the German Q-ship *Schiff 37* in the Skagerrak. In the absence of Allied attacks to account for its loss, it is probable that U 54 was lost to mining in the British Field No. 4 or Field No. 6 while outbound in the North Sea. Field No. 4 was laid on 2 January 1940 by the destroyers HMS *Ivanhoe* and HMS *Intrepid* across its exit route within an area enclosed by lines joining the positions 55°10n/05°03,5e, 55°03n/05°03,5e, 55°04,5n/04°56e and 55°09n/04°56e. Field No. 6 was also laid across its exit route within a radius of five miles around position 55°n/05°23.5e by the same two destroyers on the night of 13–14 January 1940.

9. Original postwar assessment changed by the author in August 2004. The air attack at by the Catalina C of 202 Sqn RAF and the depth charge hunt by the destroyer HMS *Wishart* starting at 2230 on 2 May 1942 were actually directed against U 375, which suffered no damage. Hence, U 74 must have been sunk by the attacks of the two destroyers earlier in the afternoon of 2 May 1942.

10. Original postwar assessment changed by author in December 1995, amended in January 2001 and February 2002. The attack by the Avenger of VC-13 Sqn USN of the escort carrier USS *Core* on 24 August 1943 in position 27°09n/37°03w, formerly credited with the destruction of U 84, was actually directed against U 172 inflicting no damage.

11. Original postwar assessment changed by Eric Zimmerman in December 1996, amended by the author in March 2004 and January 2005. The attack by the Avengers of VC-19 Sqn USN of the escort carrier USS *Bogue* on 29 November 1943 in position 39°33n/19°01w, formerly credited with destruction of U 86, was actually directed against U 764 inflicting no damage.

12. Original postwar assessment changed by FDS/NHB in December 1985.

13. Original postwar assessment changed by the FDS/NHB in April 1997. The attack by the destroyer HMS *Viscount* on 17 February 1943 in position 50°50n/40°50w, formerly credited with the destruction of U 69, actually accounted for the sinking of U 201.

14. Original postwar assessment changed by Eric Zimmerman and the author in February 2010. The attack by the Hudson V of 48 Sqn RAF on 28 March 1943 in position 38°31n/00°53w, formerly credited with the destruction of U 77, was actually directed against U 380 inflicting no damage.

15. Original postwar assessment changed by FDS/NHB in June 1988. The attack by the Hudson C of 608 Sqn RAF on 19 November 1942 in position 35°38n/11°48w, formerly credited with the destruction of U 98, was actually directed against U 413 inflicting severe damage.

16. U 132 was operating against convoy SC.107 when it reported for the last time on 3 November 1942. After having failed repeatedly to report, the boat was posted as missing effective 4 November 1942. The original postwar assessment crediting its loss to the attack of Liberator H of 120 Sqn RAF on 5 November 1942 in position 58°08n/33°13w had been changed by the FDS/NHB in January 1985 when it became known that the attack was actually directed against U 89 inflicting severe damage. In the absence of an Allied attack to account for its loss, the underwater explosion of the SS *Hatimura* carrying explosives offers a possible explanation as U 132 must have attacked that ship shortly before and was probably still nearby.

17. Original postwar assessment changed by Eric Zimmerman and the author in July 2004. The attack by the Wellington J of 179 Sqn RAF on 24 August 1943 in position 42°07n/09°30w, formerly credited with the destruction of U 134, was actually directed against U 340 inflicting no damage.

18. Original postwar assessment changed by the FDS/NHB in April 1997. The attack by the destroyer HMS *Fame* on 17 February 1943 in position 50°36n/41°07w, formerly credited with the destruction of U 201, actually accounted for the sinking of U 69.

19. Original postwar assessment changed by the author in August 1991 and the FDS/NHB in March 1992. The attack by the Whitley B of 502 Sqn RAF on 30 November 1941 in position 46°55n/07°16w, formerly credited with the destruction of U 206, was actually directed against U 71 inflicting no damage. U 206 was outbound to break through the Gibraltar Strait into the Mediterranean Sea. When it failed repeatedly to report its position, it was posted as missing effective 4 December 1941. In the absence of an Allied attack to account for its loss, it is possible that U 206 was lost to mining in the British minefield Beech, which was dropped by RAF aircraft after August 1940 off St. Nazaire.

20. Original postwar assessment and subsequent reassessment changed by the FDS/NHB in January 1986. The attack by the corvette HMS *Bluebell* on 11 December 1941 in position 36°40n/09°20w, formerly credited with the destruction of U 208, was actually directed against U 67 inflicting slight damage.

21. Original postwar assessment changed by the author in May 1990 and the FDS/NHB in October 1991. The attack by the frigate HMS *Jed* and the sloop HMS *Sennen* on 19 May 1943 in position 54°54n/34°19w, formerly credited with the destruction of U 209, actually accounted for the sinking of U 954. U 209 reported last on 6 May 1943 via U 954 from the approximate position 55°n/42°w on extensive damage and transmitter breakdown sustained from air attack. As a result the boat was recalled to Brest the same day. The reported air attack was in all probability carried out by the Canso W of 5 Sqn RCAF on 4 May 1943 in position 56°38n/42°32w. When the boat failed to return to Brest, France, or signal its position, it was posted as missing effective 19 May 1943. There is presently no known explanation for its loss. There is, however, a possibility that U 209 was already lost on or about 7 May 1943 to submarine accident as a result of the damage received in the previous air attack.

22. Original postwar assessment and reassessment by the FDS/NHB from May 1987 changed by the author in March 2008. The attack by the Coast Guard cutter USS *John C. Spencer* on 21 February 1943 in position 51°25n/27°28w, originally credited with the destruction of U 225, was actually directed against U 604 inflicting no damage, while the attack of Liberator S of 120 Sqn RAF on 15 February 1943 in position 55°45n/31°09w, subsequently credited with destruction of U 225, actually accounted for the sinking of U 529.

23 Original postwar assessment changed by the author in May 2002 with amendments in December 2002 and April 2003. The attack by the Liberator Q of 2nd A/S Sqn USAAF on 8 July 1943 in position 40°37n/13°41w, formerly credited with the destruction of U 232, was actually directed against U 183 inflicting no damage.

24. Original postwar assessment changed by the author in February 1998. The attack by the Sunderland V of 330 Sqn RAF on 16 May 1944 in position 63°05n/03°10e, formerly credited with the destruction of U 240, was actually directed against U 668 inflicting no damage. U 240 was on a transfer passage to Narvik, Norway. When it failed repeatedly to report its position after sailing, it was posted as missing to the west of Norway effective from 17 May 1944. There is presently no known explanation for its loss.

25. Original postwar assessment and subsequent reassessment changed by the author in January 1991. The attack by the destroyers HMS *Hesperus* and HMS *Havelock* on 30 April 1945 in position 53°42n/04°53w, formerly credited with the destruction of U 242, was actually directed against the wreck of U 246. The attacks from the two destroyers produced personal belongings from a crew member of U 246.

26. Original postwar assessment changed by the author in January 1991, amended in December 2004. The attack by the frigate HMS *Duckworth* on 29 March 1945 in position 49°58n/05°25w, formerly credited with the destruction of U 246, was probably directed against a non-sub contact. The sunken wreck of U 246 was located and heavily depth charged on 30 April 1945 by the destroyers HMS *Hesperus* and HMS *Havelock*. See also note 5.

27. Original postwar assessment changed by FDS/NHB in December 1979. The attack by the Catalina U of 210 Sqn RAF on 23 September 1942 in position 68°19n/13°50w, formerly credited with the destruction of U 253, was actually directed against U 255 inflicting medium damage. U 253 reported last on 24 September 1942 from the approximate position 67°30n/21°00w while operating against convoy OP.14. The following day it was directed into the North Atlantic. When the boat thereafter failed repeatedly to signal its position, it was posted as missing effective 28 September 1942. There is presently no known explanation for its loss. There is, however, a strong possibility that U 253 was lost to mining on or about 25 September 1942 in the Denmark Straits in the British anti-submarine minefields SN 11 or SN 71A off the Icelandic coast. The two fields were laid on 1 June 1942 and 21 August 1942 and crossed its onward route to its assigned operational area in the North Atlantic.

28. U 263 reported last on 20 January 1944 about its intention to return to La Pallice while being unable to dive after severe damage during a deep-diving trial. When the transmission of its last report stopped incomplete and the boat thereafter failed to signal its position upon immediate orders, U 263 was posted as missing effective 20 January 1944. In the absence of Allied attacks to account for its loss, it is probable that U 263 was lost in a marine accident as the result of severe structural damage sustained in the deep-diving test.

29. Original postwar assessment changed by the FDS/NHB in April 1990. The attack by the Liberator B of 86 Sqn RAF on 14 May 1943 in position 47°45n/26°57w, formerly credited with the destruction of U 266, was actually directed against U 403 inflicting no damage.

30. Original postwar assessment changed by the FDS/NHB in August 1994. The attack by the Liberator X of 120 Sqn RAF on 4 October 1943 in position 60°51n/28°26w, formerly credited with the destruction of U 279, actually accounted for the sinking of U 389.

31. Original postwar assessment changed by the author in September 2003. U 305 reported last early on 15 January 1944 on its intention to return to its base in France on 20 January 1944. On 2 February U-boat Command ordered the boat to report at once. When no answer was received and the boat also failed to arrive in port, U 305 was posted as missing on 3 February 1944 with effect from 2 February 1944 during the return passage to France. On the morning of 16 January 1944, an distress radio signal from an unknown German U-boat was monitored by German and Allied stations, reporting it was sinking quickly after a torpedo hit. Providing it was genuine, this signal must have come from U 305.

32. Original postwar assessment changed by the FDS/NHB in April 1986. The attack by the Sunderland A of 423 Sqn RCAF on 24 April 1944 in position 50°36n/18°36w, formerly credited with the destruction of U 311, was actually directed against U 672 inflicting severe damage.

33. Original postwar assessment changed by the author in April 2002. The attack by the destroyers HMS *Whitehall* and HMS *Meteor* on 30 January 1944 in position 73°41n/24°30e, formerly credited with the destruction of U 314, was actually directed against U 965 inflicting no damage.

34. Original postwar assessment changed by the author in November 1989. The attack by the Sunderland M of 461 Sqn RAAF on 2 May 1943 in position 44°48n/08°58w, formerly credited with the destruction of U 332, actually accounted for the sinking of U 465.

35. Original postwar assessment changed by the FDS/NHB in August 1994. The attack by the Ventura B of VB-128 Sqn USN on 4 October 1943 in position 60°40n/26°30w, formerly credited with the destruction of U 336, actually accounted for the sinking of U 279.

36. Original postwar assessment changed by the author in January 1993. The attack by the Fortress G of 206 Sqn RAF on 15 January 1943 in position 57°40n/27°10w, formerly credited with the destruction of U 337, was actually directed against U 632 inflicting no damage. U 337 reported last on 3 January 1943 from the approximate position 63°n/12°w while en route to its assigned operational area to the northeast of Newfoundland. When the boat thereafter failed repeatedly to signal its position, it was posted as missing effective 24 January 1943. There is presently no plausible explanation for its loss.

37. Original postwar assessment changed by the FDS/NHB in October 1992. The attack by the Liberator F of 120 Sqn RAF on 20 September 1943 in position 57°40n/29°48w, formerly credited with the destruction of U 338, was actually directed against U 386 inflicting no damage. U 338 reported last on 20 September 1943 from the approximate position 57°20n/30°00w while operating against convoy ON.202/ONS.18. When the boat thereafter failed repeatedly to signal its position, it was posted as missing effective 21 September 1943. There is presently no known explanation for its loss.

38. Original postwar assessment changed by FDS/NHB in September 1980. The attack by the sloop HMS *Peacock* and the frigate HMS *Loch Dunvegan* on 24 August 1944 in position 72°49n/30°41e, formerly credited with the destruction of U 344. actually accounted for the sinking of U 354.

39. Original postwar assessment changed by Eric Zimmerman in January 1997. The attack by the Catalina Y of 210 Sqn RAF on 17 July 1944 in position 68°35n/06°00e, formerly credited with the destruction of U 347, actually accounted for the sinking of U 361.

40. Original postwar assessment and reassessment by the FDS/NHB from September 1957 changed by Eric Zimmerman and the author in June 2011. The attack by the Swordfish X of 825 Sqn FAA of the escort carrier HMS *Vindex* on 22 August 1944 in position 74°54n/15°26e, originally credited with the destruction of U 354, actually accounted for the sinking of U 344. The attacks by the destroyer HMS *Keppel* and the sloop HMS *Peacock* on 25 August 1944 were actually directed against U 668 and U 365, inflicting no damage.

41. Original postwar assessment changed by the author in January 1997. The attack by the Avenger H of 846 Sqn FAA of the escort carrier HMS *Tracker* and the destroyer HMS *Beagle* on 1 April 1944 in position 73°07n/10°21e, formerly credited with the destruction of U 355, was actually directed against U 673 inflicting medium damage. U 355 reported last on 1 April 1944 from the approximate position 73°03n/13°10e while operating against convoy JW.58. When it thereafter failed repeatedly to report its position, it was posted as missing in the Arctic Sea effective 4 April 1944. There is presently no known explanation for its loss.

42. Original postwar assessment changed by the author in December 1997. The attack by the Mariner P-1 of VP-32 Sqn USN on 28 July 1943 in position 15°57n/68°30w, formerly credited with the destruction of U 359, actually accounted for the sinking of U 159.

43. Original postwar assessment changed by Eric Zimmerman in January 1997. The attack by the Liberator U of 86 Sqn RAF on 17 July 1944 in position 68°36n/08°33e, formerly credited with the destruction of U 361, actually accounted for the sinking of U 347.

44. Original postwar assessment changed by the author in March 1998, amended in April 2003. The attack by the Wellington K of 172 Sqn RAF on 31 January 1944 in position 45°25n/05°15w, formerly credited with the destruction of U 364, was actually directed against U 608 inflicting no damage. The aircraft was shot down by U 608 in the attack without being able to drop its depth charges.

45. Original postwar assessment changed by the author in March 2013. U 367 reported last on 15 March 1945 while inbound to Hela from the front-line training group area in the Danzig Bay. The mine field laid by the Soviet submarine *L-21* on 13 March 1945 across the German swept channel Weg 76 off Hela between the positions 54°35,5n/18°52e and 54°34,8n/18°51,1e was not yet discovered at that time. The previous attribution of a radio distress signal without signature about a mine hit at 2359/16 in naval grid square AO 9573 (54°51n/18°55e) to the loss of U 367 is highly unlikely as the boat was due to arrive in port already on 15 March 1945.

46. Original postwar assessment changed by the author in November 2009. The attack by the submarine chaser USS *PC 624* on 31 July 1943 in position 36°40n/12°28e, formerly credited with the destruction of U 375, was actually directed against the Italian submatrine *Velella* inflicting no damage. U 375 reported last on 25 July 1943 from the approximate position 36°39n/14°18e while operating against Allied landing forces south of Sicily. When it thereafter failed repeatedly to report its position, it was posted as missing effective 1 August 1943. In the absence of an Allied attack to account for the boat, there is presently no known explanation for its loss.

47. Original postwar assessment changed by the author in November 1996. The attack by the Wellington C of 172 Sqn RAF on 10 April 1943 in position 46°48n/09°00w, formerly credited with the destruction of U 376, was actually directed against U 465 inflicting severe damage. U 376 was outbound for a special operation code-named "Elster" to take aboard German naval officers who escaped from a Canadian POW camp at North Point on the northern tip of Prince Edward Island on the Canadian East coast. When it failed repeatedly to report its position after sailing, it was posted as missing in the Bay of Biscay effective 13 April 1943. There is presently no known explanation for its loss.

48. Original postwar assessment changed by the author in September 2003. Using U 377's last report on 15 January 1944 from 45°57n/20°15w as a reference, the attack by HMS *Wanderer* and HMS *Glenarm* on 17 January 1944, formerly credited with the destruction of U 305, took place almost exactly on U 377's direct course line towards the centre of its assigned attacking area around 51°03n/19°15w. The distance between its last known position and the location of the attack is about 220 nautical miles, which equals the expected boat's mileage. Thus it is very probable that it was in fact U 377 that was sunk by the two ships on 17 January 1944.

49. Original postwar assessment changed by the FDS/NHB in June 1992. The attacks by the corvette HMS *Snowflake* and the destroyer HMS *Duncan* on 19 May 1943 in position 54°41n/34°45w, formerly credited with the destruction of U 381, were actually directed against U 304 and U 636, inflicting minor damage. U 381 reported last on 9 May 1943 from the approximate position 51°30n/36°00w while patrolling to the south of Greenland. When the boat thereafter failed repeatedly to signal its position, it was posted as missing effective 21 May 1943. There is presently no plausible explanation for its loss.

50. U 383 reported last late on 1 August 1943 from the position 47°03n/10°35w that it was unable to dive or maneuver as the result of a previous air attack. The reported attack was in all probability carried out by the Sunderland V of 228 Sqn RAF on 1 August 1943 in the reported position 47°24n/12°10w. When U 383 thereafter failed repeatedly to report its position and was not met the following day by German air and naval forces sent to its assistance, it was posted as missing effective 1 August 1943. It is very probable that U 383 was lost on 1 August 1943 as the result of the damage received in the previous air attack.

51. Original postwar assessment changed by the FDS/NHB in June 1975. The attack by the Sunderland T of 201 Sqn RAF on 20 March 1943 in position 54°18n/26°15w, formerly credited with the destruction of U 384, was actually directed against U 631, inflicting no damage.

52. Original postwar assessment changed by the FDS/NHB in August 1994. The attack by the Hudson F of 269 Sqn RAF on 5 October 1943 in position 62°43n/27°17w, formerly credited with the destruction of U 389, actually accounted for the sinking of U 336.

53. Original postwar assessment changed by author in February 1990. The attack by the Beaufighters U, Q1, and D of 236 Sqn RAF and Beaufighters Q, F, and J of 254 Sqn RAF on 4 May 1945 in position 55°37n/10°00e, formerly credited with the destruction of U 393, was actually directed against U 2351, inflicting slight damage.

54. Original postwar assessment changed by author in June 1993. The attack by the Liberator U of 86 Sqn RAF on 23 April 1945 in position 59°29n/05°22w, formerly credited with the destruction of U 396, was very probably directed against a nonsub target. U 396 reported last early on 11 April 1945 from the approximate position 57°30n/26°00w. In its last signal U 396 reported that it had started its return trip from its weather reporting position in the North Atlantic following damage to its forward hydroplanes. When the boat thereafter failed to return to Trondheim or signal its position after the cessation of hostilities, it was posted as missing. There is presently no plausible explanation for its loss.

55. U 398 was ordered to operate against enemy shipping off the western exit of the English Channel. No signal was received from it after sailing from Kristiansund. When U 398 subsequently failed to return to Norway or signal its position after the cessation of hostilities, it was posted as missing. There is presently no known explanation for its loss. There is, however, a possibility that U 398 instead of U 1017 was sunk in the attack of the Liberator Q of 120 Sqn RAF on 29 April 1945 in position 56°04n/11°06w. Both boats disappeared without trace while outbound and should have passed through the attack area at the same time.

56. Original postwar assessment changed by the author in February 2004 with amendment in July 2008. The attack by the frigate HMS *Nyasaland* on 17 December 1942 in position 51°16n/08°05w, formerly credited with the destruction of U 400, actually accounted for the sinking of U 772.

57. Original postwar assessment changed by the author in February 2004. The attack by the destroyers HMS *Wanderer* and HNoMS *St. Albans* earlier on 3 August 1941 in position 50°27n/19°50w, formerly credited with damaging of U 401, was actually directed against U 205 inflicting slight damage.

58. Original postwar assessment changed by the FDS/NHB in June 1993. The attack by the Hudson O of 200 Sqn RAF on 17 August 1943 in position 14°11n/17°40w, formerly credited with the destruction of U 403, was very probably also directed against U 403 but without inflicting lethal damage.

59. Original postwar assessment and subsequent reassessment changed by the FDS/NHB in June 1988. The attack by the destroyer HMS *Wrestler* on 15 November 1942 in position 36°09n/07°42w, formerly credited with the destruction of U 411, actually accounted for the sinking of U 98.

60. Original postwar assessment changed by Eric Zimmerman and the author in February 2010. The attack by the Beaufighter B of 236 Sqn RAF on 1 June 1943 in position 47°05n/08°55w, formerly credited with the destruction of U 418, was actually directed against U 378 inflicting no damage.

61. Original postwar assessment changed by the author in January 1996. The attack by the Liberator A of 10 Sqn RCAF on 26 October 1943 in position 50°49n/41°01w, formerly credited with the destruction of U 420, was actually directed against U 91 inflicting no damage. U 420 reported last on 20 October 1943 from the approximate position 48°00n/21°00w while en route to its operational area to the northeast of Newfoundland. When U 420 subsequently failed to report its position or to return to Brest, France, it was posted as missing effective 17 November 1943. There is presently no known explanation for its loss.

62. Original postwar assessment changed by the author and the FDS/NHB in January 1993. The attack by several aircraft from VC-9 Sqn USN of the escort carrier USS *Card* on 4 October 1943 in position 43°18n/28°58w. formerly credited with the destruction of U 422, was actually directed against U 264 inflicting severe damage.

63. Original postwar assessment changed by the FDS/NHB in November 1987. The attack by the submarine HMS *Ultimatum* on 30 October 1943 in position 43°04n/05°57e, formerly credited with the destruction of U 431, was actually directed against U 73 inflicting no damage.

64. Original postwar assessment changed by the author in May 2002 with amendments in December 2002 and April 2003. The attack by the Wellington R of 179 Sqn RAF on 9 July 1943 in position 39°48n/14°22w, formerly credited with the destruction of U 435, actually accounted for the sinking of U 232.

65. Original postwar assessment and reassessment by the FDS/NHB from August 1996 changed by the author in August 2006. The attack by the Wellington A of 304 Sqn RAF (Polish) on 18 June 1944 in position 49°03n/04°48w, formerly credited with the destruction of U 441, was very probably directed against a nonsub target, possibly a whale.

66. Original postwar assessment changed by the author in September 2005 with amendment from July 2012.

67. Original postwar assessment and subsequent reassessments changed by the FDS/NHB in October 1989. The attack by the Sunderland G of 423 Sqn RCAF together with the destroyer HMS *Broadway* and the frigate HMS *Lagan* on 13 May 1943 in position 48°37n/22°39w, formerly credited with the destruction of U 456, actually accounted for the sinking of U 753. U 456 reported last on 12 May 1943 from the approximate position 46°40n/26°50w after previous reports on its inability to dive. When the boat thereafter failed to signal its position, it was posted as missing effective 12 May 1943. The boat was very probably lost when it attempted to dive while facing the approaching destroyer HMS *Opportune*. The destroyer was called to the scene by the Liberator B of 86 Sqn RAF after its initial crippling attack a few hours before in position 46°40n/26°20w.

68. Original postwar assessment and subsequent reassessment changed by the author in November 1989. The attack by the Sunderland W of 10 Sqn RAAF on 7 May 1943 in position 47°06n/10°58w, formerly credited with the destruction of U 465, was actually directed against U 663 inflicting severe damage.

69. Original postwar assessment changed by the author in September 2013. In the summer of 2013 the wreck of a German U-boat, tentatively identified as U 479 by the author, was located in Estonian territorial waters N.W. of Osmusaari (Odensholm), showing damage from mining.

70. Original postwar assessment changed by Innes McCartney and the FDS/NHB in January 1998. The attacks carried out by the frigates HMS *Duckworth* and HMS *Rowley* on 24 February 1945 in position 49°55n/06°08w, formerly credited with the destruction of U 480, actually accounted for the sinking of U 1208.

71. Original postwar assessment and reassessment by the FDS/NHB from August 1993 changed by the author in March 2004. The attacks carried out by the ships of 22 E.G. from 16 to 19 January 1945 in position 55°30n/05°50w, formerly credited with the destruction of U 482, were directed against a non-sub target.

72. Original postwar assessment and subsequent reassessment changed by the author in January 1994. The attacks carried out by the frigate HCMS *Dunver* and the corvette HCMS *Hespeler* on 9 September 1944 in position 56°30n/07°40w, formerly credited with the destruction of U 484, were very probably directed against a nonsub target.

73. U 553 was last seen by U 465 on 20 January 1943 in the approximate position 48°n/15°w while outbound to its operational area in the Eastern North Atlantic. When the boat thereafter failed repeatedly to signal its position, it was posted as missing effective 28 January 1943. In the absence of an Allied attack to account for its sinking, there is presently no plausible explanation for its loss.

74. Original postwar assessment changed by the FDS/NHB in November 1990. The attack by the Sunderland X of 230 Sqn RAF on 9 January 1942 in position 32°22n/26°54e, formerly credited with the destruction of U 577, was actually directed against U 568 inflicting minor damage. It should be noted, that the attack on 15 January 1942 provided no conclusive evidence for the destruction of the U-boat present, whose identity was U 577 in all probability. In the absence of other promising attacks or speculative explanations for its disappearance, the loss of U 577 was allocated to the attack for want of better information.

75. Original postwar assessment changed by the author in November 1995. The attack by the Wellington H of 311 Sqn RAF on 10 August 1942 in position 45°59n/07°44w, formerly credited with the destruction of U 578, was actually directed against U 135 inflicting minor damage. U 578 was outbound for an operation in the North Atlantic. When it failed repeatedly to report its position, it was posted as missing in the Bay of Biscay effective 11 August 1942. There is presently no known explanation for its loss.

76. Original postwar assessment and subsequent reassessments changed by the author and the NHB in June 1986. The loss of U 579 was observed and recorded by the accompanying U 1008.

77. Original postwar assessment and subsequent reassessment changed by the FDS/NHB in June 1987. The attack by the Hudson N of 269 Sqn RAF on 5 October 1942 in position 58°41n/22°58w, formerly credited with the destruction of U 582, actually accounted for the sinking of U 619.

78. Original postwar assessment changed by Claude Huan in January 1977. The attack by the destroyer HMS *Fury* on 29 March 1942 in position 72°15n/34°22e, formerly credited with the destruction of U 585, was actually directed against U 378 inflicting no damage. U 585 reported last on 29 March 1942 from the approximate position 71°05n/34°00e while operating against convoy PQ.13. When it thereafter failed repeatedly to report its position, it was posted as missing effective 5 April 1942. In the absence of an Allied attack to account for its loss, it is possible that U 585 was accidentally lost to a drifting mine from the German minefield Bantos A, which was laid on 20 March 1942 close to the assumed route.

79. Original postwar assessment changed by Eric Zimmerman and the author in December 2012. Although the attack by the Hudson F of 48 Sqn RAF on 4 June 1943 in position 35°55n/09°25w, formerly credited with the destruction of U 594, was indeed directed against U 594, damage, if any, could not have been lethal as two more known U-boat contacts/attacks in the area on the next day could only have been U 594.

80. Original postwar assessment was changed sometime afterward to the effect that the attack of the Hudson N of 500 Sqn RAF on 23 April 1943 in position 36°10n/00°30w was credited with the sinking of U 602. This attack was however directed against U 453 inflicting no damage. U 602 reported last on 19 April 1943 from its operational area north of Oran at the Algerian coast. When the boat thereafter failed repeatedly to signal its position, it was posted as missing effective 23 April 1943. In the absence of an Allied attack to account for its sinking, there is presently no plausible explanation for its loss.

81. Original postwar assessment changed by the author in January 2001. The attack by the destroyer escort USS *Bronstein* on 1 March 1944 in position 48°55n/26°10w, formerly credited with the destruction of U 603, was actually directed against a non-sub contact. The damage sustained by USS *Bronstein* in the course of the action, believed to have resulted from a nearby torpedo detonation, was clearly caused by a premature depth charge explosion due to technical failure or lack of drill. U 603 reported last late on 18 February 1944 from 48°57n/23°45w when operating as part of group "Hai" against the convoys ONS.29 and ON.224. Its nominally assigned operational area on 1 March 1944 was more than 200 nautical miles

away from the attack position. When U 603 subsequently failed to report its position, it was posted as missing effective 16 March 1944. There is presently no plausible explanation for its loss.

82. The complete crew of U 604 was taken over by U 185 which, together with U 172, was sent to its assistance. On 14 August 1943 twenty-two men were transferred at sea to U 172 and finally arrived at Lorient, France, on 7 September 1943. Twenty-three crew members including the Commanding Officer remained aboard U 185. When this boat was sunk on 24 August 1943, the Commanding Officer and thirteen men of U 604 were killed and nine men became Prisoners of War.

83. Original postwar assessment changed by the FDS/NHB in July 1987. The attack by the corvettes HMS *Poppy* and HMS *Lotus* on 13 November 1942 in position 37°04n/02°55e, formerly credited with the destruction of U 605, was actually directed against U 77 inflicting minor damage.

84. Original postwar assessment changed by author in July 2000 with amendment from January 2004. The attack by the corvette FNFL *Lobelia* on 7 February 1943 in position 55°17n/26°38w, formerly credited with the destruction of U 609, was actually directed against U 613 inflicting slight damage.

85. Original postwar assessment changed by author in October 1995. The attack by the Catalina H of VP-84 Sqn USN on 10 December 1942 in position 58°09n/22°44w, formerly credited with the destruction of U 611, was actually directed against U 609 inflicting no damage.

86. Original postwar assessment changed by the FDS/NHB in June 1987. The attack by the destroyer HMS *Viscount* on 15 October 1942 in position 53°42n/35°56w, formerly credited with the destruction of U 619, actually accounted for the sinking of U 661.

87. Original postwar assessment changed by the FDS/NHB in September 1988. The attack by the Catalina J of 202 Sqn RAF on 14 February 1943 in position 39°27n/11°34w, formerly credited with the destruction of U 620, was actually directed against U 381 inflicting no damage.

88. Original postwar assessment changed by author in January 2006. U 626 reported last in the morning of 14 December 1942 from the approximate position 58°40n/20°00w. The attacks by the USCGC *Ingham* on 15 December 1942 in position 56°46n/27°12w and 18 December 1942 in position 55°00n/35°01w, formerly credited successively with the destruction of U 626, took place some 180 and 200 nautical miles respectively away from U 626's likely position on these days. Both attacks were therefore most probably directed against non-sub targets. In the absence of a promising Allied attack to account for its sinking, there is presently no plausible explanation for its loss.

89. Original postwar assessment changed by the FDS/NHB in March 1997. The attack by the Liberator G of 224 Sqn RAF on 8 June 1944 in position 48°27n/05°47w, formerly credited with the destruction of U 629, actually accounted for the sinking of U 740. Three bodies of the crew of U 629 were washed ashore on the French coast at Quessant or picked up at sea between 19 and 21 June 1944.

90. Original postwar assessment changed by the FDS/NHB in October 1991. The attack by the Canso W of 5 Sqn RCAF on 4 May 1943 in position 56°38n/42°32w, formerly credited with the destruction of U 630, was actually directed against U 209 inflicting severe damage.

91. Original postwar assessment changed by the author in January 1993 with amendment in May 2005 and the FDS/NHB in December 1996. The attack by the Fortress J of 220 Sqn RAF on 7 March 1943 in position 57°14n/26°30w, formerly credited with the destruction of U 633, was actually directed against U 641 inflicting no damage. The collision incident reported by the British S/S *Scorton* on 10 March 1943 in position 58°51n/19°55w actually involved U 229, which escaped without damage.

92. Original postwar assessment changed by the FDS/NHB in March 1985. The attack by the frigate HMS *Tay* on 6 April 1943 in position 58°25n/29°22w, formerly credited with the destruction of U 635, was actually directed against U 306 inflicting no damage.

93. Original postwar assessment changed by the FDS/NHB in October 1991. The attack by the corvette HMS *Loosestrife* on 5 May 1943 in position 53°06n/45°02w, formerly credited with the destruction of U 638, actually accounted for the sinking of U 192.

94. Original postwar assessment changed by the FDS/NHB in June 1992. The attack by the frigate HMS *Swale* on 17 May 1943 in position 58°54n/42°33w, formerly credited with the destruction of U 640, actually accounted for the sinking of U 657.

95. Original postwar assessment changed by the author in November 1995 with amendment from June 2004. The attack by the destroyer USS *Schenck* on 24 December 1943 in position 45°20n/21°40w, formerly credited with the destruction of U 645, was actually directed against U 275 inflicting no damage. U 645 reported last on 12 December 1943 from the approximate position 49°30n/22°30w while outbound to the North Atlantic to the west of Spain. It was to operate with U-boat group "Borkum"

against convoys on the U.K.-Gibraltar route. When the boat failed repeatedly to signal its position, it was posted as missing effective 13 January 1944.

96. U 647 reported last on 28 July 1943 from the approximate position 64°00n/01°30w while outbound to the North Atlantic through the Iceland passage. When the boat thereafter failed repeatedly to signal its position, it was posted as missing effective 9 August 1943. In the absence of an Allied attack to account for its sinking, there is presently no plausible explanation for its loss.

97. Original postwar assessment changed by the author in January 1998. The attacks by the frigates HMS *Bazely*, HMS *Blackwood* and HMS *Drury* on 23 November 1943 in position 42°40n/20°37w, formerly credited with the destruction of U 648, were actually directed against U 424, U 714 and U 843 inflicting no damage. U 648 reported last early on 22 November 1943 from the approximate positon 45°09n/19°45w while operating against convoys on the UK-Gibraltar route. When the boat subsequently failed repeatedly to report its position or to arrive at the rendezvous point off St. Nazaire, it was posted as missing effective 2 December 1943. There is presently no known explanation for its loss.

98. Original postwar assessment changed by the author in July 2008 when the wreck of a U-boat already located in 1987 was positively identified as U 650. With the wreck showing signs of depth charge damage, it has however been yet unable to attribute an Allied A/S-attack to the wreck site. The nearest recorded attack was carried out by the British corvette *Dahlia* on 21 January 1945 in the historical position 49°56n/05°35w, putting it some seven miles away from the wreck position.

99. Original postwar assessment changed by the FDS/NHB in June 1992. The attack by the Catalina C of VP-84 Sqn USN on 14 May 1943 in position 60°10n/31°52w, formerly credited with the destruction of U 657, was very probably also directed against U 657 but without inflicting lethal damage.

100. Original postwar assessment changed by the FDS/NHB in June 1987. The attack by the Liberator H of 120 Sqn RAF on 15 October 1942 in position 53°58n/33°43w, formerly credited with the destruction of U 661, was actually directed against U 615 inflicting no damage.

101. Original postwar assessment changed by the author in November 1989. The attack by the Halifax S of 58 Sqn RAF on 7 May 1943 in position 46°33n/11°12w, formerly credited with the destruction of U 663, was actually directed against U 214 inflicting minor damage. U 663 reported last early on 8 May 1943 from the approximate position 46°50n/10°00w on damage received by the attack of Sunderland W of 10 Sqn RAAF on 7 May 1943 in position 47°06n/10°58w and its further intentions. When the boat thereafter failed repeatedly to signal its position, it was posted as missing effective 8 May 1943. In the absence of an Allied attack to account for its sinking, a marine accident as the result of the severe structural damage sustained in the air attack offers a possible explanation for its loss.

102. Original postwar assessment and reassessment by the FDS/NHB from May 1992 changed by the author in December 2002 with amendment from August 2003. The attack by the Wellington G of 172 Sqn RAF on 22 March 1943 in position 46°47n/09°58w, formerly credited with the destruction of U 665, was actually directed against U 448 inflicting no damage. Likewise, the attack by the Whitley Q of 10 OTU Sqn RAF on 22 March 1943 in position 48°04n/10°26w was directed against U 435 inflicting no damage. U 665 reported last on 21 March 1943 to notify Control that it was then 36 hours off the rendezvous position with her escort off La Pallice. When the boat failed to meet her escort at the prefixed time at 0930 on 23 March 1943 or to report its position, it was posted as missing with effect from 23 March 1943.

103. Original postwar assessment and reassessment by the author from September 1995 reverted to original post-war assessment by Eric Zimmerman and the author in May 2011. Fresh research had shown that the positional information included in one of U 666's last signals shortly before the attack was inadvertently misspelled, giving its position apparently some 130 nautical miles away from attack position.

104. U 667 reported last on 25 August 1944 announcing its arrival at the rendezvous point off La Pallice for the following day. When the boat thereafter failed repeatedly to show up or to signal its position, it was posted as missing effective 26 August 1944. In the absence of an Allied attack to account for its sinking, mining offers a plausible explanation for its loss.

105. Original postwar assessment changed by the author in November 1995 with amendment from February 2003 and June 2009. The attack by the Wellington W of 407 Sqn RCAF on 7 September 1943 in position 45°36n/10°13w, formerly credited with the destruction of U 669, was actually directed against U 584 inflicting no damage. U 669 was outbound for a special operation code-named "Kiebitz" to take aboard the former German U-boat commander Kptltn Heyda, who escaped from a Canadian

POW camp, at Baie de Chaleurs, New Brunswick, on the Canadian east coast. Following a deep-diving trial the boat failed to report back to its escorting vessel. When it also failed repeatedly to report its position thereafter, it was posted as missing in the Bay of Biscay effective 8 September 1943.

106. The wreck of U 676 was located in August 2002. The wreck of U 676 was located in 2002. U 676 reported last on 12 February 1945 on ice damage while staying in its operational area in the Gulf of Finland. When the boat thereafter failed repeatedly to signal its position, it was posted as missing effective 19 February 1945.

107. The wreck of U 679 was located in August 2015. Postwar reassessment by the Soviet navy reverted to original post-war assessment by the author in March 2013. The attack by the Soviet sub-chaser *MO-124* on 9 January 1945 in position 59°26n/24°07e must have been directed against a non-sub wreck, as it took place well to the East of U 679's assigned operational area and after it was ordered to return to base.

108. Original postwar assessment changed by the author and FDS/NHB in December 1989. The attack by the frigate HMS *Loch Ruthven* and the sloop HMS *Wild Goose* on 12 March 1945 in position 49°52n/05°52w, formerly credited with the destruction of U 683, was actually directed against the wreck of U 247. The target's identity was proven by personal belongings of a crew member of U 247 recovered after the attack. U 683 reported last on 20 February 1945 from the approximate position 55°00n/12°30w while en route to its operational area off Cherbourg in the English Channel. When U 683 subsequently failed to return to Stavanger, Norway, it was posted as missing effective 3 April 1945. There is a possibility that U 683 was lost on or after 28 February 1945 on the British minefield "HW A1" in position 50°31,4'n / 05°22,8'w.

109. Original postwar assessment and reassessment by the author from June 1990 changed in July 2012. On 30 March 1942 U 702 left Heligoland to the North via way 'Blau'. On 2 April 1942 it was ordered to enter Bergen after a short deployment with group Wachsam to the west of Norway. Two days later its destination was changed to Stavanger. No signal was received from it after sailing from Heligoland. The boat was posted as missing effective 4 April 1942. On 21 March 1942 the French submarine *Rubis* had laid a minefield, consisting of 21 units, right off the northern exit of way 'Blau'.

110. U 703 was ordered to operate off the east coast of Greenland to put out a floating automatic weather buoy. No signal was received from it after sailing from Narvik. The boat was posted as missing effective 6 October 1944. There is presently no plausible explanation for its loss.

111. Original postwar assessment changed by the FDS/NHB in November 1987. The attack by the Whitley V of 77 Sqn RAF on 3 September 1942 in position 47°55n/10°04w, formerly credited with the destruction of U 705, was actually directed against U 660 inflicting no damage.

112. Original postwar assessment changed by the author in January 2001. The attacks by the destroyer escorts USS *Thomas*, USS *Bostwick* and USS *Bronstein* on 1 March 1944 in position 49°10n/26°00w, formerly credited with the destruction of U 709, were actually directed against U 441 inflicting major damage. U 709 reported last early on 19 February 1944 from 49°15n/23°14w when operating as part of group "Hai" against the convoys ONS.29 and ON.224. When U 709 subsequently failed to report its position, it was posted as missing effective 16 March 1944. There is presently no known explanation for its loss.

113. Original postwar assessment changed by the author in January 2004. The attack by the destroyer HMS *Keppel* on 24 February 1944 in position 69°27n/04°53e, formerly credited with the destruction of U 713, was actually directed against U 313 inflicting no damage. U 713 reported last on 24 February 1944 from 69°21n/03°30e when operating as part of group "Werwolf" against the convoy JW-57. When U 713 subsequently failed to report its position, it was posted as missing effective 26 February 1944. There is presently no known explanation for its loss.

114. Original postwar assessment changed by the author in August 1996 with amendment from January 2009. The attack carried out by the Liberator F of 120 Sqn RAF on 9 June 1944 in position 49°09n/08°37w, formerly credited with the destruction of U 740, was very probably directed against a nonsub target.

115. Original postwar assessment changed by the author in January 1994. The attack by the corvette HMS *Portchester Castle* and the frigate HMS *Dunver* on 9 September 1944 in position 55°45n/11°41w, formerly credited with the destruction of U 743, actually accounted for the sinking of U 484. U 743 was outbound for an operation in the North Atlantic off the North Channel. When it failed repeatedly to report its position, it was posted as missing effective 10 September 1944. There is presently no known explanation for its loss.

116. The wreck of U 745 was located in 2012. U 745 was last seen by U 475 on 30 January 1945 off Narwa Bay in the Gulf of Finland. It was subsequently ordered to pass through the German defence minefield to the west. When the boat thereafter failed repeatedly to signal its position, it was posted as missing effective 4 February 1945. The body of the commanding officer was found washed ashore South of the Finnish island of Föglö in the Aland archipelago on 10 February 1945.

117. Original postwar assessment changed by the author in June 1984.

118. Original postwar assessment and subsequent reassessment changed by FDS/NHB in September 1987. The attack by the Catalina B of VP-73 Sqn USN on 1 September 1942 in position 58°08n/27°33w, formerly credited with the destruction of U 756, was actually directed against U 91 inflicting slight damage.

119. Original postwar assessment changed by the author in December 1997. The attack by the Mariner P-12 of VP-32 Sqn USN on 26 July 1943 in position 18°06n/75°00w, formerly credited with the destruction of U 759, actually accounted for the sinking of U 359.

120. Original postwar assessment changed by the author in December 1994.

121. Original postwar assessment and reassessment of the FDS/NHB from July 1999 changed by the author in March 2004. The attack by the Wellington L of 407 Sqn RCAF on 30 December 1944 in position 50°05n/02°31w, formerly credited with the destruction of U 772, was actually directed against U 486 inflicting no damage. The attack by the corvette HMCS *Calgary* on 29 December 1944 in position 50°26n/02°28w, thereafter credited with the destruction of U 772, actually accounted for the sinking of U 322.

122. Original postwar assessment changed by the author in January 1991.

123. Original postwar assessment changed by the author and FDS/NHB in 1991–92. The attack by the Liberator B of 86 Sqn RAF on 20 March 1945 in position 59°42n/04°55w, formerly credited with the destruction of U 905, was very probably directed against a nonsub target. U 905 was outbound for an operation in the North Atlantic to the southwest of Ireland. No signal was received from it after sailing from Trondheim. When it failed to report its position after the cessation of hostilities, it was posted as missing. The attack by HMS *Conn* produced the identity disc of a crew member of U 905. It remains yet unclear why U 905 did not proceed to its allocated operational area.

124. Original postwar assessment changed by author in December 1997. The attacks by the Swordfish F of 813 Sqn FAA of the escort carrier HMS *Campania* on 30 September 1944 in position 72°32n/12°55e, formerly credited with the destruction of U 921, were actually directed against U 636 and U 968, inflicting no damage. U 921 reported last on 24 September 1944 from the approximate position 74°45n/13°50e on having commenced its return trip to Narvik, Norway, owing to unspecified damage. When U 921 did not arrive at Narvik until 29 September 1944, it was redirected on the same day to take part in the operation against convoy RA.60. Following the end of the convoy operation on 1 October 1944, the boat was ordered to continue its return trip to Narvik. When U 921 thereafter failed to report its position or to arrive at Narvik, it was posted as missing effective 2 October 1944. In the absence of an Allied attack to account for its sinking, there is presently no known explanation for its loss. From its initial failure to arrive at Narvik before 29 September 1944 it is likely that U 921 was already lost before that date.

125. The date of loss was arbitrarily fixed by Admiral Commanding U-boats after U 923 went missing in the western Baltic Sea. The boat had left Travemünde on 6 February 1945 for transfer passage to Kiel. When U 923 thereafter failed to arrive at Kiel, it was posted as missing effective 9 February 1945. The bodies of three crew members have been washed ashore on the Danish island Aerö on 11 February 1945. The wreck of U 923 was located and partly raised in 1952 during clearance work. It is probable that the boat sank already on 6 or 7 February 1945.

126. U 925 was outbound via the route through the Iceland passage for an operation as a weather reporting boat in the eastern North Atlantic. No signal was received from it after sailing from Kristiansand. The boat was therefore posted as missing effective 18 September 1944. There is presently no plausible explanation for its loss.

127. There is serious doubt over the loss of U 927. Despite intensive searches by the United Kingdom Hydrographic Office and other parties no unidentified German U-boat wreck has yet been found in the area around the attack postion. U 927 reported last on 8 February 1945 from the approximate position 59°50n/05°00w while en route to its assigned operational area in the eastern English Channel. For want of better information the original postwar assessment is left unchanged.

128. Original postwar assessment changed by the FDS/NHB in October 1991. The attack by the Liberator T of 120 Sqn RAF on 19 May 1943 in position 55°09n/35°18w, formerly credited with the destruction of U 954, was actually directed against U 731 inflicting no damage.

129. Original postwar assessment changed by the author in December 1991. The attack by the frigate HMS *Conn* on 27 March 1945 in position 58°34n/05°46w, formerly credited with the destruction of U 965, very probably accounted for the sinking of U 905. The attacks by the frigates HMS *Rupert* and HMS *Conn* produced personal belongings from a crew member of U 965.

130. U 972 reported last on 15 December 1943 from the approximate position 60°30n/20°00w while en route to its assigned operational area in the eastern North Atlantic. During the following weeks, it was deployed as a member of various U-boat groups against Allied convoys. When the boat thereafter failed to report its arrival off Brest in early February 1944, U 972 was posted as missing effective 1 February 1944. There is presently no plausible explanation for its loss.

131. Original postwar assessment changed by the author and Innes McCartney in December 2001 with amendment in March 2012. The wreck of U 984 was located already before 2000. The attacks by the destroyers HMCS *Ottawa,* HMCS *Chaudiére* and HMCS *Kootenay* on 20 August 1944 in position 48°16n/05°33w, formerly credited with the destruction of U 984, were directed against a nonsub target. U 984 is likely to have arrived in its assigned operational area on or about 2 August 1944. There is presently no plausible explanation for its loss in the wreck position.

132. Original postwar assessment changed by the author in December 1999. The attack by the minesweeper USS *Swift* and the subchaser USS *PC 619* on 17 April 1944 in position 50°09n/12°51w, formerly credited with the destruction of U 986, was very probably directed against a nonsub contact. The boat reported last on 10 April 1944 from the approximate position 51°30n/20°00w about its intention to commence its return to France on 12 April 1944. On 14 April 1944, the boat was ordered to enter Lorient. When it failed to arrive at that port, it was posted as missing effective 20 April 1944. The location of the attacks made by the USS *Swift* and the USS *PC 619* is about one hundred seamiles to the north of the normal transfer route through the Bay of Biscay used by U-boats under order to enter Lorient like U 986. There is presently no plausible explanation for the loss of U 986.

133. Original postwar assessment changed by the author in December 2013. The wreck of U 988 had already been located in 1998 and has now been positively identified. The attacks by the frigates HMS *Essington*, HMS *Duckworth*, HMS *Dommett* and HMS *Cooke*, and Liberator L of 224 Sqn RAF on 29/30 June 1944 in position 49°37n/03°41w, formerly credited with the destruction of U 988, actually accounted for the sinking of U 441.

134. Original postwar assessment changed by the FDS/NHB in April 1984. On photographs taken from HMS *Aylmer* during the encounter on 26 January U 1051 was positively identified by the insignia device carried on the front of its conning tower. The attack by the frigates HMS *Tyler*, HMS *Keats*, and HMS *Bligh* on 27 January 1945 in position 52°24n/05°42w, formerly credited with the destruction of U 1051, actually accounted for the sinking of U 1172.

135. Original postwar assessment changed by the author in April 1991. The attack by the Catalina R of VP-63 Sqn USN on 30 April 1945 in position 48°00n/06°30w, formerly credited with the destruction of U 1055, actually accounted for the sinking of U 326. U 1055 reported last on 23 April 1945 from the approximate position 52°00n/11°00w while en route to its operational area in the English Channel. When U 1055 subsequently failed to return to Norway or signal its position after the cessation of hostilities, it was posted as missing. There is presently no plausible explanation for the loss of U 1055.

136. Original postwar assessment changed by the author in September 2021. The attack by the Liberator O of 224 Sdn RAF on 29 March 1945 in position 61°46n/02°16w, formerly credited with the destruction of U 1106, was very probably directed against U 1022, then home-bound to Bergen in Norway, inflicting no damage. U 1106 was outbound for a patrol against enemy shipping off the western exit of the English Channel. No signal was received from it after release from escort early on 23 March 1945. When U 1106 subsequently failed to return to Norway or signal its position after the cessation of hostilities, it was posted as missing. There is presently no known explanation for its loss.

137. Original postwar assessment and reassessment by the FDS/NHB from May 1997 changed by the author in December 2013. The wreck of U 1191 had already been located in 1995. The attacks by the destroyer escorts HMS *Affleck* and HMS *Balfour* on 25 June 1944 in position 50°03n/02°59w and by Wellington A of 304 Sqn RAF (Polish) on 18 June 1944 in position 49°03n/04°48w, formerly credited with the destruction of U 1191, were both directed against non-sub contacts.

138. Original postwar assessment changed by the author in December 2013. The wreck of U 1200 had already been located in 1999 in the given position and has now been positively identified. The boat should have arrived at the wreck position en route to its operational area in the English Channel on or

about 12 November 1944 or homebound at the end of November 1944. In the absence of an Allied A/S attack to have accounted for the boat, there is presently no plausible explanation for the loss of U 1200. The attacks by the corvettes HMS *Pevensey Castle*, HMS *Launceston Castle*, HMS *Portchester Castle* and HMS *Kenilworth Castle* on 11 November 1944 in position 50°24n/09°10w, formerly credited with the destruction of U 1200, were directed against a non-sub contact.

139. Original postwar assessment changed by the author in September 1991 with amendment from June 2009. The attack by the sloop HMS *Amethyst* on 20 February 1945 in position 51°48n/07°07w, formerly credited with the destruction of U 1208, actually accounted for the sinking of U 1276. The attacks by the frigates HMS *Loch Fada* and HMS *Labuan* and the sloop HMS *Wild Goose* on 27 February 1945 in position 49°46n/05°47w, thereafter credited with the destruction of U 1208, actually accounted for the sinking of U 1279.

140. Original postwar assessment changed by the FDS/NHB in April 1985. The attack by the Liberator B of 120 Sqn RAF on 22 March 1945 in position 55°23n/06°40w, formerly credited with the destruction of U 296, was very probably directed against a nonsubmarine target. U 296 was ordered to operate in the Firth of Clyde. No signal was received from it after sailing from Bergen. When the boat subsequently failed to return to Bergen, it was posted as missing. There is presently no known explanation for its loss. There is the possibility that U 296 was lost to mining on or about 12 March 1945 in the western entrance to the North Channel on the deep antisubmarine minefields T1 or T2, which crossed the route to its operational area.

141. Postwar reassessment changed by the FDS/NHB in April 1997. The attack by the frigates HMS *Loch Insh* and HMS *Goodall* on 6 December 1944 in position 58°44n/04°29w, formerly credited with the destruction of U 297, was actually directed against U 775 inflicting no damage. The wreck of U 297 was located in May 2000. The attack by Sunderland Y of 201 Sqn RAF on 6 December 1944 in position 58°44n/04°29w, sometimes also attributed with the destruction of U 297, was in fact directed against a meteorological phenomena (whillywaw). There is presently no plausible explanation for the loss of U 297 in the wreck position.

142. Original postwar assessment changed by the author in March 2004. The attack carried out by the frigate HMS *Ascencion* on 25 November 1944 in position 60°18n/04°52w, formerly credited with the destruction of U 322, actually accounted for the sinking of U 482.

143. Original postwar assessment and subsequent reassessment by the author and FDS/NHB from May 1993 changed by the author in July 2008.

144. Original postwar assessment and reassessment by the author from April 1991 changed by the author in June 2006.

145. Original postwar assessment and reassessment by the author from September 1991 changed by the author in July 2009. The attacks by the frigates HMS *Loch Fada* and HMS *Labuan* and the sloop HMS *Wild Goose* on 27 February 1945 in position 49°46n/05°47w, formerly credited with the destruction of U 327, actually accounted for the sinking of U 1279.

146. Original postwar assessment changed by the author and the FDS/NHB in June 1986. The attack by the Liberator G of 86 Sqn RAF on 6 May 1945 in position 57°52n/10°49w, formerly credited with the destruction of U 1008, actually accounted for the sinking of U 3523.

147. See note 55.

148. Original postwar assessment changed by the author in May 2009. The wreck of U 1020 was located in September 2007.

149. Original postwar assessment and reassessment by the FDS/NHB from November 1990 changed by the author in July 2008. The attack by the frigates HMS *Rupert* and HMS *Conn* on 30 March 1945 in position 58°19n/05°31w, formerly credited with the destruction of U 1021, actually accounted for the sinking of U 965. On 14 March 1945 the British steamer *Rolfsborg* heard a heavy explosion at the wreck position and observed patches of oil. Therefore, it is possible that U 1021 was lost to mining in the reported incident.

150. Original postwar assessment and reassessment by the author from April 1991 reverted to original postwar assessment by the author in June 2006.

151. Original postwar assessment changed by the author in January 1991 and September 2016. The mine explosion observed by the A/S-trawler HMT *Willow* on 5 April 1945 in position 52°03n/05°53w, originally credited with the destruction of U 1169, actually accounted for the sinking of U 242. U 1169 reported last on 8 March 1945 from the approximate position 57°n/13°w while en route to its assigned operational area in the eastern English Channel. On 26 March 1945 the body of a crew member from

U 1169, which had been washed ashore, was buried in Penzance Cemetery, which implies that the loss of the boat must have taken place earlier somewhere along the Cornish coast. There is a possibility that U 1169 was lost on or after 17 March 1945 on the British minefield "HW A1" in position 50°31,4'n/05°22,8'w. The attack by HMS *Duckworth* on 29 March 1945 in position 49°58n/05°25w, formerly also credited with the destruction of U 1169, was directed against a non-sub contact.

152. Original postwar assessment changed by FDS/NHB in April 1984. The loss of U 1172 was transposed with the loss of U 1051.

153. At least two incomplete pressure hulls out of U 1173–U 1179 were converted to transport barges for prefabricated Type XXI sections built in the Danzig area.

154. Original postwar assessment changed by FDS/NHB in September 1987. The attack by the Liberator U of 224 Sqn RAF on 3 April 1945 in position 61°42n/00°24w, formerly credited with the destruction of U 1276, was very probably directed against a nonsub target. The attack by the sloop HMS *Amethyst* produced clothing from a crew member of U 1276.

155. Original postwar assessment changed by the author in July 2009. The attacks by the frigates HMS *Bayntun*, HMS *Braithwaite* and HMS *Loch Eck* on 3 February 1945 in position 61°21n/02°00e, formerly credited with the destruction of U 1279, actually accounted for the sinking of U 327.

156. Original postwar assessment and subsequent reassessment changed by FDS/NHB in January 1981. The attack by the destroyer HMS *Fortune* on 20 March 1940 in position 67°33n/12°10e, formerly credited with the destruction of U 44, was very probably directed against a nonsub target. U 44 was ordered to operate in a waiting position to the west of the Orkneys and Shetlands. It made no report after sailing from Wilhelmshaven. The boat was therefore posted as missing effective 20 March 1940. In the absence of an Allied attack to account for its loss, it is probable that U 44 was lost to mining in the British mine barrage Field No. 7 while outbound in the North Sea. Field No. 7 was laid on its exit route on 3 March 1940 by the destroyers HMS *Express*, HMS *Esk*, HMS *Icarus*, and HMS *Impulsive*.

157. Original postwar assessment changed by FDS/NHB in June 1986. The attack by the corvette HMS *Gladiolus* on 28 April 1941 in position 60°04n/15°45w, formerly credited with the destruction of U 65, was actually directed against U 96 inflicting no damage.

158. Original postwar assessment changed by FDS/NHB in September 1987. The attack by the corvette HMS *Rhododendron* on 21 November 1940 in position 56°28n/14°13w, formerly credited with the destruction of U 104, was actually directed against U 103 inflicting no damage. U 104 reported for the last time on 19 November 1940 from the approximate position 60°30n/02°30e while en route into the North Atlantic to the west of Britain. When it failed repeatedly thereafter to report its position, the boat was posted as missing effective 30 November 1940. U 104, however, must have been responsible for two attacks on merchant vessels on 27 November 1940, the last taking place in position 55°45n/11°57w, as no other U-boat reported an attack. In the absence of an Allied attack to account for its sinking, there is presently no known explanation for its loss. There is, however, a possibility that U 104 was lost to mining as its last recorded position was very close to the British minefield SN 44, which was laid on 8 November 1940 to the northwest of Tory Island.

159. U 122 reported last early on 21 June 1940 from the approximate position 56°00n/10°30w while en route to its operational area west of Cape Finisterre, Spain. When the boat thereafter failed repeatedly to signal its position, it was posted as missing effective 27 July 1940. There is presently no known explanation for its loss. Based on research by the FDS/NHB from December 1985, there is a possibility that U 122 was lost by the depth charge attack of the corvette HMS *Arabis* on 23 June 1940 in position 49°21n/08°47w, but lack of details on the attack prevent a proper assessment.

160. Original postwar assessment changed by the author in October 2013. The attack carried out by the destroyer USS *Lansdowne* on 13 July 1942 in position 09°46n/81°29w, formerly credited with the destruction of U 153, were directed against a non-sub target.

161. Original postwar assessment changed by the author in December 1997. The attack by the Mariner P-10 of VP-32 Sqn USN on 15 July 1943 in position 15°58n/73°44w. formerly credited with the destruction of U 159, actually accounted for the sinking of U 759.

162. Original postwar assessment and subsequent reassessment changed by the FDS/NHB in April 1987. The attack by the submarine USS *Herring* on 21 March 1943 in position 44°13n/08°23w, formerly credited with the destruction of U 163, was very probably directed against a nonsub target, possibly a Spanish fishing boat.

163. Original postwar assessment changed by Eric Zimmerman and the author in February 2003.

164 Original postwar assessment changed by Robert Church and Dan Warren in June 2001 after the wreck of U 166 was discovered during oil exploration work. The attack by the Widgeon Y of 212 Sqn USCG on 1 August 1942 in position 28°37n/90°45w, formerly credited with the destruction of U 166, was actually directed against U 171 inflicting no damage.

165. There is presently no final proof for the distribution of the losses of U 518, U 880, and U 1235 among the individual attacks carried out during the operation "Teardrop" by the destroyer escorts USS *Stanton* and USS *Frost* on 15 and 16 April 1945 and the USS *Carter* and USS *Neal A. Scott* on the 22 April 1945. The given attribution is entirely based on the immediate postwar estimation of the U.S. Tenth Fleet Command. However, none of the attacks produced conclusive evidence to identify the target nor were there any signals from the missing boats immediately before their losses.

166. Original postwar assessment changed by the author in October 1994 with supplement from the FDS/NHB in June 1996. The attack by the Liberator T of 2 A/S Sqn USAAF on 10 February 1943 in position 47°05n/17°45w, formerly credited with the destruction of U 519, was actually directed against U 752 inflicting minor damage. U 519 was outbound for an operation in the North Atlantic. When it failed repeatedly to report its position, it was posted as missing in the Bay of Biscay effective 10 February 1943. There is presently no known explanation for its loss. According to observations made by U 183 and U 332, there is, however, a possibility that U 519 was sunk in an attack of Wellington B of 172 Sqn RAF on 4 February 1943 in the approximate position 46°40n/15°50w with the attacking aircraft in turn shot down by the U-boat.

167. Original postwar assessment changed by the FDS/NHB in January 1993. The attack by the corvette HNoMS *Potentilla* on 20 November 1942 in position 49°25n/45°25w, formerly credited with the destruction of U 184, was actually directed against U 264 inflicting no damage. U 184 was operating against convoy ONS.144 when it reported for the last time on 20 November 1942 from the approximate position 49°00n/45°30w. After having failed repeatedly thereafter to report, the boat was posted as missing effective 21 November 1942. In the absence of an Allied attack to account for its sinking, there is presenty no plausible explanation tor its loss.

168. Original postwar assessment changed by FDS/NHB in October 1991. The attack by the corvette HMS *Pink* on 5 May 1943 in position 54°56n/43°44w, formerly credited with the destruction of U 192, was actually directed against U 358 inflicting no damage.

169. Original postwar assessment changed by the author in July 1996. The attack by the Wellington W of 612 Sqn RAF on 28 April 1944 in position 45°38n/09°43w, formerly credited with the destruction of U 193. was actually directed against U 802 inflicting no damage. U 193 was outbound for an operation in the mid- or South Atlantic. When it failed repeatedly to report its position after sailing from Lorient. it was posted as missing in the Bay of Biscay effective 6 May 1944. There is presently no known explanation for its loss.

170. Original postwar assessment changed by the author in December 1987. The attack by the Liberator H of 120 Sqn RAF on 24 June 1943 in position 58°15n/25°25w, formerly credited with the destruction of U 194, actually accounted for the sinking of U 200.

171. Reassessment by the FDS/NHB from May 1987 reverted to original postwar assessment by the author in March 2008.

172. Original postwar assessment changed by FDS/NHB in October 1991. The combined attacks by the destroyer HMS *Oribi* and the corvette HMS *Snowflake* on 6 May 1943 in position 52°13n/44°50w, formerly credited with the destruction of U 531, actually accounted for the sinking of U 125.

173. Original postwar assessment changed by FDS/NHB in 1985. The attack by the Liberator T of 206 Sqn RAF on 5 May 1945 in position 56°59n/11°48e, formerly credited with the destruction of U 534, was probably directed against U 3523 inflicting severe damage.

174. Original postwar assessment changed by the author in September 1990. The attack by the Wellington L of 179 Sqn RAF on 28 November 1943 in position 39°04n/16°25w, formerly credited with the destruction of U 542, was actually directed against U 391 inflicting minor damage.

175. Original postwar assessment changed by the author in January 1990. The combined attacks by the frigate USS *Natchez* and the escort destroyers USS *Thomas*, USS *Coffman*, and USS *Bostwick* on 30 April 1945 in position 36°34n/74°00w, formerly credited with the destruction of U 548, probably accounted for the sinking of U 879. The attacks from the destroyer escorts USS *Buckley* and USS *Reuben James* produced wreckage of U 548.

176. Original postwar assessment changed by the FDS/NHB in September 1987. The attack by the Liberator A of 224 Sqn RAF on 24 September 1944 in position 61°00n/04°07e, formerly credited with the destruction of U 855, was actually directed against U 763 inflicting medium damage. U 855 reported for the last time on 11 September 1944 from the approximate position 59°30n/26°00w while on return to Kristiansand, Norway, through the Iceland passage. When it failed to arrive at that port or to report its position, the boat was posted as missing effective 15 October 1944. In the absence of an Allied attack to account for its sinking, there is presently no known explanation for its loss. There is, however, a possibility that U 855 was lost due to mining in the British Iceland-Faeroes barrage on or about 17 September 1944.

177. Original postwar assessment changed by the FDS/NHB in April 1994. The attack by the destroyer escort USS *Gustafson* on 7 April 1945 in position 42°22n/69°46w, formerly credited with the destruction of U 857, was very probably directed against a nonsub target. U 857 reported last on 7 March 1945 from the approximate position 49°n/36°w while en route to its operational area off Cape Hatteras. When U 857 subsequently failed to return to Norway or signal its position after the cessation of hostilities, it was posted as missing. There is presently no known explanation for its loss. There is, however, a possibility that U 857 was sunk on 30 April 1945 in the attacks of the frigate USS *Natchez* and the destroyer escorts USS *Bostwick*, USS *Coffman*, and USS *Thomas* in position 36°34n/74°00w, which are presently credited with the destruction of U 879. Both U-boats could have operated in the area of the attack at that time.

178. U 865 was outbound for an operation on the Canadian east coast. No signal was received from it after sailing from Trondheim. The boat was posted as missing effective 1 October 1944. The original postwar assessment crediting its loss to the attack of Liberator S of 206 Sqn RAF on 19 September 1944 in position 62°20n/02°20e had been changed by the MoD in the 1950s when it became known that the attack was actually directed against U 858 inflicting slight damage. In the absence of an Allied attack to account for its sinking, there is presently no plausible explanation for its loss. Before its last patrol, however, U 865 had three abortive attempts to reach the North Atlantic owing to schnorkel problems.

179. Original postwar assessment changed by the author in January 1994 with amendment by Harold Moyers and the author in June 2005. The attacks by the destroyer escort USS *Fowler* and the subchaser FS *L'Indiscret* on 28 February 1945 in position 34°30n/08°13w, formerly credited with the destruction of U 869, were directed against a nonsub target. The wreck of U 869 was discovered in September 1991 by a group of U.S. divers with its identity positively identified thereafter.

180. Original postwar assessment changed by the author in January 1990. The attack by the destroyer escorts USS *Buckley* and USS *Reuben James* on 19 April 1945 in position 42°19n/61°45w, formerly credited with the destruction of U 879, actually accounted for the sinking of U 548.

181. See note 164.

182. There is serious doubt over the loss of U 881. The boat reported last on 19 April 1945 from the approximate position 55°30n/14°30w while en route to its assigned operational area off the American East Coast between New York and Cape Hatteras. USS *Farquhar* obtained a sonar contact and attacked five minutes later with a single depth charge pattern set to shallow depths. Contact was lost thereafter and was not regained despite a 12-hour search with two other escorts. No evidence for damage or destruction of a U-boat was obtained. It appears that the loss of U 881 was only tentatively attributed after the war. For want of better information the original postwar assessment was left unchanged.

183. U 1226 reported last on 23 October 1944 from the approximate position 59°30n/20°00w on the failure of its schnorkel gear while en route to its operational area off the Canadian coast. When the boat thereafter failed repeatedly to signal its position, it was posted as missing effective 28 October 1944. In the absence of an Allied attack to account for its sinking, a marine accident from schnorkel failure offers a possible explanation for its loss.

184. See note 164.

185. U 180 was outbound on a transport mission to the Far East. When U 180 failed repeatedly to signal its position, it was posted as missing in the Bay of Biscay effective 15 September 1944. There is presently no known explanation for its loss. Some sources attribute its loss to mining in the RAF air-laid minefield Deodar off the mouth of the River Gironde. It is, however, unlikely that U 180 hit a mine because it had already reached the two-hundred-meter depth-line when released from its escort late on the 23 August 1944.

186. Original postwar assessment changed by the author in December 1999. The attack by the destroyer USS *Mackenzie* on 16 May 1943 in position 37°55n/20°35w, formerly credited with the destruction of U 182, was very probably directed against a nonsub target.

187. U 196 was outbound to the area to the east of Madagascar in the Indian Ocean as an auxiliary refueler for U 510. Owing to the return of U 510, it was recalled the same day it sailed. When U 196 did not return to Jakarta and failed repeatedly to signal its position, it was posted as missing in the Sunda Strait effective 12 December 1944. In the absence of an Allied attack to account for its sinking, there is presently no known explanation for its loss.

188. Original postwar assessment changed by the author in December 1987. The attack by the Liberator H of 120 Sqn RAF on 24 June 1943 in position 58°15n/25°25w, formerly credited with the destruction of U 194, actually accounted for the sinking of U 200. The identity of U 200 was proven from photographs taken from the Liberator H during the attack. The losses of U 194 and U 200 were therefore transposed.

189. U 851 reported last on 27 March 1944 from the approximate position 42°20n/46°30w while outbound to the Gulf of Aden in the Indian Ocean. When the boat thereafter failed repeatedly to signal its position, it was posted as missing effective 8 June 1944. No Allied attack is on record to account for its loss. However, early on 28 March 1944 a war emergency signal from a unidentified German U-boat, reporting bomb-damage, was picked up by German and Allied radio stations. If genuine, it could have originated only from U 851, indicating its loss on the same day by unknown reason.

190. Original postwar assessment changed by the author in January 1991.

191. U 116 reported last on 6 October 1942 from the approximate position 45°00n/31°30w while homebound to Lorient. France. When the boat thereafter failed repeatedly to show up at the rendezvous point or to signal its position, it was posted as missing effective 15 October 1942. In the absence of an Allied attack to account for its sinking, there is presently no plausible explanation for its loss.

192. There is some doubt over the loss of U 220. According to the war diary of U 256, which was accompanying U 220 at the time of the attack on 28 October 1943, U 220 contacted U 256 about thirty minutes after the attack by underwater telephone to make arrangements for a new meeting point later that day. The exchange of messages took place while both boats stayed submerged after the air attack. Moreover, the attack by the two aircraft of USS *Block Island* produced no visible indication for the destruction of U 220. Eight hours later, U 256 observed explosion plumes at the horizon and assumed that U 220 had fallen victim to air attack as it did not appear at the agreed meeting point. When the boat thereafter failed to report its position, it was posted as missing effective 31 October 1943.

193. Original postwar assessment changed by the author and the FDS/NHB in January 1993. The attack by several aircraft from VC-9 Sqn USN of the escort carrier USS *Card* on 4 October 1943 in position 43°13n/28°58w, formerly credited with the destruction of U 460, actually accounted for the sinking of U 422.

194. Original postwar assessment changed by the FDS/NHB in April 1990. The attack by the Halifax M of 58 Sqn RAF on 15 May 1943 in position 45°28n/10°20w, formerly credited with the destruction of U 463, actually accounted for the sinking of U 266.

195. Original postwar assessment changed by the author in November 1991. The attack by the Liberator K of 547 Sqn RAF on 5 May 1945 in position 56°11n/11°08e, formerly credited with the destruction of U 2521. actually accounted for the sinking of U 579.

196. Original postwar assessment changed by the author in October 1991. The attack by the Liberator K of 86 Sqn RAF on 6 May 1945 in position 57°08n/11°52e, formerly credited with the destruction of U 2534, was actually directed against U 3503 inflicting minor damage.

197. Original postwar assessment changed by the author in October 1991. The attack by the Liberator G of 86 Sqn RAF on 5 May 1945 in position 56°45n/11°52e, formerly credited with the destruction of U 3503, actually accounted for the sinking of U 534.

198. Original postwar assessment changed by the author in March 1994. The attack by the Liberator T of 224 Sqn RAF on 5 May 1945 in position 56°06n/11°06w, formerly credited with the destruction of U 3523, was actually directed against U 1008 inflicting minor damage.

199. Original postwar assessment changed by the author in October 1991. The attack by the Liberator L of 311 Sqn RAF on 5 May 1945 in position 57°27n/10°38e, formerly credited with the destruction of U 2365. was actually directed against a nonsub target.

200. Numerous postwar publications give German UIT-numbers 9 to 20 for ex-Italian submarines of the *Tritone*-class that were captured incomplete at the time of the Italian capitulation in September 1943. There is, however, no support for the allocation of UIT numbers 9 to 20 to ex-Italian submarines from German wartime documents.

SELECTED BIBLIOGRAPHY

Bagnasco, Erminio. *Submarines of World War II*. Annapolis: Naval Institute Press, 1977.

Barley, F. W., and D. Waters. *Defeat of the Enemy Attack on Shipping*. 2 vols. Admiralty-Naval Staff History. London, 1957.

British Admiralty. *German, Italian and Japanese U-boat Casualties during the War*. London: His Majesty's Stationary Office, 1946.

Carter, Kit, and Robert Mueller. *The Army Air Forces in World War II. Combat Chronology, 1941–1945*. Washington. D.C.: Albert F. Simpson Historical Research Center Air University and Office of the Air Force History Headquarters USAF, 1973. Chief of Naval Operations, Navy Department U.S. Navy. *German, Japanese, and Italian Submarine Losses World War II*. Washington. D.C., 1946.

Conway's All the World's Fighting Ships, 1922-1946. London: Conway, 1980; Annapolis: Naval Institute Press, 1981.

Elliott, Peter. *Allied Escort Ships of World War II*. London: Macdonald and Janes, 1977.

Gröner, Erich. *Die deutschen Kriegsschiffe, 1815-1945*. Vol. 1. München: J.F. Lehmanns, 1966.

—— *Die Schiffe der deutschen Kriegsmarine und Luftwaffe 1939–1945 und ihr Verbleib*. München: J.F. Lehmanns, 1954.

Gröner, Erich. Dieter Jung, and Martin Maas. *Die deutschen Kriegsschiffe, 1815-1945*. Rev. ed. Vol. 3. Koblenz: Bernard & Graefe, 1985.

Herzog, Bodo. *60 Jahre deutsche U-Boote, 1906-1966*. München: J.F. Lehmanns, 1968.

Ministry of Defence (Navy)[Hessler, Günter]. *The U-Boat War in the Atlantic, 1939–1945*. London: Her Majesty's Stationery Office, 1989.

Köhl. Fritz, and Axel Niestlé. *Uboottyp VII C—Vom Original zum Modell* Koblenz: Bernard & Graefe, 1989.

—— and —— *Uboottyp IX C—Vom Original zum Modell*. Koblenz: Bernard & Graefe, 1990.

Lenton, Henry Trevor. *Navies of the Second World War, German Submarines*. 2 vols. London: MacDonald, 1965.

Lohmann, Walter, and Hans H. Hildebrand. *Die deutsche Kriegsmarine, 1939–1945*. 3 vols. Bad Nauheim: Podzun, 1956–1964.

Macpherson. Ken, and John Burgess. *The Ships of Canada's Naval Forces, 1910–1981: A Complete Pictorial History of Canadian Warships*. Toronto: Collins, 1981.

Middlebrook, Martin, and Chris Everitt. *The Bomber Command War Diaries: An Operational Reference Book, 1939–1945*. New York: Harmondsworth, 1985.

Mielke, Erich. *Die deutschen U-Boote. 1939–45*. München: Moewig, 1959.

Mooney, James L., ed. *Dictionary of American Naval Fighting Ships*. Vol. I–VIII. Washington, D.C.: Naval Historical Center, 1959–1981.

Morison, Samuel Eliot. *The Atlantic Battle Won. May 1943-May 1945*. In *History of United States Naval Operations in World War II*. Vol. X. Boston: Little, Brown and Company, 1956.

—— *The Battle of the Atlantic, September 1939–May 1943*. In *History of United States Naval Operations in World War II*, Vol. I. Boston: Little, Brown and Company, 1947.

Naval History Division, Office of the Chief of Naval Operations (CNO). *U.S. Submarine Losses World War II*. Washington, D.C.: Government Printing Office, 1963.

Peyton-Ward, D. V. *The RAF in the Maritime War*. London: Air Ministry. Air Historical Branch Narrative, nd.

Rohwer, Jürgen, and Gerhard Hümmelchen. *Chronology of the War at Sea, 1939-1945*. Rev. ed. Annapolis: Naval Institute Press, 1992.

Roscoe, Theodore. *United States Destroyer Operations in World War II*. Annapolis: Naval Institute Press, 1953.

Roskill, Stephen Wentworth. *The War at Sea, 1939-1945*. 3 vols. London: Her Majesty's Stationery Office, 1954–1961.

Rössler, Eberhard. *Die deutschen Uboote und ihre Werften*. Koblenz: Bernard & Graefe, 1990.

—— *The U-boat: The Evolution and Technical History of German Submarines*. London: Arms & Armour Press; Annapolis: Naval Institute Press, 1981.

—— *U-Boottyp XXI*. Koblenz: Bernard & Graefe, 1986.

Rössler, Eberhard, and Fritz Kohl. *Uboottyp XVII-Vom Original zum Modell*. Koblenz: Bernard & Graefe, 1995.

—— and —— *Uboottyp XXIII—Vom Original zum Modell*. Koblenz: Bernard & Graefe, 1993.

Schoenfeld, Max. *Stalking the U-Boat, USAAF Offensive Antisubmarine Operations in World War II* Washington, D.C.: Smithsonian Institution Press, 1995.

Schull, Joseph. *The Far Distant Ships: An Official Account of Canadian Naval Operations in the Second World War*. Ottawa: Kings Printer, 1950.

Tarrant, V. E. *The U-boat Offensive: 1914-1945*. Annapolis: Naval Institute Press, 1989.

Watts, Anthony J. *Axis Submarines*. New York: Arco, 1977.

Y'Blood, William T. *Hunter-Killer: U.S. Escort Carriers in the Battle of the Atlantic*. Annapolis: Naval Institute Press, 1983.

Zeissler, Herbert. *U-Bootsliste*. Hamburg-Wandsbek: Selbstverlag, 1956.

INDEX I

U-BOAT COMMANDING OFFICERS

Name	First Name	Class	Rank	U-No.
Abel, Dr.	Ulrich	D 39	Oblt. z. S. d. Res.	U 193
Achilles	Albrecht	(34)	Kaptlt.	U 161
Ackermann	Paul	(XII/39)	Oblt. z. S.	U 1221
Ady	Gerhard	(X/40)	Oblt. z. S.	U 677
Ahlefeld, von	Hunold	(X/40)	Oblt. z. S.	U 4714
Ahlers	Kurt	(XII/39)	Oblt. z. S.	U 10
Albrecht	Fritz	(X/37)	Oblt. z. S.	U 386
Albrecht	Karl	(X/38)	Oblt. z. S. (K.O.)	U 1062
Aldegarmann	Wolfgang	(X/37)	Oblt. z. S.	U 297
Altmeier	Friedrich	(X/38)	Oblt. z. S.	U 1227, U 155
Amendolia	Angelo		TV	U 429
Andersen	Klaus	(X/37)	Kaptlt.	U 481
Angermann	Walter	(X/40)	Lt. z. S., Oblt. z. S.	U 2323, U 2334
Apel	Horst	(38)	Oblt. z. S.	U 798
Arco, Graf von	Ferdinand	(I/41)	Oblt. z. S.	U 151
Arco-Zinneberg, Graf von und zu	Ulrich-Philipp	(X/39)	Oblt. z. S.	U 29, U A
Arendt	Rudolf	(X/40)	Oblt. z. S.	U 23
Arillo	Mario		CC	U 748
Auffermann	Hans-Jürgen	(34)	Kaptlt.	U 514
Auffhammer	Leonhard	(36)	Oblt. z. S,	U 265
Augustin	Hans-Eckart	(V/41)	Lt. z. S.	U 62
Aust	Eduard	(X/39)	Lt. z. S., Oblt. z. S.	U 34, U 679
Baberg	Kurt	(36)	Kaptlt.	U 827
Bach	Joachim-Werner	(X/37)	Oblt. z. S.	U 1110
Bade	Hans-Botho	D X/39	Lt. z. S. d. Res.	U 626
Baden	Hans Heinrich	D X/38	Oblt. z. S. d. Res.	U 955
Bahn	Rolf	(36)	Kaptlt.	U 876

Name	First Name	Class	Rank	U-No.
Bahr	Rudolf	(35)	Kaptlt.	U 305
Balduhn	Ernst-Ludwig	(X/38)	Oblt. z. S.	U 1163
Baldus	Hugo	(X/39)	Oblt. z. S.	U 773
Balke	Diethelm	(X/37)	Kaptlt.	U 991
Ballert	René	(XII/39)	Oblt. z. S.	U 1196
Ballert	Sarto	(X/37)	Oblt. z. S., Kaptlt.	U 1166, U 3520
Barber	Bruno	D IV/22	Oblt. z. S. d. Res.	U 220
Bargsten	Klaus	(35)	Kaptlt.	U 521
Barleben	Curt	D I/35	Kaptlt. d. Res.	U 271
Barsch	Franz	(IV/37)	Kaptlt.	U 1235
Barschkis	Hans-Heinrich	(XII/39)	Oblt. z. S.	U 2321
Bart	Fritz	(IV/37)	Kaptlt.	UD 4, U 3060
Bartels	Robert	(34)	K. Kapt.	U 197
Barten	Wolfgang	(31)	K. Kapt.	U 40
Bartke	Erwin	D VIII/40	Oblt. z. S. d. Res.	U 1106
Basse	Georg-Wilhelm	(36)	Kaptlt.	U 314
Bauer	Hermann	(36)	Oblt. z. S.	U 169
Bauer	Max-Hermann	(30)	Kaptlt.	U 50
Baum	Heinz	D VII/40	Oblt. z. S. d. Res.	U 290
Baumann	Arend	(22)	K. Kapt.	U 131
Baumann	Heinz	D VIII/40	Oblt. z. S. d. Res.	U 2333
Baumgärtel	Friedrich	(X/40)	Oblt. z. S.	U 17, U 142
Baur	Götz	(35)	Kaptlt.	U 660
Beck	Dieter	(34)	Kaptlt.	U 3052
Becker	Klaus	(36)	Oblt. z. S., Kaptlt.	U 235, U 360
Becker	Klaus	(X/39)	Oblt. z. S.	U 260
Becker	Philipp	D IV/40	Oblt. z. S. d. Res.	U 794
Beckmann	Hans	D X/39	Oblt. z. S. d. Res.	U 2330
Beckmann	Heinz	D X/39	Oblt. z. S. d. Res.	U 159
Beduhn	Heinz	(26)	K. Kapt.	U 25
Behnisch	Günter	(XII/39)	Oblt. z. S.	U 2337
Bender	Werner	(36)	Kaptlt.	U 841
Bensel	Rolf-Rüdiger	(X/40)	Oblt. z. S.	U 120
Benthin	Karl-Dietrich	(X/40)	Oblt. z. S.	U 2335
Bentzien	Heinz	(X/37)	Kaptlt.	U 425
Berends	Fritz	D V/40	Oblt. z. S. d. Res.	U 321
Berger	Joachim	(34)	Kaptlt.	U 87
Bergner	Georg	D IX/39	Oblt. z. S. d. Res.	U 3531
Berkemann	Paul	D VII/33	Oblt. z. S. (K.O.)	U 4709

Name	First Name	Class	Rank	U-No.
Bernardelli	Richard	(32)	K. Kapt.	U 805
Bertelsmann	Hans-Joachim	(36)	Kaptlt.	U 603
Besold	Heinrich	(X/39)	Oblt. z. S.	U 1308
Biagini	Augusto		TV	U 746
Bielfeld	Heinz	(34)	Kaptlt.	U 1222
Bigalk	Gerhard	(33)	Kaptlt.	U 751
Billich	Carl	D IX/39	Kaptlt. d. Res.	U 3053
Bischoff	Gustav	(X/39)	Oblt. z. S.	U 2359
Bitter	Otto	(X/37)	Kaptlt.	U 2535
Blaich	Ferdinand	D I/40	Oblt. z. S. d. Res.	U 890, U 3024
Blaudow	Ernst-Ulrich	(IV/37)	Kaptlt.	U 1001
Blauert	Hans-Jörg	(X/37)	Oblt. z. S.	U 734
Blischke	Heinz	(X/38)	Oblt. z. S.	U 744
Block	Helmut	D IV/38	Oblt. z. S. d. Res.	U 771
Blum	Otto-Ulrich	(36)	Kaptlt.	U 760
Bode	Thilo	(36)	Kaptlt.	U 858
Boehmer	Wolfgang	(XII/39)	Oblt. z. S.	U 575
Böhm	Hermann	D X/37	Oblt. z. S. d. Res.	UIT 1, U 2341
Bohmann	Heino	(34)	Kaptlt.	U 88
Böhme	Kurt	(X/37)	Oblt. z. S.	U 450
Bokelberg	Max	(IV/37)	Kaptlt.	U 2530, U 2559
Boos	Hans-Heinz	D I/37	Oblt. z. S. d. Res.	U 1015, U 1002
Bopst	Eberhard	(33)	Kaptlt.	U 597
Borchardt	Gustav	(X/37)	Oblt. z. S.	U 563
Borcherdt	Ulrich	(31)	Kaptlt.	U 587
Borger	Wolfgang	(36)	Kaptlt.	U 394
Börner	Hans-Joachim	(X/37)	Oblt. z. S.	U 735
Bornhaupt	Konrad	(X/37)	Kaptlt.	U 285
Bornkessel	Dieter	(XII/39)	Oblt. z. S.	U 2370
Bortfeldt	Karl-Hermann	(X/39)	Oblt. z. S.	U 1167
Bothe	Friedrich	(36)	Kaptlt.	U 447
Braeucker	Friedrich	(IV/37)	Kaptlt.	U 889
Brammer	Herbert	(X/37)	Oblt. z. S.	U 1060
Brandenburg	Karl	(24)	K. Kapt.	U 457
Brandi	Albrecht	(35)	Kaptlt.	U 617, U 380
Brans	Hans-Joachim	(35)	Kaptlt.	U 801
Brauel	Wilhelm	(X/37)	Oblt. z. S., Kaptlt.	U 256, U 92, U 3530, U 975
Breinlinger	Siegfried	(XII/39)	Oblt. z. S.	U 3018

Name	First Name	Class	Rank	U-No.
Breithaupt	Wolfgang	(33)	Kaptlt.	U 599
Bremen, von	Hanskurt	(X/38)	Oblt. z. S.	U 764
Bressler	Reinhard	(X/37)	Oblt. z. S.	U 1173
Breun	Gerhard	D IV/40	Oblt. z. S. d. Res.	U 2358
Brodda	Heinrich	(33)	Kaptlt.	U 209
Brosin	Hans-Günther	(36)	Kaptlt.	U 134
Brückner	Werner	(V/41)	Oblt. z. S. (K.O.)	U 2351
Bruder	Hermann	(XII/39)	Oblt. z. S.	U 1058
Brünig	Matthias	(X/38)	Oblt. z. S.	U 108, U 3038
Brünner	Joachim	(X/37)	Oblt. z. S.	U 703
Brünning	Herbert	(35)	Kaptlt.	U 642, U 3518
Brunke	Franz	D 39	Oblt. z. S. d. Res.	U 2558
Bruns	Heinrich	(31)	Kaptlt.	U 175
Büchel	Paul	(25)	F. Kapt.	U 860
Buchholz	Heinz	(29)	K. Kapt.	U 195. U 177
Büchler	Rudolf	(36)	K. Kapt.	U 387
Budzyn	Sigmund	(V/41)	Oblt. z. S.	U 2352
Bugs	Hans-Helmuth	(IV/37)	Oblt. z. S.	U 629
Buhse	Heinz	D X/39	Oblt. z. S. d. Res.	U 399
Bürgel	Friedrich	(36)	Oblt. z. S.	U 205
Burghagen	Walter	(11)	K. Kapt. z.V.	U 219
Burmeister	Walter	(X/37)	Kaptlt.	U 1018
Buscher	Hans	(X/38)	Oblt. z. S.	U 1307
Buttjer	Johann	X/37	Oblt. z. S.	U 768
Cabolet	Servais	D X/37	Oblt. z. S. d. Res.	U 907
Callsen	Peter	D XI/39	Oblt. z. S. d. Res.	U 3033
Carlowitz, von	Dietrich	(36)	Oblt. z. S.	U 710
Carlsen	Claus-Peter	(X/37)	Oblt. z. S.	U 732
Christiansen	Helmut	D X/38	Oblt. z. S. d. Res.	U 1305
Christiansen	Uwe	(X/38)	Oblt. z. S.	U 2508, U 2365
Christophersen	Erwin	(36)	Kaptlt.	U 3028
Clausen	Nicolai	(29)	K. Kapt.	U 182
Claussen	August-Wilhelm	(X/37)	Oblt. z. S.	U 1226
Claussen	Emil	(IV/37)	Oblt. z. S.	U 469
Clemens	Johannes	D X/35	Oblt. z. S. d. Res.	U 319
Coester	Christian-Brandt	(X/37)	Oblt. z. S.	U 542
Conrad	Gerhard	(XII/39)	Oblt. z. S.	U 214
Cordes	Ernst	(36)	Kaptlt.	U 1195
Cranz	Wilhelm	D X/39	Oblt. z. S. d. Res.	U 398

Name	First Name	Class	Rank	U-No.
Cremer	Peter Erich	(32)	K. Kapt.	U 2519
Creutz	Horst	(35)	Kaptlt.	U 400
Curio	Oskar	(IV/37)	Kaptlt.	U 952, U 2528
Czekowski	Martin	(X/40)	Oblt. z. S.	U 2362
Czygan	Werner	(25)	K. Kapt.	U 118
Dahlhaus	Eberhard	(38)	Oblt. z. S.	U 634
Dahms	Hermann	(36)	Kaptlt.	U 980
Dähne	Udo-Wolfgang	(XII/39)	Oblt. z. S.	U 349
Damerow	Wolf-Dietrich	(X/37)	Oblt. z. S.	U 106
Dangschat	Günther	(35)	Kaptlt.	U 184
Dankleff	Walter	D II/35	Oblt. z. S. d. Res.	U 767
Dau	Rolf	(26)	Kaptlt.	U 42
Dauter	Helmut	(X/37)	Oblt. z. S.	U 448
Davidson, von	Heinrich	(IV/37)	Kaptlt.	U 281
De Buhr	Johann	D XII/34	Oblt. z. S. d. Res.	U 347
Deckert	Horst	(IV/37)	Oblt. z. S.	U 73
Deecke	Joachim	(33)	Kaptlt.	U 584
Deecke	Jürgen	(31)	Kaptlt.	U 1
Deetz	Friedrich	(35)	Kaptlt.	U 757
Degen	Horst	(33)	Kaptlt.	U 701
Deiring	Hugo	(X/38)	Oblt. z. S.	U 3503
De Siervo	Federico		TV	U 1161
Dick	Hans-Peter	(X/39)	Oblt. z. S.	U 612
Dierks	Hans-Joachim	(X/40)	Oblt. z. S.	U 14, U 137
Dierksen	Reiner	(33)	K. Kapt.	U 176
Dieterichs	Horst	(34)	Kaptlt.	U 406
Dietrich	Willi	(X/38)	Oblt. z. S. (K.O.)	U 286
Diggins	Kurt	(34)	Kaptlt.	U 458
Dingler	Gottfried	(XII/39)	Oblt. z. S.	U 748
Dobberstein	Erich	(X/38)	Oblt. z. S.	U 988
Dobbert	Max	D X/38	Oblt. z. S. d. Res.	U 969, U 2537, U 2546
Dobenecker	Günter	(X/40)	Oblt. z. S.	U 11
Dobinsky	Hans-Jürgen	(XII/39)	Oblt. z. S.	U 323
Döhler	Hans	(IV/37)	Oblt. z. S.	U 606
Dohrn	Erwin	(X/38)	Oblt. z. S.	U 325
Drescher	Günther	(X/38)	Oblt. z. S.	U 882, U 3026
Dresky, von	Hans-Wilhelm	(29)	Kaptlt.	U 33
Drewitz	Hans-Joachim	(33)	Kaptlt.	U 525

Name	First Name	Class	Rank	U-No.
Drews	Ulrich	(36)	Kaptlt.	U 2534
Dübler	Rudolf	(XII/39)	Oblt. z. S.	U 1101
Duis	Hans-Diederich	(XII/39)	Oblt. z. S.	U 792
Dültgen	Gert	(X/37)	Oblt. z. S.	U 391
Dumrese	Adolf	(29)	Kaptlt.	U 655
Düppe	Joachim	D I/40	Oblt. z. S. d. Res.	U 2505
Eberbach	Heinz-Eugen	(X/39)	Oblt. z. S.	U 967, U 230
Eberlein	Otto	D VIII/39	Oblt. z. S. d. Res.	U 1020
Ebert	Jürgen	(IV/37)	Kaptlt.	U 927
Eck	Heinz-Wilhelm	(34)	Kaptlt.	U 852
Eckel	Kurt	(XII/39)	Oblt. z. S.	U 2325
Eckelmann	Heinz	(IV/37)	Oblt. z. S.	U 635
Eckhardt	Hermann	(36)	Kaptlt.	U 432
Edelhoff	Ernst	D X/36	Oblt. z. S. d. Res.	U 324
Ehrhardt	Walther	(X/38)	Oblt. z. S.	U 1016
Ehrich	Heinz	(X/37)	Oblt. z. S.	U 334
Eichmann	Kurt	(IV/37)	Oblt. z. S.	U 98
Eick	Alfred	(IV/37)	Kaptlt.	U 510
Eisele	Wilhelm	(IV/37)	Kaptlt.	U 1103
Elfe	Horst	(36)	Oblt. z. S.	U 93
Ellerlage	Hermann	D VIII/40	Oblt. z. S. d. Res.	U 2344
Ellmenreich	Helmut	(35)	Kaptlt.	U 535
Elsinghorst	Josef	D IV/39	Oblt. z. S. d. Res.	U 822
Emde	Bernhard	(X/37)	Oblt. z. S.	U 299
Emmrich	Heinz	D VI/40	Oblt. z. S. d. Res.	U 320
Endler	Siegfried	D III/34	Oblt. z. S. d. Res.	U 4711
Endraß	Engelbert	(34)	Kaptlt.	U 567
Engel	Herbert	(36)	Kaptlt.	U 228
Engelmann	Kurt-Eduard	(23)	K. Kapt.	U 163
Epp	Dietrich	(IV/37)	Oblt. z. S.	U 341
Eppen	Günter	(33)	Kaptlt.	U 519
Ernst	Hans-Joachim	(X/37)	Kaptlt.	U 1022
Esch, von der	Dietrich	(34)	Kaptlt.	U 863
Ewerth	Klaus	(25)	F. Kapt.	U 850
Ey	Hans	(35)	Oblt. z. S.	U 433
Fabricius	Fritz	(X/37)	Kaptlt.	U 1028
Fabricius	Ludwig	(XII/39)	Oblt. z. S.	U 721
Falke	Hans	D XI/37	Oblt. z. S. d. Res.	U 1279
Falke	Hans	(X/39)	Oblt. z. S.	U 992

Name	First Name	Class	Rank	U-No.
Faust	Erich	(XII/39)	Oblt. z. S.	U 618
Fechner	Otto	(24)	K. Kapt.	U 164
Fehler	Johann-Heinrich	(35)	Kaptlt.	U 234
Feindt	Hans-Arend	(XII/39)	Oblt. z. S.	U 758
Fenski	Horst-Arno	(X/37)	Oblt. z. S.	U 410, U 371
Ferro	Otto	D VIII/40	Oblt. z. S. d. Res.	U 645
Fiebig	Günter	(X/38)	Oblt. z. S.	U 1131
Fiedler	Hans	(36)	Oblt. z. S., Kaptlt.	U 564, U 998, U 333
Fiehn	Helmut	(35)	Kaptlt.	U 191
Findeisen	Eberhard	(36)	Kaptlt.	U 877
Finke	Otto	(36)	Kaptlt.	U 279
Fischel, von	Unno	(34)	Oblt. z. S.	U 374
Fischer	Ernst	(X/39)	Oblt. z. S.	U 3006
Fischer	Klaus	(X/38)	Oblt. z. S.	U 961
Fischler, Graf von Treuberg	Rupprecht	(X/39)	Oblt. z. S.	U 445
Fitting	Hans-Hermann	(X/39)	Oblt. z. S.	U 1274
Fleige	Karl	(X/37)	Oblt. z. S.,Kaptlt. (K.O.)	U 18, U 4712
Folkers	Ulrich	(34)	Kaptlt.	U 125
Förster	Hans-Joachim	(X/38)	Oblt. z. S.	U 480
Förster	Heinz	D I/40	Oblt. z. S. d. Res.	U 359
Förster	Hugo	(23)	K. Kapt.	U 501
Forster	Ludwig	(36)	Oblt. z. S.	U 654
Forstner, Freiherr von	Siegfried	(30)	K. Kapt.	U 402
Forstner, Freiherr von	Wolfgang-Friedrich	(IV/37)	Oblt. z. S.	U 472
Fraatz	Georg-Werner	(35)	Oblt. z. S., Kaptlt.	U 652, U 529
Frahm	Karl	(V/41)	Oblt. z. S. (K.O.)	U 2363
Frahm	Peter	(32)	Kaptlt.	U 15
Franceschi	Gerhard	(I/41)	Oblt. z. S.	U 4704
Franke	Hans-Heino	(X/40)	Oblt. z. S.	U 2355
Franke	Heinz	(36)	Kaptlt.	U 2502
Franz	Johannes	(26)	Kaptlt.	U 27
Franz	Ludwig	(IV/37)	Oblt. z. S.	U 362
Franze	Joachim	(IV/37)	Kaptlt.	U 278
Fränzel	Otto	(X/39)	Oblt. z. S.	U 3011
Fraternale	Athos		CC	U 428
Freiwald	Kurt	(25)	Kapt. z. S.	U 181

Name	First Name	Class	Rank	U-No.
Freyberg-Eisenberg-Allmendingen, Freiherr von	Walter	(35)	Kaptlt.	U 610
Friedeburg, von	Ludwig-Ferdinand	(V/41)	Oblt. z. S.	U 4710
Friederich	Karl	(IV/37)	Oblt. z. S.	U 74
Friedrich	Rudolf	(35)	Kaptlt.	U 759
Friedrichs	Adolf	(35)	Kaptlt.	U 253
Frischke, Dr.	Karl-Heinz	D X/36	Kaptlt. d. Res.	U 881
Fritz	Detlef	(X/39)	Oblt. z. S.	U 555
Fritz	Herbert	(XII/39)	Oblt. z. S.	U 3055
Fritz	Karl-Heinz	D I/41	Lt. z. S. d. Res.	U 107
Fritze	Günther	(XII/39)	Oblt. z. S.	U 3514
Frohberg	Günther	(X/39)	Oblt. z. S.	U 1275
Fröhlich	Günther	(XII/39)	Oblt. z. S.	U 3056
Fröhlich	Wilhelm	(29)	Kaptlt.	U 36
Frömmer	Heinz	(XII/39)	Oblt. z. S.	U 923
Frömsdorf	Helmut	(XII/39)	Oblt. z. S.	U 853
Gabert	Paul	(X/37)	Kaptlt.	U 1210
Gänge	Albrecht	(X/37)	Oblt. z. S.	U 226
Ganzer	Erwin	(36)	Kaptlt.	U 871
Gaude	Hans-Ludwig	(36)	Oblt. z. S., Kaptlt.	U 19, U 2343
Gaza, von	Jürgen	(X/39)	Oblt. z. S.	U 312
Gebauer	Werner	(XII/39)	Oblt. z. S.	U 681
Gehrken	Heinrich	D III/37	Oblt. z. S. d. Res.	UF 2, U 298
Geider	Horst	(IV/37)	Oblt. z. S.	U 761
Geisler	Hans-Ferdinand	(X/38)	Oblt. z. S.	U 3049
Geissler	Heinz	D X/38	Oblt. z. S. d. Res.	U 390
Gelhaar	Alexander	(27)	Kaptlt.	U 45
Gemeiner	Gerth	(X/37)	Oblt. z. S.	U 154
Gengelbach	Dietrich	(34)	Oblt. z. S.	U 574
Gericke	Otto	(31)	Kaptlt.	U 503
Gerke	Ernst-August	(XII/39)	Oblt. z. S.	U 382, U 673, U 3035
Gerlach	Peter	(XII/39)	Oblt. z. S.	U 223
Gerlach	Wilhelm	D XI/39	Oblt. z. S. d. Res.	U 490
Gessner	Hans	(X/38)	Oblt. z. S,	U 1008
Giersberg	Dietrich	(IV/37)	Oblt. z. S.	U 419
Gilardone	Hans	(32)	Kaptlt.	U 254
Glaser	Wolfgang	(X/37)	Oblt. z. S.	U 1014
Glattes	Gerhard	(27)	Kaptlt.	U 39

Name	First Name	Class	Rank	U-No.
Gode	Heinrich	(XII/39)	Oblt. z. S.	U 3531
Göing	Walter	(34)	Kaptlt.	U 755
Goldbeck	Heinz	D X/36	Oblt. z. S. d. Res.	U 1169
Göllnitz	Heinrich	(34)	Kaptlt.	U 657
Görner	Friedrich-Karl	(XII/39)	Oblt. z. S.	U 145
Goschzik	Georg	(X/38)	Oblt. z. S. (K.O.)	U 2348
Gosejacob	Henri	(IV/37)	Oblt. z. S.	U 713
Gossler	Johann-Egbert	(35)	Kaptlt.	U 538
Gossler, von	Curt	(32)	Kaptlt.	U 49
Götze	Hans	D XI/39	Oblt. z. S. d. Res.	U 586, U 2527
Graef	Adolf	(36)	Oblt. z. S.	U 664
Gräf	Ulrich	(35)	Kaptlt.	U 69
Grafen	Karl	(X/40)	Oblt. z. S.	U 20
Gramitzky	Franz	(36)	Oblt. z. S.	U 138
Grandefeld	Wolfgang	(36)	Oblt. z. S.	U 174
Grau	Peter	(X/38)	Oblt. z. S.	U 1191
Grau	Peter Ottmar	(34)	Kaptlt.	U 872, U 3015
Grave	Günther	(IV/37)	Oblt. z. S.	U 470
Grawert	Justus	(X/40)	Oblt. z. S.	U 750
Greger	Eberhard	(35)	Oblt. z. S.	U 85
Gretschel	Günther	(36)	Oblt. z. S.	U 707
Gréus	Friedrich-August	(X/39)	Oblt. z. S.	U 737
Grimme	Wilhelm	(X/37)	Oblt. z. S.	U 116
Grosse	Harald	(25)	K. Kapt.	U 53
Grote	Heinrich	(X/38)	Oblt. z. S.	U 3516
Groth	Gerhard	(IV/37)	Kaptlt.	U 397
Gudenus	Karl-Gabriel	(X/38)	Oblt. z. S.	U 427
Guggenberger	Friedrich	(34)	Kaptlt.	U 513
Günther	Horst	(XII/39)	Oblt. z. S.	U 1281, U 2533
Guse	Joachim	(X/39)	Oblt. z. S.	U 1193
Gutteck	Hans-Joachim	(36)	Kaptlt.	U 1024
Habekost	Johannes	(33)	Kaptlt.	U 31
Hackländer	Burkhard	(33)	Kaptlt.	U 454
Hackländer	Klaus	(X/37)	Oblt. z. S.	U 423
Hagene	Georg	(32)	K. Kapt.	U 1208
Hamm	Horst	(35)	Kaptlt.	U 562
Hammer	Ulrich	(X/39)	Oblt. z. S.	U 430, U 733
Hänert	Klaus	(36)	Kaptlt.	U 550
Hanitsch	Hans-Ulrich	(XII/39)	Oblt. z. S.	U 428

Name	First Name	Class	Rank	U-No.
Hansen	Hans-Johann	(X/37)	Oblt. z. S.	U 1026
Hansen	Hermann	D XI/39	Oblt. z. S. d. Res.	U 2517
Hansen	Otto	(IV/37)	Kaptlt.	U 601
Hansmann	Bruno	(29)	Kaptlt.	U 127
Happe	Werner	(36)	Oblt. z. S.	U 192
Harms	Erich	D IX/39	Oblt. z. S. d. Res.	U 3023
Harms	Otto	(33)	Kaptlt.	U 464
Harney	Klaus	(35)	Kaptlt.	U 756
Harpe, von	Richard	(X/37)	Oblt. z. S., Kaptlt.	U 129, U 3519
Hartel	Friedrich	D VIII/40	Oblt. z. S. d. Res.	U 2356
Hartenstein	Werner	(28)	K. Kapt.	U 156
Hartmann	Curt	(X/39)	Oblt. z. S.	U 982
Hartmann	Klaus	(33)	Kaptlt.	U 441
Hartmann	Otto	(36)	Oblt. z. S.	U 77
Hartwig	Paul	(35)	Kaptlt.	U 517
Hasenschar	Heinrich	(36)	Kaptlt.	U 628
Hashagen	Berthold	D III/37	Oblt. z. S. d. Res.	U 846
Hauber	Hans-Gerold	D III/34	Oblt. z. S. d. Res.	U 170
Haupt	Hans-Jürgen	D IV/35	Oblt. z. S. d. Res.	U 665
Hause	Karl	(35)	Kaptlt.	U 211
Hechler	Ernst	(29)	K. Kapt.	U 870
Heckel	Fridtjof	(XII/39)	Oblt. z. S.	U 2322
Hegewald	Wolfgang	(IV/37)	Kaptlt.	U 671
Heibges	Wolfgang	D IV/40	Oblt. z. S. d. Res.	U 999
Heidel	Werner	(32)	Kaptlt.	U 55
Heidtmann	Hans	(34)	Kaptlt.	U 559
Heilmann	Siegfried	(36)	Kaptlt.	U 389
Hein	Fritz	(X/38)	Oblt. z. S.	U 300
Heine	Karl-Franz	(34)	Kaptlt.	U 303, U 403
Heinicke	Ernst-Günther	(27)	K. Kapt.	U 2561
Heinicke	Hans-Dieter	(33)	Kaptlt.	U 576
Heinrich	Erwin	(X/40)	Oblt. z. S.	U 2357
Heinrich	Günther	(X/38)	Oblt. z. S.	U 960
Heinrich	Helmuth	D IX/39	Oblt. z. S. d. Res.	U 255
Heinsohn	Heinrich	(33)	Kaptlt.	U 573, U 438
Heitz	Horst	(XII/39)	Oblt. z. S.	U 1407
Heller	Wolfgang	(30)	K. Kapt.	U 842
Hellriegel	Hans-Jürgen	(36)	Kaptlt.	U 543
Hellwig	Alexander	(35)	Kaptlt.	U 289

Name	First Name	Class	Rank	U-No.
Henke	Werner	(33)	Kaptlt.	U 515
Henne	Wolf	(24)	K. Kapt.	U 157
Hennig	Helmut	(36)	Kaptlt.	U 533
Hennig, von	Heinz	(X/40)	Oblt. z. S.	U 2361
Henning	Fritz	(IV/37)	Oblt. z. S., Kaptlt.	U 561, U 565, U 2560, U 668
Hepp	Horst	(36)	Oblt. z. S., Kaptlt.	U 272, U 238
Herglotz	Helmut	(X/38)	Oblt. z. S.	U 1303
Herrle	Friedrich-Georg	D XII/39	Oblt. z. S. d. Res.	U 393
Herrmann	Werner	(X/38)	Oblt. z. S.	U 2510
Hertin	Willi	(35)	Kaptlt.	U 647
Herwartz	Oskar	(35)	Kaptlt.	U 843
Herwartz	Wolfgang	(IV/37)	Kaptlt.	U 1302
Hesemann	Siegfried	(34)	Kaptlt.	U 186
Hess	Hans Georg	D IV/40	Oblt. z. S. d. Res.	U 995
Hesse	Hans-Joachim	(25)	K. Kapt.	U 442
Hesse	Hermann	(34)	Kaptlt.	U 194
Heusinger von Waldegg	Burkhard	(X/38)	Oblt. z. S.	U 198
Heyda	Wolfgang	(32)	Kaptlt.	U 434
Heydemann	Ernst	(36)	Oblt. z. S.	U 268
Hilbig	Hans	(36)	Kaptlt.	U 1230
Hilbig	Kurt	(X/38)	Oblt. z. S.	U 993, U 3526
Hilgendorf	Klaus	D X/39	Oblt. z. S. d. Res.	U 1009
Hillmann	Jürgen	(X/40)	Oblt. z. S.	U 2353
Hinrichs	Hermann	(V/41)	Oblt. Ing (K.O.)	U 2504
Hinrichs	Johannes	(X/37)	Kaptlt.	U 3005
Hinz	Rudolf	(X/39)	Oblt. z. S.	U 1004
Hippel, von	Friedrich	(34)	Oblt. z. S.	U 76
Hoeckner	Fritz	(33)	Kaptlt.	U 215
Hoffmann	Eberhard	(25)	K. Kapt.	U 165
Hoffmann	Eberhard	(33)	K. Kapt.	U 451
Hoffmann	Erich-Michael	(X/38)	Oblt. z. S.	U 738
Hoffmann	Heinrich-Dietrich	(X/40)	Oblt. z. S.	U 141
Hoffmann	Hermann	(X/39)	Oblt. z. S.	U 172
Höh, von der	Hermann	D IV/40	Oblt. z. S. d. Res.	U 2346
Hohmann	Otto	D III/37	Oblt. z. S. d. Res.	U 2526
Holleben, von	Heinrich	(X/38)	Oblt. z. S.	U 1051
Holpert	William	(X/38)	Oblt. z. S. (K.O.)	U 1021
Holtorf	Gottfried	(35)	Kaptlt.	U 598

Name	First Name	Class	Rank	U-No.
Höltring	Horst	(33)	Kaptlt.	U 604
Homann	Hans	D XI/38	Oblt. z. S. d. Res.	U 1165
Hopmann	Rolf-Heinrich	(26)	K. Kapt.	U 405
Hoppe	Joachim	(33)	Kaptlt.	U 65
Horn	Karl-Horst	(35)	Kaptlt.	U 705
Hornbostel	Klaus	(34)	Kaptlt.	U 806
Hornkohl	Hans	(36)	Kaptlt.	U 566, U 3512, U 3041
Horrer	Hans-Joachim	(32)	Kaptlt.	U 589
Horst	Friedrich	D XI/39	Oblt. z. S. d. Res.	U 121
Hossenfelder	Albert	D X/35	Oblt. z. S. d. Res.	U 342
Hübsch	Horst Dieter	(XII/39)	Oblt. z. S.	U 78
Hübschen	Otto	(X/38)	Oblt. z. S.	U 2532
				U 2542
Huisgen	Friedrich	D IX/36	Kaptlt. d. Res.	U 749, U 235
Hülsenbeck	Ewald	(X/38)	Oblt. z. S.	U 1209
Hummerjohann	Emmo	(IV/37)	Oblt. z. S.	U 964
Hunger	Hans	(35)	Kaptlt.	U 336
Hungershausen	Heinz	(36)	Kaptlt.	U 91
Hungershausen	Walter	(X/38)	Oblt. z. S.	U 280
Huth	Walther	(IV/37)	Oblt. z. S.	U 414
Hüttemann	Eberhard	(X/37)	Oblt. z. S.	U 332
Hymmen, von	Reinhard	(33)	Kaptlt.	U 408
Hyronimus	Guido	(X/37)	Obll. z. S.	U 670, U 678
Isermeyer	Hans-Adolf	(X/38)	Oblt. z. S.	U 2562
Ites	Otto	(36)	Oblt. z. S.	U 94
Ites	Rudolf	D IV/36	Oblt. z. S. d. Res.	U 709
Jäckel	Kurt	(X/40)	Oblt. z. S.	U 2366
Jacobs	Paul	(X/39)	Oblt. z. S. (K.O.)	U 560
Jacobs, von	Nikolaus	(33)	Kaptlt.	U 611
Jaenicke	Karl	D XI/39	Oblt. z. S. d. Res.	U 3533
Jäger	Walter	D I/43	Oblt. z. S. d. Res.	U 1061
Jahrmärker	Walther	(35)	Kaptlt.	U 412
Janssen	Gustav-Adolf	(36)	Kaptlt.	U 103, U 3037
Jaschke	Heinz	(X/39)	Oblt. z. S.	U 592
Jebsen	Johann	(35)	Kaptlt.	U 859
Jenisch	Hans	(33)	Oblt. z. S.	U 32
Jenisch	Karl-Heinrich	(29)	Kaptlt.	U 22
Jensen	Kurt	(IV/37)	Oblt. z. S.	U 644

Name	First Name	Class	Rank	U-No.
Jenssen	Karl-Joachim	(X/38)	Oblt. z. S.	U 477
Jeschonnek	Wolf	(X/38)	Oblt. z. S.	U 607
Jessen, von	Ralf	(35)	Kaptlt.	U 222, U 266
Jestel	Erwin	(X/40)	Lt. z. S., Oblt. z. S.	U 6, U 1204
Jewinski	Erich	(X/38)	Oblt. z. S.	U 46
Jobst	Karl	D IV/36	Oblt. z. S. d. Res.	U 2326
Johann	Johann	D III/27	Oblt. z. S. d. Res.	U 2539
Johannsen	Hans	D X/35	Oblt. z. S. d. Res.	U 569
John	Alfred	(X/38)	Oblt. z. S.	U 828
Jordan	Günther	(X/37)	Oblt. z. S.	U 274
Junker	Hanns-Joachim	(X/40)	Oblt. z. S.	U 2370, U 2332
Junker	Ottoheinrich	(24)	F. Kapt.	U 532
Jürs	Ralf	(X/37)	Kaptlt.	U 778
Jürst	Harald	(32)	Kaptlt.	U 104
Just	Paul	(36)	Kaptlt.	U 546
Justi	Friedrich	(X/37)	Kaptlt.	U 1170
Kaeding	Walter	D IV/35	Lt. z. S. (KO)	U 4713
Kaiser	Hans-Dietrich	D IV/40	Oblt. z. S. d. Res.	U 2338
Kaiser	Hermann	(25)	F. Kapt.	U 3002
Kaiser	Karl-Ernst	(X/38)	Oblt. z. S.	U 986
Kallipke	Fritz	D XI/37	Oblt. z. S. d. Res.	U 2516, U 2529
Kameke, von	Horst-Tessen	(35)	Kaptlt.	U 119
Kandler	Hans-Albrecht	(IV/37)	Oblt. z. S.	U 653
Kandzior	Helmut	(X/38)	Oblt. z. S.	U 743
Kapitzky	Ralph	(35)	Kaptlt.	U 615
Karpf	Hans	(35)	Kaptlt.	U 632
Kasch	Lorenz	(33)	Kaptlt.	U 540
Käselau	Erich	(I/41)	Oblt. z. S.	U 922
Kasparek	Walter	(XII/39)	Oblt. z. S.	U 143
Kaufmann	Wolfgang	(33)	Kaptlt.	U 79
Keerl	Hans	(X/39)	Kaptlt.	U 80
Kelbling	Gerd	(34)	Kaptlt.	U 593
Kell	Walter	(33)	Kaptlt.	U 204
Keller	Günter	(IV/37)	Kaptlt.	U 683
Keller	Günther	(XII/39)	Oblt. z. S.	U 981, U 3521
Keller	Siegfried	(IV/37)	Oblt. z. S.	U 130
Keller, Graf	Alexander	(X/38)	Oblt. z. S.	U 731
Kellerstrass	Gerhard	(IV/37)	Oblt. z. S., Kaptlt.	U 491, U 3043
Kellner	Adolf	(36)	Kaptlt.	U 357

Name	First Name	Class	Rank	U-No.
Ketelhodt, Freiherr von	Eberhard	(X/40)	Oblt. z. S.	U 712
Ketels	Hans-Heinrich	(IV/37)	Kaptlt.	U 970, U 2523, U 1162
Kettner	Paul-Hugo	(33)	Kaptlt.	U 379
Kiessling	Ulrich	D X/39	Oblt. z. S. d. Res.	U 1306
Kietz	Siegfried	(IV/37)	Oblt. z. S.	U 126
Kimmelmann	Walter	(X/40)	Oblt. z. S.	U 139
Kindelbacher	Robert	(35)	Kaptlt.	U 627
Kinzel	Manfred	(35)	Kaptlt.	U 338
Klapdor	Heinrich	(X/40)	Oblt. z. S.	U 9, U 2538
Klaus	Hans-Joachim	(IV/37)	Oblt. z. S.	U 340
Kleinschmidt	Wilhelm, gen. Peter	(30)	Kaptlt.	U 111
Klingspor	Leonhard	(X/37)	Kaptlt.	U 293
Kloevekorn	Friedrich	(IV/37)	Kaptlt.	U 471
Klot, von	Harro	(31)	Kaptlt.	U 102
Klug	Werner	(X/39)	Oblt. z. S.	U 1406
Klusmeier	Emil	(X/38)	Oblt. z. S., Kaptlt. (K.O.)	U 2340, U 2336
Kluth	Gerhard	(X/37)	Oblt. z. S.	U 377
Knackfuss	Ulrich	(X/38)	Oblt. z. S.	U 345, U 821
Knecht	Joachim	(X/37)	Kaptlt.	U 3036, U 3059
Kneip	Albert	(X/39)	Oblt. z. S.	U 1223
Knieper	Bernhard	D I/41	Oblt. z. S. d. Res.	U 267
Knoke	Helmut	D III/41	Oblt. z. S. d. Res.	U 925
Knollmann	Helmut	(IV/37)	Kaptlt.	U 1174, U 1273
Knorr	Dietrich	(31)	Kaptlt.	U 51
Koch	Heinz	(IV/37)	Oblt. z. S.	U 304
Koch	Walter-Ernst	(X/38)	Oblt. z. S.	U 1132
Kock	Uwe	D X/36	Kaptlt. d. Res.	U 249
Köhl	Kurt	D XI/39	Oblt. z. S. d. Res.	U 669
Koitschka	Siegfried	(IV/37)	Oblt. z. S.	U 616
Kolbus	Hans	(X/38)	Oblt. z. S.	U 421, U 596, U 407
Könenkamp	Jürgen	(32)	Kaptlt.	U 375
König	Gottfried	(XII/39)	Oblt. z. S.	U 316
König	Klaus-Dietrich	(X/37)	Oblt. z. S.	U 972
Koopmann	Hermann	D I/40	Oblt. z. S. d. Res.	U 1171
Köpke	Klaus	(35)	Kaptlt.	U 259
Köppe	Helmut	(31)	Kaptlt.	U 613
Korndörfer	Hubertus	(X/39)	Oblt. z. S.	U 3537

Name	First Name	Class	Rank	U-No.
Körner	Willy-Roderich	(35)	Kaptlt.	U 301
Kosbadt	Hans-Carl	(IV/37)	Oblt. z. S.	U 224
Kosnick	Fritz	D IV/36	Oblt. z. S. d. Res.	U 739
Kottmann	Hermann	(36)	Kaptlt.	U 203
Kranich	Franz	(IV/37)	Kaptlt.	U 3525
Krankenhagen	Detlev	(36)	Kaptlt.	U 549
Kraus	Hans-Werner	(34)	Kaptlt.	U 199
Krech	Günther	(33)	Kaptlt.	U 558
Kregelin	Ludo	(X/38)	Oblt. z. S.	U 3003
Krempl	Erich	(X/39)	Oblt. z. S.	U 548
Kremser	Horst	(36)	Kaptlt.	U 383
Kretschmer	Otto	(30)	K. Kapt.	U 99
Krieg	Johann Otto	(X/37)	Oblt. z. S.	U 81
Kriegshammer	Jürgen	(X/40)	Oblt. z. S.	U 8, U 150
Kronenbitter	Willy	(X/37)	Kaptlt. (K.O.)	U 3527
Kröning	Ernst	(25)	Kaptlt.	U 656
Krüer	Werner	D I/37	Oblt. z. S. d. Res.	U 590
Krüger	Erich	D X/39	Oblt. z. S. d. Res.	U 307
Krüger	Jürgen	(IV/37)	Oblt. z. S.	U 631
Kühl	Peter	(I/41)	Oblt. z. S.	U 57
Kuhlmann	Hans-Günther	(36)	Oblt. z. S.	U 580, U 160
Kuhlmann	Jürgen	(X/38)	Oblt. z. S.	U 1172
Kühn	Herbert	(X/39)	Oblt. z. S.	U 708
Kühne	Johannes	(X/40)	Oblt. z. S.	U 2371
Kummer	Heinz	(36)	Kaptlt.	U 467
Kummetat	Heinz	(IV/37)	Oblt. z. S.	U 572
Kuntze	Jürgen	(36)	Kaptlt.	U 227
Kuppisch	Herbert	(32)	Kaptlt.	U 847
Kurrer	Hellmut	(35)	Kaptlt.	U 189
Kuscher	Fedor	D XII/39	Oblt. z. S. d. Res.	U 3515
Kutschmann	Günter	(29)	Kaptlt.	U 54
Kuttkat	Martin	(X/40)	Oblt. z. S.	U 429
La Baume	Günter	(29)	K. Kapt.	U 355
Lamby	Hermann	(36)	Kaptlt.	U 437, U 3029
Landt-Hayen	Martin	D X/39	Oblt. z. S. d. Res.	U 4705
Lange	Georg	(11)	Kaptlt.	UC 1
Lange	Gerhard	(X/37)	Oblt. z. S.	U 418
Lange	Hans	(35)	Kaptlt.	U 261
Lange	Hans-Günther	(IV/37)	Kaptlt.	U 711

Name	First Name	Class	Rank	U-No.
Lange	Harald	D IX/39	Oblt. z. S. d. Res.	U 505
Lange	Helmut	(IV/37)	Oblt. z. S.	U 1053
Lange	Karl-Heinz	(IV/37)	Kaptlt.	U 667
Langenberg	Bruno	D XI/38	Oblt. z. S. d. Res.	U 366
Langfeld	Albert	(IV/37)	Oblt. z. S.	U 444
Lau	Kurt	(XII/39)	Oblt. z. S.	U 1197
Laubert	Helmut	(X/37)	Kaptlt.	U 3048
Laudahn	Karl-Heinz	(IV/37)	Kaptlt.	U 262
Lauterbach-Emden	Hans-Jürgen	(IV/37)	Kaptlt.	U 539
Lauth	Hermann	(XII/39)	Oblt. z. S.	U 1005
Lauzemis	Albert	(IV/37)	Oblt. z. S.	U 68
Lawaetz	Ulf	(X/37)	Oblt. z. S.	U 672
Lawrence	Peter	(X/38)	Oblt. z. S.	U 2328
Leder	Joachim	D I/40	Oblt. z. S. d. Res.	U 4707
Lehmann	Hans	D XI/38	Oblt. z. S. d. Res.	U 997
Lehmann-Willenbrock	Heinrich	(31)	K. Kapt.	U 256
Lehsten, von	Detlev	(X/37)	Oblt. z. S., Kaptlt.	U 996, U 373, U 3508, U 3044
Leimkühler	Wolfgang	(IV/37)	Oblt. z. S.	U 225
Leisten	Arno	(X/38)	Oblt. z. S.	U 346
Lemcke	Hans	(IV/37)	Kaptlt.	U 327
Lemcke	Rudolf	(33)	K. Kapt.	U 210
Lemp	Fritz-Julius	(31)	Kaptlt.	U 110
Lenkeit	Paul Ehrenfried	(35)	Kaptlt.	U 1301
Lenzmann	Dieter	D X/39	Oblt. z. S. d. Res.	U 24, U 3522
Lerchen	Kai	(33)	Kaptlt.	U 252
Leupold	Günter	(X/38)	Oblt. z. S.	U 1059
Ley	Wolfgang	(X/38)	Oblt. z. S.	U 310
Liesberg	Ernst	(X/37)	Oblt. z. S.	U 962
Lilienfeld, von	Eric	(35)	Oblt. z. S.	U 661
Linck	Gerhard	(X/37)	Oblt. z. S.	U 1013
Lindemann	Kurt	D VII/40	Oblt. z. S. d. Res.	U 1207
Linder	Gerhard	(X/38)	Oblt. z. S.	U 2515, U 2554
Lindschau	Rudolf	D X/36	Oblt. z. S. d. Res.	U 3017
Link	Günther	(X/37)	Oblt. z. S.	U 240
Loeder	Herbert	(X/38)	Oblt. z. S.	U 309
Loeschke	Günther	(X/39)	Oblt. z. S.	U 7
Loewe	Odo	(34)	Kaptlt.	U 256, U 954
Lohmann	Dietrich	(30)	Kaptlt., K. Kapt.	U 579, U 89

Name	First Name	Class	Rank	U-No.
Lohmeyer	Peter	(32)	Kaptlt.	U 651
Lohse	Bernhard	(32)	Kaptlt.	U 585
Longhi	Alberto		TV	U 749
Looff	Hans-Günther	(25)	K. Kapt.	U 122
Looks	Hartwig	(36)	Kaptlt.	U 264
Loos	Johann-Friedrich	(XII/39)	Oblt. z. S.	U 248
Lorentz	Günther	(32)	Oblt. z. S.	U 63
Lott	Werner	(26)	Kaptlt.	U 35
Lottner	Ernst	(X/39)	Oblt. z. S.	U 746
Lübcke	Olaf	(X/37)	Kaptlt.	U 826
Lube	Günter	(X/39)	Oblt. z. S.	U 552
Lübsen	Robert	(IV/37)	Kaptlt.	U 277
Lüdden	Siegfried	(36)	Kaptlt.	U 188
Lüders	Günter	(X/38)	Oblt. z. S.	U 424
Lüders	Gustav	D IV/41	Oblt. z. S. d. Res.	U 884
Lührs	Dierk	(X/38)	Oblt. z. S.	U 453
Luis	Wilhelm	(35)	Kaptlt.	U 504
Lüssow	Gustav	(IV/37)	Oblt. z. S.	U 571
Lüth	Günter	D III/37	Oblt. z. S. d. Res.	U 1057
Luther	Otto	(X/37)	Oblt. z. S.	U 135
Luttmann	Bernhard	(X/39)	Oblt. z. S.	U 3030
Lutz	Friedrich	(X/37)	Kaptlt. (K.O.)	U 485
Mackeprang	Hans-Peter	D X/35	Oblt. z. S. d. Res.	U 244
Mäder	Erich	(36)	Kaptlt.	U 378
Mahn	Bruno	(11)	F. Kapt.	U B
Makowski	Kurt	(36)	Oblt. z. S.	U 619
Manchen	Erwin	(36)	Kaptlt.	U 879
Mangels	Hinrich	(X/38)	Oblt. z. S.	U 1200
Manhardt von Mannstein	Alfred	(25)	K. Kapt.	U 753
Manke	Rolf	(35)	Kaptlt.	U 358
Mannesmann, Dr.	Gert	D V/33	Kaptlt. d. Res.	U 545
Manseck	Helmut	(34)	Kaptlt.	U 3007, U 3008
Marbach	Karl-Heinz	(IV/37)	Kaptlt.	U 3014
March	Jürgen	(33)	Kaptlt.	U 452
Marienfeld	Friedrich-Wilhelm	(X/38)	Oblt. z. S.	U 1228
Marks	Friedrich-Karl	(34)	Kaptlt.	U 376
Märtens	Hans	(IV/37)	Kaptlt.	U 243
Martin	Lothar	(IV/37)	Kaptlt.	U 776

Name	First Name	Class	Rank	U–No.
Maßenhausen, von	Wilhelm	(35)	Kaptlt.	U 258
Maßmann	Hanns Ferdinand	(36)	Oblt. z. S.	U 409
Mathes	Ludwig	(28)	Kaptlt.	U 44
Matschulat	Gerhard	(X/38)	Oblt. z. S.	U 247
Matthes	Peter	(X/37)	Kaptlt.	U 326
Mattke	Willy	(35)	Kaptlt.	U 544
Matuschka, Graf von Freiherr von Topolczan und Spaetgen	Hartmut	(34)	Kaptlt.	U 482
Matz	Joachim	(32)	Kaptlt.	U 70
Mäueler	Heinrich	D IV/40	Oblt. z. S. d. Res.	U 3020
Maus	August	(34)	Kaptlt.	U 185
Mayer	Karl-Theodor	(XII/39)	Oblt. z. S.	U 72
Meenen	Karlheinz	(X/39)	Oblt. z. S.	U 1192
Meentzen	Bernhard	D X/38	Oblt. z. S. d. Res.	U 3016
Meermeier	Johannes	(IV/37)	Kaptlt.	U 979
Meeteren, van	Kurt	D X/39	Oblt. z. S. d. Res.	U 3021
Mehne	Karl	(IV/37)	Oblt. z. S., Kaptlt.	U 1280, U 891, U 3027
Meier	Alfred	D VII/39	Oblt. z. S. d. Res.	UIT 25
Meier	Friedrich	(X/37)	Kaptlt. (K.O.)	U 3012
Meinlschmidt	Rudolf	(XII/39)	Oblt. z. S.	U 2544
Melzer	Volker	D X/39	Oblt. z. S. d. Res.	U 994
Menard	Karl-Heinz	(IV/37)	Kaptlt.	U 1282, U 237
Merkle	Reinhold	(XII/39)	Oblt. z. S.	U 1201
Methner	Joachim	(IV/37)	Oblt. z. S.	U 2521
Metz	Helmut	D I/35	Oblt. z. S. d. Res.	U 487
Meyer	Fritz	(34)	Oblt. z. S.	U 207
Meyer	Gerhard	D X/35	Oblt. z. S. d. Res.	U 486
Meyer	Heinrich	(XII/39)	Oblt. z. S.	U 287
Meyer	Herbert	D III/37	Oblt. z. S. d. Res.	U 804
Meyer	Rudolf	(X/38)	Oblt. z. S.	U 1055
Meyer	Willy	D X/36	Oblt. z.S. d. Res.	U 288
Mittelstaedt, von	Gert	(32)	Kaptlt.	U 144
Möglich	Hans	(35)	Kaptlt.	U 526
Mohr	Eberhard	(35)	Oblt. z. S.	U 133
Mohr	Johann	(34)	K. Kapt.	U 124
Mohr	Kurt	D IV/40	Oblt. z. S. d. Res.	U 930
Mohs	Hans-Dieter	(X/37)	Kaptlt.	U 956
Möller	Günther	(X/37)	Oblt. z. S.	U 844

Name	First Name	Class	Rank	U-No.
Morstein, von	Hans-Joachim	(28)	Kaptlt. z.V.	U 483
Müffling, Freiherr von	Hans-Bruno	(X/39)	Oblt. z. S.	U 2545
Mugler	Gustav-Adolf	(31)	Kaptlt.	U 41
Mühlendahl, von	Arved	(23)	Kapt. z. S.	U 867
Mühlenpfordt	Karl	D VIII/40	Oblt. z. S. d. Res.	U 308
Muhs	Harald	(X/38)	Oblt. z. S.	U 674
Müller	Bernhard	(IV/37)	Oblt. z. S.	U 633
Müller	Hans-Georg	(X/40)	Oblt. z. S.	U 2349
Müller	Heinrich-Eberhard	(36)	Kaptlt.	U 662
Müller	Rudolf	(X/37)	Oblt. z. S.	U 282
Müller	Werner	(XII/39)	Oblt. z. S.	U 2327
Müller	Willi	D IX/39	Oblt. z. S. d. Res.	U 1000, U 3523
Müller-Bethke	Erich	(X/37)	Kaptlt.	U 1278
Müller-Koelbl	Harro	(X/38)	Oblt. z. S.	U 3051
Müller-Stockheim	Günther	(34)	K. Kapt.	U 67
Mumm	Friedrich	(36)	Kaptlt.	U 594
Mumm	Herbert	(X/39)	Oblt. z. S.	U 236
Münnich	Ralph	(35)	Kaptlt.	U 187
Münster	Helmut	(X/37)	Oblt. z. S., Kaptlt.	U 101
				U 3517
Musenberg	Werner	(25)	F. Kapt.	U 180
Nachtigall	Otto-Heinrich	D VIII/37	Oblt. z. S. d. Res.	U 3513
Nagel	Karl-Heinz	(IV/37)	Oblt. z. S.	U 640
Neckel	Herbert	(35)	Kaptlt.	U 531
Nees	Werner	(X/37)	Kaptlt.	U 363
Neitzsch	Wilhelm	(X/39)	Oblt. z. S.	U 3509
Neuerburg	Hellmut	(36)	Kaptlt.	U 869
Neuland	Carl	D IX/39	Oblt. z. S. d. Res.	U 3054
Neumann	Hans-Werner	(25)	K. Kapt.	U 117
Neumann	Heinz-Joachim	(30)	Kaptlt.	U 372
Neumann	Hermann	(X/38)	Oblt. z. S.	U 3057
Neumeister	Hermann	(X/40)	Lt. z. S., Oblt. z. S.	U 3, U 291
Ney	Günter	(XII/39)	Oblt. z. S.	U 283
Nibbe	Hans-Heinrich	(X/37)	Oblt. z. S.	U 2557
Nielsen	Karl	D X/35	Oblt. z. S. d. Res.	U 370
Niemeyer	Heinrich	(X/39)	Oblt. z. S.	U 547, U 1233, U 3532
Niester	Erich	(X/39)	Oblt. z. S.	U 350
Niethmann	Otto	(X/38)	Oblt. z. S.	U 476, U 3507

Name	First Name	Class	Rank	U-No.
Niss	Hellmut	D X/39	Kaptlt. d. Res.	U 2531
Nissen	Jürgen	(36)	Kaptlt.	U 105
Noack	Hans-Dietrich	(34)	Kaptlt. (Ing)	U 2501
Nölke	Kurt	(35)	Kaptlt.	U 263
Nollau	Herbert	(36)	Kaptlt.	U 534
Nollmann	Rolf	(36)	Kaptlt.	U 1199
Nolte	Gerhard	(XII/39)	Oblt. z. S.	U 704
Nordheimer	Hubert	(36)	Kaptlt.	U 237, U 990, U 2512
Norita	Sadatoshi	IJN	Lt. Comdr.	U 1224
Oesten	Jürgen	(33)	K. Kapt.	U 861
Oestermann	Johannes	(32)	Kaptlt.	U 754
Offermann	Hans	(X/39)	Oblt. z. S.	U 518
Ohlsen	Prosper	(IV/37)	Oblt. z. S.	U 855
Oldörp	Hans-Jürgen	(35)	Kaptlt.	U 90
Opitz	Herbert	(34)	Kaptlt.	U 206
Ostrowitzky	Clemens	(XII/39)	Oblt. z. S. (KO)	U 4716
Otto	Hermann	(36)	Oblt. z. S.	U 449
Otto	Paul-Friedrich	(IV/37)	Kaptlt.	U 270, U 2525
Paepenmöller	Klaus	(IV/37)	Oblt. z. S.	U 973
Pahl	Hans-Walter	(X/38)	Oblt. z. S.	U 2331, U 2369
Pahls	Heinrich	(X/39)	Oblt. z. S.	UIT 24
Palmgren	Gerhard	(X/38)	Oblt. z. S.	U 741
Panitz	Johannes	D VIII/37	Oblt. z. S. d. Res.	U 1065
Parduhn	Fritz	(X/37)	Kaptlt.	U 1107
Pauckstadt	Hans	(26)	Kaptlt.	U 18
Paulshen	Ottokar	(34)	Kaptlt.	U 557
Pelkner	Hans-Hermann	(34)	Kaptlt.	U 335
Perleberg	Rüdiger	(X/37)	Oblt. z. S. (K.O.)	U 1104
Peschel	Otto	(IV/37)	Kaptlt.	U 3004
Peters	Georg	(30)	K. Kapt.	U 38
Peters	Gerhard	(XII/39)	Oblt. z. S.	U 1198
Peters	Wilhelm	(X/37)	Kaptlt.	U 3045, U 3001
Petersen	Klaus	(36)	Kaptlt.	U 3042
Petersen	Kurt	(36)	Kaptlt.	U 541
Petersen	Theodor	(X/37)	Oblt. z. S. (K.O.)	U 874
Petran	Friedrich	(X/38)	Oblt. z. S.	U 516
Pfeffer	Günther	(34)	Kaptlt.	U 171
Pfeifer	Werner	(33)	Kaptlt.	U 581

Name	First Name	Class	Rank	U-No.
Pich	Helmuth	(34)	Kaptlt.	U 168
Pick	Ewald	D XII/34	Oblt. z. S. d. Res.	U 1025
Pietsch	Ulrich	(36)	Kaptlt.	U 344
Pietschmann	Walter	(X/37)	Oblt. z. S.	U 762
Pietzsch	Werner	(35)	Kaptlt.	U 523
Plohr	Helmut	(I/41)	Oblt. z. S. (K.O.)	U 149
Poeschel	Hans-Wolfgang	(X/38)	Oblt. z. S.	U 422
Pommer-Esche, von	Gerd	(IV/37)	Oblt. z. S.	U 160
Popp	Günther	(X/39)	Oblt. z. S.	U 4717
Poser	Günter	(36)	Kaptlt.	U 202
Prellberg	Wilfried	(33)	Kaptlt.	U 31
Premauer	Rudolf	(X/37)	Kaptlt.	U 857
Pressel	Karl	(X/37)	Kaptlt.	U 951
Preuß	Georg	(36)	Kaptlt.	U 1224, U 875
Preuss	Joachim	(33)	Kaptlt.	U 568
Prien	Günther	(31)	K. Kapt.	U 47
Pückler und Limpurg, Graf von	Wilhelm-Heinrich	(34)	Kaptlt.	U 381
Pulst	Günther	(X/37)	Kaptlt.	U 978
Pultkamer, von	Konstantin	(36)	Oblt. z. S.	U 443
Quaet-Faslem	Jürgen	(34)	Kaptlt.	U 595
Queck	Horst-Thilo	(35)	Kaptlt.	U 622, U 2522
Raabe	Ernst	(36)	Kaptlt.	U 246
Raabe	Karl-Heinz	(X/38)	Oblt. z. S.	U 1007
Rabenau, von	Georg	(36)	Oblt. z. S.	U 528
Rabenau, von	Wolf-Rüdiger	(33)	Kaptlt.	U 702
Racky	Ernst-August	(X/38)	Oblt. z. S.	U 52, U 3019
Rademacher	Ewald	(IV/37)	Kaptlt.	U 772
Rademacher	Rudolf	(X/37)	Oblt. z. S.	U 478
Rahe	Heinz	(35)	Kaptlt.	U 257
Rahlf	Peter	D IX/39	Oblt. z. S. d. Res.	U 317
Rahmlow	Hans-Joachim	(28)	Kaptlt.	U 570
Rahn	Hermann	(X/38)	Lt. z. S.	U 5
Rahn	Wolfgang	(X/38)	Oblt. z. S.	U 343
Ranzau	Emil	D I/39	Oblt. z. S. d. Res.	U 71
Rappard, von	Konstantin	(36)	Kaptlt.	U 2324
Rasch	Karl-Heinz	(34)	Kaptlt.	U 296
Rathke	Hellmut	(30)	Kaptlt.	U 352
Ratsch	Heinrich	(34)	Kaptlt.	U 583

Name	First Name	Class	Rank	U–No.
Reese	Hans-Jürgen	(IV/37)	Oblt. z. S.	U 420
Reff	Reinhard	D XI/37	Oblt. z. S. d. Res.	U 736
Rehren	Hellmut	(XII/39)	Oblt. z. S.	U 926
Rehwinkel	Ernst-August	(23)	K. Kapt.	U 578
Reich	Christian	(36)	Oblt. z. S., Kaptlt.	U 416, U 426
Reichenbach-Klinke	Kurt	(35)	Kaptlt.	U 217
Reichmann	Wilfried	(24)	K. Kapt.	U 153
Reimann	Ernst	(X/39)	Oblt. z. S.	U 3050
Reimers	Hans	D VIII/39	Lt. z. S. d. Res., Oblt. z. S. d. Res.	U 983, U 722
Reisener	Wolfgang	(X/38)	Oblt. z. S.	U 608
Reith	Hans-Edwin	(X/39)	Oblt. z. S.	U 190
Remus	Gerhard	(36)	Kaptlt.	U 2364
Remus	Werner	(X/39)	Oblt. z. S.	U 339, U 554
Rendtel	Horst	(36)	Kaptlt.	U 641
Rex	Wilhelm	D X/35	Oblt. z. S. d. Res.	U 1405
Richard	Hellmuth	(36)	Oblt. z. S.	U 446
Richter	Freimut	(XII/39)	Oblt. z. S.	U 2547
Riecken	Werner	D III/34	Oblt. z. S. d. Res.	U 1017
Riedel	Heinrich	(XII/39)	Oblt. z. S.	U 242
Rieger	Eberhard	(X/40)	Oblt. z. S.	U 416
Rieger	Hubert	(XII/39)	Oblt. z. S.	U 4
Riekeberg	Wolfgang	(IV/37)	Kaptlt.	U 1054
Riesen, van	Friedrich	D I/38	Oblt. z. S. d. Res.	U 1109
Riesen	Rolf	(X/38)	Oblt. z. S.	U 180
Rigoli	Roberto		TV	U 747
Rinck	Hans	D VII/41	Oblt. z. S. d. Res.	U 1019
Ringelmann	Helmuth	(31)	Kaptlt.	U 75
Rix	Robert	D VIII/38	Oblt. z. S. d. Res.	U 96
Robbert	Heinz	D X/39	Oblt. z. S. d. Res.	U 3040
Rodig	Johannes	(36)	Kaptlt.	U 878
Rodler von Roithberg	Hardo	(IV/37)	Oblt. z. S., Kaptlt.	U 24, U 989
Rogowsky	Peter	(X/38)	Oblt. z. S.	U 866
Rollmann	Siegfried	(34)	Kaptlt.	U 82
Rollmann	Wilhelm	(26)	K. Kapt.	U 848
Römer	Wolfgang	(36)	Oblt. z. S.	U 353
Ropp, von der	Dietrich	(29)	Kaptlt.	U 12
Rosenberg	Günther	(36)	Oblt. z. S.	U 201
Rosenberg-Gruszczynski, von	Hans-Achim	(IV/37)	Oblt. z. S.	U 384

Name	First Name	Class	Rank	U-No.
Rosenstiel, von	Jürgen	(33)	Kaptlt.	U 502
Rossetto	Mario		TV	U 430
Roßmann	Hermann	(X/37)	Oblt. z. S.	U 273
Rostin	Erwin	(33)	Kaptlt.	U 158
Roth	Götz	(X/38)	Oblt. z. S.	U 368, U 1232
Rothkirch und Panthen, von	Siegfried	(X/38)	Oblt. z. S.	U 717
Röttger	Helmut	(IV/37)	Kaptlt.	U 715
Rudloff	Klaus	(35)	Kaptlt.	U 609
Rudolph	Johannes	(X/37)	Kaptlt.	U 2552
Ruperti	Günter	(IV/37)	Oblt. z. S., Kaptlt.	U 777, U 3039
Ruppelt	Günther	(X/37)	Oblt. z. S.	U 356
Ruwiedel	Kurt	(36)	Oblt. z. S.	U 337
Sach	Heinrich	D X/38	Oblt. z. S. d. Res.	U 3031
Sachse	Dietrich	(X/39)	Oblt. z. S.	U 28, U 413
Säck	Franz	(X/37)	Oblt. z. S. (K.O.)	U 251
Sammler	Karl-Heinz	(X/37)	Oblt. z. S.	U 675
Sass	Paul-Heinrich	(X/38)	Oblt. z. S.	U 364
Sass	Werner	(X/37)	Kaptlt.	U 676
Sauerberg	Ernst	(XII/39)	Oblt. z. S.	U 1225
Sauerbier	Joachim	(X/39)	Oblt. z. S.	U 56
Sausmikat	Werner	(IV/37)	Kaptlt.	U 774
Schaar	Gerhard	(X/37)	Oblt. z. S., Kaptlt.	U 957, U 2551
Schacht	Harro	(26)	K. Kapt.	U 507
Schad von Mittelbiberach	Berchtold	D IX/39	Oblt. z. S. d. Res.	U 2342
Schaefer	Wolff-Axel	(30)	K. Kapt.	U 484
Schäffer	Heinz	(XII/39)	Oblt. z. S.	U 977
Schamong	Klemens	(IV/37)	Oblt. z. S.	U 468
Schatteburg	Hans	(XII/39)	Oblt. z. S.	U 1272
Schauenburg	Günther	(XII/39)	Oblt. z. S.	U 1409
Schauenburg	Herbert	(31)	Kaptlt.	U 577
Schauenburg	Rolf	(34)	Kaptlt.	U 536
Schauer	Werner	(X/40)	Oblt. z. S.	U 2350
Schauroth	Karl	(X/40)	Oblt. z. S.	U 146
Scheibe	Hans-Martin	(36)	Kaptlt.	U 455
Scheltz	Hans Ulrich	D X/34	Oblt. z. S. d. Res.	UD 5
Schendel	Eberhard	(XII/39)	Oblt. z. S.	U 636
Schendel	Rudolf	(32)	K. Kapt.	U 2509, U 2520

Name	First Name	Class	Rank	U-No.
Schepke	Joachim	(30)	Kaptlt.	U 100
Scherfling	Wolfgang	(X/40)	Oblt. z. S.	U 140
Scheringer	Heinz	(27)	Kaptlt.	U 26
Schetelig	Robert	(IV/37)	Oblt. z. S.	U 229
Schild	Hans-Jürg	(X/38)	Oblt. z. S.	U 924
Schimmel	Günter	(XII/39)	Oblt. z. S.	U 30, U 382
Schimpf	Karl	(36)	Kaptlt.	U 803, U 3009
Schley	Hans-Jürgen	(XII/39)	Oblt. z. S.	U 3507
Schlieper	Alfred	(34)	Oblt. z. S.	U 208
Schlitt	Karl-Adolf	(IV/37)	Kaptlt.	U 1206
Schlömer	Fokko	(X/37)	Kaptlt. (KO)	U 3061
Schlott	Heinrich	(X/40)	Oblt. z. S.	U 2329
Schmandt	Adalbert	D I/40	Oblt. z. S. d. Res.	U 489
Schmid	Heinrich	(34)	Kaptlt.	U 663
Schmidt	Friedrich	(XII/39)	Oblt. z. S.	U 793
Schmidt	Hellmut	(X/40)	Oblt. z. S.	U 60
Schmidt	Karl-Heinz	D V/36	Oblt. z. S. d. Res.	U 3529
Schmidt	Werner	(X/39)	Oblt. z. S.	U 292
Schmidt	Werner Karl	(35)	Kaptlt.	U 250
Schmidt-Weichert	Hans-Joachim	(36)	Oblt. z. S.	U 9, U 3501
Schmoeckel	Helmut	(36)	Kaptlt.	U 802
Schnee	Adalbert	(34)	K. Kapt.	U 2511
Schneewind	Fritz	(36)	Kaptlt.	U 511, U 183
Schneider	Herbert	(34)	Kaptlt.	U 522
Schneider	Manfred	(XII/39)	Oblt. z. S.	U 4706
Schneidewind	Karl-Hermann	(27)	K. Kapt.	U 1064
Schnoor	Ebe	D XII/15	Kaptlt. d. Res.	U 460
Schöler	Clemens	(36)	Oblt. z. S.	U 20
Scholle	Hans-Ulrich	D I/38	Oblt. z. S. d. Res.	U 328
Scholz	Günther	(X/38)	Oblt. z. S.	U 284, UD 2, U 1052
Scholz	Hans-Ulrich	D I/40	Oblt. z. S. d. Res.	U 4703
Schönberg	Adolf	(X/37)	Oblt. z. S.	U 404
Schonder	Heinrich	(34)	Kaptlt.	U 200
Schöneboom	Dietrich	(IV/37)	Oblt. z. S.	U 431
Schötzau	Gerhard	(36)	Kaptlt.	U 880
Schramm	Joachim	(36)	Oblt. z. S.	U 109
Schreiber	Gerd	(31)	Kaptlt.	U 95
Schreiber	Heinrich	(X/37)	Oblt. z. S.	U 270

Name	First Name	Class	Rank	U-No.
Schreiner	Wolfgang	(IV/37)	Oblt. z. S.	U 417
Schrenk	Hans	(IV/37)	Kaptlt.	U 901
Schrenk	Hermann	(IV/37)	Kaptlt.	U 3511
Schrewe	Peter	(34)	Kaptlt.	U 537
Schreyer	Hilmar	(X/38)	Oblt. z. S. (K.O.)	U 987
Schrobach	Kurt	(I/41)	Oblt. z. S.	U 2360
Schröder	Gustav	(XII/39)	Oblt. z. S.	U 1056
Schröder	Heinrich	D IX/39	Oblt. z. S. d. Res.	U 2367
Schröder	Hermann	(36)	Oblt. z. S.	U 623
Schroeteler	Heinrich	(36)	Kaptlt.	U 1023
Schroeter	Karl-Ernst	(34)	Kaptlt.	U 752
Schroeter, von	Horst	(X/37)	Oblt. z. S., Kaptlt.	U 123, U 2506
Schröter	Karl-Heinz	(X/39)	Oblt. z. S.	U 763, U 3062
Schrott	Karl	(32)	Kaptlt.	U 551
Schug	Walter	(34)	Kaptlt.	U 86
Schüler	Philipp	(34)	Kaptlt.	U 602
Schüler	Wolf-Harald	(X/39)	Oblt. z. S.	U 2325
Schulte	Max	(33)	Kaptlt.	U 13
Schulte	Werner	(31)	Kaptlt.	U 582
Schultz	Diedrich	D VIII/40	Oblt. z. S. d. Res.	U 4708
Schultz	Hermann	(X/38)	Oblt. z. S.	U 3502
Schultz	Karl-Otto	(34)	Kaptlt.	U 216
Schultze	Heinz-Otto	(34)	Kaptlt.	U 849
Schultze	Rudolf	(XII/39)	Oblt. z. S.	U 2540
Schultze	Wolfgang	(30)	Kaptlt.	U 512
Schulz	Hermann	(38)	Oblt. z. S.	U 2327
Schulz	Richard	D X/39	Oblt. z. S. d. Res.	U 58
Schulz	Werner	D XI/39	Oblt. z. S. d. Res.	U 929
Schulz	Wilhelm	(32)	Kaptlt.	U 64
Schümann	Henning	(X/37)	Oblt. z. S.	U 392
Schumann-Hindenberg	Friedrich	(32)	K. Kapt.	U 245
Schunck	Hans-Norbert	(X/38)	Oblt. z. S.	U 348, U 369
Schütt	Heinz	D X/36	Oblt. z. S. d. Res.	U 294
Schütze	Herbert-Viktor	(35)	Kaptlt.	U 605
Schwaff	Werner	(36)	Oblt. z. S.	U 440
Schwalbach	Bruno	(X/37)	Kaptlt.	U 1161
Schwantke	Hans-Joachim	(36)	Oblt. z. S.	U 43
Schwarting	Bernhard	D X/36	Oblt. z. S. d. Res.	U 1102, U 905
Schwartzkopff	Volkmar	(34)	Kaptlt.	U 520

Name	First Name	Class	Rank	U-No.
Schwarz	Hans-Joachim	(X/38)	Oblt. z. S.	U 1105
Schwarzenberg	Hans-Dietrich	(X/40)	Oblt. z. S.	U 579
Schwarzkopf	Wolfgang	(XII/39)	Oblt. z. S.	U 2, U 21
Schwaßmann	Heinz	(35)	Kaptlt.	U 742
Schwebcke	Hans-Joachim	(IV/37)	Kaptlt.	U 714
Schweichel	Hans-Adolf	(36)	Oblt. z. S.	U 173
Schweiger	Friedhelm	(IV/37)	Kaptlt.	U 313
Schwirley	Ernst-Werner	(XII/39)	Oblt. z. S.	U 3510
Seeger	Joachim	D X/39	Oblt. z. S. d. Res.	UD 3
Seeger	Sigurd	(X/39)	Oblt. z. S.	U 1203
Seehausen	Gerhard	(IV/37)	Oblt. z. S.	U 66
Seeliger	Edgar	D IV/40	Oblt. z. S. d. Res.	U 4702
Seibicke	Günther	(32)	Kaptlt.	U 436
Seidel	Hans	(IV/37)	Kaptlt.	U 361
Seiler	Wolfgang	(X/39)	Oblt. z. S.	U 3047
Sell	Erwin	D IV/40	Oblt. z. S. d. Res.	U 1102
Selle	Horst	(XII/39)	Oblt. z. S.	U 795, U 1408
Senkel	Hans	(32)	Kaptlt.	U 658
Sickel	Herbert	(35)	Kaptlt.	U 302
Siebold	Karl Hartwig	(36)	Kaptlt.	U 3504
Sieder	Heinz	(X/38)	Oblt. z. S.	U 984
Siegmann	Paul	(35)	Kaptlt.	U 612, U 2507
Siemon	Hilmar	(34)	Kaptlt.	U 396
Simmermacher	Volker	(IV/37)	Kaptlt,	U 3013
Siriani	Emerico		TV	U 750
Slevogt	Horst	(XII/39)	Oblt. z. S.	U 3032
Sobe	Ernst	(24)	F. Kapt.	U 179
Soden-Fraunhofen, Graf von	Ulrich	(35)	Kaptlt.	U 624
Sons	Friedrich	D I/40	Oblt. z. S. d. Res.	U 479
Spahr	Wilhelm	(35)	Kaptlt.	U 178
Speidel	Hans Harald	(36)	Kaptlt.	U 643
Spindlegger	Johann	(35)	Kaptlt.	U 411
Staats	Georg	(35)	Kaptlt.	U 508
Stahl	Peter	D I/38	Oblt. z. S. d. Res.	U 648
Stähler	Helmuth	(IV/37)	Kaptlt.	U 928
Stark	Günther	(36)	Kaptlt.	U 740
Staudinger	Oskar	(36)	Kaptlt.	U 638
Steen	Hans	(IV/37)	Kaptlt.	U 233

Name	First Name	Class	Rank	U-No.
Steffen	Karl	D VII/40	Oblt. z. S. d. Res.	U 2345
Steffens	Klaus-Dietrich	(IV/37)	Kaptlt.	U 719
Stege	Friedrich	(X/39)	Oblt. z..S.	U 958
Stegemann	Hasso	(X/39)	Oblt. z. S.	U 367
Stegmann	Johann	D X/35	Oblt. z. S. d. Res.	U 779
Stein	Heinz	(36)	Kaptlt.	U 620
Steinaecker, Freiherr von	Walter	(35)	Kaptlt.	U 524
Steinbeck	Ernst-Georg	D X/39	Oblt. z. S. d. Res.	U 1027
Steinbrink	Erich	(X/38)	Oblt. z. S.	U 953
Steinert	Hermann	(36)	Kaptlt.	U 128
Steinfeldt	Friedrich	D IV/40	Oblt. z. S. d. Res.	UIT 21, U 195
Steinhoff	Friedrich	(35)	Kaptlt.	U 873
Steinmetz	Karl-Heinz	(XII/39)	Oblt. z. S.	U 993
Stellmacher	Dietrich	D IV/39	Oblt. z. S. d. Res.	U 865
Stephan	Karl-Heinz	D V/36	Kaptlt. d. Res.	U 1063
Sternberg	Heinz	(36)	Kaptlt.	U 473
Stever	Ehrenreich	(X/37)	Kaptlt.	U 1277
Sthamer	Hans-Jürgen	(X/37)	Oblt. z. S.	U 354
Stiebler	Wolf-Harro	(32)	Kaptlt., K. Kapt.	U 21, U 461
Stipriaan, van	Johannes	D IV/40	Oblt. z. S. d. Res.	U 3046
Stock	Hans	(35)	Kaptlt.	U 659
Stock	Rupprecht	(IV/37)	Kaptlt.	U 218
Stoeffler	Otto	(X/39)	Kaptlt.	U 475
Stoelker	Gerhard	D XI/39	Oblt. z. S. d. Res.	U 825
Stolzenburg	Gottfried	D I/38	Oblt. z. S. d. Res.	U 2543
Sträter	Wolfgang	(35)	Kaptlt.	U 614
Straub	Siegfried	(X/39)	Oblt. z. S.	U 625
Strauch	Günter	(33)	Kaptlt.	U 1010
Strehl	Hugo	(XII/39)	Oblt. z. S.	U 351
Strelow	Siegfried	(31)	Kaptlt.	U 435
Striegler	Hans-Werner	(X/37)	Oblt. z. S.	UIT 23, U 196
Strübing	Werner	D I/42	Oblt. z. S. d. Res.	U 1003
Stuckmann	Hermann	(X/39)	Oblt. z. S.	U 621
Studt	Bruno	D X/39	Oblt. z. S. d. Res.	U 488
Stührmann	Günter	(X/40)	Oblt. z. S.	U 904
Sturm	Kurt	(25)	K. Kapt.	U 167
Sues	Peter	(X/38)	Oblt. z. S.	U 388
Sureth	Kurt	(XII/39)	Oblt. z. S.	U 2549

Name	First Name	Class	Rank	U-No.
Süß	Walter	D I/40	Oblt. z. S. d. Res.	U 1304
Tammen	Renko	(I/41)	Oblt. z. S.	U 148
Taschenmacher	Erich	(X/38)	Oblt. z. S.	U 775
Teichert	Max-Martin	(34)	Kaptlt.	U 456
Thäter	Gerhard	(36)	Kaptlt.	U 466, U 3509
Thiel	Gemot	(X/40)	Oblt. z. S.	U 152
Thienemann	Sven	D X/39	Oblt. z. S. d. Res.	U 682, U 1271
Thimme	Jürgen	(IV/37)	Oblt. z. S.	U 716
Thomsen	Rolf	(36)	Kaptlt.	U 1202
Thurmann	Helmut	(36)	Kaptlt.	U 1234
Thurmann	Karl	(28)	K. Kapt.	U 553
Tiesenhausen, Freiherr von	Hans-Diedrich	(34)	Kaptlt.	U 331
Tiesler	Raimund	(X/37)	Oblt. z. S.	U 649, U 976
Timm	Heinrich	(32)	K. Kapt.	U 862
Tinschert	Otto	(35)	Kaptlt.	U 267, U 903
Tippelskirch, von	Helmut	(IV/37)	Oblt. z. S.	U 439
Todenhagen	Diether	(X/37)	Oblt. z. S.	U 365
Topp	Erich	(34)	Oblt. z. S., F. Kapt.	U 57, U 3010, U 2513
Trojer	Hans	(36)	Kaptlt.	U 221
Trotha, von	Claus	(36)	Kaptlt.	U 306
Trotha, von	Wilhelm	(36)	Oblt. z. S., Kaptlt.	U 733, U 745
Trox	Hans-Georg	(36)	Kaptlt.	U 97
Turre	Eduard	(X/39)	Oblt. z. S.	U 868
Uebel	Johannes	D IV/40	Oblt. z. S. d. Res.	U 883
Ufermann	Fritz	(V/41)	Oblt. z. S. (K.O.)	U 2368
Uhl	Georg	(X/37)	Oblt. z. S.	U 269
Uhlig	Herbert	(35)	Kaptlt.	U 527
Ulber	Max	(XII/39)	Oblt. z. S.	U 680
Ulbing	Willibald	(XII/39)	Oblt. z. S.	U 2347
Umlauf	Hans Hugo	(IV/37)	Kaptlt.	U 1168
Unterhorst	Ernst Günther	(X/37)	Oblt. z. S.	U 395
Unverzagt	Günter	(XII/39)	Oblt. z. S.	U 965
Uphoff	Horst	(35)	Kaptlt.	U 84
Utischill	Karl-Erich	(X/39)	Oblt. z. S.	U 2548
Valentiner	Hans Guido	(IV/37)	Kaptlt.	U 385
Vanselow	Jürgen	(X/37)	Kaptlt.	U 2555
Varendorff, von	Amelung	(35)	Oblt. z. S.	U 213

Name	First Name	Class	Rank	U-No.
Verpoorten	Hubert	(X/40)	Oblt. z. S.	U 19
Vöge	Ulrich	(X/38)	Oblt. z. S.	U 239, U 2536
Vogel	Hans	(X/37)	Kaptlt.	U 3025
Vogel	Viktor	(32)	Kaptlt.	U 588
Vogelsang	Ernst	(31)	Kaptlt.	U 132
Vogler	Helmut	(35)	Kaptlt.	U 212
Voigt	Horst	(X/38)	Oblt. z. S.	U 1006
Vowe	Bruno	D X/23	Oblt. z. S. d. Res.	U 462
Wächter	Karl-Jürg	(36)	Kaptlt.	U 2503
Wäninger	Ludwig	D VII/40	Oblt. z. S. d. Res.	U 4715
Wahlen	Rolf-Birger	(36)	Kaptlt.	U 23, U 2514, U 2541
Waldkirch	Heinz	D X/36	Oblt. z. S. d. Res.	UC 2
Walther	Herbert	(V/41)	Lt. z. S. (K.O.)	U 59
Warnecke	Heinrich	D X/39	Oblt. z. S. d. Res.	U 4718
Wattenberg	Jürgen	(21)	F. Kapt.	U 162
Weber	Klaus	(I/41)	Oblt.(Ing)	U 637
Weber	Paul	(IV/37)	Kaptlt.	U 3022
Weber	Werner	(32)	K. Kapt.	U 845
Wehrkamp	Helmut	(XII/39)	Oblt. z. S.	U 275
Weidner	Friedrich	(X/37)	Oblt. z. S., Kaptlt.	UD 1, U 2518
Weiher	Horst	(36)	Kaptlt.	U 854
Weingaertner	Hannes	(27)	K. Kapt.	U 851
Weitz	Friedrich	(X/38)	Oblt. z. S.	U 959
Wellner	Horst	(29)	Kaptlt.	U 16
Wendelberger	Erhard	(XII/39)	Oblt. z. S.	U 720
Wenden, von	Eberhard	(IV/37)	Kaptlt.	U 37
Wendt	Karl-Heinz	(X/38)	Oblt. z. S.	U 1276
Wendt	Werner	D IV/38	Oblt. z. S. d. Res.	U 765
Wengel	Hans	(35)	Kaptlt.	U 1164
Wentz	Rolf-Werner	(X/39)	Oblt. z. S.	U 963
Wenzel	Wolfgang	(34)	Kaptlt.	U 231
Wermuth	Otto	(X/39)	Oblt. z. S.	U 530
Werner	Alfred	D X/38	Oblt. z. S. d. Res.	U 921
Werner	Herbert	(XII/39)	Oblt. z. S.	U 415
Werr	Arno	(X/39)	Oblt. z. S.	U 241
Westphalen	Otto	(X/38)	Oblt. z. S.	U 968
Wetjen	Eberhard	(35)	Oblt. z. S.	U 147
Wex	Dieter	(XII/39)	Oblt. z. S.	U 2354

Name	First Name	Class	Rank	U-No.
Wichmann	Walter	(X/37)	Oblt. z. S.	U 639
Wicke	Helmut	(X/39)	Oblt. z. S.	U 1231
Wieboldt	Günter	(X/37)	Kaptlt.	U 295
Wiechmann	Arnold	D IX/39	Oblt. z. S. d. Res.	U 4701
Wieduwilt	Helmut	(X/38)	Oblt. z. S.	U 718
Wigand	Wolf	D XII/39	Oblt. z. S. d. Res.	U 1108
Wilamowitz-Moellendorff, von	Georg	(12)	K. Kapt. z. V.	U 459
Wilberg	Ernst-August	D I/38	Oblt. z. S. d. Res.	U 666
Wilke	Hans-Dietrich	D V/32	Oblt. z. S. d. Res.	U 766, U 2553
Will	Josef	D X/39	Oblt. z. S. d. Res.	U 318
Willner	Horst	(X/38)	Oblt. z. S.	U 3505, U 3034
Winkler	Werner	(36)	Oblt. z. S.	U 630
Wißmann	Friedrich-Wilhelm	(35)	Oblt. z. S.	U 18
Witt	Hans-Ludwig	(29)	K. Kapt.	U 3524
Witte	Werner	(35)	Kaptlt.	U 509
Wittenberg	Friedrich	(X/37)	Oblt. z. S.	U 856
Witzendorff, von	Ernst	(IV/37)	Kaptlt.	U 2524
Woermann	Germanus	D VIII/40	Oblt. z. S. d. Res.	U 2339
Wohlfarth	Herbert	(33)	Kaptlt.	U 556
Wolf	Eckehard	(X/37)	Oblt. z. S., Kaptlt.	U 966, U 2556
Wolf	Heinz	(34)	Kaptlt.	U 465
Wolfbauer	Leo	13 (K.u.K.)	K. Kapt. z.V.	U 463
Wolff	Günter	D X/39	Oblt. z. S. d. Res.	U 2550
Wolff	Heinz	(IV/37)	Oblt. z. S., Kaptlt.	U 974, U 985, U 3534
Wolfram	Ralf-Reimar	(30)	K. Kapt.	U 864
Wollschläger	Otto	(X/37)	Oblt. z. S.	UC 2
Wörißhoffer	Ulrich	(36)	Oblt. z. S.	U 83
Wrede	Hans-Christian	(X/39)	Oblt. z. S.	U 1234
Wulff	Heinrich	D VIII/40	Oblt. z. S. d. Res.	U 646
Wunderlich	Karl	D II/41	Oblt. z. S. d. Res.	UIT 22
Würdemann	Erich	(33)	Kaptlt.	U 506
Wurmbach	Reinhard	(IV/37)	Kaptlt.	U 3058
Wysk	Gerhard	(X/38)	Oblt. z. S.	U 322
Zahnow	Günter	(X/39)	Oblt. z. S.	U 747
Zander	Hermann	(X/37)	Kaptlt.	U 1205
Zander	Joachim	(36)	Kaptlt.	U 311
Zapf	Werner	(V/41)	Lt. z. S.	U 61

Name	First Name	Class	Rank	U-No.
Zeißler	Herbert	(X/38)	Oblt. z. S.	U 1194
Zenker	Walter	(X/38)	Oblt. z. S. (K.O.)	U 3535
Zeplien	Walter	(X/37)	Oblt. z. S.	U 971
Ziehm	Ernst	(33)	Kaptlt.	U 232
Ziesmer	Reimar	(IV/37)	Oblt. z. S.	U 236, U 591
Zimmermann	Gero	(29)	Kaptlt.	U 401
Zimmermann	Heinrich	(30)	Kaptlt.	U 136
Zinke	Armin	(32)	K. Kapt.	U 1229
Zitzewitz, von	Alexander	(34)	Kaptlt.	U 706
Zoller	Herbert	(X/38)	Oblt. z. S.	U 315
Zorn	Rudolf	(X/37)	Oblt. z. S. z.V.	U 650
Zurmühlen	Bernhard	(33)	Kaptlt.	U 600
Zwarg	Heinz	(IV/37)	Kaptlt.	U 276, U 3528

INDEX 2

ALLIED AND AXIS COMMANDING OFFICERS AND PILOTS

Name	U-No.	Name	U-No.
Abbot, Evelyn David John, Lt. Comdr. RN	U 213	Armstrong, William Norman, P/O RCAF	U 231
Abel, Brent Maxwell, Lt. Comdr. USNR	U 66	Atkinson, Robert, Lt. RNR	U 878
Abel-Smith, Edward Michael Conolly, Capt. RN	U 89, U 203	Aubrey, Robert Marriott, Lt. Comdr. RN	U 449, U 504, U 462
Abram, Rider Stewart, Lt. Comdr. RN	U 238, U 592	Auslander, Stanley E., Lt.(jg) USNR	U 590
Adams, John F., Lt. Comdr. USNR	U 575	Austen, Nigel Hubert George, Lt. RN	U 79
Akins, R. T., Major USAAF	U 848	Austin, Bernhard Lige, Comdr. USN	U 173
Alexander, Robert Love, Lt. Comdr. RN	U 308	Avery, Howard Malcolm, Lt. Comdr. USN	U 402, U 860
Allan, John Alfred Robert, A/Lt. Comdr. RCNVR	U 1302	Ayles, Sydney, Lt. RNR	U 82
Allen, Conway Benning, Comdr. RN	U 82, U 135, U 204, U 213	Ayre, Albert, Lt. Comdr. RNR	U 89, U 753
Allon, James Joseph, T/Lt. RNR	U 744	Babanov, Wasilij Alexandrowitsch, Kl. Soviet Navy	U 362
Allsop, Gordon Campbell., F/Sgt RAAF	U 336	Baines, Edward Francis, Lt. RN	U 1191
Anderson, Charles Courtney, Lt. RN	U 714	Baker, Francis John Torrence, Lt. Comdr. USNR	U 518
Anderson, Jack D., Ens. USNR	U 509	Baker, Howard Jefferson, Lt.(jg) USN	U 761
Anderson, Wilbert, F/Sgt RNZAF	U 535		
Ardern, Frank, T/A/Lt. Comdr. RNR	U 390	Baker-Cresswell, Addison Joe, Comdr. RN	U 110
Armstrong, Harold Thomas, Capt. RN	U 223, U 589	Baldwin, Charles Arba, Lt.[jg], Lt. USNR	U 598, U 848

Name	U-No.	Name	U-No.
Balfrey, Charles Patrick, A/Lt. Comdr. RCNR	U 1006	Beloe, Isaac William Trant, Lt. Comdr. RN	U 286
Ballantine, John Holme Jr., Lt.(jg) USNR	U 160	Bennett, Gordon, Lt. RNVR	U 344
Balliett, Letson. Samuel, Lt.(jg) USN	U 584	Bennett, Edwin Brian, Sub-Lt. RNVR	U 973
Banks, William Eric, Comdr. RN	U 65	Bennett, Sidney William Floyd, Lt. Comdr. RN	U 443
Barling, John William, P/O \ F/L RAF	U 605, U 441	Bennington, Leslie William Abel, Lt. Comdr. RN	UIT 23
Barnard, David Thomas, F/Sgt RAAF	U 97	Benson, Arthur James, F/Sgt RAAF	U 564
Barnes, William Roy, Lt. Comdr. USN	U 960	Bentinck, Wolf Walter Rudolf, Capt. RN	U 277, U 674, U 959
Barnett, Lionel Oscar, F/L RAFVR	U 197	Berdine, Harold Sloop, Comdr. USCG	U 175
Barton, Claude N., Lt.(jg) USN	U 509	Beresford, Peter John, T/Sub-Lt. RNVR	U 472
Barwood, Andrew William, F/L RAFVR	U 331	Beverley, Herbert James, Lt. Comdr. RNR	U 252, U 414
Bass, Harry Brinkley, Lt. USN	U 160	Bickford, Edward Oscar, Lt. Comdr. RN	U 36
Bastable, Brian, F/O RAFVR	U 241	Bidwell, Vivian Dickerson Hamlin, Lt. Comdr. RNR	U 1279
Batcheller, James Harvey Jr., Lt. USN	U 490	Bigo, Ernest Henri Paul Marie, Ensign de vaisseau 1, FAFL	U 403
Bateman, Cecil Julian, Lt. RN	U 453	Billingsley, Edward Baxter, Comdr. USN	U 616
Bateman, Lorenco John, F/O RCAF	U 846	Birch, Anthony John Wyndham, F/O RAFVR	U 463
Bates, Geoffrey Hamilton, Lt. RNVR	U 81	Birch, John Dudley, Comdr. RN	U 257, U 536
Baveystock, Leslie Harold, F/O \ F/L RAFVR	U 955, U 107	Birch, John Travis Beaufroy, Lt. Comdr. RN	U 568
Bayliss, Horace Temple Taylor, Capt. RN	U 344, U 394, U 653, U 765	Bishop, Albert Alton, F/O RCAF	U 489
Beach, Joseph F., Lt. USNR	U 194	Biskupski, Boleslaw, Comdr. ORP	U 407
Beatty, David Creagh, Lt. RN	U 413	Black, Peter Claud Shipton, Lt. RN	U 965
Beaty, Arthur David, F/O RAFVR	U 575	Blackburn, Reginald John, Sub-Lt. RNVR	U 1060
Beck, Frederick Allan, T/Lt. RCNVR	U 356	Blake, Charles Benjamin, T/A/Lt. Comdr. RN	U 300
Behague, Albert Charles Comdr. RN	U 407	Bland, Eric Arthur, F/L RAFVR	U 844
Bell, Charles Leigh de Hauteville, Lt. Comdr. RNR	U 306	Blyth, Robert Edwin, A/Lt. Comdr RNVR	U 765
Bell, James Nicolson Pratt, F/O RAF	U 273		

Name	U-No.	Name	U-No.
Bockett-Pugh, Ian Hamilton, Comdr. RN	U 581	Brooke, Ronald de Leighton, Lt. Comdr. RN	U 443
Bodden, Keith Desmond, W/O RAFVR	U 1007	Brooks, Edward John, F/O RAF	U 55
Bodinet, Philip A., Lt.(jg) USNR	U 640	Broom, James Reginald Turner, T/Lt. RNVR	U 617
Bone, David Drummond, Lt. Comdr. RN	U 1199	Brown, Bernard Henry, Lt. RN	U 371
Bonner-Davis, George Graham, T/Lt. RNVR	U 212	Brown, Harold Hinksman, Lt. RNR	U 135, U 1199
Bookless, John Henderson, F/O RAAF	U 280	Brown, Kenneth Binfield, T/A/ Lt. Comdr. RNVR	U 731
Bostock, John, Lt. Comdr. RN	U 63	Brownell, Ralph Bliss, Lt.(jg) USNR	U 508
Bourke, Leo Patrick, Lt. Comdr. RNZNR	U 327, U 757, U 989, U 1278	Brownsill, Anthony Gerald, F/L RAFVR	U 927
Bovell, Henry Cecil, Capt. RN	U 517	Brunini, William Herbert, P/O RCAF	U 617
Bowerman, Harold Godfroy, Lt. Comdr. RN	U 207, U 587	Bruneau, Arthur Andrew, F/O RCAF	U 579
Bowles, Walter George, Sub-Lt. RNZN	U 752	Buer, John, Lt. RNAF	U 482
Boys-Smith, Humphrey Gilbert, Comdr. RNR	U 136	Bulloch, Terence Malcolm, S/L RAF	U 597, U 611, U 514
Bradshaw, Harold George, Lt.(jg) USN	U 850	Bulmer, K. H. N., P/O RCAF	U 960
Brent, Trevor Montague, F/Sgt RAFVR	U 573	Burcher, Cyril Wallace, F/O RAAF	U 632, U 643
		Burfield, John Blackmore, Lt. RN	U 722, U 1001
Brewer, Charles Walter, Lt. Comdr. USN	U 378. U 185, U 487	Burhanna, Howard, Jr., Capt. USAAF	U 512
Brewer, Godfrey Noel, Comdr. RN	U 334, U 438	Burnett, James Arbouin, Lt. Comdr. RN	U 845
Bridge, James, T/Sub-Lt. RNVR	U 331	Burton, John Thomas, Lt. USNR	U 863
Bridgman, Clement Edward, Lt. Comdr. RNR	U 379	Butler, Ian Bishop, F/O RAFVR	U 562
Brilliant, Stanley, Lt. RNVR	U 288	Butler, Sidney William, F/L RAFVR	U 625
Brinton, C. R., Capt.	U 205	Buxton, Winslow H., Lt. Comdr. USCG	U 866
Brock, John, T/A/Lt. Comdr. RCNVR	U 1302	Buzzard, Anthony Wass, Comdr. RN	U 53
Brock, Jeffry Vanstone, Lt. Comdr. RCNVR	U 600	Byrd, Thomas Hugh, Lt. Comdr. USNR	U 613
Brocklehurst, C. M., F/Sgt	U 1007	Byron, John, Lt. Comdr. RNR	U 131
Brokas, Alex X., Lt.(jg) USNR	U 1229	Cadle, John W., Jr., Ens. USNR	U 505
Bromage, John Henry, Lt. RN	U 301	Caemmerer, Ernst von, Oblt. z. S. d. Res.	U 416
Bromley, Douglas Henry Read, Lt. Comdr. RN	U 450		

Name	U-No.	Name	U-No.
Callaway, Arthur Henry, Lt. Comdr. RANVR	U 111	Clayton, John Every, T/Lt. RCNR	U 87
Camacho, Vivian Evelyn, F/O RCAF	U 292	Clerke, Frederick John, P/O RAAF	U 77
Cambridge, Robert Arthur Dillon, Lt. Comdr. RNR	U 1024	Cochrane, Dundonald Nelson, F/O RAFVR	U 372
Campbell, Allan Donald Peter, Lt. RN	U 765, U 1051	Cockroft, Irving G., Lt.(jg) USN	U 850
		Cole, William H., Lt.(jg) USNR	U 1059
Capey, John, F/O RAFVR	U 981	Coleman, Albert Robert Ernest, Lt. Comdr. RCNR	U 224
Caple, Reginald Lacey, Lt. RN	U 358		
Carey, Harold C., Lt.(jg) USN	U 128	Collinson, Frank Bentley, Lt. Comdr. RNR	U 436
Carmichael, John William, F/L RAF	U 629		
		Colquhoun, Kenneth Stuart, A/Capt. RN	U 711
Case, Richard Vere Essex, Lt. Comdr. RNR	U 134		
Casement, Peter Reginald, F/L RAF	U 751	Colthurst, Anthony Paul, Comdr. RN	U 589
Cassleman, George Washington, Lt. Comdr. USNR	U 505, U 515, U 546	Conder, Edward Reignier, Comdr. RN	U 55
Castell, Edgar Frederick, F/O RAFVR	U 77	Conkey, George Lissant, Lt. Comdr. USN	U 549
Castens, George William Emil, Comdr. RN	U 634	Conner, Ray Russell, Comdr. USN	U 960
Chair, Henry Graham Dudley de, Lt. Comdr. RN	U 162	Cooke, John Malcolm, W/O RAFVR	U 616
Chamberlain, William F., Lt.(jg) USNR	U 569, U 860, U 118	Cooke, Thomas Charles, F/O RCAF	U 342
Chapman, Cecil St.George William, W/C RCAF	U 715	Cooper, Jack Winston, A/Lt. Comdr. RNR	U 636
Chapman, Lewis William, F/Sgt RAFVR	U 533	Cooper, Leslie George, Sub-Lt. RNVR	U 277, U 959
Chesterman, Harold Geeves, Lt. RNR	U 125	Cooper, Thomas, T/Lt. RN	U 436
		Cornish, Donald Mervin, Sgt/F/Sgt RCAF	U 431, U 566, U 542
Chevasse, Evelyn Henry, Comdr. RN	U 89	Coughlin, Clifton Rexford, Lt. Comdr. RCNVR	U 744
Church, William John Patrick, Lt. Comdr. RN	U 562	Coumbis, Alexander, F/Sgt RAFVR	U 126
Clark, Leslie George, P/O RAFVR	U 384	Coventry, Cecil Dick Bluett, Lt. Comdr. RNR	U 672, U 1191
Clarke, Irwin Alexander Fraser, F/L RAAF	U 106	Cowell, Patrick James, Lt. Comdr. RN	U 394
Clarke, John Richard, T/A/Lt. Comdr. RNVR	U 1195	Cowey, Robert Leonard, P/O \ F/O RAFVR	U 627, U 710
Claudius, Herbert Gordon, Lt Comdr. USNR	U 166	Cowherd, Grant, Lt. Comdr. USNR	U 548

Name	U-No.	Name	U-No.
Cox, Clifford C., Lt.(jg) USN	U 572	Delgado, Mario Ramirez, Alférez de Fregata Cuban Navy	U 176
Crawford, George, A/S/L RAFVR	U 391	Dempster, Edward William Charles, T/A/Lt. Comdr. RNVR	U 307
Crist, Marion Edward, Capt. USN	U 860	Deneys, James Godfrey Wood, Lt. Comdr. RN	U 100
Crocker, Joseph Clement, Lt. Comdr. USNR	U 879	Denison, Orville B., Lt. USNR	U 1279
Crockett, Lewis D., Lt. USNR	U 615	Denne, John Richard Alured, Lt. RN	U 722
Cruickshank, John Alexander, F/O RAF	U 361	Denny, Leslie Perman, Lt. \ A/Lt. Comdr. RCNR	U 753, U 877
Chrutchfield, Robert Reynolds, Lt. USNR	U 548	DeWolf, Henry George, Comdr. RCN	U 971
Crutchley, Victor Alexander Charles, Capt. RN	U 64	Diggens, Allen Augustus, A/Lt. Comdr. RN	U 212
Culme-Seymour, Sir Michael, Lt. Comdr. RN	U 49	Dobbs, William A., Lt. Comdr. USCG	U 1062
Cumberland, Peter Earnest, T/Sub-Lt. RNVR	U 653	Dobson, Andrew Hedley, A/Lt. Comdr. RCNR	U 87, U 90
Cundy, Peter John, S/L RAF	U 628	Donaghy, Alan Victor, Lt. RNR	U 1060
Currie, Robert Alexander, Comdr. RN	U 767	Doran, Andrew Edward, A/Comdr. RN	U 300
Curry, Ralph R., Comdr. USCG	U 371	Dowty, Norman Taylor, Lt.(jg) USNR	U 1059, U 801
Dalison, John Stanley, Comdr. RN	U 448	Draney, Robert William, Lt. Comdr. RCNR	U 575
Dallmeyer, William Alexander, Comdr. RN	U 32	Dresbach, John William, Lt.(jg) USNR	U 615
Dalton, Kelvin Reginald, F/Sgt RAAF	U 167	Drummond, James Ralph, Lt. RN	U 303
Daniel, Charles Saumarez, Capt. RN	U 39	Drummond, Roderick Patrick, F/L AAF	U 707
D'Arcy, Kenneth Judge, A/Capt. RN	U 711	Dryden, John E. Jr., Lt. USNR	U 156
Darling, Stanley, Lt. Comdr. RANVR	U 333, U 736, U 1063	Duck, Norman Winder, Comdr. RNR	U 333, U 385
Davidson, Jack R., Lt. Comdr. USNR	U 879	Dudley, James Robert, Capt. USN	U 378
Davies, Thomas D., Lt. Comdr. USN	U 604	Duff, Howard Carlton, Lt. Comdr. USNR	U 546
Davis, Howland S., Lt. USNR	U 128	Dulm, Johannes Frans van, Lt. Comdr. RNN	U 95
Dawkins, Marion Vance Jr., Lt.(jg) USNR	U 849	Dundas, Alexander Derek Stewart, F/L RAFVR	U 821
Dawson, James Crosbie, Lt. Comdr. RNR	U 198	Dunkerley, E. D., Sub-Lt. RNVR	U 577
Delap, Miles Villiers, S/L RAF	U 31	Dunn, James Alexander, Lt. RCNVR	U 536

Name	U-No.	Name	U-No.
Dunn, Joseph Brantley, Capt. USN	U 575, U 172, U 525, U 850	Fisher, Robert Frank, F/L RCAF	U 341
		Fiss, Gordon R., Lt. USN	U 94
Dyer, Kenneth Lloyd, Lt. Comdr. RCN	U 588	Fleming-Williams, Donald Charles, F/O RAFVR	U 304
Dyer, Richard, Lt. Comdr. RN	U 744	Fletcher, Graham Reynal Philips, Sub-Lt. RNVR	U 131
Eaden, John Henry, Lt. Comdr. RN	U 314, U 409, U 767	Flynn, Walter T., Lt. USNR	U 521
Eadie, David William, F/L RAFVR	U 418	Foley, James Louis, Lt. Comdr. USN	U 515
Eames, William Edward James, Comdr. RN	U 207	Foley, Joseph Ferall, Comdr. USN	U 616
Edwards, George E. Jr., Ens. USNR	U 860	Ford, William Render, Lt. USNR	U 598, U 164, U 848
Egan, Rupert Cyril, Lt. Comdr. RN	U 372	Forney, Junior C, Lt.(jg) USNR	U 664, U 117
Ellis, Arthur Hubert, F/O RAFVR	U 340	Forrester, James R., F/O RCAF	U 852
		Fowler, Wilma William, Lt.(jg) USNR	U 584, U 118
Ellison, Henry Bramhall, Comdr. RN	U 55	Foxall, Leslie Lewendon, Lt. Comdr. RCNR	U 356
Enloe, George Albert, Lt. USNR	U 271	Franks, Robert Denys, Lt. RN	U 651
Ensor, John Bernard, S/L	U 411	Fraser, Alexander William, A/F/L RAAF	U 200
Ensor, Maechel Anthony, F/O RNZAF	U 259	Fraser, James Philip, Lt. Comdr. RCNR	U 257
Erskine, John M., Lt.(jg) USNR	U 615	Freaker, Ronald Clifford, Lt. Comdr. RNR	U 327, U 334, U 556, U 954, U 989, U 1278
Evans, Martin James, Comdr. RN	U 229		
Evenou, Jules, Capt. de frègate FNFL	U 136		
Evershed, Walter, Lt. Comdr. RN	U 102	Freeth, John Samuel, F/Sgt RAAF	U 227
Evert, Thomas Rudolph, Lt. USNR	U 84	French, Frank John, S/L RAFVR	U 601
Feldman, Herbert, Lt. Comdr. USCGR	U 866	French, William Maynard, F/O RCAF	U 563
Fick, Harold Foster, Capt. USN	U 43, U 160, U 509	Frizell, Thomas Frederick Peter, F/O RAAF	U 675
Field, Russell Norman, Lt. USNR	U 681	Fry, Kenneth Gregson, F/L RAAF	U 454
Fifas, Dimitrios, Lt. Comdr. RHN	U 458		
Finch, John, F/L RAFVR	U 761	Fryatt, Harry E., Lt.(jg) USNR	U 118
Finnessy, Joseph Patrick, F/O RAFVR	U 575	Gall, Douglas Muir, F/L RAFVR	U 440
		Gallery, Daniel Vincent, Capt. USN	U 68, U 515, U 505, U 544
Finnie, Robert J., Lt. USNR	U 135		
Firth, Charles Leslie, Comdr. \ Capt. RN	U 63, U 407	Gallmeier, Charles F., Lt. USAAF	U 558
Fisher, Eric Joseph, F/O RAFVR	U 232	Gambetta, Mario, TV Regia Marina	U 557

Name	U-No.	Name	U-No.
Gamble, George Douglas, F/O RAFVR	U 964	Grubb, Frederick Ernest, Lt. RCN	U 501
Garwood, Robert Cecil Somers, Cdr. RN	U 1051	Gunn, Ian Donald, W/O RAFVR	U 966
Gates, Richard Thomas Fairfax, W/C RAF	U 608	Gurnette, Byron Lawrence, Comdr. USN	U 616
Gaylord, Elisha C., Lt.(jg) USNR	U 172	Gwinner, Clive, Lt. \ A/Comdr. \ Comdr. RN	U 91, U 226, U 358, U 392,
Gex, Virgil Edward, Lt. Comdr. USNR	U 546		U 462, U 1191
Gibbs, Edward Albert, Comdr. RN	U 27, U 203, U 162	Hadow, Philip Henry, Lt. Comdr. RN	U 39
Gibson, William Norman, F/L RAAF	U 26	Hall, Daniel Alfred, Lt. Comdr. SANF(V)	U 714
Gladstone, Gerold Vaughan, Cdr. RN	U 136	Hall, Harry John, Lt. \ Lt. Comdr. RNR	U 660, U 671
Goldie, Thomas Hugh Evelyn, F/L RAFVR	U 3523	Hamilton, Joseph L., Capt.	U 706
		Hammer, Arthur J., Lt. USAAF	U 404
Goodfellow, William Patterson, Lt. Comdr. RNVR	U 413, U 671, U 1191	Hanbury, Reader Dennison, F/O RAFVR	U 607, U 106
Goodwin, Glendon C., Lt.(jg) USN	U 850	Hanbury, Ross Malcolm, Lt. Comdr. RCNVR	U 1003
Goord, Anthony Brian, Cdr. RIN	U 198	Hance, Kenneth Perry, Lt. USN	U 850
Goossens, Hendrikus Abraham Waldemar, Lt. Comdr. RNN	U 168	Hancock, Cecil William, A/T/Lt. Comdr. RNR	U 1014
Gordon, Bernard John, T/Lt. RNVR	U 343	Hands, Thomas Henry, T/Sub-Lt. RNVR	U 517
Gordon, Stirling, T/A/Lt. Comdr. RNVR	U 441	Handshuh, Harold L., Ens. USNR	U 220
Gould, Richard Kaynor, Lt. Comdr. USN	U 68	Harkness, Archibald Ferguson, Lt. RNR	U 205
Grant, John William, Capt. RN	U 711	Harkness, Kenneth Lanyon, Comdr. RN	U 49
Green, Howard Morley Saville, F/O RAF	U 595	Harris, Bryan Webster, T/A/Lt. RNVR	U 741
Green, James Chalmers, P/O RAFVR	U 109	Harris, Morgan Hamilton, Comdr. USNR	U 549
Green, Percy, W/C RAF	U 852	Harrison, Aislabie, T/Lt. Comdr. RNR	556
Greer, Marshall Raymond, Capt. USN	U 67, U 185, U 847, U 487	Hart, Raymond, Lt. \ Lt. Comdr. RN	U 274, U 282, U 630, U 767,
Gregory-Smith, William Frank Niemann, Lt. Comdr. RN	U 568		U 905, U 965, U 531
Gretton, Peter William, Cdr. RN	U 274, U 282	Hartley, Eric Leeming, F/O RAFVR	U 221
Groos, Harold Victor William, A/ Lt. Comdr. RCN	U 744	Hatherly, Gordon Leslie, F/L RAFVR	U 635

Name	U-No.	Name	U-No.
Hay, Sidney M., Lt. Comdr. USCGR	U 550	Hogan, Gerald G., Lt.(jg) USNR	U 664
Hayes, John Douglas, Lt. Comdr. RN	U 617	Holden, Philip Dana, Lt. Comdr. USNR	U 518
Hayman, Robert W., Lt.(jg) USNR	U 378	Holderness, Harold Hardwicke Clarke, S/L RAFVR	U 1060
Headland, Edwin Harvey, Lt. Comdr. USN	U 515	Holdsworth, John Arundell, Lt. RN	U 761
Heathcote, Ralph, Comdr. RN	U 69, U 353	Holland, Thomas Venables, F/Sgt RAAF	U 447
Heckey, Albert Rossville, Comdr. USN	U 616	Holmes, Theodore M., Lt.(jg) USNR	U 615
Heim, Elbert Stewart, Lt.(jg) USNR	U 422, U 118, U 460	Hoodless, Colin Arthur, T/Lt. RNR	U 215
Henderson, Stuart, T/Lt. RCNR	U 356	Hopgood, Robert B., Lt.(jg) USNR	U 464
Henley, Maurice William, Sub-Lt. RNVR	U 365	Hornell, David Ernest, F/L RCAF	U 1225
Heron, Peter William, F/O RCAF	U 283	Horrocks, Harry, A/T/Sub-Lt. RNVR	U 752
Herrick, Terence Desmond, Lt. RN	U 79	Howard-Johnston, Clarence Dirsmore, Comdr. RN	U 651
Hewitt, Charles G., Lt.(jg) USNR	U 525	Howe, Hamilton Wilcox, Lt. Comdr. USN	U 85
Hezlet, Arthur Richard, Lt. Comdr. RN	U 859	Howell, Wiley Basil, F/O RAFVR	U 502
Higgins, Edward Matthews, Lt. USNR	U 172	Huber, Oblt. z.S.	U 18
Hill, Harold, Lt. Comdr. RNR	U 213	Huey, Fred, Lt. Comdr. USNR	U 248
Hill, Henry Knox, A/T/Lt. Comdr. RCNVR	U 536	Hughes, Alwyn Phillips, T/A/Lt RNR	U 731
Hill, Leonard Charles, Lt. Comdr. RNR	U 441, U 214	Hughes, Francis Massie, Capt. USN	U 1059, U 66, U 801
Hill, William Edward, Lt. USNR	U 848	Hugonin, Rowland Etienne Sinclair, Lt. Comdr. RN	U 449, U 504, U 462
Hilliard, Aubrey Henry, F/O RAFVR	U 976	Hunt, Anthony Reece Arthur, P/O RAFVR	U 751
Hirshfield, James A., Comdr. USCG	U 606	Hunter, William, F/L RAF RAFVR	U 364
Hodgkinson, David Beatty, S/L RCAF	U 617	Huntley, John Hubert, A/Capt. RN	U 288
Hodgkinson, John James, Lt. RCNR	U 756	Hutchins, Charles Harris, Lt. USNR	U 405
Hodson, Norman D., Lt. USN	U 664, U 117	Hutchinson, George, Lt. Comdr. USN	U 616
Hoerner, Helmuth Ernest, Lt. USNR	U 68	Hutchison, William Joseph Lennox, Sub-Lt. RNVR	U 365
Hoffman, George Dewey, Lt. Comdr. USN	U 801		
Hoffman, Norman Cutten, Lt. Comdr. USNR	U 233		

Name	U-No.	Name	U-No.
Ingram, John Charles Anthony, Lt. Comdr. RN	U 125, U 988	Kellogg, David M., Lt. Comdr. USNR	U 879, U 233
Irvine, James McCabe, Lt. Comdr. USNR	U 248	Kent, Arthur Horace, Lt. RNR	U 660
Isbell, Arnold Jay, Capt. USN	U 402, U 422, U 584, U 664, U 525, U 117, U 460	Kerrigan, Harold Fleming, F/L RCAF	U 470
		Kiley, John C. Jr., Lt. Comdr. USNR	U 880, U 1235
Iselin, Lewis, Lt. Comdr. USNR	U 853	Kinaszczuk, Thomas, Lt.(jg) USNR	U 174
Israel, Neil Frederick, Lt. \ T/A/ Lt. Comdr. RNR	U 225, U 285, U 1172	King, Clarence Aubrey, A/Lt. Comdr. \ A/Cdr. RCNR	U 94, U 311, U 448, U 845
Isted, Desmond James, S/L RAF	U 623	King, Henry Alexander, Comdr. RN	U 35
Jakimov, Gregory, Sgt. RAAF	U 83		
Jackson, Ernest E., Lt.(jg)	U 117	King, Hugh Valentine, Cdr. RN	U 135
Jackson, John, Lt. Comdr. RNR	U 302, U 657	Kinney, Sheldon Hoard, Lt. USN	U 801
James, Francis Henry William, F/Sgt RAF	U 646	Kirkwood, Henry, Lt. Comdr. RN	U 593
		Kitkat, John Percy de Winton, Lt. Comdr. RN	U 286, U 1014
Jefferies, John, Comdr. RN	U 450		
Jenkins, Ralph Grosvenor, Lt. Comdr. RN	U 962, U 538	Knapton, Eric Guy Philip Bromfield, Lt. Comdr. RN	U 1024
Jennings, William Thomas Henry, F/O RAFVR	U 459	Knowles, Eric, F/L RAF	U 540
		Knox, Dudley S., Lt. Comdr. USNR	U 505, U 546
Jester, Maurice D., Lt. Comdr. USCG	U 352	Koenig, Penev A., Lt. USAAF	U 654
Jewiss, Edward Arthur, F/O	U 452	Kolenko, Alexander Petrowitsch, Obltn. Soviet Navy	U 250
Johansen, Erling Ulleberg, Lt.	U 998		
Johansen, John Edwin, Lt. Comdr. USNR	U 1224/ RO-501	Krafft, Carl Frederik, Lt. RNAF	U 423
		Krug, Edward Arthur, Lt. USNR	U 863
Johns, Hugh Richard Lewis, Sub-Lt. RNZNVR	U 1060	Kuenning, Thomas E., Lt. USN	U 435
		Lacon, Reginald William Beecroft, Lt. RN	U 74, U 98
Johnson, Robert J., Lt.(jg) USNR	U 118		
Johnston, Means Jr., Lt. Comdr. USN	U 515	LaFleur, Wallace A., Lt.(jg) USNR	U 850
Jones, Basil, Comdr. RN	U 45	Lake, Frederick George, Lt. USNR	U 1107
Jones, Frederick John Gwynn, Lt. Comdr. RNR	U 1208		
		Lambert, Wilfred, A/Lt. Comdr. RNVR	U 618, U 441
Josselyn, John William, Comdr. RN	U 45	Lambton, Hedworth, Cdr. RN	U 425
Judson, Charles Sterling, Lt. Comdr. USN	U 869	Lampen, David, Lt. Comdr. RN	U 655
		Lanyon, Norman, Lt. Comdr. RN	U 86, U 223
Kabbe, Karl, Kapitän	U 580	Laughland, Andrew Russell, F/L RAF	U 332
Kamlah, Kurt, K. Kpt.	U 737		
Kane, Harry J., Lt. USAAF	U 701	Launders, James Stuart, Lt. RN	U 711, U 864

Name	U-No.	Name	U-No.
Lawrence, John Thornett, F/L RAFVR	U 1008	MacBride, Robert Ernest, F/L RCAF	U 477, U 478
Layard, Arthur Frank Capel, Comdr. RN	U 247, U 311, U 309	MacBryde, Ernest P., Lt. Comdr. USCGR	U 866
Leadbitter, Charles William, A/Lt. Comdr. RNR	U 1014	MacInnes, A. A., F/Sgt	U 705
Lee-Barber, John, Comdr. RN	U 456	MacIntyre, Donald George Frederick Wyville, Comdr. RN	U 99, U 100, U 269, U 357, U 765, U 186, U 191
Levasseur, Jean, Capt. de frègate FLNL	U 432, U 444		
Lewis, Frank C., Ens. USNR	U 576	MacIver, Peter Graeme, Lt. Comdr. RNR	U 147
Lewis, John David Walter, T/Lt. RNVR	U 246	MacKendrick, Douglas William, Comdr. RN	U 131
Liddington, Bernard Potter, P/O RAFVR	U 599	MacLean, Donald Murdo, Comdr. RN	U 962
Liermann, Heinz, Kptlt.	U 235	Main, Philip, Capt. USAAF	U 848
Lingle, Van A. T., Lt.(jg) USNR	U 392	Mainprize, Maxwell Stanley, F/L RAAF	U 563
Little, Donald Arthur, F/O RAAF	U 270		
Livingstone, Charles Alexander, P/O RAFVR	U 595	Majendie, Lewis Bernard Alexander, A/Comdr. RN	U 445
Lloyd-Williams, Hugh, Lt. Comdr. RNVR	U 70	Malins, Charles Wickham, Lt. Comdr. RN	U 458
Loney, Wesley Glen, P/O RAAF	U 470	Manners, John Errol, Lt. RN	U 1274
Long, Ralph W., Lt. USN	U 847	Mansfield, Donald Emberton, Lt. Comdr. RN	U 538
Longton, Ernest William, Comdr. USN	U 616	Marczak, Rudolf, W/O RAFVR	U 321
		Markham, James, F/O RAFVR	U 619
Lord, George Alfred Bertram, F/O RAFVR	U 595	Markham, Lewis Merrill Jr., Lt. Comdr. USN	U 173
Loveland, Kenneth, Lt. Comdr. USN	U 575	Marrows, Dudley, F/L RAAF	U 461
		Marshall, James Gilbert, Comdr. USN	U 172
Lucas, Richard David, A/F/L RAAF	U 571	Martin, Arthur Desmond Stanley, F/Sgt RAFVR	U 412
Luce, John David, Lt. Comdr. RN	U 51		
Ludwig, Lloyd, Lt.(jg)	U 507	Martin, Desmond Samuel Royst, Lt. RN	U 644
Luke, Manuel, Chief Aviation Pilot USAAF	U 582	Mason, Donald Francis, CPO ACMM (AA)	U 503
Lumby, Michael Geoffrey Rawson, Lt. RN	U 335	Mason, James Francis, Sub-Lt. RNVR	U 366
Lundon, Gordon David Arthur, F/O RAFVR	U 268	Mathews, Jerry A., Lt. Comdr. USNR	U 575
Mabley, Louis Christopher Lt. Comdr. \ Comdr. USNR	U 248, U 546	Matuski, Anthony R., Lt. USNR	U 615
		Maud, Colin Douglas, Lt. Comdr. RN	U 35, U 45

Name	U-No.	Name	U-No.
Maxwell, F. W. L., Capt. SAAF	U 476	Mills, Ronald George, Comdr. RN	U 399, U 441 U 618, U 1208, U 1169
Mayhew, Geoffrey Richard, F/O RAFVR	U 442		
Mayo, Robert C., Lt.	U 759	Mitchell, David Reynolds, Lt. Comdr. RN	U 562
McAuslan, Alexander C., Lt.(jg) USNR	U 584, U 217	Mitchell, Roy Howard, F/O RAFVR	U 852
McCabe, Frank M., Lt. Comdr. USCG	U 866	Moffat, John Knox, F/O RAFVR	U 189
McCabe, Gordon Wallis, Sub-Lt. RNVR	U 288	Moffat, William Purves, A/Lt. Comdr. RCNVR	U 744
McClintock, Hubert Victor Perry, Capt. RN	U 366, U 472, U 973	Moffit, Barry Haig, S/L RCAF	U 209
McCormick, Nelson C., Lt.(jg) USCG	U 157	Mogilevskij, Sergej Sergejewitsch, Kpt 3.Rg Soviet Navy	U 367
McCullen, Colin William, Comdr. RN	U 484	Moore, Frederick Lee, Ens. USNR	U 543
McDonell, Walter S., Lt. USAAF	U 951	Moore, Kenneth Owen, F/O RCAF	U 373, U 740
McEwen, John Finch, F/L RAFVR	U 389	Moore, Ronald James, F/Sgt RAFVR	U 559
Mackintosh, Lachlan Donald, Capt. RN	U 1060	Moore, William Josselyn, Comdr. RNR	U 482
McIssac, Wilfred, Lt. RCNVR	U 163	Moran, William Francis, Lt. USNR	U 172
McLane, William M., Ens. USNR	U 544	Morrison-Payne, Christopher, T/A/Lt. Comdr. RNVR	U 286
McMahon, Richard E., Ens. USNR	U 860	Morsier, Pierre de, Capt. De frègate FNFL	U 609
McQueen, J. W., F/Sgt	U 447	Moseley, Michael Grange, P/O RAFVR	U 347
McRae, Donald Farquhar, F/O RCAF	U 211	Mosse, John Pemberton, Lt. Comdr. RN	U 354, U 394
McWhorter, John H., Lt. Comdr. USNR	U 154, U 488, U 490	Mulhe, Joseph, Master Roosevelt Steamship Co., Inc	U 576
Melson, Charles Leroy, Lt. Comdr. USN	U 130	Mundy, E. A. K., W/O	U 960
Merriman, Peter Gordon, Lt. Comdr. RN	U 340	Murphy, Geoffrey, F/L RAF	U 1007
Micklethwait, St. John Aldrich, Capt. RN	U 372	Murray, Franklin M., Lt. USNR	U 220
		Murray, Kenneth McKenzie, F/L RAFVR	U 320
Millard, Robert C, Lt. USN	U 408, U 467	Musgrave, John, F/L RAFVR	U 753
Miller, Herman Edward, Lt. Comdr. USN	U 183	Musson, Rowland Gascoigne, W/C RAF	U 614
Miller, Roger Francis, Lt. Comdr. USNR	U 172	Myerscough, John, Sub-Lt. RNVR	U 331

Name	U-No.	Name	U-No.
Myhre, Leonard A., Lt. Comdr. USNR	U 248, U 546	Parker, Norman John, Lt. Comdr. RN	U 636
Nash, F/Sgt	U 568	Parry, Gerald Joseph, Lt. RNR	U 1191
Nash, Edgar Shepherd Stow, F/L RAF	UIT 22	Parsons, Samuel G., Lt. USNR	U 68
Nicholson, Kenneth Montgomery, Lt. Comdr. RNR	U 651	Patrick, Willis W., Lt. Comdr. USNR	U 546
Nickerson, Roger Brown, Lt. Comdr. USN	U 173	Patterson, Harry B., Lt.(jg) USNR	U 161
Nicol, John Douglas, W/O RAFVR	U 534	Patterson, Ian Costin, S/L RAF	U 331
		Pavelka, Josef, F/O RAFVR	U 1060
Nixon, Charles Patrick, A/Lt. Comdr. RCN	U 621, U 744	Pavillard, Louis Raymond, A/Lt. Comdr. RCNR	U 757
Nixon, John M., Lt. USCG	U 869	Paynter, Maxwell Henry, P/O RAAF	U 545
Noall, William Robert Boyce, Lt. RNR	U 204	Pearson, Frederick John, F/O RAFVR	U 1007
Noble, Allan Herbert Percy, Lt. Comdr. RN	U 162	Pearson, Randolph Brougham, Lt. RN	U 331
Norrie, Keith, F/O RAFVR	U 821	Peck, Barry Edwards, F/L RAFO	U 470
Norris, Stephen Hugh, Lt. Comdr. RN	U 39	Pennell, John Henry, Lt. RN	U 719
Northey, Adrian Paul, Lt. RN	U 76	Perabo, Phil Jr., Lt.(jg) USNR	U 118
Nott, Dwight Dee, Lt. USNR	U 326	Petch, William Napier, Lt. Comdr. RN	U 559
Null, Robert S., Lt. Comdr. USNR	U 615	Peters, James Ernest Louis, Lt. RNR	U 135
Nunn, Stanley George, F/L RAFVR	U 821	Petrov, Nikolaj Iwanowitsch, Kl. Soviet Navy	U 144
Nutter, Reginald Charles, F/L RAFVR	U 52, U 101, U 276	Phibbs, Karl Henry John Lynals, Lt. Comdr. RN	U 732
Ogilvie, George Alexander Kinloch, F/O RAFVR	U 755	Phillips, Lionel Haultain, Lt. Comdr. RN	U 841
Oliver, Hedley James, F/O RAFVR	U 1017	Piggott, William Brown, Comdr. RNR	U 340, U 528
O'Neill, Martin G., Lt.(jg) USNR	U 185	Pinholster, David C., Lt.(jg) USNR	U 159
Ormsby, Gerald Anthony Gore, Lt. Comdr. RN	U 386, U 406	Pinnell, Carrell Ivan, Lt.(jg) USN	U 177
Orpen, Arthur Frederick St.George, Comdr. RN	U 147	Pitulko, Franciszek, Lt. Comdr. ORP	U 606
Osbourne, Frederick Meares, Lt. Comdr. RANVR	U 878	Playne, Edward, A/T/Lt. Comdr. RNVR	U 774, U 1051
Oulton, Wilfred Ewart, W/C RAF	U 266, U 563	Pleydell-Bouverie, Anthony Hon, Comdr. RN	U 472, U 988
Parish, William Wells, Lt. USNR	U 966	Pickard, Anthony Fenwick, T/Lt. Comdr. RCNR	U 744
Parker, Geoffrey William Tyndall, F/L RAFVR	U 317		

Name	U-No.	Name	U-No.
Plomer, James, Lt. Comdr. RCNVR	U 282, U 631, U 638	Reeves-Brown, John Vivian, Lt. RN	U 91, U 358
Pomeroy, Arthur Shubrook, Lt. RN	U 587	Rendell, Amos John, F/O RAF	U 843
Poncet, Pierre Marie André, Capt. de corvette FNFL	U 371	Renken, Henry Algernon, Comdr. USN	U 616
Potier, Gilbert George, F/L RAFVR	U 618	Renwick, James, T/Lt. RNR	U 433
		Rice, Frederick Charles, PO RN	U 64
Powell, William Garth, F/L RAFVR	U 1060	Rich, Lawrence St.George, Lt. Comdr. RN	U 131
Powers, Earle A., Lt. USAAF	U 182	Richmond, Maxwell, Capt. RN	U 289
Powlett, Philip Frederick, Lt. Comdr. RN	U 434, U 131	Richmond, Robert Fern, Lt.(jg) USNR	U 43
Prentice, James Douglas, Comdr. RCN	U 621, U 678, U 501	Ritchie, Andrew E., Lt. Comdr. USNR	U 880, U 1235
Price, Hugh Percival, Lt. Comdr. RN	U 33	Roberts, Howard S., Lt. USNR	U 569
		Roberts, John Parker, F/O RAAF	U 426
Price, Rodney Athelstan, Lt. Comdr. RN	U 187	Roberts, Wolffe W., Lt. USNR	U 505
Proctor, James Richard Eastham, S/L RAF	U 258	Roberson, George Peter, P/O RAFVR	U 624
Pryse, Henry Leslie, Comdr. RNR	U 264, U 424, U 762	Robertson, James Ian, Capt. RN	U 752
		Robertson, James McIntosh, Lt. USN	U 371
Puckett, David O., Lt.(jg) USNR	U 422, U 460	Robin, Clarence Ernest, F/O RCAF	U 197
Purse, Cuthbert Richard, Lt. Comdr. RN	U 443	Robinson, B. G. H., F/O	U 960
Putt, Willie Furneaux, Master British India Steam Navigation Co Ltd.	U 132	Robinson, Edward LaPage, F/O RCAF	U 658
Quinn, Howard Lee, Lt. Comdr. RCNVR	U 1302	Roddick, Frederick James, F/L RCAF	UIT 22
Quinn, James, F/L RAFVR	U 970	Rodgers, Bryan Humphrey Craig, T/A/Lt. Comdr. RNVR	U 732
Ramsden, Kenneth Ludlam Holmes, P/O RAFVR	U 265	Rodney, Nigel Robert Harley, Lt. Comdr. RN	U 450
Ramsey, Logan Carlisle, Capt. USN	U 220	Rogers, Benjamin Andrew, Lt. Comdr. RNR	U 1279, U 1018
Rankin, Christopher Henry, Lt. Comdr. RN	U 1172	Rogers, Richard S., Lt. USN	U 217, U 118
Rawson, Ralph W., Lt. USN	U 359	Roper, Edward Greason, Lt. Comdr. RN	U 457
Raymes, Daniel Francis, F/O RCAF	U 520	Rosenthal, Alvord Sydney, Comdr. RAN	U 127
Rayner, George James, F/L RAF	U 867	Rossiter, Geoffrey George, F/L RAAF	U 663
Read, Ernest William, F/O RAFVR	U 852	Rossum, August van, F/O RAF	U 462

Name	U-No.	Name	U-No.
Rountree, Frederick Manning, Lt.(jg) USN	U 847	Scott, Alexander Gordon, Lt. RNR	U 484
Rousselot, Henri L. G.. Lt. FNFL	U 702	Scott, Humphrey Gilbert, Comdr. RN	U 74
Rowland, James Marjoribanks, Lt. Comdr. RN	U 76	Scott, John, T/A/Lt. Comdr. RNVR	U 772, U 1014
Rowland, Richard H., Lt.(jg) USNR	U 662	Scott, Walter, Lt. \ Lt. Comdr. RN	U 559, U 568
Roxburgh, John Charles Young, Lt. RN	U 486	Scott, Walter William, F/Sgt RAFVR	U 821
Roxburgh, William, F/L RAFVR	U 469	Scott-Elliott, Ninian, Lt. Comdr. RN	U 1276
Rubinow, Sysney Godfrey, Jr., Lt. Comdr. USNR	U 546	Scott-Moncrieff, Alan Kenneth, Capt. RN	U 88
Russell, Alfred Herbert, F/O RCAF	U 610	Šedivý, Alois, S/L RAFVR	U 1060
Ruttan, Charles Graham, S/L RCAF	U 706	Segrave, William Francis Roderick, Lt. Comdr. RN	U 226, U 238, U 449, U 462
Ryall, J. P., W/O	U 852	Sellars, Jimmie J., Lt.(jg) USNR	U 66
Rycroft, Henry Richard, Lt. Comdr. RN	U 372	Sessions, William A., Lt. Comdr. USNR	U 550
Rylands, James Wolferstan, Lt. Comdr. RN	U 587	Shaffer III, John Jackson, Comdr. USN	U 856
Salis, Anthony Fane de, Capt. RN	U 138	Shaw, David Alexander, Lt. Comdr. RN	U 559
Sallenger, Asbury H., Lt.(jg) USNR	U 117	Shaw, David Byam, Lt. Comdr. RN	U 131
Salm, Ernest, Lt. USAAF	U 506	Sheardown, Harry R., F/L RCAF	U 620
Salz, Julius, Kapitän	U 670	Sheela, Barton C., Ens. USNR	U 402
Samuel, Adrian Christopher Ian, F/O RAFVR	U 169	Sheen, Charles Edward, Lt. RN	U 357
Sanders, Harry Marcus Crews, Lt. Comdr. RNR	U 26, U 556	Sheffield, Frederick George Barrington, Lt. Comdr. RNVR	U 394, U 765
Sanford, William L., Lt. USAAF	U 524	Sherbring, Milton J., Lt.(jg) USNR	U 1229
Saumarez, Philip Lionel, Lt. Comdr. RN	U 42	Sherman, Laurence, F/O RCAF	U 980
Sawtell, Goeffrey Allan., F/L RAFVR	U 558	Short, Giles Ezra, Capt. USN	U 569, U 217, U 118
Scatchard, John Percival, Lt. Comdr. RN	U 453	Short, Kenneth Albert, A/Capt. RN	U 365
Schapler, Walter-Gustav, Kptlt.	U 34	Simpson, John Howard, P/O RAFVR	U 595
Schnoor, Sergio Candido, Lt. FAB	U 199	Sinclair, Erroll Norman, Lt. Comdr. RN	U 971
Schoby, James F., Lt.(jg) USNR	U 487		
Schreder, Richard E., Lt. USN	U 158	Sissler, Bernard C., Lt.(jg) USNR	U 1229
Schuur, Heinrich, Kptlt.	U 15	Sisson, Brian Aubrey, S/L RAFO	U 990

Name	U–No.	Name	U–No.
Sleep, David Mackie, F/O RAFVR	U 216	Stearns, Robert Lloyd, Lt.(jg) USNR	U 422, U 527, U 118, U 460
Sly, Leslie Tillman, Lt. Comdr. RNR	U 600	Steiger, Earl Henry, Lt. USNR	U 487
Small, Norville Everett, S/L RCAF	U 754	Stephen, George Hay, Lt. Comdr. RCNR	U 845
Smith, Egbert Campbell, A/F/L RAAF	U 465	Stevens, Eric Barry Kenvyn, Comdr. / Capt. RN	U 559, U 42
Smith, Norman Edward Mace, F/L RAFVR	U 478	Stevens, James Edward, Comdr. USN	U 537
Smith, Thomas Hartley, Lt. RANR	U 617	Stewart, Charles Napier, Lt. RNR	U 641
Smith, Vivian Funge, Lt. Comdr. RNR	U 110	Stewart, Jack H., Ens. USN	U 525, U 847
Smith, William E., Lt.(jg) USN	U 199	Stewart, John Parker, Lt. Comdr. RNR	U 651
Smithwick, Michael Robert Standish, Lt.	U 86	Stiesberg, Frederick Max, Lt. Comdr. USN	U 616
Smythe, John Patrick, Lt. Comdr. RNR	U 634, U 124	Stonehouse, Herbert Arthur, A/Lt. Comdr. RNR	U 425, U 192
Snell, Basil Furness, F/Sgt RAFVR	U 261	Stoner, Percival John, Lt. Comdr. RN	U 327, U 989
Somerville, Philip, Lt. Comdr. RN	U 35	Strohbehn, Walter William, Comdr. USN	U 593
Sorenson, Paul, Lt.(jg) USNR	U 801	Strong, Lawrence Vezey, T/Lt. RNVR	U 561
Southall, Ivan Francis, P/O RAAF	U 385	Stuart, Daniel Alfriend, Comdr. USN	U 450
Sowell, Jesse Clyborn, Comdr. USN	U 128	Stuart, Orme Gordon, Lt. Comdr. RCNVR	U 722, U 1001
Spalding, Ralph David Jr., Lt. USNR	U 988	Stuart-Menteth, Henry Alexander, Lt. RN	U 587
Spear, Moncrieff J., Ens. USNR	U 860	Stubbs, John Hamilton, A/Lt. Comdr. RCN	U 210
Spears, Ralph C., Lt. USNR	U 392	Student, Vaclav, F/O RAFVR	U 165
Spotswood, Denis Frank, A/W/C RAFO	U 595	Sullivan, Eugene Thomas Bradley, Lt. Comdr. USN	U 488
Stacey, William Roland, Lt. Comdr. RCNVR	U 247	Sulton, John Jr., Lt.(jg) USNR	U 1229
Stafford, John H., Lt. USNR	U 879	Surridge, Albert Henley, F/L RAFVR	UIT 22
Stannard, Richard Been, Lt. Comdr. RNR	U 394, U 187	Swanson, Norman W., Lt. Comdr. USNR	U 488
Stapler, Charles Ramsay, Lt. USN	U 117	Sweeny, Robert Vincent, F/O RAFVR	U 404
Stark, James Braidwood, P/O RAFVR	U 528	Tague, James Robert, Capt. USN	U 543
St. Clair-Ford, Aubrey, Comdr. RN	U 75	Tait, Arthur Andre, Lt. Comdr. / Comdr. RN	U 93, U 208, U 444

Name	U-No.	Name	U-No.
Talbot, Arthur George, Capt. RN	U 331	Trigg, Lloyd Allan, F/O RNZAF	U 468
Tancock, Edward Bernard, Lt. Comdr. RN	U 27	Trofimov, Jewgenij Nikolajewitsch, Kl. Soviet Navy	U 639
Taylor, Bertram Wilfrid, Cdr. RN	U 1172	Tufts, David A., Lt. Comdr. USNR	U 154, U 490
Taylor, Samuel Kyle Jr., Lt. USNR	U 848	Tuke, Seymour Charles, Lt. Comdr. RN	U 13
Taylor, Thomas, Lt. Comdr. RN	U 110	Turnbull, Bryan Walker, A/W/O RNZAF	U 540
Tedder, Fondville Lee, Comdr. USN	U 128	Turner, Douglas Jackson, F/O RAFVR	U 976
Tennant, Robert Basil Stewart, Lt. Comdr. RN	U 340	Turner, Reginald Thomas Frederick, F/O RAFVR	U 529
Tennant, Raymond J., Lt.(jg) USNR	U 118	Turquand-Young, David, T/A/Lt. Comdr. RNVR	U 285
Tepuni, William, Ens. USNR	U 656	Tyson, Ismay James, Lt. Comdr. / Comdr. RNR	U 360, U 394, U 523
Thomas, Walter James, F/O RAF	U 844	Ungoed, Daniel William, Lt. RN	U 91, U 358
Thomkinson, Michael Wilfred, Lt. Comdr. RN	U 179	Valvatne, Sigurd, Lt. RNoN	U 974
Thompson, James Herbert, A/S/L RAFO	U 570	Vauchez, Pol, L.V. FAFL	U 105
Thompson, Ronald Bain, A/W/C AAF	U 417	Vaughan, Ronald William George, F/O	U 742
Thomson, Rodney Charles Vesey, Lt. Comdr. RN	U 124	Vella, Jan, F/O RAFVR	U 971
Thomson, William Harvie, T/Sub-Lt. RNVR	U 666	Vibert, Bruce Fraser, Sub-Lt. RNVR	U 674
Thornton, Frederick Harold, Lt. Comdr. RNR	U 954	Vivian, The Hon. Douglas David Edward, RN	U 1191
Thornton, Mark, Lt. Comdr. RN	U 32, U 208, U 559	Vopatek, Matthias J., Lt.(jg) USN	U 392, U 731
Thynne, Brian Winslow, F/O RAFVR	U 319	Vosseller, Aurelius Bartlett, Capt. USN	U 1229
Tilley, William Boris, F/O RAAF	U 243	Vranken, Edward van, Lt.(jg) USNR	U 43
Tilston, Arthur Robert James, T/Lt. RNR	U 306	Wade, James Yorke, F/L RAFVR	U 852
Todd, Percy, Capt. RN	U 63, U 45	Wadsworth, Thomas J., Ens. USNR	U 860
Tollaksen, Leslie Bliss, Lt. Comdr. USCG	U 853	Walgate, Richard, Lt. RNR	U 452
Toner, John Stannard, T/Lt. RNVR	U 288	Walker, Frederic John, Comdr. / Capt. RN	U 202, U 226, U 238, U 252, U 264, U 449, U 473, U 574, U 592, U 653, U 734, U 961, U 131, U 504, U 842, U 119, U 462
Toone, Louis George, Lt. RN	U 223		
Torres, Alberto Martins, Cadet FAB	U 199		
Townsend, David Franks, Lt. Comdr. RN	U 453		
Travell, Wilfred Roland, F/O RAFVR	U 575	Wallace, Arthur Francis, F/L RAFVR	U 871

Name	U-No.	Name	U-No.
Wallace, John Henry, Lt. Comdr. RN	U 761	Wicht, Edgar Jacques, A/S/L RAFO	U 274
Walter, Delton E., Lt. Comdr. USNR	U 881	Wilcox, Robert, Lt. Comdr. USCGR	U 550
Walters, Ivan Francis Bryant, F/L RAFVR	U 1222	Wilkinson, Peter McQuhae, Sub-Lt. RN	U 451
Wanless, Robert Hume, Lt. Comdr. USNR	U 856, U 488	Williams, George, F/O RAFVR	U 595
Ward, Peter Ronald, Lt. Comdr. RN	U 293	Williams, Robert Pershing, Lt. USNR	U 67, U 185, U 487
Warren, Edgar George, Lt. Comdr. RN	U 223, U 450	Williams, Russel Champion Jr., Cdr. USN	U 73
Waterhouse, John Valentine, Lt. Comdr. RN	U 201, U 661, U 1051	Willits, William Edward, A/F/L RAF	U 167
Watson, John B., Lt. USNR	U 1229	Willoughby, Guy, A/Capt. RN	U 288
Watson, John Manuel, Lt. RCN	U 845	Willson, William Herbert, Lt. Comdr. RCN	U 621, U 678
Waugh, Goree Edward, Lt.(jg) USNR	U 598	Wilmott, Alfred Ernest, Lt. Comdr. RNR	U 70
Webb, Charles D., Ens. USNR	U 576	Winder, Ralph Spearing, Lt. RNR	U 551
Webber, Denis Charles Leslie, F/O RAFVR	U 643	Windeyer, Guy Stanley, Lt. Comdr. RCN	U 356, U 588
Weigle, Donald E., Lt.(jg) USNR	U 860, U 460	Wolf, Henry George de, Capt. RCN	U 971
Wier, Henry Robert, Comdr. USN	U 73	Wolfendon, Richard, Lt. RNR	U 678
Wemyss, David Edward Gillespie, Lt. Comdr. RN	U 424, U 473, U 592, U 653, U 734, U 762, U 1279, U 504, U 842	Wood, Everett Waite, Lt. USNR	U 388
		Wooddell, Charles A., Lt.(jg) USNR	U 801
		Woodhouse, Leslie Ernest, Lt. Comdr. RN	U 522
Westhofen, Charles L., Comdr. USN	U 279	Woods, Sidney Richard James, Lt. Comdr. RNR	U 473, U 608
Weston, Tobin Subremont, Lt. RN	U 987	Woodward, Edward Arthur, Lt. RN	U 374
Wheeler, Edward, Comdr. RNR	U 354, U 989	Woolfenden, Joseph Eric, Lt. RNR	U 401
Whinney, Reginald Fife, Lt. Comdr. RN	U 377, U 390, U 523	Woolley, George Stephen, A/T/ Lt. Comdr. RNVR	U 413
Whitcomb, Roy Selden, Lt.(jg) USN	U 513	Woolley, Thomas Russell, Lt.(jg) USNR	U 761
White, Hugh Robert, Lt. Comdr. RN	U 567	Work, Magnus Spence, T/Lt. RNR	U 387
White, Richard Taylor, Comdr. RN	U 31, U 372, U 41	Worrell, Hubert L., Lt. USN	U 731
White, Stanley, F/O RAFVR	U 383	Worth, Peter Reginald George, A/ Lt. Comdr.	U 636, U 774
Whyte, James, F/O RNZAF	U 459		

Name	U-No.	Name	U-No.
Wright, John, F/L RAFVR	U 419, U 456	Young, F/Sgt	U 331
Wright, Henry Ward Beecher, F/O RAFVR	U 594	Young, Walter C., Lt.(jg) USNR	U 591
Wright, Kenneth Leon, Lt.(jg) USNR	U 966	Youngs, Joseph John, Lt. Comdr. RNR	U 651
Yeates, Gerald Norman Edgar, F/O RAFVR	U 821	Zanta, Otakar, F/Sgt RAFVR	U 966

INDEX 3

ALLIED AND AXIS SHIPS

Name	U-No.
Aconit (K.58), French corvette Flower I class [British] (ex *Aconite*)	U 432, U 444
Active (H. 14), British destroyer A class	U 340, U 179
Activity, British escort carrier *Activity* class	U 288
Affleck (K.462). British destroyer escort Captain class (ex American DE 71)	U 91, U 358, U 392
Ahrens (DE 575), American destroyer escort *Buckley* class	U 549
Aldenham (L.22), British destroyer escort Hunt III class	U 587
Alnwick Castle (K.405), British corvette Castle class	U 425
Alpino Bagnolini, Italian submarine *Console Generale Liuzzi* class	s. UIT 22
Amethyst (U.16), British sloop *Black Swan* [modified] class	U 1276
Angelburg, German target ship (ex Norwegian M/V *Viator*)	U 580
Anguilla (K.500), British frigate Colony class (ex American PF 72)	U 286
Annan (K.404), Canadian frigate River class	U 1006
Antelope (H.36), British destroyer A class	U 31, U 41
Anthony (H.40), British destroyer A class	U 761
Anton (ex *Mars*), German steam trawler	U 1234
Arabis (II)(K.73), British corvette Flower I class	U 651
Arbutus (K.86), British corvette Flower I class	U 70
Archer, British escort carrier *Archer* class (ex American AVG 1, ex M/V *Mormacland*)	U 752
Ascension (K.502), British frigate Colony class (ex American PF 74)	U 482
Assiniboine (1.18). Canadian destroyer River class (ex British *Kempenfelt*)	U 210
Atherton (DE 169). American destroyer escort *Cannon* class	U 853
Atule (SS 403), American submarine *Balao* class	U 977
Aubretia (K.96), British corvette Flower I class	U 110
Audacity, British escort carrier *Audacity* class	U 131
Avenger, British escort carrier *Avenger* class (ex American AVG 2, ex M/V *Rio Hudson*)	U 589
Aylmer (K.463), British frigate Captain class (ex American DE- 72)	U 765, U 1051

Name	U-No.
B 5, Norwegian submarine Holland class	s. UC 1
B 6, Norwegian submarine Holland class	s. UC 2
B-26, Soviet submarine	s. U 1231
B-27, Soviet submarine	s. U 2529
B-28, Soviet submarine	s. U 3035
B-29, Soviet submarine	s. U 3041
B-30, Soviet submarine	s. U 3515
B-100, Soviet test submarine	s. U 3515
Baker (DE 190), American destroyer escort *Cannon* class	U 233
Balfour (K.464), British frigate Captain class (ex American DE 73)	U 672
Balsam (K.72), British corvette Flower I class	U 135
Bamborough Castle (K.412), British corvette Castle class	U 387
Barber (DE 161), American destroyer escort *Buckley* class	U 488
Batiray, Turkish submarine *Saldiray* class	s. UA
Battleford (K.l65), Canadian corvette Flower I class	U 356
Bayntun (K.310), British frigate Captain class (ex American DE 1)	U 757, U 989, U 1278, U 327
Bazely (K.311), British frigate Captain class (ex American DE 2)	U 600, U 636
Bentinck (K.314), British frigate Captain class (ex American DE 52)	U 636, U 774, U 1051
Besugo (SS 321), American submarine *Balao* class	U 183
Beverly (H.64), British destroyer Town class (ex American DD 197)	U 187
Bicester (L.34), British destroyer escort Hunt II class	U 443
Bickerton (K.466), British frigate Captain class (ex American DE 75)	U 269, U 765
Biter, British escort carrier *Avenger* class (ex American, ex M/V *Rio Parana*)	U 89, U 203
Blackfly (FY.117), British A/S trawler (ex *Barnett*)	U 731
Black Swan (U.57), British sloop *Black Swan* class	U 124, U 600
Blackwood (K.313), British frigate Captain class (ex American DE 4)	U 600
Blaison, French submarine	s. U 123
Blankney (L.30), British destroyer escort Hunt II class	U 371, U 434, U 450, U 131
Blencathra (L.24), British destroyer escort Hunt I class	U 223, U 450
Bligh (K.467), British frigate Captain class (ex American DE 76)	U 765, U 1172
Block Island (CVE 21), American escort carrier *Bogue* class	U 1059, U 66, U 801, U 220
Blyskawica (H.34), Polish destroyer *Grom* class	U 278, U 363, U 368, U 481, U 825, U 1198, U 295, U 155, U 806, U 861, U 2321, U 2322, U 2324, U 2325, U 2341, U 2361

Name	U-No.
Bogue (CVE 9), American escort carrier *Bogue* class	U 569, U 575, U 217, U 172, U 527, U 1229, U 850, U 118
Bolkoburg, German target ship (ex German motor passenger ship *Ostwind*, ex Polish *Warszawa*)	U 670
Borie (DD 215), American destroyer *Clemson* (Flushdecker) class	U 405
Bostwick (DE 103), American destroyer escort *Cannon* class	U 879
Bouan, French submarine	s. U 510
Braithwaite (K.468), British frigate Captain class (ex American DE 77)	U 989, U 327
Brazen (H.80), British destroyer B class	U 49
Brecon (L.76), British destroyer escort Hunt IV class	U 450
Brissenden (L 79), British destroyer escort Hunt IV class	U 1191
Broadway (H.90), British destroyer Town class (ex American DD 194)	U 89, U 110
Bronstein (DE 189), American destroyer escort *Cannon* class	U 801
BSh-28, Soviet block ship	s. U 2529
Buckley (DE 51), American destroyer escort *Buckley* class	U 66, U 548
Bulldog (H.91), British destroyer B class	U 719, U 110
Burza (F.73), Polish destroyer *Burza* class	U 606
Byard (K.315), British frigate Captain class (ex American DE 55)	U 841
Byron (K.509), British frigate Captain class (ex American DE 79)	U 722, U 1001
Cachalot (N.83), British submarine *Porpoise* class	U 51
Calder (K.349), British frigate Captain class (ex American DE 58)	U 774, U 1051
Calgary (K.231), Canadian corvette Flower I class	U 322, U 536
Calpe (L.71), British destroyer escort Hunt II class	U 593
Camellia (K.31), British corvette Flower I class	U 70
Campania, British escort carrier *Campania* class	U 365
Campbell (WPG 32), American Coast Guard Cutter Treasury class	U 606
Camrose (K.154), Canadian corvette Flower I class	U 757
Card (CVE 11), American escort carrier *Bogue* class	U 402, U 422, U 584, U 664, U 525, U 847, U 117, U 460
Carter (DE 112), American destroyer escort *Cannon* class	U 518
Celandine (K.75). British corvette Flower I class	U 556
Chambly (K.116), Canadian corvette Flower I class	U 501
Champlin (DD 601), American destroyer *Bristol* class	U 130, U 856
Chaser, British escort carrier *Attacker* class	
(ex American *Breton* (ACV 10), ex M/V *Mormacgulf*)	U 366. U 472, U 973
Chatelain (DE 149), American destroyer escort *Edsall* class	U 505, U 515, U 546
Chaudière (H.99), Canadian destroyer River II class (ex British *Hero*)	U 621, U 744

Name	U-No.
Chilliwack (K.131), Canadian corvette Flower I class	U 356, U 744
Clemson (DD 186), American destroyer *Clemson* (Flushdecker) class	U 172
CM 1, Italian submarine CM class	s. UIT 7
CM 2, Italian submarine CM class	s. UIT 8
Coffman (DE 191), American destroyer escort *Cannon* class	U 879
Comandante Cappellini, Italian submarine *Marcello* class	s. UIT 24
Conn (K.509), British frigate Captain class (ex American DE 80)	U 905, U 965
Cooke (K.471), British frigate Captain class (ex American DE 267)	U 441, U 214
Core (CVE 13), American escort carrier *Bogue* class	U 378, U 67, U 185, U 487
Corry (DD 463), American destroyer *Bristol* class	U 801
Cotton (K.510), British frigate Captain class (ex American DE 81)	U 286
Crane (U.23), British sloop *Black Swan* [modified] class	U 962, U 538
Croome (L.62), British destroyer escort Hunt II class	U 372
CS 13, Cuban submarine chaser 83 ft-cutter class (ex American CG)	U 176
Cubitt (K.512), British frigate Captain class (ex American DE 83)	U 779, U 298, U 1230
Curzon (K.513), British frigate Captain class (ex American DE 84)	U 212
Cygnet (U.38), British sloop *Black Swan* [modified] class	U 962
Deptford (U.53), British sloop *Grimsby* class	U 567
Dianthus (K.95), British corvette Flower I class	U 225, U 379
Dommett (K.473), British frigate Captain class (ex American DE 269)	U 441
Douglas (I.90), British destroyer Admiralty Leader class	U 65
Drumheller (K.167), Canadian corvette Flower I class	U 753
Drury (K.316), British frigate Captain class (ex American DE 46)	U 636
Duckworth (K.351), British frigate Captain class (ex American DE 61)	U 399, U 441, U 618, U 1169, U 1208
Dulverton (L.63), British destroyer escort Hunt II class	U 559
Duncan (I.99), British destroyer *Duncan* class	U 274, U 282
DuPont (DD 152), American destroyer *Wickes* (Flushdecker) class	U 172
Easton (L.09), British destroyer escort Hunt III class	U 458
Ekins (K.552), British frigate Captain class (ex American DE 87)	U 212
Ellyson (DD 454), American destroyer *Bristol* class	U 616
Emmons (DD 457), American destroyer *Bristol* class	U 616
Eridge (L.68), British destroyer escort Hunt II class	U 568
Erna, German steam freighter	U 738
Erne (U.03), British sloop *Black Swan* class	U 213
Escort (H.66), British destroyer E class	U 63
Eskimo (F.75), British destroyer Tribal class	U 971
Essington (K.353), British frigate Captain class (ex American DE 67)	U 618, U 441

Name	U-No.
Eugene E. Elmore (DE 686), American destroyer escort *Rudderow* class	U 549
Exmoor (II)(L.08), British destroyer escort Hunt II class	U 450, U 131
Fame (H.78), British destroyer F class	U 69, U 353, U 767
Farquhar (DE 139). American destroyer escort *Edsall* class	U 881
Faulknor (H.62), British destroyer *Exmouth* class	U 138, U 88, U 39
Fearless (H.67), British destroyer F class	U 49
Fencer, British escort carrier *Attacker* class (ex American *Croatan* [ACV 14])	U 277, U 666, U 674, U 959
Fennel (K.194), Canadian corvette Flower I class	U 744
Fessenden (DE 142), American destroyer escort *Edsall* class	U 1062
Findhorn (K.301), British frigate River class	U 198
Firedrake (H.79), British destroyer F class	U 39
Fitzroy (K.553), British frigate Captain class (ex American DE 88)	U 722, U 1001
Flaherty (DE 135). American destroyer escort *Edsall* class	U 515, U 546
Fleetwood (U.47), British sloop *Grimsby* class	U 340, U 528
Flounder (SS 251), American submarine *Gato* class	U 183
Foley (K.474), British frigate Captain class (ex American DE 270)	U 538
Forester (H.74), British destroyer F class	U 27, U 413, U 845
Formidable, British fleet carrier *Illustrious* class	U 331
Fortune (H.70). British destroyer F class	U 27
Fowey (L.15), British sloop *Shoreham* class	U 150, U 55, U 427, U 720, U 1102
Foxhound (H.69), British destroyer F class	U 39
Francis M. Robinson (DE 220), American destroyer escort *Buckley* class	U 1224
Frost (DE 144), American destroyer escort *Edsall* class	U 154, U 880, U 1235, U 488, U 490
G 7, Spanish submarine	s. U 573
Gandy (DE 764), American destroyer escort *Cannon* class	U 550
Garland (H.37), Polish destroyer G class [British] (ex *Garland*)	U 407, U 1010
Garlies (K.475), British frigate Captain class (ex American DE 271)	U 358
Gatineau (H.61), Canadian destroyer River II class (ex British *Express*)	U 744
George E. Badger (DD 196). American destroyer *Clemson* (Flushdecker) class	U 613, U 172
Geranium (K.16), British corvette Flower I class	U 306
Giuseppe Finzi, Italian submarine *Pietro Calvi* class	s. UIT 21
Gladiolus (K.34), British corvette Flower I class	U 26, U 556
Gleaner (N.83), British minesweeper *Bramble* class	U 33
Gleaves (DD 423), American destroyer *Benson* class	U 616
Glenarm (K.258), British frigate River class	U 305
Godavari (U.52), Indian sloop *Bittern* [RIN modified] class	U 198

Name	U-No.
Gloxinia (K.22), British corvette Flower I class	U 205
Gore (K.481), British frigate Captain class (ex American DE 277)	U 91, U 358
Gould (K.476), British frigate Captain class (ex American DE 272)	U 91, U 358
GR 522, Italian floating oil tank	s. UIT 2
GR 523, Italian floating oil tank	s. UIT 3
Graph, British submarine	s. U 570
Greenfish (SS 351), American submarine *Balao* class	U 234
Griep, German salvage vessel	U 2532
Grindall (K.477), British frigate Captain class (ex American DE 273)	U 285
Grongo, Italian submarine *Tritone* class	s. ex Italian U-boats
Grove (L.77), British destroyer escort Hunt II class	U 587
Guadalcanal (CVE 60), American escort carrier *Casablanca* class	U 68, U 505, U 515, U 544
Gurkha (F.20), British destroyer Tribal class	U 53
Haarlem (FY.306) British A/S trawler	U 617
Hai, German submarine	s. U 2365
Haida (G.63), Canadian destroyer Tribal (II) class	U 971
Hambledon (L.37), British destroyer escort Hunt I class	U 223
Hambleton (DD 455), American destroyer *Bristol* class	U 616
Harvester (H.19), British destroyer H class [Brazilian] (ex *Handy*, ex *Guru*)	U 32, U 208, U 444
Hasty (H.24), British destroyer H class	U 79
Hatimura, British steam ship	U 132
Havelock (H.88), British destroyer H class [Brazilian] (ex *Jutahy*)	U 767
Haverfield (DE 393), American destroyer escort *Edsall* class	U 575
Hayter (DE 212). American destroyer escort *Buckley* class	U 248
Hecht, German submarine	s. U 2367
Helmi Söhle, German trawler	U 2
Helmsdale (K.253), British frigate River class	U 484
Hero (H.99), British destroyer H class (*Chaudière*)	U 559, U 568
Hesperus (H.57), British destroyer H class [Brazilian] (ex *Hearty*, ex *Juruena*)	U 93, U 208, U 357, U 186, U 191
Hiev, German salvage vessel	U 2532
Highlander (H.44), British destroyer H class [Brazilian] (ex *Jaguaribe*)	U 32
Hilary P. Jones (DD 427), American destroyer *Benson* class	U 616
Hobson (DD 464), American destroyer *Bristol* class	U 575
Hotspur (H.01), British destroyer H class	U 79
Hursely (L.84), British destroyer escort Hunt II class	U 562
Howard D. Crow (DE 252), American destroyer escort *Edsall* class	U 869
Hurworth (L.28), British destroyer escort Hunt II class	U 559, U 568

Name	U-No.
Huse (DE 145), American destroyer escort *Edsall* class	U 856, U 488, U 490
Hyacinth (K.84), British corvette Flower I class	U 617
Hyderabad (K.212). British corvette Flower I class	U 436
Hydrangea (K.39), British corvette Flower I class	U 401
I-501, Japanese submarine	s. U 181
I-502, Japanese submarine	s. U 862
I-503, Japanese submarine	s. UIT 24
I-504, Japanese submarine	s. UIT 25
I-505. Japanese submarine	s. U 219
I-506, Japanese submarine	s. U 195
Icarus (I.03), British destroyer I class	U 35, U 45, U 744, U 1199
Icarus (WPC 110), American Coast Guard Cutter *Thetis* class	U 352
Ilex (I.61), British destroyer I class	U 42
Iltis, German torpedo boat Raubtier class	U 15
Imogen (D.44), British destroyer I class	U 63, U 42
Imperialist (FY. 126), British A/S trawler	U 732
Implacable, British fleet carrier *Implacable* class	U 1060
Impulsive (I.11), British destroyer I class	U 457
Inch (DE 146), American destroyer escort *Edsall* class	U 154, U 490
Inconstant (H.49), British destroyer I class [Turkish] (ex *Muavenet*)	U 409, U 767
Inglefield (D.02), British destroyer *Inglefield* class	U 63, U 45
Intrepid (D.10), British destroyer I class	U 45
Isis (I.87), British destroyer I class	U 562
Ivanhoe (D.I6), British destroyer I class	U 45
Janssen (DE 396), American destroyer escort *Edsall* class	U 546
Jed (K.235), British frigate River class	U 334, U 954
Joseph C. Hubbard (DE 211), American destroyer escort *Buckley* class	U 248, U 546
Joseph E. Campbell (DE 70), American destroyer escort *Buckley* class	U 371
Jouett (DD 396), American destroyer *Somers* class	U 128
Joyce (DE 317), American destroyer escort *Edsall* class	U 550
Kashmir (F. 12), British destroyer K class	U 35
Kaura, Norwegian submarine	s. U 995
KBP 33, Soviet combat training hulk	s. U 1231
Keats (K.482), British frigate Captain class (ex American DE 278)	U 285, U 1172
Keith (DE 241), American destroyer escort *Edsall* class	U 546
Kenilworth Castle (K.420), British corvette Castle class	U 744
Keppel (I.84), British destroyer Shakespeare class	U 229, U 360, U 394
Kilmarnock (5.11), British corvette Kil class (ex American PCE 837)	U 731

Name	U-No.
Kingston (F.64), British destroyer K class	U 35
Kinn, Norwegian submarine	s. U 1202
Kipling (G.91), British destroyer K class	U 75
Kite (U.87), British sloop *Black Swan* [modified] class	U 226, U 238, U 449, U 504, U 462
Knerten, Norwegian submarine	s. U 4706
Koiner (DE 331) American destroyer escort *Edsall* class	U 869
Kootenay (H.75), Canadian destroyer River II class (ex British *Decoy*)	U 621, U 678
Kortenaer, Dutch destroyer (ex British *Scorpion II*)	U 219
Kya, Norwegian submarine	s. U 926
L-21, Soviet submarine L class	U 367
Labuan (K.584), British frigate Colony class (ex American PF 80)	U 1279
Lady Shirley, British A/S trawler	U 111
Lady Madeleine (FY.283), British A/S trawler	U 246
La Favorite, French submarine *Aurore* class	s. UF 2
Laforey (G.99), British destroyer L class	U 223
L'Africaine, French submarine *Aurore* class	s. UF 1
Lagan (K.259), British frigate River class	U 89, U 753
La Hulloise (K.668), Canadian frigate River class	U 1302
Lamerton (L.88), British destroyer escort Hunt II class	U 443
Lark (U.88), British sloop *Black Swan* [modified] class	U 425
L'Astree, French submarine *Aurore* class	s. UF 3
Laubie, French submarine	s. U 766
Launceston Castle (K.397), British corvette Castle class	U 1200
Leamington (G.19), British destroyer Town class (ex American DD 127)	U 207, U 587
Lech, German submarine tender (ex German M/V *Panther*)	U 34
Léopard, French destroyer *Jaguar* class	U 136
Le Tiger (FY.243), British A/S trawler	U 215
Liddesdale (L.100), British destroyer escort Hunt I class	U 453
Lobelia (K.05), French corvette Flower I class [British](ex *Lobelia*)	U 609
Loch Arkaig (K.603), British frigate Loch class	U 975, U 3514
Loch Dunvegan (K.425), British frigate Loch class	U 354, U 989
Loch Eck (K.422), British frigate Loch class	U 989, U 327, U 1278
Loch Fada (K.390), British frigate Loch class	U 1279, U 1018
Loch Glendhu (K.619), British frigate Loch class	U 1024, U 181, U 862
Loch Inch (K.433), British frigate Loch class	U 307
Loch Killin (K.391), British frigate Loch class	U 333, U 736, U 1063

Name	U-No.
Loch Lomond (K.437), British frigate Loch class	U 181, U 862
Loch More (K.639), British frigate Loch class	U 1024
Loch Scavaig (K.648), British frigate Loch class	U 1014
Loch Shin (K.421), British frigate Loch class	U 286, U 1014
Loosestrife (K.105), British corvette Flower I class	U 192
Lotus (II)(K.130), British corvette Flower I class	U 660
Louis (K.515), British frigate Captain class (ex American DE 517)	U 445
Lowe (DE 325), American destroyer escort *Edsall* class	U 866
Ludlow (DD 438), American destroyer *Benson* class	U 960
Luigi Torelli. Italian submarine *Marconi* class	s. UIT 25
M-31, Soviet submarine	s. U 2353
M-120, Soviet submarine M class	U 18, U 24
M 203, German minesweeper Type 35 class	U 416
Macomb (DD 458), .American destroyer *Bristol* class	U 616
Madison (DD 425), American destroyer *Benson* class	U 450
Magpie (U.82), British sloop *Black Swan* [modified] class	U 238, U 592
Malcolm (I.19), British destroyer Admiralty Leader class	U 651
Mallow (K.81), British corvette Flower I class	U 204
Manners (K.568), British frigate Captain class (ex American DE 523)	U 1051
Marigold (K.87), British corvette Flower I class	U 433
Matane (K.444), Canadian frigate River class	U 311
Menges (DE 320), American destroyer escort *Edsall* class	U 866
Mermaid (U.30), British sloop *Black Swan* [modified] class	U 354, U 394
Meteorite, British submarine	s. U 1407
Mignonette (K.38), British corvette Flower I class	U 136, U 1199
Millé, French submarine	s. U 471
Milne (G.14), British destroyer M class	U 289
MO-103, Soviet A/S cutter Type MO-IV class	U 250
Moberly (PF 63), American frigate *Ashville-Tacoma* class	U 853
Moffett (DD 362), American destroyer Porter class	U 128
Moosejaw (K.164), Canadian corvette Flower class	U 501
Morden (K.170), Canadian corvette Flower class	U 756
Mosley (DE 321), American destroyer escort *Edsall* class	U 866
MRS 25, German mine sweeping vessel (ex German M/V *Nordraum*)	U 737
MTB 81, British Vosper type motor torpedo boat	U 561
Mull (T.110), British A/S trawler	U 343
Murena, Italian submarine *Tritone* class	s. ex Italian U-boats
N 16, British submarine	s. U 1105
N 19, British submarine	s. U 1171

Name	U-No.
N 21, British submarine	s. U 2348
N 22, British submarine	s. U 1057
N 23, British submarine	s. U 1058
N 24, British submarine	s. U 1064
N 25, British submarine	s. U 1305
N 26, British submarine	s. U 1231
N 27, British submarine	s. U 2529
N 28, British submarine	s. U 3035
N 29, British submarine	s. U 3041
N 30, British submarine	s. U 3515
N 31, British submarine	s. U 2353
N 41, British submarine	s. U 3017
N 46, British submarine	s. U 570
N 83, British submarine	s. U 1023
N 85, British submarine	s. U 249
Nairana, British escort carrier *Campania* class	U 1052, U 1203, U 1272, U 1307
Napanee (K.118). Canadian corvette Flower class	U 356
Nasturtium (K.107), British corvette Flower 1 class	U 556
Natal (K.430), South African frigate Loch class (ex British *Loch Cree*)	U 714
Natchez (PF 2), American frigate *Ashville* class (ex Canadian *Annan*)	U 879
Neal A. Scott (DE 769), American destroyer escort *Cannon* class	U 518
Nemo, American submarine	s. U 505
Nene (K.270), British frigate River class	U 257, U 536
Nestor (G.02), Australian destroyer N class [British]	U 127
Neunzer (DE 150), American destroyer escort *Edsall* class	U 546
New Glasgow (K.320), Canadian frigate River class	U 1003
New Liskeard (J.397), Canadian minesweeper *Algerine* class	s. U 190
Niblack (DD 424), American destroyer *Benson* class	U 960
Nields (DD 616), American destroyer *Bristol* class	U 616
Nootka (R.96). Canadian destroyer Tribal (II) class	U 190
Nyasaland (K.587), British frigate Colony class (ex American PF 83)	U 772, U 1014
O.8, Dutch submarine Holland class	s. UD 1
O.12, Dutch submarine *O.12* class	s. UD 2
O.21, Dutch submarine *O.21* class	U 95
O.25, Dutch submarine *O.25* class	s. U D3
O.26, Dutch submarine *O.25* class	s. U D4
O.27, Dutch submarine *O.25* class	s. U D5
Oakville (K.178), Canadian corvette Flower class	U 94

Name	U-No.
Offa (G.29), British destroyer O class	U 294, U 1165, U 874, U 875, U 883, U 2336, U 2351
Onslaught (G.04), British destroyer O class	U 150, U 291, U 369, U 720, U 826, U 901, U 928, U 1191, U 1102, U 1103, U 1004, U 1019, U 170, U 541, U 1233, U 2506, U 2329, U 2334, U 2335, U 2337, U 2341, U 2350, U 2356, U 2363
Onslow (G.17), British destroyer O class	U 143, U 145, U 312, U 427, U 472, U 589, U 668, U 680, U 775, U 779, U 1194, U 298, U 930, U 1009, U 1110, U 1061, U 1230, U 2321, U 2322, U 2324, U 2325, U 2354, U 2361
Opportune (G.80), British destroyer O class	U 456
Orchis (K.76), British corvette Flower I class	U 741
Oribi (G.66), British destroyer O class	U 125, U 1191
Orione (ON), Italian torpedo boat *Orsa* class	U 557
Orwell (G.98), British destroyer O class	U 293
Osmond Ingram (DD 255), American destroyer *Clemson* (Flushdecker) class	U 172
Ottawa (II)(H.31), Canadian destroyer River II class (ex British *Griffin*)	U 621, U 678
Otter (DE 210), American destroyer escort *Buckley* class	U 248
Owen Sound (K.340), Canadian corvette Flower class	U 845
P.715, British submarine	s. U 570
Pakenham (G.06), British destroyer P class	U 559
Paladin (G.69), British destroyer P class	U 205
Papua (K.588), British frigate Colony class (ex American PF 84)	U 1014
Pathfinder (G.10), British destroyer P class	U 203, U 162
PC 565, American submarine chaser PC 461 class	U 521
PC 566, American submarine chaser PC 461 class	U 166
Peacock (U.96), British sloop *Black Swan* [modified] class	U 394
Pelican (U.86), British sloop *Egret* class	U 136, U 334, U 438, U 448
Pentstemon (K.61), British corvette Flower I class	U 131
Periwinkle (K.55), British corvette Flower I class	U 147

Name	U-No.
Petard (G.56), British destroyer P class	U 559
Peterson (DE 152), American destroyer escort *Edsall* class	U 550
Peter Wessel, Norwegian motor passenger ship	U 1054
Pillsbury (II)(DE 133), American destroyer escort *Edsall* class	U 505, U 515, U 546
Pincher (J.294), British minesweeper *Algerine* class	U 300
Pindos (L.65), Greek destroyer escort Hunt III class (British] (ex *Bolebroke*)	U 458
Piorun (G.65), Polish destroyer N class [British] (ex *Nerissa*)	U 149, U 244, U 427, U 720, U 764, U 826, U 1102, U 318, U 1004, U 1022, U 1061, U 170, U 2502, U 2329, U 2334, U 2335, U 2337, U 2350, U 2363
Pope (DE 134), American destroyer escort *Edsall* class	U 515
Portchester Castle (K.362), British corvette Castle class	U 484
Prescott (K.161), Canadian corvette Flower class	U 163
Pride (DE 323), American destroyer escort *Edsall* class	U 371, U 866
Prince Rupert (K.324), Canadian frigate River class	U 575
PZS 31, Soviet floating torpedo firing station	s. U 3041
PZS 32, Soviet floating torpedo firing station	s. U 1058
PZS 33, Soviet floating torpedo firing station	s. U 1064
PZS 34, Soviet floating torpedo firing station	s. U 3035
PZS 35, Soviet floating torpedo firing station	s. U 3515
Q 165	s. U 123
Q 176	s. U 510
Q 335	s. U 766
Q 339	s. U 471
Q 426	s, U 2518
Queen, British escort carrier *Ameer* class (ex American *St. Andrews* [CVE 49])	U 711
Quentin (G.78), British destroyer Q class	U 162
Quick (DD 490), American destroyer *Bristol* class	U 173
R 7, Italian submarine Romolo class	s. UIT 4
R 8, Italian submarine Romolo class	s. UIT 5
R 9, Italian submarine Romolo class	s. UIT 6
R 10, Italian submarine Romolo class	s. UIT 1
R 11, Italian submarine Romolo class	s. UIT 2
R 12, Italian submarine Romolo class	s. UIT 3
R-1, Soviet submarine	s. U 3535
R-2, Soviet submarine	s. U 3536

Name	U-No.
R-3, Soviet submarine	s. U 3537
R-4, Soviet submarine	s. U 3538
R-5, Soviet submarine	s. U 3539
R-6, Soviet submarine	s. U 3540
R-7, Soviet submarine	s. U 3541
R-8, Soviet submarine	s. U 3542
Recruit (J.98), British minesweeper *Algerine* class	U 300
Redmill (K.554), British frigate Captain class (ex American DE 89)	U 722
Reginaldo Giuliani, Italian submarine *Console Generale Liuzzi* class	s. UIT 23
Reuben James (II)(DE 153), American destroyer escort *Buckley* class	U 548
Ro-500, Japanese submarine	s. U 511
Ro-501, Japanese submarine	s. U 1224
Robert A. Owens (DD 827), American destroyer *Gearing* class	U 2513
Rochester (U.50), British sloop *Shoreham* class	U 82, U 135, U 204, U 213
Rocket (H.92), British destroyer R-class	U 86
Rodman (DD 456), American destroyer *Bristol* class	U 616
Roland Morillot, French submarine	s. U 2518
Rona, Norwegian steam salvage tug (ex *Securitas*)	U 57
Roper (DD 147), American destroyer *Wickes* (Flushdecker) class	U 85
Rother (K. 224), British frigate River class	U 134
Rowley (K.560), British frigate Captain class (ex American DE 95)	U 1208
Rubis (H4, 202, P15), French submarine *Saphir* class	U 702
Rupert (K.561), British frigate Captain class (ex American DE 96)	U 965
S 1, Italian submarine	s. U 428
S 2, Italian submarine	s. U 746
S 3, Italian submarine	s. U 747
S 4, Italian submarine	s. U 429
S 5, Italian submarine	s. U 748
S 6, Italian submarine	s. U 430
S 7, Italian submarine	s. U 749
S 8, Italian submarine	s. U 1161
S 9, Italian submarine	s. U 750
S 01, Spanish submarine	s. U 573
S-81, Soviet submarine	s. U 1057
S-82, Soviet submarine	s. U 1058
S-83, Soviet submarine	s. U 1064
S-84, Soviet submarine	s. U 1305
S-101, Soviet submarine S class	U 639

Name	U-No.
Sahib (P.212), British submarine	U 301
Saint John (K.456), Canadian frigate River class	U 247, U 309
Salmon (65.S), British submarine S class	U 36
Sandwich (U.12), British sloop *Bridgewater* class	U 213
Santee (CVE 29), American escort carrier *Sangamon* class	U 43, U 160, U 509
Saracen (P.247), British submarine S class	U 335
Satyr (P.214), British submarine S class	U 987
Shch -307, Soviet submarine SC class	U 144
Scarborough (U.25), British sloop *Hastings* class	U 76
Scimitar (H.21), British destroyer Admiralty S class	U 651
Seal (37.M), British submarine *Porpoise* class	s. UB
Searcher, British escort carrier *Attacker* class (ex American ??)	U 711
Sénégalais (T 22), French destroyer escort *Algerien* class (ex American DE 106)	U 371
Sennen, British sloop (ex American Coast Guard Cutter *Champlain*)	U 954
Seymour (K 563), British frigate Captain class (ex American DE 98)	U 1191
Sharpshooter (N.68), British minesweeper *Bramble* class	U 655
Shediac (K.l10), Canadian corvette Flower class	U 87
Shoemaker, American steam freighter	U 1406
Sickle (P.224), British submarine S class	U 303
Sikh (G.82), British destroyer Tribal class	U 372
Skeena (I.59), Canadian destroyer River class	U 588
Snowberry (K.166), Canadian corvette Flower class	U 536
Snowden (DD 246), American destroyer escort *Edsall* class	U 488
Snowflake (K.211), British corvette Flower I class	U 125
Solebay (R.70), British destroyer 1942 Battle class	U 2511
Solomons (CVE 67), American escort carrier *Casablanca* class	U 860
Sparide, Italian submarine *Tritone* class	s. ex Italian U-boats
Speedwell (N.87), British minesweeper *Bramble* class	U 651
Spencer (WPG 36), American Coast Guard Cutter Treasury class	U 175
Spey (K.246), British frigate River class	U 136, U 386, U 406
Stanley (I.73), British Town class [long range] (ex American DD 252)	U 434, U 131
Stanton (DE 247), American destroyer escort *Edsall* class	U 880, U 1235
Starling (U.66), British sloop *Black Swan* [modified] class	U 202, U 226, U 238, U 264, U 333, U 385, U 473, U 592, U 653, U 734, U 961, U 842, U 119
Starwort (K.20), British corvette Flower 1 class	U 660
Statice (K.281), British Flower class [modified]	U 678

Name	U-No.
Stayner (K.573), British frigate Captain class (ex American DF 564)	U 671
St. Catharines (K.325), Canadian frigate River class	U 744
St. Croix (I.81), Canadian destroyer Town class (ex American DD 252)	U 87, U 90
St. Laurent (H.83), Canadian destroyer River class (ex British *Cygnet*)	U 356, U 845
Stonecrop (K.142), British corvette Flower I class	U 634, U 124
Stork (U.81), British sloop *Bittern* class	U 252, U 574, U 634, U 131
Strathadam (K.682), Canadian frigate River class	U 1302
St. Thomas (K.488), Canadian corvette Castle class (ex British *Sandgate Castle*)	U 877
Sunflower (K.41), British corvette Flower I class	U 282, U 631, U 638
Swale (K.217), British frigate River class	U 302, U 657
Swansea (K.328), Canadian frigate River class	U 247, U 311, U 448, U 845
Swanson (DD 443), American destroyer *Benson* class	U 173
T 17, German torpedo boat Type 37 class	U 235
T-116, Soviet minesweeper *Admirable* class (ex American *Arcade* [AM 143])	U 362
T 156, German torpedo boat	U 18
Talybont (L 18), British destroyer escort Hunt III class	U 1191
Tally Ho (P.317), British submarine T class	UIT 23
Tamarisk (K.216), British corvette Flower I class	U 82
Tantivy (P.319), British submarine T class	U 249, U 485, U 739, U 773, U 978, U 991, U 992, U 1002, U 532
Tapir (P.335), British submarine T class	U 486
Tavy (K.272), British frigate River class	U 380
Templar (P.316), British submarine T class	U 1109
Tenacious (R.45), British destroyer T class	U 453
Termagant (R.89), British destroyer T class	U 453
Terpsichore (R.33), British destroyer T class	U 407
Test (K.239), British frigate River class	U 436
Tetcott (L.99), British destroyer escort Hunt II class	U 372
Thetford Mines (K.459), Canadian frigate River class	U 1302
Thetis (WPC 115), American Coast Guard Cutter *Thetis* class	U 157
Thomas (DE 102), American destroyer escort *Cannon* class	U 879, U 233
Tintagel Castle (K.399), British corvette Castle class	U 878
Toro (SS 422), American submarine *Tench* class	U 530
Totland (Y.88), British sloop (ex American Coast Guard Cutter *Cayuga*)	U 522
Tracker, British escort carrier *Attacker* class (ex American M/V *Mormacmail*)	U 288
Trenchant (P.331), British submarine T class	U 859

Name	U-No.
Trippe (DD 403), American destroyer *Benham* class	U 73
Troubridge (R.00), British destroyer T class	U 407
Truculent (P.315), British submarine T class	U 308
Trumpeter, British escort carrier *Ameer* class (ex American *Bastian* (CVE 37])	U 711
TS-5, Soviet submarine	s. U 3535
TS-6, Soviet submarine	s. U 3536
TS-7, Soviet submarine	s. U 3537
TS-8, Soviet submarine	s. U 3538
TS-9, Soviet submarine	s. U 3539
TS-10, Soviet submarine	s. U 3540
TS-11, Soviet submarine	s. U 3541
TS-12, Soviet submarine	s. U 3542
TS-13, Soviet submarine	s. U 3543
TS-14, Soviet submarine	s. U 250
TS-15, Soviet submarine	s. U 3544
TS-16, Soviet submarine	s. U 9
TS-17, Soviet submarine	s. U 3545
TS-18, Soviet submarine	s. U 3546
TS-19, Soviet submarine	s. U 3547
TS-32, Soviet submarine	s. U 3548
TS-33, Soviet submarine	s. U 3549
TS-34, Soviet submarine	s. U 3550
TS-35, Soviet submarine	s. U 3551
TS-36, Soviet submarine	s. U 3552
TS-37, Soviet submarine	s. U 3553
TS-38, Soviet submarine	s. U 3554
Tumult (R.11), British destroyer T class	U 86, U 223
Tuna (N.94), British submarine T class	U 644
Tyler (K.576), British frigate Captain class (ex American DE 567)	U 1172
Ula, Norwegian submarine V class (ex British *Varne*)	U 974
Unbeaten (N.93), British submarine U class	U 374
Unicoi, American motor freighter	U 576
UTS-3, Soviet training hulk	s. U 2529
UTS-23, Soviet training hulk	s. U 1231
UTS-49, Soviet training hulk	s. U 1064
UW 20, German submarine	s. U 2365
Vanessa (D.29), British destroyer V & W class [long range]	U 357
Vanoc (H.33), British destroyer V & W class [long range]	U 100, U 392
Vanquisher (D.54), British destroyer V & W class [long range]	U 878

Name	U–No.
Vansittart (D.64), British destroyer V & W class	U 102
Varian (DD 798), American destroyer escort *Buckley* class	U 248, U 546
Vascama (FY.185), British A/S trawler	U 452
Venturer (P.88), British submarine V class	U 771, U 864
Vetch (K.132), British corvette Flower I class	U 252, U 414
Veteran (D.72), British destroyer V & W class	U 207
Viceroy (L.21), British destroyer V & W class	U 1274
Victorious, British fleet carrier *Illustrious* class	U 517
Vidette (D.48), British destroyer V & W class [long range]	U 274, U 282, U 413, U 630, U 531
Ville de Quebec (K.), Canadian corvette Flower class	U 224
Vimy (D.33), British destroyer V & W class [long range]	U 162, U 187
Vindex, British escort carrier *Campania* class	U 344, U 394, U 653, U 765
Violet (K.35), British corvette Flower I class	U 641, U 651
Viscount (D.92), British destroyer V & W class [long range|	U 201, U 661
Visenda, British A/S trawler	U 551
Volunteer (D.71). British destroyer V & W class [long range]	U 587
Wainwright (DD 419), American destroyer *Sims* class	U 593
Wake Island (CVE 65), American escort carrier *Casablanca* class	U 543
Walker (D.27), British destroyer V & W class [long range]	U 99, U 100
Wallflower (K.44). British corvette Flower I class	U 523
Wanderer (D.74), British destroyer V & W class [long range]	U 147, U 305, U 390, U 523
Warspite. British battleship *Queen Elizabeth* class	U 64
Waskesiu (K.330), Canadian frigate River class	U 257
Watchman (D.26), British destroyer V & W class [long range]	U 1195
Wensleydale (L.86), British destroyer escort Hunt III class	U 413, U 671, U 1191
Westcott (D.47), British destroyer V & W class	U 581
Weston (U.72), British sloop *Falmouth* class	U 13
Wetaskiwin (K.175), Canadian corvette Flower class	U 588
Wheatland (L.122), British destroyer escort Hunt II class	U 443
Whitehall (D.94), British destroyer V & W class [long range]	U 306, U 394
Whitshed (D.77), British destroyer V & W class [long range]	U 55
Wild Goose (U.45), British sloop *Black Swan* [modified] class	U 424, U 449, U 473, U 592, U 653, U 734, U 762, U 1279, U 504, U 842, U 462
Wilhelm Bauer, German submarine	s. U 2540
Wishart (D.67), British destroyer V & W class	U 74, U 761

Name	U-No.
Witherington (D.76), British destroyer V & W class	U 340
Wivern (D.66), British destroyer V & W class	U 714
Wollongong (J.172), Australian minesweeper *Bathurst* class	U 617
Wolverine (D.78), British destroyer V & W class	U 76
Woodcock (U.90), British sloop *Black Swan* [modified] class	U 226, U 462
Woodpecker (U.08), British sloop *Black Swan* (modified] class	U 264, U 424, U 449, U 762, U 504, U 462
Woolsey (DD 437), American destroyer *Benson* class	U 73, U 173
Wren (U.28), British sloop *Black Swan* |modified] class	U 449, U 473, U 608, U 504, U 462
Wrestler (L.10), British destroyer V & W class [long range]	U 74, U 98
Zetland (L.59), British destroyer escort Hunt II class	U 427, U 720, U 1102
Zulu (F. 18), British destroyer Tribal class	U 372
Zwaardvisch, Dutch submarine T class (ex British *Talent*)	U 168

INDEX 4

ALLIED AIR FORCE UNITS

Sqn	U-No.	Sqn	U-No.
Royal Air Force (RAF)		209	U 452
8	U 852	210	U 241, U 320, U 361, U 418 U 476, U 601, U 742
36	U 616, U 960		
38	U 562	220	U 265, U 575, U 624, U 707, U 871
47	U 559	221	U 372
48	U 442, U 447, U 594	224	U 216, U 274, U 332, U 373, U 404, U 441, U 514, U 599, U 628, U 740, U 867
53	U 391, U 535, U 608, U 618, U 629		
58	U 221, U 261, U 266, U 463, U 528, U 558, U 563	228	U 55, U 106, U 383, U 563, U 607, U 970
59	U 292, U 470, U 540, U 844, U 990	233	U 77, U 167, U 447, U 573, U 605
61	U 751	235	U 251, U 804, U 843, U 1065, U 2359
77	U 256, U 705	236	U 2338, U 2503
82	U 31	244	U 533
86	U 109, U 280, U 317, U 347, U 419, U 456, U 478, U 534, U 632, U 643, U 844, U 964, U 1008, U 3523	245	U 1007, U 2521
		248	U 251, U 804, U 821, U 976, U 2359
		254	U 2338, U 2503
120	U 189, U 200, U 258, U 304, U 389, U 470, U 529, U 540, U 597, U 611, U 623, U 635, U 643, U 1017	259	U 197
		262	UIT 22
143	U 251, U 804, U 1065, U 2359	265	U 197
172	U 126, U 231, U 268, U 459, U 502, U 575, U 614	269	U 273, U 336, U 570, U 619, U 646
		304 (Pol)	U 321
175	U 52, U 101, U 276	311 (Cz)	U 966, U 971, U 1060, U 165
179	U 211, U 232, U 340, U 412, U 431, U 542, U 566, U 617, U 927	330 (Nor)	U 482
		333 (Nor)	U 423, U 998
184	U 2521, U 3032	500	U 77, U 83, U 259, U 331, U 411, U 595, U 960
200	U 468		
201	U 107, U 440, U 955, U 1222	502	U 364, U 462, U 751, U 981, U 1060
202	U 620, U 761	547	U 459, U 579
203	U 568, U 652	608	U 595, U 755
206	U 169, U 319, U 384, U 417, U 469, U 575, U 627, U 710, U 821	612	U 545, U 966
		621	U 852

Sqn	U-No.
4 OTU(C)	U 675
10 OTU	U 564

Bomber Command area bombing attacks

U 228, U 239, U 677, U 735, U 777, U 982, U 993, U 1164, U 1227, (U 1408)*, (U 1409)*, U 2509, U 2514, U 2516, (U 2550)*, (U 3052)*, U 3512, U 4708, UIT 6

Royal Australian Air Force (RAAF)

10	U 26, U 243, U 426, U 454, U 563, U 663
455	U 227
459	U 97
461	U 106, U 270, U 385, U 461, U 465, U 571

Royal Canadian Air Force (RCAF)

5	U 209
10	U 341, U 520
113	U 754
145	U 658
162	U 342, U 477, U 478, U 715, U 980, U 1225
407	U 283, U 846
415	U 706
422	U 625
423	U 489, U 610, U 753

Royal Navy—Fleet Air Arm (FAA)

700	U 64
802	U 131
811	U 89, U 203
812	U 451
813	U 365
815	U 577, U 652
816	U 366, U 472, U 973
817	U 517
819	U 288, U 752
820	U 331
825	U 344, U 394, U 589, U 653, U 765
842	U 277, U 666, U 674, U 959
846	U 288, U 711
853	U 711
882	U 711

Sqn	U-No.
892	U 752
893	U 331
1771	U 1060

South African Air Force (SAAF)

15	U 205

United States Army Air Force (USAAF)

1st A/S	U 435, U 506, U 951
2ndt A/S	U 524, U 182
4th A/S	U 404, U 706
19th A/S	U 558
1st Comp	U 848
45th B.	U 654
59th B.	U 153
99th B.	U 512
396th B.	U 701

8 AF area bombing attacks

U 72, U 96, U 108, U 235, U 236, U 237, U 345, U 348, U 350, U 429. U 430, U 474, U 622, U 682, (U 723)*, (U 724)*, U 749, U 758, U 870, U 872, U 882, U 884, U 890, U 891, U 902, U 906, (U 908)*, U 996, (U 1011)*, (U 1012)*, U 11.31, U 1167, U 1221, U 1238, U 2340, U 2515, U 2523, U 2530, U 2532, U 2537, U 2542, U 2547, (U 2550)*, U 3003, U 3007, U 3036, U 3045, U 3046, U3505, U 3508

9 AF XXIX TAC (probably)

U 393, U 733, U 746, U 1210, U 3012

15 AF area bombing attack

U 81, U 380, U 410, U 421, U 471, U 586, U 596, U 642, U 952, U 969, UIT 1, UIT 4, UIT 5

United States Navy (USN)

VB-103	U 271, U 326, U 508, U 681, U 966
VB-105	U 84
VB-107	U 177, U 598, U 848, U 849, U 863
VB-110	U 966, U 988
VB-112	U 1279
VB-125	U 174
VB-127	U 591
VB-128	U 279
VB-129	U 604
VB-130	U 615
VC-1	U 117, U 220, U 525, U 664, U 847

Sqn	U-No.	Sqn	U-No.
VC-6	U 801, U 1059	VP-84	U 194, U 388, U 408, U 467, U 640
VC-8	U 505	VP-92	U 94, U 135, U 590, U 662, U 615
VC-9	U 118, U 217, U 402, U 422, U 460,	VP-94	U 590, U 662
	U 527, U 569, U 584, U 860	VP-204	U 615
VC-13	U 67, U 185, U 378, U 487, U 544	VP-205	U 572, U 615
VC-19	U 172, U 850	VS-9	U 576
VC-29	U 43, U 160, U 509	VS-62	U 176
VC-42	U 1229		
VC-55	U 66		
VC-58	U 68, U 515, U 543		
VC-95	U 575		
VP-32	U 159, U 359, U 759		
VP-53	U 156		
VP-63	U392, U 731, U 761, U 1107		
VP-73	U 464, U 582		
VP-74	U 128, U 158, U 161, U 199, U 513		
VP-82	U 503, U 656		
VP-83	U 164, U 507		

Forces Aériennes Françaises Libres (FAFL)

4. Escadrille d' Aviation	U 105
2nd Flottille de Bombardement	U 403

Brazilian Air Force (FAB)

7th Air Base Corps	U 199

Soviet Air Force area bombing attack

U 9

* U-boat numbers in ( ) ≈ U-boat destroyed on slip while under construction